Indian Reservations: A State and Federal Handbook

# INDIAN RESERVATIONS
## A State and Federal Handbook

*Compiled by*
The Confederation of American Indians
New York, N.Y.

McFarland & Company, Inc., Publishers
*Jefferson, North Carolina, and London*

**Library of Congress Cataloguing-in-Publication Data**

*Indian reservations.*

Includes index.
1. Indians of North America—Reservations—Directories.
I. Confederation of American Indians.
E93.I3828   1986     973′.0497002573     85-43573

ISBN 0-89950-200-8 (acid-free natural paper)

Manufactured in the United States of America

McFarland   Box 611   Jefferson NC 28640

# TABLE OF CONTENTS

## New Mexico

# INTRODUCTION

Major questions have always existed concerning the role and status of Indian tribes and Indian peoples within the fabric of life in the United States. There is a relatively consistent body of law whose origins flow from precolonial America to the present day. This body of law is neither well-known nor well-understood by the American public. Federal Indian law—or, more accurately, United States constitutional law concerning Indian tribes and individuals—is unique and separate from the rest of American jurisprudence. Analogies to general constitutional law, civil rights law, public land law, and the like are misleading and often erroneous. Indian law is distinct. It encompasses Western European international law, specific provisions of the United States Constitution, precolonial treaties, treaties of the United States, an entire volume of the United States Code, and numerous decisions of the United States Supreme Court and lower federal courts.

Indian tribes are governmental units that have a "special" political (trust) relationship with the government of the United States. As with any government whose power is inherent rather than specifically delegated, it is not possible to catalog precisely all the powers that the tribes retain. Some powers may not have been exercised in recent years, and others may become apparent only in the context of changing needs and circumstances. It is, however, safe to say that tribal powers include most normal powers incidental to internal governmental functioning, for example, the power to define and enforce criminal laws, the power to determine matters of family law, the power to regulate hunting and fishing, the power to tax, the power to zone and otherwise determine land use, and the power to determine the form of the tribe's governmental institutions.

Indian reservations were established for the most part in the 19th century as an adjunct to federal policy that encouraged white settlement and westward expansion of the new nation. To the extent that the presence of Indian tribes impeded that process, they were removed and restricted to reserved land. This was done through a series of treaties between various tribes and the federal government that guaranteed federal protection for the tribes and their remaining assets.

The nature of the federal, state, and tribal relationship was defined in a highly politicized setting, when the Supreme Court of the United States, led by Chief Justice John Marshall, struck down an entire series of state statutes as violative of tribal-state and tribal-federal relations. These cases established the principles that Indian tribes possessed sovereignty over their members and territory and that the federal government protects tribal sovereignty, land, and resources from states and non–Indian interests.

When initially established, Indian reservations were enclaves almost exclusively occupied by Indians. As the population makeup and legislation have changed, the states have acquired some jurisdiction over some reservations.

The concept that states do not possess jurisdiction in Indian country was premised on international law and the constitutional fact that tribal relations were a matter of federal jurisdiction, to the exclusion of the states. Prior to the Revolutionary War, the power to deal with Indian tribes resided in the British crown; such power was transferred to the federal government, first in the Articles of Confederation and then in the Constitution. In fact, many of the states admitted to the Union, after the original 13 colonies, came into the Union with the express understanding, contained either in their enabling legislation or in their constitution, that they had no jurisdiction over tribal lands.

States do not have inherent power (jurisdiction) within Indian reservations. Congress is viewed in American jurisprudence as possessing plenary power with respect to Indian affairs. Although Indian tribes were not parties to the United States Constitution, much of federal Indian law is controlled by a single clause in the Constitution giving Congress the power to "regulate Commerce with Foreign Nations, and among several states, and with the Indian Tribes."

States are specifically excluded by Congress from alienating, taxing or probating trust property and infringing upon hunting, fishing, and trapping rights.

Today, most Indian tribes operate their own local government and court systems, and the Navajo have recently passed an income tax law. The U.S. Internal Revenue Code provides that Indian tribes shall be considered equivalent to state governments for tax purposes—thus the tribe is exempt from federal tax and tribal taxes are deductible from federal taxes to the same extent that state taxes are deductible.

The Supreme Court of the United States has specifically addressed the issue of whether specialized treatment of Indians by the federal government is unconstitutional racial discrimination. The clear answer of the Court was that it is not. For the purpose of dealing with the federal government, Indian tribes are not racial groupings but rather political groupings—governments.

This directory provides a unique source of information on the land areas controlled by these governments that many citizens do not even realize exist.

The Confederation of American Indians would be grateful for information that might be used in possible future editions of this handbook, and data should be sent to:

Confederation of American Indians
Box 5474
New York, New York 10163-5474.

# ALASKA

ANNETTE ISLANDS RESERVE                    Federal Reservation
Southeast Region
Tsimpshian Tribe
Tribal Headquarters: Metlakatla, Alaska

**Land Status.** Tribal land: 86,471 acres. Total area: 86,471 acres.

**History.** The ancestral home of the Tsimpshians is on the Skeena River in British Columbia and the coast to the southward. In 1887, a Church of England missionary, the Rev. William Duncan, persuaded a number of the Indians to move to Annette Islands. A grant of land was later obtained from the U.S. Government by an Act of May 30, 1891, and the Tsimpshians have continued to reside there, principally in the Village of Metlakatla. Along with the land grant, the Tsimpshians received U.S. citizenship and certain fishing rights.

**Culture.** Establishment of the Metlakatla Indian Community was based on religious freedom and self-expression, and this attitude is prevalent today. Metlakatla is a modern and progressive community with youthful, vigorous, and hard-working residents who participate in the social, economic, and political life of the State.

**Government.** The Metlakatla Indian Community is organized under the Indian Reorganization Act and is incorporated under a Federally-approved charter. The governing body is the popularly elected Annette Islands Reserve Council consisting of 15 members.

**Population Profile. 1969:** Indian resident 1,000; Unemployment 10%; Underemployment 60%. **1980:** Indian resident 942; Non-Indian resident 253; Percent Indian of total population 78.8; Total housing units 353; Occupied housing units 321. Education level: 10 years.

**Tribal Economy.** The average annual income is $250,000. This income is derived 90 percent from fishing, 5 percent from forestry, and 5 percent from land leases.

**Climate.** Rainfall averages 120 inches per year. The temperature ranges from a high of 58 degrees to a low of 22 degrees.

**Transportation.** There is only an internal road system on the island. Commercial air service is available on the island, and the nearest bus and truck transportation is located in Ketchikan, a distance of 15 miles.

**Utilities.** All utilities are tribally-owned including the Metlakatla Water System and the Metlakatla Power and Light Company.

**Recreation.** The tribally-owned community center includes a basketball court, theatre, auditorium, and numerous meeting rooms. Recreational activities are limited primarily to hunting and fishing.

1

CRAIG                                                Native Village
Prince of Wales Island, Southeast Region
Tlingit Tribe
Tribal Headquarters:  Craig, Alaska

**Land Status.** Craig is incorporated as a town in Alaska. The term "Indian Reservation" has been applied generally to any lands in Alaska set aside for the benefit of Indians. The lands in established native townsites are held in trust by the Federal Government for disposal as provided by the 1926 Alaska Native Townsite Act which authorizes the townsite trustee to issue a restricted deed to an Alaskan native for a tract of land occupied by and set apart for him in a townsite established under the 1891 Townsite Act.

**History.** The Tlingit were formerly one of North America's most powerful tribes, crossing the mountains from Canada to seek the seacoast. Russian explorers found them there in 1741 and exerted a harsh and oppressive rule over them. The Tlingit continued to live in this area, dividing into villages, each with hunting and fishing grounds. Today they participate actively in Alaska's political affairs.

**Culture.** The Tlingit developed a rich economy based upon the abundant resources of the ocean and coast. They constructed very seaworthy boats and canoes and appear to have carried on fairly active trade with the Orient. War captives from other tribes were enslaved. Individuals had a clearly defined rank and status within the society; however, they were quite mobile from generation to generation. Social status among the Tlingit depended upon elaborate feasts called "Potlatches" at which the heads of families or clans vied for prestige by destroying or giving away vast quantities of valuable goods. The goat wool and cedar bark ceremonial blanket has always been in great demand as a trade item with each house having its own design. Totem poles were important to the Tlingit culture, serving as the decorative record of outstanding events of a family or clan.

**Population Profile. 1969:** Total population 220.

**Tribal Economy.** The three major industries in the area, Columbia Ward Packing Company, Big Harbor Cold Storage, and West Coast Cold Storage, are all privately owned. In addition, there are a variety of retail businesses in Craig.

**Climate.** The Prince of Wales Island lies in the Pacific currents which cause a mild and moist climate year round. The rainfall averages 106 inches per year and temperatures vary from a high of 80 degrees to a low of 15 degrees.

**Transportation.** The nearest transportation center for the area is Ketchikan, some 80 miles from the reservation. Commercial transportation by air, bus, and truck is available here.

**Community Facilities.** Craig has a municipal water and sewer system. Electricity is provided by the Alaska Power and Telephone Company. The nearest medical care is located in Ketchikan.

**Recreation.** Trout and salmon fishing, and bear and deer hunting in this mild climate attract many tourists and sportsmen.

HOONAH                                    Native Village
Chicagof Island, Southeast Region
Tlingit Tribe
Tribal Headquarters: Hoonah, Alaska

**Land Status.** Hoonah is incorporated as a town in Alaska. The term "Indian Reservation" has been applied generally to any lands in Alaska set aside for the benefit of Indians. The lands in established native townsites are held in trust by the Federal Government for disposal as provided by the 1926 Alaska Native Townsite Act which authorizes the townsite trustee to issue a restricted deed to an Alaskan native for a tract of land occupied by and set apart for him in a townsite established under the 1891 Townsite Act.

**History.** The Tlingit were formerly one of North America's most powerful tribes, crossing the mountains from Canada to seek the seacoast. Russian explorers found them in 1741 and exerted a harsh, oppressive rule over them. The Tlingit continued to live in this area, dividing into villages, each with hunting and fishing grounds. Today they participate actively in Alaska's political affairs.

**Culture.** Social status among the Tlingit depended on elaborate feasts called "Potlatches" at which the heads of families or clans vied in destroying or giving away vast quantities of valuable goods. The goat wool and cedar bark ceremonial blanket has always been in great demand as a trade item with each clan house having its own design. Totem poles were important to the culture of the Tlingit, serving as the decorative record of outstanding events of a family or clan. The Tlingit developed a rich economy based largely on the abundant resources of the sea and coast. War captives from other tribes were enslaved. The Tlingit constructed seaworthy boats and canoes, and seem to have carried on active trade with the Orient.

**Government.** Hoonah was incorporated in 1946 with a mayor and council form of government. Primary income is from sales tax and revenue from electricity and water collections.

**Population Profile. 1969:** Indian resident 704; Non-Indian resident 130; Unemployment 70%. Education level: 9.5 grades. The median family income is quite low, as 78 percent of the families earn less than $3,000 each year.

**Tribal Economy.** Two industries, Coastal Glacier Sea Foods and Thompson's Cold Storage, are privately owned. Small businesses include three general stores, two fuel oil dealers, a coffee shop, hotel, and theater. The community owns a liquor store. Municipal water and electricity are supplied by the tribe.

**Climate.** The area's climate is modified by the Pacific, having a low temperature of only -5 degrees and a high of 70 degrees. Rainfall averages 93 inches per year.

**Transportation.** Hoonah is 30 miles from Juneau, one of the larger Alaskan cities. Although there is no train service, air, truck, and bus companies serve Juneau.

**Community Facilities.** Water and sewer systems are maintained by the municipal government. The Municipal Electric Service provides the electric power to the area. Fuel oil is supplied by private dealers.

The Public Health Service operates a hospital in Juneau which serves Hoonah residents.

**Recreation.** Glacier Bay National Monument lies across icy straits from Hoonah. Fishing in 14 major salmon and trout streams, and hunting bear, deer, mountain goat, and waterfowl attract the sportsman. The native arts and crafts also have much attraction for tourists.


HYDABURG                                              Native Village
Prince of Wales Island, Southeast Region
Haida Tribe
Tribal Headquarters: Hydaburg, Alaska

**Land Status.** Hydaburg is incorporated as a town in Alaska. The term "Indian Reservation" has been applied generally to any lands in Alaska set aside for the benefit of Indians. The lands in established native townsites are held in trust by an employee of the Federal Government for disposal as provided by the 1926 Alaska Native Townsite Act which authorizes the townsite trustee to issue a restricted deed to an Alaskan native for a tract of land occupied by and set apart for him in a townsite established under the 1891 Townsite Act.

**History.** The Haida Indians were emigres from Canada in the early 18th century. Hydaburg was established in 1911 by Indians from the villages of Klinkwan and Howkan with the common interest of bettering their conditions. Many live today in Hydaburg and derive their income from fishing. They take an active interest in Alaska's political affairs.

**Culture.** According to tradition, totem carving originated among the Haida. Their carvers were sometimes hired or enslaved by the Tlingit to provide totems or carved embellishments for Tlingit homes and villages. They also produced fine slate carvings and delicately worked articles of wood, bone, and shell.

**Government.** Incorporated as a city in 1915, Hydaburg is governed by a mayor and council form of government.

**Population Profile. 1969:** Indian resident 237; Average family income $3,000; Unemployment 88%.

**Tribal Economy.** The tribal cannery, Hydaburg Cooperative Association, is not operating at present. There are various retail businesses in the city.

**Climate.** The climate which attracted the Haida to the area is modified by warm Pacific currents. The average annual rainfall of 105 inches encourages the lush natural growth. Temperatures range from a high of 80 degrees to a low of 15 degrees.

**Transportation.** The transportation center for the area is Ketchikan, which lies 70 miles from Hydaburg. Commercial transportation by air, truck, and bus is available here.

**Community Facilities.** The water and sewer system is municipal. Electricity is supplied by the Alaska Power and Telephone Company. The nearest hospital and health care facility is located in Ketchikan.

**Recreation.** Trout and salmon fishing is a tourism attraction, as are bear and deer hunting.

KAKE                                          Native Village
Kupreanof Island, Southeast Region
Tlingit Tribe
Tribal Headquarters:  Kake, Alaska

**Land Status.** Kake is incorporated as a town in Alaska. The term "Indian Reservation" has been applied generally to any lands in Alaska set aside for the benefit of Indians. The lands in established native townsites are held in trust by the Federal Government for disposal as provided by the 1926 Alaska Native Townsite Act which authorizes the townsite trustee to issue a restricted deed to an Alaskan native for a tract of land occupied by and set apart for him in a townsite established under the 1891 Townsite Act.

**History.** The Tlingit were formerly one of North America's most powerful tribes, crossing the mountains from Canada to seek the seacoast. Russian explorers found them there in 1741 and exerted a harsh and oppressive rule over them. The Tlingit continued to live in this area, dividing into villages, each with hunting and fishing grounds. Today they participate actively in Alaska's political affairs.

**Culture.** The Tlingit developed a rich economy based upon the abundant resources of the ocean and coast. They constructed very seaworthy boats and canoes and appear to have carried on fairly active trade with the Orient. War captives from other tribes were enslaved. Individuals had a clearly defined rank and status within the society; however, they were quite mobile from generation to generation. Social status among the Tlingit depended upon elaborate feasts called "Potlatches" at which the heads of families or clans vied for prestige by destroying or giving away vast quantities of valuable goods. The goat wool and cedar bark ceremonial blanket has always been in great demand as a trade item with each house having its own design. Totem poles were important to the Tlingit culture, serving as the decorative record of outstanding events of a family or clan.

**Government.** Kake is governed by a popularly-elected common council with a mayor as chief administrative officer.

**Population Profile.  1969:** Indian resident 417; Non-Indian resident 40; Unemployment 70%. Education level: 9.5 grades. While the average family income is $3,000, 65 percent of the families earn less than that amount each year.

**Tribal Economy.** The tribe has formed the Kake Cooperative Association, the Kake Totem Committee, and an Arts and Crafts Cooperative. The tribe operates the Kake Electrical Utility System, Keku Canning, and Kupreanof Packing, Inc. The Clear Creek Logging Company is privately owned. Retail businesses include a general merchandise store, fuel oil dealer, motel, sporting goods store, short order restaurant, and a theater.

**Climate.** Although in the northern latitudes, the climate is modified by warm Pacific currents. Temperatures range from a high of 85 degrees to a low of −5 degrees.

**Transportation.** Kake is located 30 miles from Petersburg where transportation by air, bus, and truck is available.

**Community Facilities.** The water and sewer system is municipal

as is the Kake Electric Utility System. The Public Health Service operates a hospital in Kake to meet the health needs of residents.

**Recreation.** Sport fishing is developing in the area surrounding
Kake. At Keku Point, tourists are attracted by white, sandy beaches
and unusual rocks. Fishing for salmon, snapper, cod, bass, and trout,
and hunting for bear, wolf, deer, and wildfowl attract many sportsmen.

KLAWOCK                                           Native Village
Prince of Wales Island, Southeast Region
Tlingit Tribe
Tribal Headquarters: Klawock, Alaska

**Land Status.** Klawock is incorporated as a town in Alaska. The
term "Indian Reservation" has been applied generally to any lands
in Alaska set aside for the benefit of Indians. The lands in established
native townsites are held in trust by the Federal Government for disposal
as provided by the 1926 Alaska Native Townsite Act which authorizes
the townsite trustee to issue a restricted deed to an Alaskan native
for a tract of land occupied by and set apart for him in a townsite
established under the 1891 Townsite Act.

**History.** The Tlingit were formerly one of North America's more
powerful tribes, crossing the mountains from Canada to seek the seacoast. Russian explorers found them there in 1741 and exerted a harsh
and oppressive rule over them. The Tlingit continued to live in this
area, dividing into villages, each with hunting and fishing grounds. Today they participate actively in Alaska's political affairs.

**Culture.** The Tlingit developed a rich economy based upon the
abundant resources of the ocean and coast. They constructed very
seaworthy boats and canoes and appear to have carried on fairly active
trade with the Orient. War captives from other tribes were enslaved.
Individuals had a clearly defined rank and status within the society;
however, they were quite mobile from generation to generation. Social
status among the Tlingit depended upon elaborate feasts called "Potlatches" at which the heads of families or clans vied for prestige by
destroying or giving away vast quantities of valuable goods. The goat
wool and cedar bark ceremonial blanket has always been in great demand
as a trade item with each house having its own design. Totem poles
were important to the Tlingit culture, serving as the decorative record
of outstanding events of a family or clan.

**Government.** Klawock is governed by a popularly elected common
council with the mayor functioning as chief administrative officer.

**Population Profile. 1969:** Indian resident 200; Unemployment
68%.

**Tribal Economy.** The tribe owns and operates the Klawock Oceanside
Packing Company. There are a variety of retail businesses in Craig.

**Climate.** The mild and moist climate created by the Pacific currents
attracted the ancestors of the people now living in Craig. The rainfall
measures close to 105 inches each year. Temperatures reach highs
of 80 degrees and lows of 15 degrees.

**Transportation.** The nearest city with adequate transportation service is Ketchikan, 85 miles from Craig. Commerical transportation by air, truck, and bus is available here.

**Community Facilities.** Craig has a municipal water and sewer system. Electricity is provided by the Alaska Power and Telephone Company. The hospital in Ketchikan is the nearest source of health care.

**Recreation.** The Prince of Wales Island attracts numerous sportsmen to the excellent trout and salmon fishing and bear and deer hunting.

# ARIZONA

AK CHIN RESERVATION                    Federal Reservation
Pinal County
Papago Tribe
Tribal Headquarters: Ak Chin Community, Arizona

**Land Status.** Total area: 21,840 acres. All the land is tribally-owned. The tribal members refused to accept the assignments of allotments to individuals when the Bureau of Indian Affairs policies so dictated.

**History.** The Papago, or Bean People, reside in the southern part of Arizona including the Ak Chin Reservation. Until the coming of the Spaniards from whom they learned stock raising, the Papago Indians were farmers using fields irrigated only by flash floods. Although many of the Papagos are better known today as cattlemen, those on the Ak Chin Reservation still rely on their 10,000-acre farm for jobs and income.

**Culture.** The Ak Chin Papago are much more advanced than the majority of the Papagos due to their proximity to semiurban influences. The Papago speak a language unrelated to other Indian languages in the area but Pima. They were agricultural, but moved frequently to find new water sources. Tribal government was based on autonomous related villages which were governed by head men and councils. The Papago extend from Ak Chin to Sonora, Mexico.

**Government.** The governing body is the tribal council as provided under the Articles of Association, approved December 1961. The active committees include the Farm Board; Education, Health and Welfare; and Housing. Profits from the tribal farm are used for community betterment.

**Population Profile. 1969:** Tribal enrollment 289; Indian resident 230; Underemployment 26%. The education level is 7.0 grades. No one in the tribe has attended college; however, unlimited scholarship money is available from the farm profits.

**Tribal Economy.** The tribal income of $180,000 per year is composed completely of tribal farm profits. The tribe currently operates the farm and a tribal store and service station.

**Climate.** In this arid section of the country, rainfall averages 8 inches annually, and temperatures range from a high of 110 degrees to a low of 30 degrees.

**Transportation.** A county road connects the reservation with Interstate 10 to the north and Interstate 8 to the south. Commercial train, truck, and bus lines serve Maricopa, 5 miles from the reservation. The nearest commercial air service is at the Phoenix Airport, 40 miles from Ak Chin.

**Utilities.** The tribe provides its own water and sewage service, and its own electricity. The PHS hospital in Sacaton, Arizona, provides medical care for the Ak Chin residents.

CAMP VERDE RESERVATION                    Federal Reservation
Yavapai County
Yavapai-Apache Tribe
Tribal Headquarters: Middle Verde, Arizona

**Land Status.** Tribal land: 560 acres. Allotted land: 80 acres. Total area: 640 acres.

**History.** Between 1000 and 1500 A.D., fierce nomadic bands of Athapascan Indians came from the North to roam the area which is now Arizona and New Mexico. These bands were the ancestors of the Apache, a feared group of raiders and killers. In 1873, most hostile bands of Apaches were rounded up and placed on reservations, including the San Carlos Reservation in Arizona. Subsequently, a small group left and moved northeast to found the Camp Verde Reservation.

**Culture.** The Apache made their living as nomadic raiders. They were influenced culturally by the area in which they lived. Their religion was shamanistic, and their mythology rich. They believed in mountain spirits which had great powers over people for good or evil. They also feared witches and the dead who they believed could influence the living. The Apache lived in easily-moved thatched wickiups which they covered with hide in the winter. Clothing was made from hides. Baskets sealed with pitch to be waterproof were used as cooking vessels.

**Population Profile. 1969:** Tribal enrollment 682; Indian resident 607; Unemployment 77%; Median family income $2,830. **1980:** Indian resident 173; Non-Indian resident 27; Percent Indian of total population 86.5; Total housing units 51; Occupied housing units 51.

**Tribal Economy.** The tribal income of $1,700 is derived from farming leases of reservation land to non-Indians. The tribe is a member of the Indian Development District of Arizona and hopes, through this organization, to achieve for Indians a greater share of the State's growth.

**Climate.** The reservation is located in central Arizona, where the climate is semiarid, averaging 12 inches of rain annually. The temperature ranges from a high of 95 degrees to a low of 15 degrees.

**Transportation.** The Camp Verde Reservation is located on State Highway No. 279 which connects with Interstate 17 which is the major north-south highway for the area. Phoenix is 75 miles to the south by this highway. Commerical air and train companies serve Flagstaff, Arizona, which lies 50 miles from the reservation. Bus and trucklines serve Camp Verde, only 5 miles from the reservation.

**Community Facilities.** The reservation has its own water system which was installed by the Public Health Service. Individuals provide their own septic tanks. Electricity is supplied by the Arizona Public Service. There is a private hospital in Cottonwood and a PHS hospital in Camp Verde. Prescott and Phoenix both have larger hospitals.

**Recreation.** Of interest to visitors is the historic fort at Camp Verde. Also a major tourist attraction is the Montezuma Cattle National Monument, located 10 miles from the reservation.


COCOPAH RESERVATION                    Federal Reservation
Yuma County
Yuma Tribe
Tribal Headquarters: Somerton, Arizona

**Land Status.** Tribal land: 528 acres. Total area: 528 acres. The Cocopah Reservation was established by Executive Order in 1917. The reservation consisted of two parts, the larger part being northwest of the community of Somerton and the smaller part, the southeast. By an agreement between the Bureau of Reclamation and the Bureau of Indian Affairs of March 21, 1956, two lots covering 62 acres were set aside from public domain for the use of Cocopah Indians on a temporary basis.

**History.** The Cocopah Indians were one of the Yuman Tribes living along the Colorado River. In earlier times they came from Mexico and Baja, California. About the year 1760, the Yuma, Cocopah, and Maricopa composed one tribe known as the Coco-Maricopa Tribe. They occupied the country about the head of the Gulf of California, and for some distance up the Colorado River. At that time, a dispute resulted in the Cocopah Tribe's splitting from the main group. They were allowed to secede in peace. This pacific policy soon afterward induced the party, now known as the Maricopa, to secede also. However, the secession incurred the severe displeasure and hostility of the remainder who now form the Yuma Tribe.

**Culture.** The Yuman Tribe expertly farmed the fertile flatlands along the Colorado River. The tribe was divided into clans and families. These subunits of the tribe owned sections of land. The Yuman men, who were generally quite large, were widely known as fierce fighters. Although the tribe was sedentary, they had summer houses which were opensided to let the breeze through in the very hot climate.

**Government.** The Cocopah Tribe is governed by a popularly elected tribal council consisting of five members. Its authority is derived from the constitution approved under the Indian Reorganization Act of 1934.

**Population Profile. 1969:** Indian resident 48; Non-Indian resident 41; Underemployment 35%. **1980:** Indian resident 349; Non-Indian resident 6; Percent Indian of total population 98.3; Total housing units 89; Occupied housing units 68. Education level: 8.0 grades.

**Tribal Economy.** The annual tribal income of $2,400 comes entirely from farming. The tribe is a member of the Indian Development District of Arizona.

**Climate.** The climate in the reservation area is very hot and arid. Rainfall averages only 3 inches per year. The temperature goes as high as 115 degrees and only as low as 33 degrees.

**Transportation.** State Highway No. 95 crosses the reservation north-south. The nearest commercial transportation by air, bus, train, and truck, serves Yuma, Arizona, 17 miles from Cocopah.

**Utilities.** Cocopah has a community water system, installed by PHS, and individual septic tanks. Residents use bottled gas or electricity available from the Arizona Public Service. For medical care, tribal members can go to a private hospital in Yuma, or a PHS hospital in Winterhaven, California, on the Yuma Reservation.

COLORADO RIVER RESERVATION                    Federal Reservation
Yuma County
San Bernardino and Riverside Counties, California
Mojave and Chemehuevi Tribes
Tribal Headquarters: Parker, Arizona

**Land Status.** Tribal land: 258,134 acres. Allotted land: 5,958 acres. Total Area: 264,092 acres. Of the total acreage, 225,995 acres lie in Arizona and 38,096 in California.

**History.** The Mojave and Chemehuevi Indians have lived on the Lower Colorado River since recorded history. The Mojave controlled both sides of the river from Needles, California, to Black Canyon. The Chemehuevi controlled lands lying between the Mojave and the Quechan who lived farther to the south. The Mojave at first welcomed the Spanish but soon changed their position when the Spaniards tried to impose a new way of life upon them. The Mojave then became widely feared for their bellicosity. Upon acquiring this territory under the Treaty of Guadalupe Hidalgo in 1848, the U.S. agreed to preserve recognition of the Indian people's right to their land. The Colorado River Reservation was created as an inducement to the Mojave and Chemehuevi to abandon the tactics of war and adopt agriculture. The Colorado River Tribes include not only the Mojave and Chemehuevi but also some Hopi and Navajo who were located here following World War II.

**Culture.** The Mojave and Chemehuevi were other subgroups of the Yuman tribe which lived along the Colorado River and farmed the rich bottomlands there. Their major crops were corn, melons, pumpkins, native beans, roots, and mesquite beans. The Yuman lived in scattered groups in homes made of brush placed between upright mesquite logs or "sandwich houses" made of mud and wood. For traveling along the river, these Indians constructed rafts from bundles of reeds instead of making boats or canoes. The Mojave were the most populous and warlike of the Yuman tribes.

**Government.** The Colorado River Tribes adopted a constitution in 1937 under the Indian Reorganization Act. The tribal council, the governing body for the Colorado River Tribes, meets monthly, with additional meetings called. Council members are elected every 2 years on a staggered basis.

**Population Profile. 1969:** Indian resident 1,668; Unemployment 53%; Underemployment 10%; Median family income $4,500. **1980:** Indian resident 1,965; Non-Indian resident 5,908; Percent Indian of total population 25%; Total housing units 3,905; Occupied housing units 2,641. On the Colorado River Reservation, most members of the family work and pool their resources so that the median family income figure is substantially higher than the actual earning level of the head of the family. The median education level for the reservation was 11 years of school. In the 1968 school year, 16 tribal members were in colleges or junior colleges. There are no Bureau of Indian Affairs' schools on the reservation; all students must attend public or private schools.

**Tribal Economy.** The annual average tribal income of $600,000 is earned almost wholly from farming. Companies now located on the reservation include an aluminum lawn furniture manufacturer; three concrete, sand, and gravel contractors; a marina sales and service company; a tire center; and a farm machinery sales and service dealer. The Blue Water Marina was constructed by the tribe. The tribe is a member of the Indian Development District of Arizona through which it hopes to augment its development trends. Sand and gravel deposits are currently being exploited. Clay deposits, gypsum, and small amounts of gold are also found on this reservation.

**Climate.** The weather in this area is usually warm and sunny. The average July high is 93 degrees. Agriculture in this area is encouraged by the 259-day growing season; however, the low rainfall of 5.5 inches per year makes irrigation necessary.

**Transportation.** The reservation is located along a major east-west transportation corridor, Interstates 40 and 10. Train, bus, and truck service are available in Parker on the reservation; however, for commercial air service, residents must travel 60 miles to Blythe, California.

**Community Facilities.** The infrastructure on the reservation is obsolete and a deterrent to growth. The reservation's industrial park, however, has utilities adequate for any industry. The Arizona Public Service Company supplies electricity and natural gas to Parker and other parts of the reservation. A 20-bed hospital in Parker is operated by the Indian Health Service. Additional hospitals are located in Yuma, Arizona, 125 miles south of Parker. Tribal activities are centered in the modern tribal community buildings.

**Recreation.** The tremendous appeal of the Colorado River to hunters, fishermen, and tourists is only now being recognized and exploited. The area is a natural paradise for year-round activities. To take advantage of their natural industry, the Colorado River Tribes have constructed the Blue Water Marina and continue to develop facilities for vacationers. The area is excellent for water sports and other outdoor activities year round. Facilities for overnight visitors are available in Parker.

FORT APACHE RESERVATION                    Federal Reservation
Apache, Gila, and Navajo Counties
White Mountain Apache Tribe
Tribal Headquarters: Whiteriver, Arizona

**Land Status.** Total area: 1,664,872 acres. All the land is tribally-owned. This reservation was originally established in 1871 as a part of the White Mountain Indian Reservation which was divided into the San Carlos Reservation and the Fort Apache Reservation in 1897.

**History.** The Apache were a nomadic people who were attracted to the Southwest by the abundance they saw there. They usually lived in mountainous areas and raided the pueblo villages for food, crops, and material goods. There were, however, peaceful periods when the two groups traded without hostility. The Spanish also became a target of Apache raids, and adopted the Zuni word "Apache" meaning enemy. Harsh treatment by whites increased animosity. Because they had not settled in any given area and lived by raiding other people, the Apache were difficult to subdue, and were the last tribe to be defeated by the United States Government. The Apache wars ended finally in the late 19th century. The White Mountain Apache donated the Nation's Christmas tree for 1965, a 70-foot blue spruce. It was the largest tree ever to stand on the ellipse.

**Culture.** The Apache were large, well-built people trained from childhood to be hunters and fighters. They were not horsemen and never fully adopted the use of the horse. Religious beliefs were centered upon the shaman, who was the religious leader. Mountain spirits, believed to possess great powers of both good and evil over people, are impersonated in the mountain spirit dances. The thatched wickiups in which the Apache lived were covered with hide in the winter. Clothing was made out of skins. The people were also skilled in basketry, sealing some with pitch to be watertight.

**Government.** The tribe adopted a constitution in August 1938, according to the provision of the Indian Reorganization Act of 1934, and amended the constitution in June 1958. The reservation is governed by an elected tribal council which holds office for a term of 2 years.

**Population Profile. 1969:** Tribal enrollment 6,288; Indian resident 5,855; Non-Indian resident 2,000; Unemployment 54%; Underemployment 7%; Median family income $3,800. **1980:** Indian resident 6,880; Non-Indian resident 894; Percent Indian of total population 88.5; Total housing units 2,962; Occupied housing units 1,797. The education level for the reservation is about eighth grade. There are currently 64 tribal members in college. The tribe has established an ample scholarship fund, and money for education is also available from the Bureau of Indian Affairs.

**Tribal Economy.** Eighty percent of the annual tribal income of $1 million represents forest industry profits. The remainder of the tribe's income is derived from farming and business profits. The tribe employs a total of 200 persons in various enterprises. The White Mountain Apache Enterprise and the White Mountain Recreation Enterprise are organizations to develop the recreational potential of the reservation.

The Fort Apache Timber Company works the reservation's impressive forest resources. Other tribal associations are the Whiteriver Construction Enterprise, and the Livestock Association, which manages a 2,000-head herd. Three private lumber companies are also located on the reservation: The Southwest Forest Industries, Western Wood Products, and Western Pine Sales. The tribe, through its membership in the Indian Development District of Arizona, has access to professional planning, technical skills, and funding assistance. Timber is the primary resource on the reservation and there are deposits of asbestos and cinders.

**Climate.** The climate of the reservation is strongly affected by the topography. Much of the reservation is mountainous with elevations ranging from 2,700 to 11,490 feet. The Mogollon Rim passes through the reservation. Rainfall averages from 12 to 30 inches yearly, varying with the elevation. The climate is mild, much cooler in the summer than the nearby desert area. Temperatures range from 90 degrees to 15 degrees.

**Transportation.** U.S. Route 60 is the major north-south route through the reservation. U.S. Route 70 comes into the reservation from the southeast and junctions with 60 to continue west to Phoenix. Other smaller roads connect the towns of the reservation. Train, bus, and trucklines serve the industries and residents of the reservation. A commerical air shuttle to Phoenix is located in Show Low, 10 miles off the reservation.

**Community Facilities.** Where there are no municipal or local water systems, water is drawn from wells. Residents buy L.P. gas. The Arizona Public Service Company and the Navopache Electric Coop. provide electricity to the reservation. The hospital in Whiteriver is operated by the U.S. Public Health Service.

**Recreation.** The cool mountain climate is a welcome change from the hot, dry regions surrounding the reservation. There are numerous campsites where activities include water recreation, hunting, and sightseeing. The tribe runs a narrow-gauge sightseeing train. Of interest to visitors are Fort Apache, a military outpost for the territory, and the Kinishba Ruins, an ancient Indian village. The tribal fair and rodeo are held annually. Numerous tourist facilities on the reservation, including the Hon-Dah Motel and Restaurant operated by the tribe, provide accommodations for non-campers.


FORT MCDOWELL RESERVATION                    Federal Reservation
Maricopa County
Mojave, Apache, and Yavapai Tribes
Tribal Headquarters: Scottsdale, Arizona

**Land Status.** Tribal land: 24,680 acres. Total area: 24,680 acres. Approximately two-thirds of the land will be inundated by the Orme Dam, a diversion dam for the Central Arizona Project. Negotiations are being made to transfer an equivalent amount of acreage from adjoining Federal lands.

**History.** These people are descended from the Apache bands, Mojave, and Yavapai who were assigned to the Fort McDowell Military Reservation at the end of the Indian Wars. These tribes were known as strong, brave fighters.

**Government.** Under the constitution and bylaws of the Fort McDowell Mohave-Apache Community and under the corporate charter of the community, the tribal council is the popularly elected organization which carries out the program of the tribe. They are assisted by a Planning Commission, Citizens Advisory Committee, Housing Authority, and various other committees.

**Population Profile. 1969:** Tribal enrollment 402; Indian resident 327; Unemployment 20%; Underemployment 34%. **1980:** Indian resident 345; Non-Indian resident 4; Percent Indian of total population 98.9; Total housing units 94; Occupied housing units 84. The education level on the reservation is the 11th grade. Three members are college graduates.

**Tribal Economy.** Annual tribal income: $16,000 is derived largely from recreation fees and the City of Phoenix rental for a water facility. The remaining 10 percent comes from farming. There are four full-time tribal employees. The only commercial establishment on the reservation is a service station which is tribally owned.

**Climate.** Located near the Phoenix area, the climate is dry and sunny. Rainfall averages 7 inches per year. Temperatures range from a high of 110 degrees to a low of 30 degrees.

**Transportation.** State Highway No. 87 runs through the reservation east-west. Commercial transportation by air, train, truck, and bus, are all readily available in Phoenix which lies 28 miles from the reservation.

**Utilities.** The water system was provided by USPHS. Ample electricity comes from the Salt River Project. Indians are given health care at the PHS hospital in Phoenix.


GILA RIVER RESERVATION                          Federal Reservation
Maricopa and Pinal Counties
Pima-Maricopa Tribes
Tribal Headquarters: Sacaton, Arizona

**Land Status.** Tribal land: 274,492 acres; Government land: 3 acres; Allotted land: 97,438 acres; Total area: 371,933 acres.

**History.** The Pima, or River People, have occupied the same locality for centuries, continuing the Hohokam tradition of irrigated farming, industriousness, peacefulness, and artistic excellence. The original reservation of 64,000 acres was designated by an Act of Congress in 1859. Subsequent Executive Orders have increased it to its present size. As a result of their extensive use of irrigation as a community project, and the necessity of uniting for their mutual protection against the Apaches, their government structure was well organized.

**Culture.** The Spaniards, first encountering the Pimas in the late 16th century, found them to be advanced in agriculture. The Spaniards introduced new farm crops such as wheat, and a religion new to the

Indians, Christianity. The Pima were always peace-loving, and developed a highly organized culture. They were wealthy compared to the neighboring tribes.

**Government.** The 17-member, popularly-elected tribal council represents the seven districts of the reservation. The sources of power for the governing body are granted in the constitution adopted and approved in accord with the Indian Reorganization Act of 1934.

**Population Profile. 1969:** Tribal enrollment 7,200; Indian resident 7,555; Unemployment 25%; Underemployment 32%. **1980:** Indian resident 7,067; Non-Indian resident 313; Percent Indian of total population 95.8; Total housing units 1,733; Occupied housing units 1,677. Education level: 8.5 grades. The tribe has invested $100,000 from which it offers limited grants for students continuing their education. Scholarships are also available from the Bureau of Indian Affairs and private sources.

**Tribal Economy.** Average annual tribal income: $374,000. Tribal associations/cooperatives: Pima Community Farm; North Santan Development Enterprise; Fox Butte Feed Pens; Maricopa Indian Coop. Association, Inc.; Maricopa Indian Village Association, Inc.; San Tan Economic Development Corporation; Pima-Coolidge Economic Development Corp.; Lone Butte Economic Development Corp. Commercial/industrial establishments: Pima Valve Company - private; Nu-Pak Corp. (subsidiary of Sovereign Industries) - private; Baron Container Corp. - private; Spur Feeding Company - private; Adams Foods, Inc. - private; Dela Enterprises - private.

**Climate.** The Phoenix area is noted for its year-round dry, sunny climate. Rainfall averages 7 inches per year. The temperature ranges from a high of 110 degrees to a low of 30 degrees.

**Transportation.** State Highway No. 87 (northeast-southeast) crosses the reservation. State Highway No. 93 is a north-south route. Interstate 10 is a major north-south route for the area. Commercial airlines at the Phoenix airport serve the area. Trains stop in Phoenix, 25 miles from the reservation, although tracks pass through the reservation. Commercial bus and trucklines stop in Sacaton.

**Utilities.** The water and sewer system was constructed by the USPHS. Nearby communities also supply water. Gas can be obtained from the Arizona Public Service and Southwest Gas. Electricity is provided for the reservation by the San Carlos Project and the Salt River Project. The PHS Hospital located in Sacaton serves the eastern portion of the reservation. Additional hospital facilities are available at the Phoenix Indian Hospital and other private hospitals in Phoenix.

**Recreation.** Adjacent to the reservation is the Casa Grande Ruins National Monument. The Snaketown Ruins on the reservation are the most famous of Hohokam ruins and are being considered as a national monument. The reservation features some of the best dove hunting in the state. All types of recreational and cultural activities are also available in nearby Phoenix.

HAVASUPAI RESERVATION                    Federal Reservation
Coconino County
Havasupai Tribe
Tribal Headquarters: Supai, Arizona

**Land Status.** Total area: 3,058 acres. All the reservation land is tribally-owned. The reservation, which lies at the bottom of the Grand Canyon, 3,000 feet deep, is surrounded by Forest Service and parkland. An 1880 Executive Order created the reservation of 60 square miles. This area was reduced to 518.6 acres in 1882. Because of this land loss, the tribe was granted grazing rights on 245,760 acres of Federal land.

**History.** The Havasupai have for centuries made their home in the bottom of this extremely rugged section of the Grand Canyon. Their reservation lies 3,000 feet below the canyon rim and averages one-quarter mile in width.

**Culture.** The "People of the Blue-Green Water" were a sedentary tribe living along the Colorado River. They practiced agriculture with a planting stick similar to the pueblo method, irrigated their fields, and made baskets and pottery. They are probably related to the basin culture rather than to the rancheria or pueblo, but they have adopted some farming methods and ceremonies from the Hopi. Havasupai social organization was simple, the family being the sole unit. Chiefs were hereditary and patrilineal. Havasupai religion was shamanistic, and there was an absence of organized religious rites. The people have a very peaceful disposition. They are closely related to the Hualapai.

**Government.** The Havasupai Council is composed of seven members, four selected and three hereditary chiefs. The chairman and vice-chairman appoint a secretary from within the council. The constitution and bylaws were adopted in 1939, and the tribe incorporated under a corporate charter in 1946. The council is assisted by a general manager, tourist enterprise manager, trading company manager, and stocktender manager.

**Population Profile.** **1969:** Tribal enrollment 365; Indian resident 219; Unemployment 38%. **1980:** Indian resident 267; Non-Indian resident 15; Percent Indian of total population 94.7; Total housing units 87; Occupied housing units 69.

**Tribal Economy.** Tribal income averages $40,000 per year, and is earned wholly through tourism. The tourism industry is promoted by the Havasupai Tourist Enterprise, a tribal association. The tribe also operates the Havasupai Trading Company.

**Climate.** The bottom of the Grand Canyon is hot and arid, with spectacular scenery. Temperatures range from 112 degrees to -20 degrees, but average a moderate 62 degrees low temperature. Rainfall is 8 inches per year.

**Transportation.** A dirt road connects the canyon rim with U.S. Highway No. 66, 60 miles away. The remainder of the trip down the canyon wall to Havasupai can be made only by foot or by mule. Train, bus, and trucklines stop in Peach Springs, 70 miles from Havasupai. Air service is located in Kingman, 120 miles from Havasupai.

**Community Facilities.** The school on the reservation has classes through second grade only. For further education, students are sent to boarding school at Fort Apache. The USPHS maintains a clinic in Peach Springs; however, for more intensive medical care, the Havasupai must go to the USPHS hospital in Phoenix, Arizona. A HUD community building was recently completed.

**Recreation.** Tourism is the tribal industry. The area is very attractive and provides excellent hunting and fishing. The number of tourists visiting the canyon is limited only to the extent of facilities. The tribe provides both facilities and guides.


HOPI RESERVATION                                    Federal Reservation
Coconino and Navajo Counties
Hopi Tribe
Tribal Headquarters: Oraibi, Arizona

**Land Status.** Total area 2,472,254.26 acres. All land is tribally-owned. An Executive Order of 1882 granted the Hopi Tribe 2,600,000 acres in northeastern Arizona, entirely surrounded by the Navajo Reservation. The Hopi are presently living on only 650,000 acres, the remainder being occupied by the Navajo. Conflicting tribal claims to land have led to a series of ownership and boundary disputes. A 1963 court decision provided for an area of joint-use land and negotiation of disputes. The Navajo, however, have not cooperated and the case will have to be returned to the courts.

**History.** The precise origin of the Hopi is unknown. Their own legends relate that their ancestors climbed upward through four underground chambers or kivas, living in many places before settling in their present location on the Black Mesa of the Colorado Plateau, where the Hopi have lived for nearly 1,000 years. Old Oraibi, built at least by 1150 is probably the oldest continuously occupied city in the United States today. The Spanish visited the Hopi area several times from 1540 until the Pueblo Revolt in 1680. During the revolt, the Hopi moved many of their villages to mesa tops for defense purposes, and sheltered other refugees from other pueblos such as Isleta. The Hopi destroyed the Spanish missions, and killed many of the priests. The Spanish made no effort to re-establish control of the Hopi. In the early 20th century, several new towns were founded. Many Hopi are moving from mesa tops to the new towns at the foot of the mesas.

**Culture.** The Hopi, westernmost of the pueblos, speak a Uto-Aztecan language rather than the Tanoan or Keresan spoken by most other pueblos. The old towns are constructed in typical adobe architecture. Each village is autonomous, an individual being a lifetime resident of his village even if he marries someone from another village. Both property inheritance and residence are matriarchal. Hopi as a whole is a closed community. The tribal members have a distinct pride in their nation or tribe which may be an important factor in maintaining the vibrancy and vitality of the culture. Considered by many to be outstanding intellectuals of Indian tribes, the Hopi are patient, peaceful, industrious people. They have developed a complex system of gods or kachinas which are impersonated in many of the dances. These intricate dances, representative of their belief, are usually closed to the public. Kachina dolls, carved and decorated to resemble the gods, are used to teach children. Hopi also produce excellent silverwork and silver overlay, polychrome pottery, baskets, and other art forms.

**Government.** Each of the villages is organized independently, having either an elected governor or a hereditary village chief. The first tribal constitution was adopted in 1935; however, a tribal council was not elected until 1955. There is much resistance to change which might undermine their tradition and religion. Some of the more conservative villages still do not accept the authority of the tribal council. The Hopi Tribe is a member of the Indian Development District of Arizona, through which it obtains planning and development funding assistance.

**Population Profile. 1969:** Tribal enrollment 6,000; Indian resident 5,876; Unemployment 49%; Underemployment 22%; Median family income $2,000. **1980:** Indian resident 6,591; Non-Indian resident 305; Percent Indian of total population 95.6; Total housing units 2,553; Occupied housing units 1,597. Hopi usually prefer to live on the reservation in spite of limited job opportunities there. The unemployed labor force thus has an unusually high skill level. There are five BIA elementary schools on the reservation. Non-Indians attend school in Keams Canyon. All high school students are bussed from Keams Canyon to schools in Ganado or Tuba City. There are now more than 400 Hopis in high school and 185 in higher education.

**Tribal Economy.** The Hopi economy is extremely limited, being removed from economic centers and surrounded by the Navajo Reservation. Some Hopi own and operate small businesses, including arts and crafts shops, which produce excellent work. Many families farm at subsistence level to supplement their living. Government agencies and the tribal members employ some Indians on the reservation; however, because of the scarcity of jobs on the reservation, many Hopi men commute daily or weekly to nearby areas for skilled or semiskilled jobs. The tribe has established an industrial park near Winslow. A garment factory has located here and employs many Hopi women. The tribe is working to develop an economy on the reservation capable of employing all tribal members seeking work. The Black Mesa on which the reservation lies, is a rich coal deposit. There is also oil under reservation land.

**Climate.** The climate is generally mild with few seasonal extremes. Nights are much cooler than the days as is typical of desert or semi-desert areas. Rainfall averages 10 inches annually.

**Transportation.** State Highway No. 264 crosses the reservation east-west. State Highway No. 77 runs south from 264. Holbrook, which is located 75 miles from the reservation, is served by commercial train and buslines. Winslow, 108 miles from Hopi, is the nearest available commercial air service.

**Community Facilities.** There is no gas piped to the reservation, the nearest pipeline being 20 miles southeast of the reservation. Electricity is provided by the Arizona Public Service Company. The U.S. Public Health Service operates a hospital on the reservation. Other hospitals are located in Holbrook, Winslow, Flagstaff, and Ganado.

**Recreation.** There is much of interest to visitors on the reservation. Old Oraibi at the top of Third Mesa is the oldest continuously occupied town in the United States. There are also many other villages on the reservation built in the traditional style from stones and adobe. Highway No. 264 winds along the base of the three mesas, passing through and by many of the other villages. The Hopi people are warm and friendly, usually eager to greet visitors. Their ceremonies are colorful, intricate, and inspiring. The Hopi consider any observer to be a participant.


HUALAPAI RESERVATION                    Federal Reservation
Mohave, Coconino, and Yavapai Counties
Hualapai Tribe
Tribal Headquarters: Peach Springs, Arizona

**Land Status.** Tribal land: 991,680 acres; Government land: 783 acres; Total area: 992,463 acres. A January 1883 Executive Order established a reservation of 500,000 acres. In June 1911, 60 acres in the Big Sandy area were added by Executive Order. The Santa Fe Railroad deeded 6,440.68 acres in Clay Springs to the reservation in 1947. In May 1943, the Secretary of the Interior ordered odd sections which were released by the Santa Fe Railroad to be added to the reservation.

**History.** The Hualapai Indians formerly lived in northeastern Arizona occupying an area much larger than they do today. The mid-19th century was a period of friction with whites. Peace ended abruptly when the Indians felt the treaty had been violated. A stable peace was finally achieved in 1870. The Hualapai fulfilled their promise to preserve the peace. The Hualapai objected to their removal by the Bureau of Indian Affairs which placed them in the hot, arid Colorado River Basin. Illness for many members resulted from living in the climate unlike that of their former cool mountain home. The principal Chief Schrum was instrumental in achieving the final settlements.

**Culture.** The Hualapai are of Yuman stock and closely related to the Havasupai. Ancient inhabitants of the Southwest, they lived mainly by hunting and gathering. They lived in mountainous areas and were described by whites as brave and enterprising. They are part of the Colorado River cultural group, less advanced in agriculture and architecture than the Pueblos. They also exhibit traits of the Great Basin area in their simplicity of social organization, ritual, and material culture. Religion is shamanistic. Clothing was made of bark or buckskin. They harvested seeds, grasses, pinon nuts, and game.

**Population Profile. 1969:** Tribal enrollment 410; Indian resident 1,030; Unemployment 45%. **1980:** Indian resident 809; Non-Indian resident 40; Percent Indian of total population 95.3; Total housing units 218; Occupied housing units 175.

**Tribal Economy.** The annual tribal income of $83,000 is made up largely of business profits, with forestry, farming, mineral use, and government income also contributing. The tribe employs four full-time employees. Tribal associations include the Hualapai Tribal Herd and the Peach Springs Livestock Association. The tribe also operates the Hualapai Trading Company.

**Climate.** The rainfall averages only 8 inches annually in this dry neighborhood of the Grand Canyon. The temperature ranges from a high of 100 degrees to a low of 10 degrees, although the winter average low is 31 degrees.

**Transportation.** U.S. Highway No. 66 crosses the reservation east-west. Train, bus and trucklines stop in Peach Springs. Reservation residents must drive 50 miles to Kingman, Arizona, for commercial air service.

**Community Facilities.** The USPHS operates a clinic in Peach Springs. For further medical care, residents must drive to Kingman or Williams.

**Recreation.** There are a motel and restaurant in Peach Springs. This is also the access to the Havasupai Reservation and the Grand Canyon. Hunting on the reservation is excellent and varied.


KAIBAB RESERVATION                    Federal Reservation
Mohave County
Paiute Tribe
Tribal Headquarters: Fredonia, Arizona

**Land Status.** Tribal land: 120,413 acres. Total area: 120,413 acres.

**History.** The Paiute Indians of the Kaibab Reservation were known as the "Digger Indians" because they maintained a gathering culture, digging edible roots for food, unlike the agricultural groups south of them. The reservation was established in 1907 for the Kaibab band of Southern Paiute and was reshaped by Executive Orders in 1913 and 1916.

**Culture.** The Kaibab Paiute are considered by anthropologists and linguists to be tribally distinct. Their language is of the Shoshonean language group and closely related to Hopi, Chemehuevi, Comanche, and Mojave. The tribal religion is primarily ethical rather than ritual.

**Government.** The popularly-elected Kaibab Paiute Tribal Council consists of six persons with an appointed secretary-treasurer. This body is responsible for the policy decisions of the tribe. They are assisted by a Finance Commission, a Code Review Committee, and a Citizens Participation Committee and Claims Committee.

**Population Profile. 1969:** Tribal enrollment 140; Indian resident 140; Unemployment 42%; Underemployment 16%. **1980:** Indian resident 93; Non-Indian resident 80; Percent Indian of total population 53.8; Total housing units 51; Occupied housing units 44. Education level: 8.0 grades. The tribe has set aside $100,000 in judgment funds for scholarships for students continuing their education.

**Tribal Economy.** The annual tribal income is $14,000. This income is derived almost entirely from farming. The only minerals present on the reservation are sand and gravel and they account for about 10 percent of the tribal income.

**Climate.** Rainfall averages 14 inches per year. The temperature ranges from a high of 80 degrees to a low of 20 degrees.

**Transportation.** State Highway No. 389 passes east-west through the reservation. U.S. north-south Highway No. 89 lies just east of the reservation. Commercial bus and trucklines serve Fredonia, 1 mile east of the reservation; however, residents must drive 80 miles to Cedar City, Utah, for air and trainlines.

**Utilities.** Water and sewer facilities for the reservation were installed by PHS. Gas is supplied by the Northern Arizona Gas Company in Fredonia. The Garkane Power Company of Utah provides electricity for the area. Tribal members contract for health care through the USPHS at Kanab, Utah.


NAVAJO RESERVATION                    Federal Reservation
Apache, Navajo, and Coconino Counties, Arizona
San Juan and McKinley Counties, New Mexico
San Juan County, Utah
Tribal Headquarters: Window Rock, Arizona

**Land Status.** Tribal land: 12,940,191 acres. Allotted land: 722,854 acres. Government land: 326,177 acres. Jointly-Owned: 1,950,000 acres. Total area: 13,989,212 acres.

**History.** In the early 1600's, the Navajo were an aggressive and powerful tribe. During this time, they acquired horses and sheep from the Spaniards as well as knowledge of working with metal and wool. The U.S. Government after misunderstandings, raids, and retaliations, decided to round up all Navajos and send them to Fort Sumner, New Mexico, where they would be taught a sedentary agricultural life patterned after that of the Pueblo Indians. In 1868, recognizing that the Fort Sumner experiment was a failure and acceding to Navajo appeals, the Government concluded a treaty and established the Navajo Reservation. The discovery of oil on the reservation in 1921 provided the stimulus for development.

**Culture.** The extended kin group, made up of two or more families, is an important unit of Navajo social organization. It is a cooperative unit of responsible leadership bound together by ties of marriage and close relationship. Women hold an important position in the tribe. Religion is still the core of Navajo culture, and the traditional sand paintings are used in healing ceremonies. Navajo are widely known for their silverwork and rug weaving. The tribe's industry, stamina, urge to succeed, and exceptional adaptability are central to the progress Navajo made within the century.

**Government.** The Navajo Tribe is governed by a council consisting of 74 members representing the 96 chapters which make up the reservation. This includes the Alamo, Canoncito, and Ramah Reservations in New Mexico as well as the Eastern Administrative Area. All programs and projects are processed through the Advisory Committee, which is also the Overall Economic Development Program Committee, before submission to the council. The popularly elected tribal chairman is administrative head of the tribe. The Navajos organized a General Council (Assembly) in 1921 to negotiate a development lease with the discovery of oil on the reservation. The present council draws its authority from a set of rules promulgated by the Secretary of the

Interior in 1938. Many tribal leaders have expressed the desire for the development of a formal constitution, but the council which was authorized by the Navajo-Hopi Rehabilitation Act of 1950 to draft such a document has never done so. The constitution matter is a major issue on the Navajo as is the issue of jurisdiction over 1,950,000 acres of land presently under the joint ownership of the Navajo and Hopi tribes.

**Population Profile. 1969:** Indian resident 119,546; Unemployment 51%; Underemployment 23%. **1980:** Indian resident 104,978; Non-Indian resident 5,465; Percent Indian of total population 95.1; Total housing units 35,580; Occupied housing units 24,422. The estimated education attainment level for the tribe as a whole is eighth grade. However, there is a major new thrust in emphasizing continuing education, and the tribe has just opened the Navajo Community College with an Indian enrollment of over 600 young people. In addition, 700 are enrolled in vocational training, and over 600 are engaged in on-the-job training. The tribe has over $10 million invested in securities; the proceeds are used for scholarships available to the young people.

**Tribal Economy.** The tribe receives an annual income of approximately $16 million annually with 69 percent from oil, gas, and minerals; 3 percent from forestry; 16 percent from business; and 22 percent from investments. There are approximately 1,000 full-time employees of the tribal government and 400 part-time employees. Organizations established by the tribal government include: Office of Navajo Economic Opportunity, Navajo Tribal Housing Authority, Navajo Arts and Crafts Guild, Wingate Indian Village, Na-Tani-Nez Motel at Shiprock, Window Rock Motel, Cameron Arts and Crafts, and Agricultural Cooperatives. Business operations on the Navajo Reservation owned both by the tribe and private interests include:

| Company | Owner |
|---|---|
| Navajo Forest Products Industries | Navajo Tribe |
| Navajo Tribal Utility Authority | Navajo Tribe |
| Fairchild Semiconductor | Private |
| General Dynamics | Private |
| EPI Vostron | Private |
| Navajo Furniture | Private |
| Utah Construction and Mining | Private |
| Four Corners Power Plant | Private |
| W.R. Grace - Davidson Chemical Division | Private |

**Natural Resources.** There are substantial oil and natural gas reserves on the Navajo Reservation. In addition, a large coal mining operation has been started with others being planned. Other minerals are found in lesser quantity. Timber resources managed on a sustained yield basis provide 40 million board feet of lumber annually. Average annual precipitation is low, and temperatures tend to be moderate.

**Transportation.** U.S. Highway No. 89 crosses the western part of the reservation running north-south, while U.S. Highway No. 164 runs from U.S. Highway No. 89 at a point near Tuba City to the northeast part of the reservation near Shiprock, New Mexico. U.S. Highway No.

666 runs north–south crossing the east end of the reservation, and State Highway No. 265 (Navajo Route 3) crosses the reservation east–west in the southern half of the reservation. Motor freight carriers serve all major reservation communities. Nearest commercial airline and train service are at Gallup, New Mexico; and Flagstaff, Winslow, Grand Canyon, and Page, Arizona.

**Utilities.** The Navajo Tribal Utility Authority is the major supplier of electricity, natural gas, water, and sewer services on the reservation. In a few areas, Arizona Public Service supplies electricity; LP gas is marketed by private companies. Hospitals and clinics on the reservation are operated by the Public Health Service and provide necessary medical services to the residents.

**Recreation.** Parks pointing out the history of the area and camping sites in scenic places are provided by the tribe. These parks include the Grand Canyon Navajo Tribal Park, Bowl Canyon Creek Dam Recreational Area, Tsegi Canyon Tribal Park, Kinlichee Tribal Park, Window Rock-Tse Bonito Tribal Park, Little Colorado River Tribal Park, Lake Powell Tribal Park, and Monument Valley Tribal Park. In addition, the U.S. Government operates the following National Monuments within the reservation: Canyon De Chelly, Chaco Canyon, Rainbow Bridge, and Navajo. Other tribal tourism activities include the Navajo Tribal Museum Visitors Center, Research Library and Zoo at Window Rock, and Navajo Tribal Fairs held annually at Window Rock and Tuba City, Arizona, and Shiprock, New Mexico.

PAPAGO RESERVATION                    Federal Reservation
Maricopa, Pima, and Pinal Counties
Papago Tribe
Tribal Headquarters: Sells, Arizona

**Land Status.** Tribal land: 2,814,396 acres. Individual land: 41,003 acres. Government land: 30 acres. Total area: 2,855,430 acres. The Papago Reservation is composed of four segments: The main reservation, the Sells Reservation, is 2,773,358 acres. The Gila Bend Reservation which lies northwest of Sells, is 10,337 acres. Ajo lies immediately west of Sells and totals 640 acres. The San Xavier Reservation lies northeast of the Sells Reservation near Tucson and has an area of 71,095 acres.

**History.** The Papago may be descendants of the Hohokam Indians who reached a high cultural level and flourished around 1400 A.D. Other theories are that the Papago returned to their lands when the Hohokam disappeared. The Papago were agricultural and seminomadic moving to new locations in search of water. Under the U.S. the Papago suffered greatly as their few sources of water were used by others. They became the poorest Indian nation in the Southwest. The Papago, together with the Pima and Maricopa, helped the United States to force the Apache to peace in the 1860's. Because of their location in the extreme southwest desert, the Papago have been removed from the activity elsewhere in the country and are now making efforts to participate in the area's growth.

**Culture.** The Papago, a Piman tribe, are closely related to the Pima in Arizona. They made their home in the rather inhospitable desert, practicing agriculture. Fields were irrigated by flooding. Presently the Papago raise grains and stock. They were not, however, sedentary village dwellers as some other tribes because of the continual need to locate new sources of water. "Papago" means beans, referring to their staple crop. They also raised maize and cotton. To supplement the food they raised, the women gathered foods in the desert. The Papago are tall, dark-complected people who speak a language related to Pima. The women make excellent baskets of yucca and other natural fibers. Their houses are usually round, flat-topped with a shade ramada attached. Tribal organization was based on autonomous, related villages which were governed by headmen and councils. There are also Papago living in Sonora, Mexico.

**Government.** The Sells, San Xavier, Ajo, and Gila Bend Papago Reservations recently joined together for tribal government. The tribal council, which governs all the reservations, is composed of 22 members representing separate districts. A chairman and council are selected each year, the council selecting the chairman by majority vote. The tribal constitution of 1937 organized the tribe into a federal structure of government.

**Population Profile.** **1969:** Tribal enrollment N.A.; Indian resident 6,216; Unemployment 40%; Underemployment N.A.; Median family income $2,377. **1980:** Indian resident 6,959; Non-Indian resident 244; Percent Indian of total population 96.6; Total housing units 2,095; Occupied housing units 1,615. The education level for the Papago was 4.8 years in 1960. There is a public high school at Sells, three parochial schools and three BIA schools elsewhere on the reservation. There is an increasing emphasis on education within the tribe. There are currently 10 Papagos continuing their education beyond high school.

**Tribal Economy.** Minerals on the reservation include copper, gravel, building stone, and clay. The annual tribal income of $138,000 is a product of the mineral leases granted by the tribe. Commercial and industrial development on the reservation is minimal. The eight small stores on the main reservation charge higher prices than the other area stores. There are also five auto service stations and two cafes on the reservation. The copper mine and mill near Ajo employ the Papago. On the San Xavier Reservation, an industrial park is under construction. The park is located along State Highway No. 93, near Interstate Highway No. 19.

**Climate.** The reservation land is an arid desert with hot days and cool nights. Rainfall varies from less than 7 inches to 20 inches in the mountains. The growing season is 300 days, with temperatures varying from an average high of 90 degrees to an average low of 50 degrees.

**Transportation.** Arizona Highway No. 86 runs through the reservation from Tucson to Ajo. Arizona Highway No. 93 joins No. 86 northwest of Sells and runs north to Casa Grande. Interstate 19, a major route into Mexico, passes through the San Xavier Reservation. Interstate 8 connects the Gila Bend Reservation with Interstate 19 and 10, and Yuma, Arizona. Gravel surfaced roads connect towns on the reservation.

Tucson serves as a major transportation center for the region south of Phoenix, and air, bus, train, and trucklines provide ample service. A truckline serves Sells.

**Community Facilities.** Water for the reservation's residents is obtained only by digging deep wells, and from springs in the mountains. Natural gas is available only on San Xavier. Electricity is provided by the Trico Electric Cooperative with REA lines running along the highways. The Public Health Service operates a 50-bed hospital in Sells for the Papago. There is a Health Center Clinic in Santa Rosa. Papagos living on Gila Bend go to the PHS hospital in Phoenix, and those on San Xavier go to the PHS hospital in Tucson.

**Recreation.** The reservation is presently underdeveloped for recreation. There is some hunting of wild desert game. The old Spanish Xan Xavier del Bac Mission, located on the San Xavier Reservation, attracts many visitors. A good number of attractions are near the reservation, such as the Saguaro National Monument with Kitt Peak Observatory.


SALT RIVER RESERVATION                     Federal Reservation
Maricopa County
Pima-Maricopa Tribes
Tribal Headquarters: Scottsdale, Arizona

**Land Status.** Tribal land: 21,465 acres. Allotted land: 25,158 acres. Total area: 46,624 acres.

**History.** The Pima, or River People, have occupied the same locality for centuries, continuing the Hohokam tradition of irrigated farming, industriousness, peacefulness, and artistic excellence. Pima County became U.S. territory in 1853 through the Gadsden Purchase. The Salt River Reservation was established by Executive Order in 1879.

**Culture.** The early Spaniards found the Pimas advanced in agriculture as was indicated in the earliest recorded history of the Pima by Marcos de Niza in 1589 and Father Kino in 1694. Father Kino then introduced livestock, wheat, and other new farm crops as well as Christianity to the Pima. The tribe developed a highly organized culture.

**Government.** The official governing body of the tribe is the Salt River Pima-Maricopa Indian Community Tribal Council. It consists of seven popularly elected members and is authorized by the constitution approved under the Indian Reorganization Act of 1934.

**Population Profile.** **1969:** Tribal enrollment 2,265; Indian resident 2,282; Unemployment 19%; Underemployment 40%. **1980:** Indian resident 2,624; Non-Indian resident 1,465; Percent Indian of total population 64.2; Total housing units 1,577; Occupied housing units 1,331. Education level: 8.5 grades.

**Tribal Economy.** Average annual tribal income: $131,000. Commercial/Industrial establishments: Defiance of Arizona, Inc. - private ownership; Van's Evergreen Golf Course - private ownership. Sand and gravel are mined on the reservation.

**Climate.** In this arid section of the country, the rainfall averages only 7 inches each year. The temperature ranges from a high of 110 degrees to a low of 30 degrees.

**Transportation.** State Highway No. 87 crosses the reservation east-west. Bus and trucklines stop on the reservation. For commercial air and train service, the residents must go 10 miles to Phoenix.

**Utilities.** Water for the reservation is drawn from wells and from the City of Scottsdale. Sewage is disposed of in septic tanks. Arizona Public Service provides electricity and gas to the reservation area. Electricity is also available through the Salt River Project. Hospital care is provided to the tribe at the PHS hospital in Phoenix. Other private hospitals are also in Phoenix.

**Recreation.** The Salt River Reservation is adjacent to the tourism center of Scottsdale, Arizona, which is part of the metropolitan Phoenix area. The Tribe has constructed a gymnasium, swimming pool, and a community building which includes a tourist center and library. Upon completion of the Central Arizona Project, it is expected that the Orme Dam will be constructed on the Salt River Reservation and a major water-oriented tourism potential will result.


SAN CARLOS RESERVATION                    Federal Reservation
Gila and Graham Counties
Apache Tribe
Tribal Headquarters: San Carlos, Arizona

**Land Status.** Tribally-owned land: 1,853,841 acres. Government land: 22,415 acres. Allotted land: 960 acres. Total area: 1,877,216 acres.

**History.** A southern branch of the Athapascan family, the Apaches came to the Southwest probably around the 10th century. By the 17th century, they were known as savage warriors among other Indian tribes. The Apaches, named from the Zuni word meaning "enemy," engaged in widespread attacks on the white settlers until they were rounded up and sent to the San Carlos Reservation in 1873. The traditional traits of aggressiveness and individualism have been carried over by the Apache Tribe, and are being utilized today in establishing tribal enterprises and promoting the welfare of their people.

**Culture.** The Apache were nomadic raiders who never fully adopted the use of the horse except as meat. Each band's culture was affected by the area it lived in. The Apache lived in thatched wickiups which were covered with hide in the winter for greater protection. Clothing was made out of skins. The tribe was skilled in basketry, sealing some baskets with pitch to be watertight. Religion was shamanistic, and the tribe developed a rich mythology. Mountain spirits were believed to possess great power of both good and evil over people. The spirits are impersonated in the Mountain Spirit dances.

**Government.** The 12-member tribal council supervises all programs and activities on the reservation. Its authority is derived from the constitution of the tribe, approved under the Indian Reorganization Act of 1934.

**Population Profile. 1969:** Tribal enrollment 4,350; Indian resident 4,672; Unemployment 40%; Underemployment 18%. **1980:** Indian resident

5,872; Non-Indian resident 232; Percent Indian of total population 96.2; Total housing units 1,523; Occupied housing units 1,311. Education level: 8th grade.

**Tribal Economy.** Asbestos is the only mineral currently being mined on the reservation. The average tribal income is $459,000. Tribal associations and cooperatives include the Agriculture and Livestock Enterprise, Point of Pines Livestock Association, and the Tribal Farm Enterprise. The commercial and industrial establishments on the reservation include Bylas Trading Enterprise and the San Carlos Trading Enterprise, both tribally owned.

**Climate.** Rainfall averages 16 inches per year. The temperature ranges from a high of 95 degrees to a low of 30 degrees.

**Transportation.** U.S. Highway No. 60 crosses the reservation north-south. U.S. Highway No. 70 crosses the reservation east-west. Commercial air service is available in Phoenix, 100 miles from San Carlos. Train, bus, and trucklines serve Globe, 10 miles from the reservation.

**Utilities.** The water and sewer systems are provided by the USPHS. The Arizona Public Service Company provides both gas and electricity. The USPHS operates a hospital in San Carlos.

**Recreation.** The San Carlos Reservation has much potential for recreation and tourism development. The San Carlos Lake behind the Coolidge Dam is being developed into a major tourist center. Additional facilities are being planned. Boating, fishing, and hunting on the reservation are excellent.


YAVAPAI RESERVATION                    Federal Reservation
Yavapai County
Yavapai Tribe
Tribal Headquarters: Prescott, Arizona

**Land Status.** Tribally-owned land: 1,399 acres. Allotted land: 160 acres. Total area: 1,559 acres. By Congressional Act of 1935, 75 acres of the north edge of Prescott were transferred from the Veterans Administration to the Interior Department to be an Indian reservation for the Yavapai living in the area. A later act of Congress in May of 1965 added 1,298 acres to the reservation.

**History.** The Yavapai inhabited a vast area in Arizona embracing some 20,000 square miles. This territory had formerly been occupied by an agricultural people, but the Yavapai were hunters and gatherers. The three primary groups of Yavapai maintained good relations with one another. They cooperated in war and hunted and gathered in one another's territory. There was some hostility toward tribes to the south, namely the Pima, Maricopa, and other Yuman tribes. The Yavapai conducted some trade with the Navajo and tribes of the Lower Colorado River.

**Culture.** Linguistically and culturally the Yavapai have much in common with their neighbors the Hualapai and Havasupai. The Yavapai groups were nomadic, moving from place to place as wild crops ripened. Mescal, saguaro fruit, sunflower seed, and deer were important staples.

Some members sporadically cultivated maize and tobacco. The Yavapai lived in caves or huts which could be assembled quickly. Their religion was shamanistic. Basketry and pottery were not as well developed among the Yavapai as by some of their neighbors.

**Government.** The tribe is governed by the Yavapai-Prescott Community Council which is the Board of Directors of the Yavapai-Prescott Community Association. The tribe does not have a constitution but operates under Articles of Association bylaws approved in 1962. The governing board includes five persons elected to 2-year terms.

**Population Profile.** **1969:** Indian resident 85; Unemployment 35%; Underemployment 46%; Median family income $4,139. **1980:** Indian resident 66; Non-Indian resident 10; Percent Indian of total population 86.8; Total housing units 26; Occupied housing units 24.

**Tribal Economy.** The tribal income averages $5,000 per year. The tribe is a member of the Indian Development District of Arizona, an organization to promote development of the reservations in this State.

**Climate.** The rainfall in this area averages 14 inches per year. The temperature ranges from an average summer high of 95 degrees to a winter low of 10 degrees.

**Transportation.** State Highway No. 69 runs east-west through the reservation, and U.S. Highway No. 89 runs north-south. Prescott is a major transportation hub for this region northwest of Phoenix and air, rail, bus, and truck transportation are readily available just 1 mile from the reservation.

**Community Facilities.** Water for residents is drawn from wells installed by the Public Health Service. Septic tanks provide for waste disposal. The Arizona Public Service supplies electricity to the area. Gas can be obtained from the Southern Union Gas Company. A private hospital is located in Prescott.

CALIFORNIA

AGUA CALIENTE RESERVATION                    Federal Reservation
Riverside County
Agua Caliente Band
Tribal Headquarters: Palm Springs, California

**Land Status.** Tribally-owned land: 2,056 acres. Allotted land: 24,761 acres. Total area: 26,817 acres. The Agua Caliente Reservation is located in the center of the Palm Springs desert resort. The reservation was established on May 14, 1896, under the Act of January 12, 1891.

**Culture.** The Agua Caliente Band were part of the California cultural group. Much of the native culture was destroyed by the Spanish missionaries when the tribes were forced to live in rancherias at Spanish catholic missions. The Agua Caliente Band retain to the present day their language, songs, traditional foods and cooking, and the kinship pattern.

**Government.** The Agua Caliente Band's constitution and bylaws were approved in 1915 and amended in 1966. The tribe is governed by a five-member council which meets twice monthly. The chairman, vice-chairman, and secretary, and two members form the council. The treasurer is not a council member.

**Population Profile. 1969:** Tribal enrollment 117; Indian resident 74; Unemployment 10%; Underemployment 2 persons. **1980:** Indian resident 65; Non-Indian resident 13,678; Percent Indian of total population 0.5; Total housing units 13,369; Occupied housing units 6,943. The average education level for tribal members is 12th grade. There are presently between six and eight college graduates in the tribe. Students travel from 3 to 5 miles to attend public schools.

**Climate.** The reservation is located in a moderate climate. The land is rolling foothills and desert. Rainfall averages 3.6 inches per year. Temperatures reach highs of 122 degrees and lows of 26 degrees.

**Transportation.** The reservation lies 3 miles from Palm Springs. The resort city is served by bus, train, truck, and airlines. The train station is in North Palm Springs, 11 miles from Agua Caliente. State Highway No. 111 runs through the reservation to connect with Interstate 10 and Los Angeles.

**Community Facilities.** The reservation is connected to the city water and sewer system. South California Edison is the regional supplier for electricity and gas. Health care is available in Palm Springs from either private hospitals and doctors or from the Public Health Service.

**Recreation.** The Indian name for this area, Agua Caliente or Warm Water, describes the springs which have made Palm Springs a major resort area. The reservation itself has much potential for recreational development. There are ample facilities for recreation and amusements. The tribe has a community hall and there are six theaters in the area. A fiesta and Easter events are annual festivities.


ALTURAS RANCHERIA                    Federal Reservation
Modoc County
Pitt River Tribe
Tribal Headquarters: Alturas, California

**Land Status.** Total area: 20 acres. The rancheria was established by the Act of June 21, 1906, which appropriated funds for purchase of lands for California Indians. The rancheria was purchased on September 8, 1924. The rancheria is located 1 mile east of Alturas. The population is predominantly old people. Housing is substandard and land rights have been jeopardized by non-Indian ranchers.

**Culture.** The older people speak the Pitt-River language and practice traditional arts and crafts, which are made for gifts and personal use.

**Government.** The tribe has a spokesman and delegate to the Inter-Tribal Council of California.

**Population Profile. 1969:** Tribal enrollment 12; Indian resident 12; Unemployment 100%. **1980:** Indian resident 7; Non-Indian resident 0; Percent Indian of total population 100%; Total housing units 5; Occupied housing units 5. The average educational attainment is 7th grade. The elementary and high schools are 1 mile from the reservation.

**Climate.** Alturas lies in northeastern California where the land is quite flat and the climate is damp and rainy, averaging 12.8 inches of rainfall per year. Temperatures reach a high of 95 degrees and a low of -29 degrees.

**Transportation.** Alturas, 1 mile from the Indian land, has bus and truck service. Redding, 145 miles from the reservation is served by commercial air and trainlines. U.S. highway No. 395 runs north-south. State Highway No. 299 runs southwest to Redding and junctions with Interstate 5.

**Community Facilities.** The Modoc Health Center in Alturas provides medical care to the Indians. There are also a welfare clinic and a rest room here. The reservation is served by the Alturas Water Department. Gas is purchased from a local distributor. Pacific Power and Light supplies electricity. The tribe is a member of the Modoc Indian Health Project. The one tribal building is used for arts and crafts. The tribe meets weekly for Indian dancing and meetings.


AUGUSTINE RESERVATION                       Federal Reservation
Riverside County
Augustine Band of Mission Indians
Tribal Headquarters: Thermal, California

**Land Status.** Total area: 502 acres. The reservation was established in February 1893 under authority of the Act of January 12, 1891. It is located in a desert.

**Population Profile.** **1969:** Tribal enrollment 2; Indian resident 0.

**Climate.** The reservation is situated on flat, desert land, where the rainfall averages just under 4 inches per year. Temperatures in this warm and arid climate reach as high as 120 degrees and as low as 22 degrees.

**Transportation.** The nearest city to the reservation is Indio, 15 miles from Augustine. State Highway No. 111 runs north-southwest through Thermal. Trucklines stop in Coachella, 5 miles from Augustine. Other transportation by air, bus, and train is available in Indio. There is a private airstrip in Thermal, 5 miles from the Indian land.

**Community Facilities.** The tribe maintains the water system. There is no sewer system. Southern California Edison supplies electricity. Medical care and hospital facilities are available at Indio, 15 miles from the reservation.


BARONA RANCHERIA                            Federal Reservation
San Diego County
Barona Group of Capitan Band of Mission Indians
Tribal Headquarters: Lakeside, California

**Land Status.** Total area: 5,800 acres. The Capitan Grande Reservation was established by Executive Order of December 27, 1875. Executive Order of May 3, 1877, restored portions to public domain.

Executive Order of June 19, 1883, set apart certain lands for the reservation. The Barona Tract was purchased for the Barona group. The reservation is excellent for tourist, recreational and housing development.

**Population Profile. 1969:** Tribal enrollment 156; Indian resident 118; Unemployment 25%; Median family income less than $3,000. **1980:** Indian resident 222; Non-Indian resident 78; Percent Indian of total population 74; Total housing units 84; Occupied housing units 80. The average education level attained is 12th grade. A distance of 12 miles must be travelled to elementary school and 17 miles to high school in El Cajon. College can be attended at San Diego, 31 miles west of the reservation.

**Tribal Economy.** The reservation is centrally located in San Diego County on land that is rocky and hilly and not conducive to farming or grazing. Land is used for homesites, cattle grazing, and dry farming.

**Climate.** The climate is moderate, with a rainfall of about 6 inches per year. Temperatures range from a high of 103 degrees to a low of 20 degrees.

**Transportation.** Commercial airline and train service are available at San Diego, 31 miles west of the reservation. Bus service can be obtained in El Cajon 17 miles south and trucklines are available in Ramona, 12 miles south of the reservation. State Highway No. 67 runs north-south, 8 miles west of the reservation.

**Community Facilities.** Water is drawn from wells. Electricity is provided by the San Diego Gas and Electric Company. The sewer system consists of indoor plumbing with septic tanks.

The county hospital, county welfare clinics, and private dental facilities are available in El Cajon.


BERRY CREEK RANCHERIA                          Federal Reservation
Butte County
Maidu Tribe
Tribal Headquarters: Berry Creek, California

**Land Status.** Total area: 33 acres. All land is tribally owned. The tract of land was purchased in March, 1916, by the government from the Central Pacific Railway Company for the Dick Harry Band of Indians. Title to the land was vested in the U.S. with Indians having only a right to occupancy and use of the lands unless otherwise authorized by Congress.

**Culture.** Individual members host grass games on various occasions throughout the year. Indian foods such as acorn soup and mush are still eaten.

**Government.** There is no organized tribal government.

**Population Profile.** There are seven Indians and one non-Indian living on the reservation. The average education level is 9th grade. There is an elementary school nearby, but the high school is 28 miles away.

**Climate.** The reservation lies in northern California in a moderate climate. Rainfall measures 30 inches per year. Temperatures vary from a high of 90 degrees to a low of 20 degrees.

**Transportation.** Access to the reservation by four-wheel vehicles in the winter and rainy season is very difficult. A 2½-mile dirt road is the only access. Highway No. 70 runs 15 miles from the reservation. Oroville, 18 miles from the rancheria, has commercial air, train, truck, and bus service.

**Community Facilities.** There is only spring water on the reservation, and no provisions for sewage other than outhouses. There is also no electricity. Medical care is offered at the County Hospital in Oroville. The two houses on the reservation are both in poor condition.


BIG BEND RANCHERIA                          Federal Reservation
Shasta County
Pitts Tribe
Tribal Headquarters: Big Bend, California

**Land Status.** Total area: 40 acres. The reservation was established by the Secretary of the Interior on July 28, 1916.

**Culture.** The older people in the tribe still speak their native language, and eat some traditional foods such as acorn mush.

**Government.** The tribal government has three officers: a president, vice-president, and secretary-treasurer who were elected in 1965.

**Population Profile. 1969:** Indian resident 10; Unemployment 0. **1980:** Indian resident 8; Non-Indian resident 3; Percent Indian of total population 72.7; Total housing units 5; Occupied housing units 5. The average education is 10th grade. The children attend public schools 10 miles away.

**Climate.** The reservation lies in north-central California where the climate is moderate. Rainfall averages 13 inches annually, and temperatures reach a high of 95 degrees and a low of 29 degrees.

**Transportation.** Highway No. 299 runs 10 miles from the reservation. Redding, 58 miles from the rancheria, is served by commercial air, bus, train, and trucklines.

**Community Facilities.** Residents use well water. Septic tanks were installed by the USPHS. Pacific Gas and Electric is the electric company serving the area. There are no gas lines to the rancheria. The five houses are in poor condition, and the water is unsuitable for drinking. The county hospital in Redding provides medical care and hospitalization for the tribe.


BIG PINE RANCHERIA                          Federal Reservation
Inyo County
Paiute-Shoshone Tribes
Tribal Headquarters: Big Pine, California

**Land Status.** Total area: 279 acres. The U.S. Government and the City of Los Angeles exchanged 3,000 acres of property for 1,500 acres of level valley land in 1939. The land and the houses constructed thereon are tribally owned, the Board of Trustees being responsible for assignments and maintenance.

**Culture.** The tribal members still practice traditional ceremonial rituals such as the Cry Dance for the deceased and the Sweat House ceremonial.

**Government.** The Big Pine Reservation operates under the Trust Agreement of April 1, 1939, and the Assignment Ordinance of April 1962. The Owens Valley Board of Trustees, governing three reservations, has a membership of seven: five from Bishop, one from Big Pine, and one from Lone Pine Reservations.

**Population Profile. 1969:** Tribal enrollment 100; Indian resident 50; Unemployment 45%; Underemployment 3%. **1980:** Indian resident 269; Non-Indian resident 127; Percent Indian of total population 67.9; Total housing units 125; Occupied housing units 116. The average education level attained is 12th grade. The elementary and high schools are located adjacent to the reservation.

**Climate.** The Big Pine Reservation lies at the easterly base of the Sierra Nevada Mountain Range at altitudes varying from 3,700 to 4,200 feet, and with rainfall averaging only 5 inches per year. Temperatures reach a high of 101 degrees and a low of 0 degrees.

**Transportation.** U.S. Highway No. 395 runs through the reservation north-south. The City of Big Pine, which lies 1 mile outside the reservation has bus and truck service. There is an airport at Bishop, 18 miles from the reservation. The nearest train station is in Lone Pine, 42 miles from Big Pine.

**Community Facilities.** The City of Los Angeles provides the reservation with water and electricity. Individuals utilize septic tanks. Propane gas is purchased from B shop dealers.

The county maintains a sanitorium in Big Pine and a public health service facility at Independence, 28 miles from Big Pine. Private medical care is available in Bishop, 15 miles away.


BISHOP RANCHERIA                    Federal Reservation
Inyo County
Paiute-Shoshone Tribes
Tribal Headquarters: Bishop, California

**Land Status.** Total area: 875 acres. Only 90 acres are tribally owned. Most of the land is irrigated for agricultural production, the remainder being used for homesites or grazing, or is idle. An Executive Order of March 11, 1912 set apart lands for the Bishop Colony and Big Pine Colony Reservations. An Act of April 20, 1937 authorized the Secretary to exchange Indian lands and water rights for land owned by the City of Los Angeles in Inyo and Mono Counties. This exchange was consummated in 1939. Three thousand acres of trust property were exchanged for 1,500 acres of level valley surface. The Board of Trustees is responsible for the assignment. Title to the land is held in trust and the Bureau of Indian Affairs exercises authority. The Bishop Indian Reservation operates under the Trust Agreement of April 1939 and the Assignment Ordinance of April 1962. The Owens Valley Board of Trustees is comprised of seven trustees: five from Bishop, one from Lone Pine, and one from Big Pine.

**Government.** The tribe has a chairman and a four-member committee. The secretary is hired by the tribe.

**Population Profile. 1969:** Tribal enrollment 675; Indian resident 685; Non-Indian resident 110; Unemployment 19%; Underemployment 6.4%; Median family income $4,000 ca. **1980:** Indian resident 784; Non-Indian resident 341; Percent Indian of total population 69.7; Total housing units 401; Occupied housing units 346. The average education level is 12th grade. One tribal member is a college graduate. Children attend elementary school and high school 6 miles from the reservation.

**Tribal Economy.** The reservation lies in Owens Valley at the easterly base of the Sierra Nevada Mountain Range. The altitude varies from region to region and generous amounts of irrigation are required to sustain agricultural production. The tribal income of $9,500 per year is earned largely through rentals and water rights. The remainder is interest from trust funds. There are a number of commercial establishments on the reservation. The Jolly Rogers Trailer Park, Martin's Electric, and Town and County Trailer Park are all Indian owned. A used-car lot and Howard Lumber Company are leased. Clyde's Electric is owned by a non-Indian.

**Climate.** The temperature ranges from a high of 101 degrees to a low of –5 degrees. Rainfall averages only 5.4 inches annually.

**Transportation.** U.S. Highway No. 395 runs north-south and U.S. Highway No. 6 runs east-west. Bishop, 6 miles from the reservation, is served by air, bus, and trucklines. The nearest train station is in Lone Pine, 60 miles from the reservation.

**Community Facilities.** Residents use well water and individual septic tanks. The reservation is also connected to the City of Los Angeles water system; however the water distribution system is in poor condition. The Southern California Edison provides electricity. Hospitalization and medical care are available in Bishop through the USPHS. Community events are held in the Owens Valley Indian Education Center, the Four Square Mission, a community hall, and a V.F.W. hall.


CABAZON RESERVATION                    Federal Reservation
Riverside County
Cabazon Band of Mission Indians
Tribal Headquarters: Indio, California


**Land Status.** Total area: 1,706 acres. This reservation is located in an agricultural community and has good potential for agriculture development. An Executive Order of May 15, 1876, established this reservation and Executive Order of May 3, 1877, restored one section to public domain. In 1895, the area was increased under the authority of the Act of 1891.

**Culture.** Traditional culture continues to keep the people together.
**Population Profile. 1969:** Tribal enrollment 94; Indian resident 22; Unemployment 1 person. **1980:** Indian resident 8; Non-Indian resident 807; Percent Indian of total population 1.0; Total housing units 224; Occupied housing units 209. The average educational level attained is 12th grade, and there is one college graduate. Elementary and high schools are located in Indio, 7 miles from the reservation. The nearest college or university is located at Riverside, 30 miles from the reservation.

**Climate.** The climate is warm and arid and the land is flat and dry. The average rainfall is about 3.4 inches per year. Temperatures range from a high of 112 degrees to a low of 21 degrees.

**Transportation.** All commercial transportation facilities can be obtained at Indio, 7 miles from the reservation. U.S. Highway No. 60 is 3 miles south of the reservation.

**Community Facilities.** Water is provided for the reservation by the tribe. Bottled butane gas is purchased. Electricity is provided by Southern California Edison. The reservation is without a sewer system. Hospital, clinics, and dental facilities at Indio serve the reservation.


CAHUILLA RESERVATION                     Federal Reservation
Riverside County
Cahuilla Band of Mission Indians
Tribal Headquarters: Hemet, California

**Land Status.** Total area: 18,272 acres. An Executive Order of December 27, 1875, established the reservation. The area was decreased by a subsequent Executive Order in 1877, and lands were added in other such orders. The land has no allotments or assignments. The Indians, themselves, claim assignments ranging from 40 to 640 acres without the interference of other members.

**Culture.** Religious trends play an important role in the lives of the residents. Kinship ties remain strong, and the native language is sometimes spoken.

**Government.** The tribe has a non-Indian Reorganization Act constitution and bylaws which were approved in 1960 and amended the following year. The Band Council is composed of five members, a spokesman, secretary-treasurer, and three committee members.

**Population Profile. 1969:** Tribal enrollment 89; Indian resident 27; Non-Indian resident 2; Unemployment 21%; Underemployment 1 person. **1980:** Indian resident 29; Non-Indian resident 27; Percent Indian of total population 51.8; Total housing units 30; Occupied housing units 24. The average education level is 10th grade. The elementary and high schools are 38 miles from the reservation, and there is a junior college 60 miles away.

**Transportation.** State Highway No. 74 runs east-west through the reservation. Hemet is 38 miles from the reservation along Highway No. 74. Commercial air, train, bus, and truck companies serve Hemet.

**Climate.** The reservation lies in the south-central part of California in Riverside County, where the land is flat and low and the climate is warm and sunny. Rainfall averages 5.4 inches annually, and temperatures reach a high of 112 degrees and a low of 23 degrees.

**Community Facilities.** The tribe maintains the water system. Bottled gas is available and electricity is supplied by the Southern California Edison. Medical care is available at the county hospital in Hemet. This tribe holds a regular fiesta.


CAMPO RESERVATION                           Federal Reservation
San Diego County
Mission Band of Indians of Campo Community
Tribal Headquarters: Campo, California

**Land Status.** Total area: 15,010 acres. The reservation was established on February 10, 1893, under authority of the Act of 1891. The reservation was enlarged by 80 acres on February 2, 1907 and by 13,610 acres on December 14, 1911. The reservation is located in southern San Diego County at the far east portion of the county. All of the land is under trust status. Much of the land is hilly and good grazing land.

**Culture.** There is potential for a wide variety of development such as tourism and recreation, but so far the people have not united and have not grasped community action programs. The culture of these people such as Indian burials, songs, language, games, foods, arts and crafts, and medicine forms the backbone of their society.

**Population Profile. 1969:** Tribal enrollment 103; Indian resident 50; Unemployment 40%. **1980:** Indian resident 86; Non-Indian resident 14; Percent Indian of total population 86.0; Total housing units 46; Occupied housing units 32. The average educational level is 8th grade. Elementary school can be attended 2 miles from the reservation. The high school is located in El Cajon, 37 miles from the reservation. A college is available at San Diego, 52 miles from the reservation.

**Climate.** The reservation is located in the eastern part of San Diego County where the land is dry and hilly, with hot summers and mild winters. The average rainfall is about 6.2 inches per year, with temperatures as high as 95 degrees and as low as 28 degrees.

**Transportation.** The nearest airlines, trains, and bus facilities are located 54 miles from the reservation in San Diego. Trucklines are available in El Cajon, 37 miles away. State Highways No. 94 and No. 8 run east and west of the reservation.

**Community Facilities.** A well provides the people with water. The reservation does not have gas, electricity, or a sewer system. A hospital, clinic, dental, and PHS facilities are available in El Cajon, 37 miles away. Housing conditions are very poor.

CAPITAN GRANDE RESERVATION          Federal Reservation
San Diego County
Mission Tribes
Tribal Headquarters: Alpine, California

**Land Status.** Total area: 15,753 acres. An Executive Order of December 27, 1875, established the reservation, and an Executive Order of May 3, 1877, restored portions to public domain. An Executive Order of June 19, 1883, separated certain lands for the reservation. On March 10, 1894, a patent was issued to the Capitan Grande Band for lands selected by the Indian Mission Commission. All the land is tribally owned. There are three groups: Viejas, Barona, and nonreservation who are considered shareholders on the Capitan Grande Reservation. The people on Viejas and Barona have reservation land of their own, but they also have a share of the 15,753 acres. No one lives on the Capitan Grande Reservation, but the three groups share equal thirds.

**Climate.** The reservation is located in southern California in a mountainous area which is generally mild and warm. Rainfall averages 15 inches per year. The high temperature is 100 degrees; the low is 29 degrees.

**Transportation.** Alpine, 15 miles from the reservation, is the nearest city. Bus and trucklines stop here. The nearest train and airline service is 38 miles away in San Diego. Three miles of dirt road lead from the State highway to tribal land.

CEDARVILLE RANCHERIA          Federal Reservation
Modoc County
Paiute Tribe
Tribal Headquarters: Cedarville, California

**Land Status.** Total area: 17 acres. All land is tribally-owned. The land was purchased for the California Indians in 1915 under authority of the June 1906 Act.

**Culture.** Most of the permanent residents are old people who still speak the language and practice some of the arts and crafts. Indian religion is dominant. The younger people usually leave during the summer months.

**Government.** There is no tribal government structure. All residents are on welfare.

**Population Profile.** Thirteen persons, all tribal members, live on the reservation. None are employed. The average educational attainment level is 8th grade.

**Climate.** The reservation is located in northeastern California on flat land where the rainfall averages 12 inches annually, and temperatures reach a high of 85 degrees and a low of 30 degrees.

**Transportation.** Highway No. 299 runs 25 miles from the reservation and junctions with U.S. Highway No. 99 at Redding, 164 miles from the reservation. The nearest commercial air and train transportation are located in Redding. Trucks stop in Cedarville, 2 miles from the reservation. Alturas, 29 miles away, is the nearest bus stop. There is an unpaved airstrip next to the reservation.

**Community Facilities.** The USPHS dug wells and installed septic tanks. Gas can be purchased from Alturas Bottle. Electricity is supplied by the Pacific Power Company. The Modoc Medical Center is located in Cedarville. There is additional health care available in Alturas. There are seven homes on the reservation.

COLD SPRINGS RANCHERIA                    Federal Reservation
Fresno County
Mono Tribe
Tribal Headquarters: Tollhouse, California

**Land Status.** Tribal land: 53 acres. Allotted land: 45 acres. Total area: 98 acres.

**Culture.** These people were good hunters and trappers. After obtaining horses from the Spanish, they became excellent horse breeders. They crafted baskets, made ropes out of milkweed, baby cradles from roots, and wove beads. They ate acorn soup after processing the acorn to remove the toxic juices.

**Government.** The Articles of Association were approved in October 1961. The president and secretary-treasurer are elected at the annual meeting in February.

**Population Profile.** **1969:** Tribal enrollment 39; Indian resident 39; Unemployment 90%; Underemployment 10 persons. **1980:** Indian resident 63; Non-Indian resident 2; Percent Indian of total population 96.9; Total housing units 14; Occupied housing units 14. Seven of the nine families have an income of less than $1,000. The average education level is 8th grade. One tribal member is a college graduate.

**Climate.** The reservation is in a mountainous area of central California where the climate is mild and sunny. Rainfall averages 13 inches per year. Temperatures reach a high of 100 degrees and a low of 25 degrees.

**Transportation.** Fresno, 42 miles from the rancheria, is the nearest city. Fresno is served by commercial bus, train, truck, and airlines. There is also a private airstrip at Fresno. State Highway No. 168 is a badly paved, steep and curvy road leading into the rancheria.

**Community Facilities.** The rancheria water and sewer system was installed by the Bureau of Indian Affairs. Van Gas Butane Company supplies the area with gas. Electricity is available from Edison Power Plant. The Fresno County Hospital in Fresno provides health care to tribal members. The nine houses on the rancheria are in poor condition.

COLUSA RANCHERIA                                    Federal Reservation
Colusa County
Cahil Dehe Band of Wintun Indians
Tribal Headquarters: Colusa, California

**Land Status.** Total area: 269 acres. Land purchased by the Secretary of the Interior on June 21, 1907, established the Colusa Rancheria, and additional lands were acquired under the authority of the Howard-Wheeler Act in 1938. The Sacramento River runs through the rancheria often flooding the land and causing a great deal of inconvenience.

**Culture.** Very little of the culture of these people remains.

**Population Profile. 1969:** Tribal enrollment 16; Indian resident 17; Unemployment 12%; Median family income $1,000. The average educational level attained is 9th grade. Elementary and high school facilities are available 7 miles from the rancheria and college is available 34 miles away.

**Climate.** The Colusa Rancheria is located in central California where the topography is hilly and mountainous and the climate is generally mild. Summers are hot and dry. The temperatures vary from a high of 100 degrees to a low of 32 degrees. The average rainfall is about 15.7 inches per year.

**Transportation.** Sacramento, 60 miles away, has the nearest commercial airlines. Train service is available at Williams, 10 miles away. Commercial and local bus services are available in Colusa, 4 miles from the rancheria.

**Community Facilities.** Wells provide the rancheria with water. Gas and electricity are provided by the Pacific Gas and Electric. The sewer system consists of outdoor facilities. Hospital, clinic, and dental facilities are available in Colusa.


CORTINA RANCHERIA                                   Federal Reservation
Colusa County
Wintun Tribe
Tribal Headquarters: Williams, California

**Land Status.** Total area: 640 acres. The lands were purchased by the Secretary of the Interior on June 25, 1907, adding 480 acres of purchased land to withdrawn Government land. All the land is tribally-owned and in the process of being terminated. Only one person is living on the land. The remaining 48 members are living off the reservation. The off-reservation residents bury their dead on the rancheria but must hand-carry the casket one-half mile over hills and valleys when all extant roads are passable; when roads are impassable, the "carry" is much longer.

Ranchers around the rancheria let their cattle graze on the Indian land without permission of anyone. Because of fear of the ranchers, the Indians do not object, but must build fences to keep the cattle off the graveyard.

**Climate.** The reservation lies in north central California where the land is both mountainous and flat and the climate is usually mild and sunny. The rainfall averages 14 inches annually. The high temperature is 100 degrees; the low is 20 degrees.

**Transportation.** The reservation can be reached only by 11 miles of paved road and 4 miles of trail. No roads are maintained, so people are discouraged from going to the rancheria because of the difficulty of getting there. Williams, which lies 20 miles from the rancheria, is served by train, bus, and trucklines. Although there is an airstrip at Williams, the nearest commercial air service is in Yuba City, 50 miles away.

**Community Facilities.** There are no public or private utilities serving the rancheria. The nearest health care is 38 miles away in Colusa.

CUYAPAIPE RESERVATION                          Federal Reservation
San Diego County
Cuyapaipe Band of Mission Indians
Tribal Headquarters:  Mount Laguna, California

**Land Status.** Total area: 4,100 acres. This reservation was established on February 10, 1893, under authority of the Act of 1891. Much of the area surrounding the reservation is settled by the U.S. Park Service.

**Population Profile. 1969:** Tribal enrollment 1; Indian resident 1. **1980:** Indian resident 2; Non–Indian resident 0; Percent Indian of total population 100.0; Total housing units 3; Occupied housing units 1.

**Climate.** The climate is generally mild and cool, with temperatures ranging from a high of 89 degrees to a low of 10 degrees. The average rainfall is about 18 inches per year.

**Transportation.** Airline and train facilities are available in San Diego, 75 miles away. Bus service is available in Alpine, 13 miles away. El Cajon, 50 miles from the reservation, has trucking and private airport facilities. A county road serves the reservation.

**Community Facilities.** A spring provides water for the reservation. There are no gas, electric, or sewer facilities available on the reservation. Hospital and dental facilities are available in Alpine, 13 miles away. Clinics are provided by the county of San Diego, 75 miles from the reservation.

ENTERPRISE RANCHERIA                          Federal Reservation
Butte County
Maidu Tribe
Tribal Headquarters:  Oroville, California

**Land Status.** Total area: 33 acres. A portion of the previous rancheria is now under the water of Oroville Lake. The land was purchased in 1915 by the Secretary of the Interior under the Acts of 1906 and 1908.

**Culture.** The Indian language is spoken regularly. Songs and hand games are played frequently. Traditional foods are eaten and most traditional ways are followed. A hand-game festival is the only organized tribal recreation. There is no organized government.

**Population Profile. 1969:** Indian resident 3. **1980:** Indian resident 16; Non-Indian resident 0; Percent Indian of total population 100.0; Total housing units 2; Occupied housing units 2. The level of educational attainment is 11th grade. The elementary school is 5 miles away; the high school, 20 miles from the rancheria.

**Climate.** The rancheria lies in northern California in forested and mountainous terrain. The winters are cold but moderate. Rainfall averages 30 inches per year. The temperature reaches a summer high of 90 degrees and a winter low of 20 degrees. The land is used for homesites only.

**Transportation.** Highway No. 70 is 20 miles from the rancheria and is reached by a county or dirt road. Oroville, 20 miles away, is served by commercial train, bus, and truck companies. There is a private airstrip in Oroville; however, the nearest regularly scheduled air service is in Sacramento, 87 miles from Enterprise.

**Community Facilities.** The water is piped in from the spring. Septic tanks are used for sanitary facilities. There is no gas supplied to the reservation. Electricity is provided by the Pacific Gas and Electric Company. Hospital and medical care are available through the county at Oroville.


FORT BIDWELL RESERVATION                    Federal Reservation
Modoc County
Paiute Tribe
Tribal Headquarters: Fort Bidwell, California

**Land Status.** Total area: 3,335 acres. All land is tribally owned. Thirty-five acres have been assigned to residential use. A joint resolution of January 30, 1897, authorized the Secretary of the Interior to use former lands of the Fort Bidwell Military Reserve for an Indian training school. The reservation was enlarged in 1913 and in 1917.

**Culture.** The population varies with seasonal employment. The Indian language is spoken by the elderly. Indian religion is still practiced. Arts and crafts are produced in the individual homes.

**Government.** The tribe is governed under an Indian Reorganization Act constitution and bylaws approved in 1936 and amended in 1940 and 1942. The nine members of the governing body are elected each November to staggered 2-year terms.

**Population Profile. 1969:** Tribal enrollment 112; Indian resident 55; Unemployment 50%; Underemployment 50%. **1980:** Indian resident 93; Non-Indian resident 5; Percent Indian of total population 94.9; Total housing units 33; Occupied housing units 26. All families earn between $2,000 and $3,000 each year. The education attainment level is 10th grade. The elementary and high schools are 30 miles from the reservation.

**Tribal Economy.** The reservation, located in northeastern California, is rocky, hilly land covered with sage. The elevation varies from 4,550 to 7,000 feet. The tribe has an income of $3,400 per annum, half from forestry, and the other half from leases and farming. The tribal members have formed the Fort Bidwell Indian Cattleman's Association which is the only commercial enterprise on the reservation.

**Climate.** The winter snowfall is heavy and summers are warm. Rainfall averages 14 inches per year. Temperatures vary from a high of 80 degrees to a low of 20 degrees.

**Transportation.** County road No. 18 runs north to Alturas, 59 miles, to junction with Route No. 299. Alturas is served by buslines. The nearest truckline stop is Cedarville, 30 miles from Fort Bidwell. Redding, 194 miles from the reservation is the nearest available air and train service. There is also a private airstrip in Cedarville.

**Community Facilities.** The water is drawn from wells which are maintained by the USPHS as are the septic tanks. Gas is purchased from Alturas Bottle; electricity from Pacific Power and Electric. The Modoc Indian Health Project is located in Alturas. Hospitalization and other medical care are also available in Alturas. The 23 houses on the reservation are in poor condition.


FORT INDEPENDENCE RESERVATION          Federal Reservation
Inyo County
Paiute Tribe
Tribal Headquarters: Independence, California

**Land Status.** Tribally-owned land: 234 acres. Allotted Land: 122 acres. Total area: 356 acres. The Fort Independence Reservation consists of 356 acres of open, level land. U.S. Highway No. 395 bisects the reservation. Currently a problem are the allotments fractionated by heirship. Most of the land is used for homesites, the remainder is leased. Camp Independence was established during the Indian Way on July 4, 1862, and later abandoned. The Fort Independence Reservation was established by Executive Orders in 1915 and 1916.

**Culture.** The only remaining aspect of Indian culture is the Paiute language which is still spoken.

**Government.** The Articles of Association were approved in May 1965. The tribe operates under a constitution and bylaws. Officers include the chairman and the secretary-treasurer.

**Population Profile. 1969:** Tribal enrollment 62; Indian resident 46; Non-Indian resident 26; Unemployment 33%; Underemployment 2 persons; Median family income $5,000. **1980:** Indian resident 31; Non-Indian resident 30; Percent Indian of total population 50.8; Total housing units 28; Occupied housing units 25.

**Tribal Economy.** The Sherwood Forest Animal Farm is leased from the tribe, providing the tribal income of $1,200 per year.

**Climate.** Because of its location in Owens Valley at the eastern base of the Sierra Nevada Range, the climate of the reservation is arid and irrigation is necessary to sustain agriculture. Rainfall measures only 5 inches per year. The temperature ranges from 100 degrees to 5 degrees.

**Transportation.** Independence, the nearest city, lies 3 miles from the reservation. Highway No. 395 runs north–south through Independence. Bus service is available in Independence. The nearest train stop is 18 miles away in Lone Pine. Bishop, 43 miles from the reservation, has the nearest commercial air service.

**Community Facilities.** The reservation has a central water system and septic tanks. Gas is supplied by both the Lone Pine Gas Company and Suburban Gas. The Los Angeles Department of Water and Sewer provides electricity to the reservation. There are 10 homes and 7 mobile homes on the reservation; nine are in poor condition. Public Health Clinics are held in Independence. The nearest hospital is the South Inyo Hospital in Lone Pine. The community holds a yearly parade.


FORT MOJAVE RESERVATION                    Federal Reservation
Clark County, Nevada
San Bernardino County, California
Mohave County, Arizona
Mojave Tribe
Tribal Headquarters: Needles, California

**Land Status.** Total area: 38,384 acres.

**History.** In the early 16th Century, the Mojave Indians were not part of the Mission way of life instituted by the Spaniards. The members were known as "wild" Indians. Originally they welcomed the Padres and soldiers, but forced Indian labor and Spanish raids soon changed their attitudes. The 1848 Treaty of Guadalupe Hidalgo, which ended the war with Mexico, ceded California and other territories to the United States. Under that treaty, the U.S. Government agreed to preserve recognition of the Indian people's right to the land they inhabited. The Mojaves have lived since prehistoric times engaged in small–scale farming, gathering wild foods, hunting, and fishing.

**Population Profile.** **1969:** Population 511; Unemployment 40%; Underemployment 35%. **1980:** Indian resident 127; Non–Indian resident 92; Percent Indian of total population 58.0; Total housing units 73; Occupied housing units 62.

**Climate.** The temperatures in this geographical location range from a low of 35 degrees to a high of 110 degrees, with an average rainfall of 8 inches per year.

**Transportation.** The nearest commercial airline facilities are available in Kingman, 25 miles away. Needles has train, bus, and trucking facilities. U.S. Highway No. 95 and Interstate 40 serve the reservation.

**Community Facilities.** PHS provides a water and sewer system. Gas and electricity are provided by the California Pacific Utility Company. Medical care is available in Needles at a private hospital.

FORT YUMA RESERVATION                    Federal Reservation
Imperial County, California
Mohave County, Arizona
Quechan Tribe
Tribal Headquarters: Fort Yuma, Arizona

**Land Status.** Tribally-owned land: 617.17 acres. Allotted land: 8,629 acres. Government land: 25.71. Total area: 9,281 acres. The reservation lies along both sides of the Colorado River. The land in Arizona, 480 acres, is entirely allotted.

**History.** The Yuman tribes had lived along the Colorado River for centuries before the arrival of the Spanish. The Fort Yuma Reservation was established in 1884, and included acreage in Arizona and California. Since that time, the tribe has lost most of the lands in Arizona and retains only a major portion of its California lands.

**Culture.** The Quechan, a subgroup of the Yuman Indians, lived in small farming communities along the Colorado River bottomlands. Principal crops included corn, beans, pumpkins, tobacco, and gourds. Both men and women tended fields. Their crops were supplemented through hunting, fishing, and gathering wild plants. Strong tribal unity with little formal government was characteristic of the Yuman tribes. Because of the hot climate, summer houses were principally roofs with open sides. Winter homes were more substantial earth-covered, rectangular buildings. These tribes were widely known as fierce, excellent warriors; they divided into two groups: archers and club men. Fighting well and bravely brought prestige. Dreams were considered important in the foretelling of events and the indicating of abilities.

**Government.** In 1964, the tribe elected a paid president to devote full time to the socio-economic development of the reservation. The Quechan Tribe is organized according to the 1934 Indian Reorganization Act. The Quechan Tribal Council, as established by the tribe's constitution, administers all tribal affairs.

**Population Profile. 1969:** Tribal enrollment 1,625; Indian resident 1,200; Non-Indian resident 425; Unemployment 50%; Underemployment 21%; Median family income $2,800. **1980.** Indian resident 1,105; Non-Indian resident 4,056; Percent Indian of total population 21.4; Total housing units 2,281; Occupied housing units 1,834. The average education level attained is 10th grade. Five tribal members are college graduates.

**Tribal Economy.** Almost half of the tribal income, $11,300 annually, is earned in farming, the remainder coming from business and other sources.

**Climate.** The climate is mild and dry, but extremely hot in summer. The land is rich when irrigated. Rainfall averages 3 inches per year. The high temperature is 115 degrees; the low is 33 degrees.

**Transportation.** The Fort Yuma Reservation has excellent highway connections. U.S. Highway No. 80 and Interstate 8 are major east-west roads and U.S. Highway No. 95 is a north-south artery. Yuma is served by train, bus, and trucklines as well as the airlines which fly into the Yuma airport several miles outside the city.

**Community Facilities.** The Fort Yuma Reservation obtains water from the community water system and the USPHS. Gas is supplied by the Arizona Public Service Company. Electricity is provided by the Imperial Irrigation District. There are three hospitals in Yuma: the Parkview Baptist Hospital, the PHS Fort Yuma Indian Hospital, and the Yuma County Hospital.

**Recreation.** Located on the reservation is Fort Yuma, a military establishment dating to 1875. It has been renovated, and a museum and tourist facilities are available. There are hunting and fishing on some parts of the reservation, and water recreation on the Colorado River. Hotel and motel accommodations as well as theaters and restaurants are available in Yuma.

GRINDSTONE CREEK RANCHERIA                    Federal Reservation
Glenn County
Nomalaki-Wailaki Tribe
Tribal Headquarters: Elk Creek, California

**Land Status.** Total area: 80 acres. The rancheria was purchased under Acts of 1906 and 1908 by the Secretary of the Interior on January 7, 1909. The rancheria is located 7 miles from Elk Creek City.

**Culture.** Their culture still exists on the rancheria such as Indian burials, songs, language, games, foods, arts and crafts, and medicine.

**Government.** The general council is the governing body of the rancheria consisting of a chairman, vice-chairman, and a secretary-treasurer. Tribal officials are elected to serve 1 year.

**Population Profile. 1969:** Tribal enrollment 50; Indian resident 50; Unemployment 32%; Median family income under $1,000. **1980:** Indian resident 72; Non-Indian resident 1; Percent Indian of total population 98.6; Total housing units 18; Occupied housing units 17. The average educational level attained is 8th grade. The elementary and high schools are 7 miles from the reservation.

**Climate.** The weather is generally mild and sunny with warm summers. The average rainfall is 16 inches per year with temperatures as high as 105 degrees and as low as 24 degrees.

**Transportation.** Red Bluff, 50 miles away, is the nearest commercial airline. Willows, 29 miles away, has a private airport. The nearest train, bus, and trucklines are at Willows. The nearest highways are Interstate 5 and access road 306, 28 miles away. A dirt and gravel road leads into the reservation.

**Community Facilities.** Health facilities are available at Willows, 29 miles away. The water system is inadequate—one small pump to furnish the needs of all. Electricity is provided by Pacific Gas and Electric. The sewer system consists of septic tanks and outhouses. Housing conditions are poor.

HOOPA VALLEY EXTENSION RESERVATION     Federal Reservation
Humboldt County
Yurok Tribe
Tribal Headquarters: Hoopa, California

**Land Status.** Total area: 7,015.69 acres. The reservation was established by an Executive Order of October 16, 1891, adding the Klamath
strip, a tract 1 mile in width on each side of the Klamath River, from
the Hoopa Valley Reservation to the Pacific Ocean. The tribal land
is checker-boarded with a considerable amount of non-Indian land.
The Hoopa Valley Extension has a claim filed in the U.S. Court of
Claims to be included as a part of the Greater Hoopa Valley
Reservation.

**Culture.** The Yurok Tribe still practice traditional hunting and
fishing, and many of the people speak their native language.

**Population Profile.** **1969:** Indian resident 142; Unemployment
82%; Median family income $3,500. **1980:** Indian resident 411; Non-
Indian resident 671; Percent Indian of total population 38.0; Total
housing units 567; Occupied housing units 426. The average education
level attained is 10th grade. The elementary school is 12 miles from
the reservation and the high school is 26 miles from the reservation.
The nearest college is 81 miles away.

**Climate.** There is very little seasonal change in this geographical
location which has mild winters and summers. The average rainfall
is 45 inches per year, with temperatures ranging from a low of 30
degrees to a high of 95 degrees.

**Transportation.** The City of Eureka, 75 miles from the reservation,
has the nearest commercial air and land transportation. Hoopa has
the nearest private airport. Two State secondary roads, numbers 18
and 96, serve the reservation.

**Community Facilities.** Water is provided by the U.S. Public Health
Service. Gas and electricity are provided by the Pacific Gas and Electric.
The sewer system is provided by individuals. Hospitals and clinics are
available in Hoopa, about 15 miles away.


HOOPA VALLEY RESERVATION     Federal Reservation
Humboldt County
Hoopa Tribe
Tribal Headquarters: Hoopa, California

**Land Status.** Tribal land: 84,703 acres. Allotted land: 1,353 acres.
Non-Indian land: 918 acres. Total area: 86,974 acres. Much of the reservation land is owned in a complicated heirship pattern. Several non-
Indians have inherited undivided interests in the property. Due to the
land status, the members of the tribe are unable to establish homesites.

**History.** The Hoopa Reservation was established on June 23, 1876.
The tribes placed here included Huntsatung, Hoopa, Klamath River,
Meskeet, Redwood, Raiaz, Sermolton, and Sish Langton. The Hoopa
Valley lies along the banks of the Trinity River in Humboldt County.
The Hoopas are of Athapascan language stock.

**Culture.** The Hoopa Indians have maintained their culture to the extent of performing their cultural dances such as the White Deerskin Dance and the Jump Dance which is held every two years. The Brush Dance is held annually. The Hoopa still practice and encourage basket weaving and beadwork. Tribal members hunt and fish and prepare native foods such as acorns.

**Government.** The constitution and bylaws were adopted by the tribe on May 5, 1950, and approved by the Commissioner of Indian Affairs on September 4, 1954. The seven-member Hoopa council is elected from tribal membership by referendum vote of the members over 21 years of age. The council members select their chairman. The council votes on all resolutions presented to them; however, any resolution passed by them must have final approval by the Bureau of Indian Affairs. Five members constitute a quorum.

**Population Profile. 1969:** Tribal enrollment 1,271; Indian resident 950; Non-Indian resident 2,050; Unemployment 58%; Underemployment 40 persons; Median family income $3,000. **1980:** Indian resident 1,502; Non-Indian resident 539; Percent Indian of total population 73.6; Total housing units 781; Occupied housing units 651. The average education level is 10th grade. Ten tribal members are college graduates. The tribe provides three scholarships each year. The Educational Opportunity Program also provides scholarships. Hoopa children attend elementary and high schools in the valley. The nearest college is 55 miles from the reservation.

**Tribal Economy.** Ninety percent of the land is heavily forested, and the remainder is used for homesites, gardens, and grazing. The valley is heavily forested and the terrain is mountainous. The tribal income of $1,525,000 per annum is largely earned through forestry. A small amount, 2 percent, comes from farming, and the remaining 20 percent is income from leases and minerals. The three lumber mills on the reservation are owned by non-Indians. Of the nine retail businesses, one, an arts and crafts shop, is owned by an Indian.

**Climate.** The reservation is located in northwestern California where summers are hot and winters are mild. Rainfall measures 45 inches per year. Temperatures reach a high of 108 degrees and a low of 20 degrees.

**Transportation.** The reservation lies 60 miles from Eureka where ample public transportation facilities by air, train, bus, and truck are available. There is a tribal airport on the reservation. Twelve miles to the southeast at Willow Creek, Highway No. 96 connects with Route 299. U.S. Highway No. 99 is 108 miles to the east at Redding, where there is also a main-line railroad.

**Community Facilities.** The U.S. Public Health Service installed the water system. Residents have individual sewer systems. Residents purchase gas from a private distributor. Electricity is supplied by Pacific Gas and Electric. The well and water filter systems are inadequate as repaired by the PHS after the 1964 flood. Private hospitals and medical care are located in Hoopa. The tribe has four community buildings.

**Recreation.** The tribe holds spring and fall dances and various celebrations throughout the year.

INAJA-COSMIT RESERVATION                    Federal Reservation
San Diego County
Inaja-Cosmit Tribe
Tribal Headquarters: Julian, California

**Land Status.** Total Area: 880 acres. An Executive Order of December 27, 1875, established the reservation. On February 10, 1893, the Inaja Reservation was enlarged under authority of the Act of 1891. This reservation is situated in the heart of an area with high potential for recreational development.

**Culture.** The Inaja-Cosmit culture, such as Indian burials, songs, language, games, foods, arts and crafts, and medicine, is still used.

**Population Profile.** 1969: Tribal enrollment 21; Indian resident 2; Unemployment 0%; Median family income $1,000 to $2,000. The average educational level attained is 4th grade. The nearest elementary and high schools are located in Escondido, 20 miles from the reservation. The nearest college is located in San Diego, 75 miles from the reservation.

**Climate.** The reservation is located in southern California in western San Diego County, where the land is flat and sandy and the climate is mild and moderate. Rainfall averages about 4 inches per year. Temperatures run as high as 85 degrees and as low as 15 degrees.

**Transportation.** Commercial airlines and train facilities are available at San Diego, 75 miles away. Lakeside, 50 miles away, has the nearest bus and trucklines. Ramona, 40 miles away, maintains the nearest private airport. State Highway No. 78 runs east-west of the reservation.

**Community Facilities.** Water is provided by a spring. Wood stoves are used for heating. There is no electricity and no sewer system; outhouses are used. Hospitals, clinics, and dental facilities are available in Escondido. PHS is also located in Escondido.

JACKSON RANCHERIA                          Federal Reservation
Amador County
Me-Wuk Tribe
Tribal Headquarters: Jackson, California

**Land Status.** Total area: 331 acres. An Act of March 3, 1893, appropriated $10,000 for the Digger Indians of central California at Jackson. The rancheria was established on January 7, 1895. The rancheria is in process of termination by authority of the Rancheria Act, P.L. 85-671, as amended by P.L. 88-419. The Jackson Rancheria is located in central California in the foothills of the Sierra Nevada Mountains.

**Climate.** The humidity here is about 58 percent year-round. The area has an average rainfall of about 30 inches per year with temperatures ranging from a high of 76 degrees to a low of 46 degrees.

**Population Profile.** 1980: Indian resident 15; Non-Indian resident 0; Percent Indian of total population 100.0; Total housing units 4; Occupied housing units 4.

LA JOLLA RESERVATION                    Federal Reservation
San Diego County
La Jolla Band of Mission Indians
Tribal Headquarters: Escondido, California

**Land Status.** Total area: 8,233 acres. Of the total area, 7,279 acres are tribally owned. Nearly all of the agricultural land is allotted. Executive Orders of December 27, 1875 and May 15, 1876, established the Potrero or La Jolla Reservation and an Executive Order of May 3, 1877, restored a portion to public domain. The reservation was established in 1892.

**Culture.** Cultural traditions are practiced not only by those members living on the reservation, but by the whole tribal membership. This includes language, foods, kinship, religion, and other traditions.

**Government.** The tribe's Articles of Association were approved in 1962. The governing body, the general council, is composed of all adults over 21 years of age. A committee of five is elected, including the four tribal officers.

**Population Profile.** 1969: Tribal enrollment 280; Indian resident 53; Non-Indian resident 4; Unemployment 11 persons; Underemployment 1 person; Median family income $3,000. **1980:** Indian resident 141; Non-Indian resident 10; Percent Indian of total population 93.4; Total housing units 53; Occupied housing units 45. The average education level is 9th grade. The elementary and high schools are 25 miles from the reservation.

**Tribal Economy.** Eighty percent of the tribe's annual income of $2,500 is earned in farming. The tribe has formed the La Jolla Reservation Recreation Enterprise.

**Climate.** The reservation lies in southern California just south of the Cleveland National Forest where rainfall measures 15 inches per year. The climate is warm and sunny, with temperatures ranging from 110 degrees to 28 degrees.

**Transportation.** State Highway No. 76 runs east-west and is the nearest highway to the reservation. Bus, train, and truck transportation are available in Escondido, 25 miles west of the reservation. The nearest commercial air service is in San Diego, 55 miles from the reservation.

**Community Facilities.** The water is drawn from wells and springs. Septic tanks are the only provisions for sewage. The San Diego Gas and Electric Company supplies electricity to the area. The Palomar Memorial Hospital in Escondido and the County Welfare service extend medical care to reservation residents.

**Recreation.** This reservation is perhaps the best in recreation development in this area. The river is being developed for recreation and a campsite, which will compare with national park sites, is being prepared. There is also ample timber land ideal for recreation. Highway frontage is an encouraging factor in this development.

LA POSTA RESERVATION           Federal Reservation
San Diego County, California
La Posta Band of Mission Indians       Unoccupied

**Land Status.** Total area: 3,672.29 acres. The La Posta Reservation is situated between two canyons. There are more mountains than level land and the area is excellent for pasture. This reservation was inhabited about 20 years ago, but due to an enrollment problem, residents were removed by the Bureau of Indian Affairs. They also left to find better living conditions.


LAYTONVILLE RANCHERIA          Federal Reservation
Mendocino County
Cahto Tribe
Tribal Headquarters: Laytonville, California

**Land Status.** Total area: 200 acres. The land was bought by missionaries for landless Indians, but when trouble developed regarding titles to the land, the Bureau of Indian Affairs purchased the 200 acres. Acts of June 21, 1906, call for the title to the land to be held in trust by the Federal Government. All of the land is tribally-owned.

**Government.** The tribe's Articles of Association were approved in 1967. These provide for a governing body of three members who are elected annually. The tribes meet three times annually. The chairman, vice-chairman, and secretary-treasurer are the three officers.

**Population Profile. 1969:** Indian resident 77; Non-Indian resident 8; Unemployment 25%; Median family income $1,500. **1980:** Indian resident 105; Non-Indian resident 6; Percent Indian of total population 94.6; Total housing units 28; Occupied housing units 27. The average education achievement level is 8th grade.

**Climate.** The reservation lies in northwest California in rolling hills where the rainfall in this moderate climate averages 43 inches per year. The temperature reaches a high of 100 degrees and a low of 29 degrees.

**Transportation.** Bus and trucklines stop in Laytonville, 2 miles from the reservation. There is train service in Willits, 24 miles from the reservation. Willits has an airstrip; however, the nearest commercial air service is in Ukiah, 59 miles away. U.S. Highway No. 101 passes 5 miles from the reservation.

**Community Facilities.** There is water on the reservation, and septic tanks are utilized for sewage disposal. Pacific Gas and Electric provides the electricity. Residents also purchase bottled gas. The 14 houses are in good condition. Medical care is available at the hospital in Willits.

LIKELY RANCHERIA                          Federal Reservation
Modoc County
Pitt River Tribe
Tribal Headquarters: Likely, California

**Land Status.** Total area: 1.32 acres. This reservation was purchased on June 28, 1922, by authority of Acts of 1906 and 1908.

**Culture.** The culture of these people is presently being revived.

**Population Profile. 1969:** Tribal enrollment 4; Indian resident 2; Unemployment 100%; Median family income $1,000 to $2,500. The average educational level attained is 5th grade. The people who reside on this reservation are over 50 years of age.

**Climate.** The climate is mild and moderate, with temperatures ranging from a high of 90 degrees to a low of 28 degrees. The average rainfall is 12 inches per year.

**Transportation.** Reno, Nevada, 169 miles from the reservation, has the nearest commercial airline and train facilities. Bus and truck service are available in Likely, 6 miles away.

**Community Facilities.** Water is provided by private well. Bottled gas is purchased. There is no electricity or sewer system. A hospital and clinics are provided by Modoc Memorial Hospital and Modoc Department of Social Welfare located in Alturas, 20 miles away.


LONE PINE RANCHERIA                       Federal Reservation
Inyo County
Paiute-Shoshone Tribe
Tribal Headquarters: Lone Pine, California

**Land Status.** Total area: 237 acres. The Lone Pine Reservation was acquired through a land exchange consummated in 1939 between the city of Los Angeles and the Federal Government. Three thousand acres of trust property were exchanged for 1,500 acres of level valley land.

**Culture.** The culture of the Paiute-Shoshone still exists, such as ceremonial dances. Some of the Indian language is spoken and traditional foods are eaten.

**Population Profile. 1969:** Tribal enrollment 123; Indian resident 115; Unemployment 19.2%; Median family income $3,500. **1980:** Indian resident 172; Non-Indian resident 76; Percent Indian of total population 69.4; Total housing units 79; Occupied housing units 78. The average educational level attained is 12th grade. The elementary and high school facilities are available within 2 miles of the reservation.

**Climate.** The reservation, located in Owens Valley on the eastern base of the Sierra Nevada Mountains, ranges from 3,700 to 4,200 feet altitude, and receives about 5 inches rainfall per year. Temperatures range from 100 degrees to 5 degrees.

**Transportation.** The City of Bishop has the nearest commercial airline facilities; train, bus, trucking, and private aircraft facilities are available at Lone Pine. U.S. Highway No. 395 runs north-south through the reservation.

**Community Facilities.** Water is provided by the city of Los Angeles. Propane gas is purchased from local dealers. Electricity is provided by the Los Angeles Department of Water and Power. The sewer system consists of septic tanks which are in generally poor condition.


LOOKOUT RANCHERIA                                    Federal Reservation
Modoc County
Pitt River Tribe
Tribal Headquarters: Lookout, California

**Land Status.** Tribal land: 0 acres. Allotted land: 30 acres. Non-Indian land: 10 acres. Total area: 40 acres. Lookout Rancheria was purchased on October 11, 1913, by authority of Acts of 1906 and 1908 appropriating funds for purchase of lands for California Indians. Approximately 30 years ago there were a large number of Indians living on this rancheria, but due to lack of work for the young and death among the aged, the rancheria has been abandoned.

**Culture.** The Indian language is still used although the younger generation does not speak it. Arts and crafts are non-existent today. There is slight indication that some Indian religion is still present.

**Population Profile. 1969:** Tribal enrollment 8; Indian resident 8; Non-Indian resident 0; Unemployment 10%; Underemployment 0; Median family income $3,000. **1980:** Indian resident 12; Non-Indian resident 1; Percent Indian of total population 92.3; Total housing units 4; Occupied housing units 4. The average educational level attained is 7th grade. No members have continued education beyond high school. The elementary and high schools are 12 miles away.

**Climate.** Temperatures reach a high of 85 degrees and a low of 29 degrees. Rainfall averages 10 inches annually.

**Transportation.** The nearest city is Adin, 6 miles from Lookout. Buslines stop in Adin, and trucklines serve Bieber, 12 miles distant. The nearest train and air service is in Redding, 108 miles from the rancheria. There is a private airstrip in Bieber. Highway No. 299 is 6 miles from the rancheria. This junctions with U.S. Highway No. 99 in Redding.

**Community Facilities.** The water system was installed by the USPHS. There are no inside bathroom facilities, and the wells installed by PHS are often dry. Bottled gas is purchased. The Meyers Hospital in Fall River, 32 miles from the reservation, offers medical services. The PHS Modoc Indian Health Center is in Alturas where private medical care is also provided.


LOS COYOTES RESERVATION                              Federal Reservation
San Diego County
Los Coyotes Band of Mission Indians
Tribal Headquarters: Warner Springs, California

**Land Status.** Total area: 25,049.63 acres. An Executive Order of May 6, 1889, set apart lands for this reservation. On June 19, 1900, the present reservation was established under authority of the Act of 1891. Executive Order of April 13, 1914, transferred lands from the Cleveland National Forest to the Los Coyotes Reservation.

**Culture.** Indian burials, songs, language, games, foods, arts and crafts, and medicine are still a major part of these people's lives.

**Population Profile. 1969:** Tribal enrollment 146; Indian resident 35; Unemployment 45%; Median family income $2,500. **1980:** Indian resident 45; Non-Indian resident 6; Percent Indian of total population 88.2; Total housing units 17; Occupied housing units 17. The average educational level attained is 8th grade. All school facilities are off the reservation.

**Climate.** The weather is usually mild and moderate, with temperatures ranging from a low of 15 degrees to a high of 95 degrees.

**Transportation.** Commercial airlines are available in San Diego, train facilities are available in Escondido, bus service is available in Warner Springs, and a truckline serves Ramona. State Highway No. 78, running north-south, serves the reservation.

**Community Facilities.** Water for the reservation is provided by a spring. Bottled gas may be purchased and electricity is purchased from the San Diego Gas and Electric Company. The sewer system consists of septic tanks and outhouses. Hospital, clinics, dental care, and PHS facilities are available in Escondido, 40 miles from the reservation.


MANZANITA RESERVATION                    Federal Reservation
San Diego County
Manzanita Band of Mission Indians
Tribal Headquarters: Boulevard, California

**Land Status.** Total area: 3,379 acres. This reservation was established on February 10, 1893, under the authority of the Act of 1891. Lack of industry and employment opportunities have forced most of these people to leave their reservation.

**Culture.** The Manzanita Band still have their Indian culture, such as Indian burials, songs, language, games, foods, arts and crafts, and medicine.

**Population Profile. 1969:** Tribal enrollment 69; Indian resident 25; Unemployment 5%; Median family income $2,000. **1980:** Indian resident 13; Non-Indian resident 1; Percent Indian of total population 92.9; Total housing units 8; Occupied housing units 5. The average educational level attained is 8th grade. There are no school facilities available on this reservation. Students attend public schools.

**Transportation.** San Diego, 57 miles from the reservation, has the nearest airline, train and private airport facilities. Bus and trucking are available in Boulevard and El Cajon. U.S. Highway No. 80 serves the reservation.

**Community Facilities.** There are no water, gas, electricity, or sewer systems available on the reservation. Hospitals, clinics, and dental health care are provided by county and private facilities.


MESA GRANDE RESERVATION                    Federal Reservation
San Diego County
Mesa Grande Band of Mission Indians
Tribal Headquarters: Pala, California

**Land Status.** Total area: 120 acres. This reservation was established under Executive Orders of December 27, 1875, and June 19, 1883, which set apart lands for this reservation. Executive Order 4297 of August 25, 1925, set apart additional lands. An Act of May 10, 1926, provided that lands set apart were to become a part of the reservation.
**Population Profile. 1969:** Tribal enrollment 261; Indian resident 30; Unemployment 20%; Median family income $2,000. The average educational level attained is 8th grade. Elementary and high schools are available at Ramona, 10 miles away. A college is located in Escondido, 40 miles away.
**Climate.** Mesa Grande Reservation is located in the southwest portion of California, containing flatlands with a moderate climate. Rainfall is about 3 inches per year with temperatures ranging from a high of 110 degrees to a low of 28 degrees.
**Transportation.** The nearest commercial airlines are located in San Diego, 70 miles away. Train, bus, and trucking service are available at Escondido, 40 miles away. Ramona, 10 miles away, has a private airport. State Highway No. 76 runs northeast of the reservation about 8 miles from the reservation.
**Community Facilities.** Springs and wells provide water for the reservation. Bottled and tank gas are used for heating. Presently there is no electricity on the reservation. There is no sewer system on the reservation; outhouses are still used. Housing conditions are poor. Hospital and dental facilities can be obtained in Escondido. The reservation has a tribal clinic but it needs repairs.


MIDDLETOWN RANCHERIA                        Federal Reservation
Lake County
Pomo-Patwin Tribe
Tribal Headquarters: Middletown, California

**Land Status.** Total area: 109 acres. The rancheria was established by the Secretary of the Interior on July 30, 1910.
**Culture.** Traditional burials are still performed, and their language is still spoken.
**Population Profile. 1969:** Indian resident 33; Unemployment 25%; Median family income $2,000. **1980:** Indian resident 39; Non-Indian resident 1; Percent Indian of total population 97.5; Total housing units 10; Occupied housing units 8. The average educational level attained

is 11th grade. Elementary and high school facilities are available 2 miles from the rancheria and a college is available 45 miles away.

**Climate.** The seasons in this geographical location are moderate, with temperatures ranging from a high of 90 degrees to a low of 30 degrees. The average rainfall is 17 inches per year.

**Transportation.** The city of Ukiah, 90 miles from the rancheria, provides air, train, bus, and trucklines. Highway No. 53 and Highway No. 29 serve the rancheria.

**Community Facilities.** Water for the rancheria is provided by the community. Gas and electricity are provided by Pacific Gas and Electric. The tribe has its own sewer system. Hospital, clinics, and PHS facilities are available in Lakeport, 40 miles away. Dental care facilities are available in Middletown, 1 mile from the rancheria.


MISSION CREEK RESERVATION                    Federal Reservation
Riverside County
Mission Creek Band of Mission Indians
Tribal Headquarters: Whittier, California

**Land Status.** Total area: None. An Executive Order of May 15, 1876, established a reservation in this area. The present reservation was established on January 28, 1921, under authority of the Act of 1891. The Act of August 1, 1914, appropriated funds for purchase of lands for homeless California Indians. The reservation is in process of termination by authority of the Rancheria Act, P.L. 85-671,25, as amended by P.L. 88-419.

**Culture.** Very little of Mission Creek Reservation's culture still exists.

**Population Profile. 1969:** Tribal enrollment 15; Indian resident 0.

**Climate.** The climate is mild and moderate with an average rainfall of about 5.8 inches per year. The temperatures range from a high of 111 degrees to a low of 23 degrees.

**Transportation.** Commercial transportation such as airlines, trains, buses, and trucks is available at Palm Springs, 17 miles from the reservation. U.S. Highway No. 60 runs east-west through White River.

**Community Facilities.** Water is obtained from surface supplies. Bottled gas is purchased, and there is no electricity, nor a sewer system on the reservation. The county hospital at White River serves the reservation.


MONTGOMERY CREEK RANCHERIA                    Federal Reservation
Shasta County
Pitt River Tribe
Tribal Headquarters: Montgomery Creek, California

**Land Status.** Total area: 72 acres. The reservation was established by the Secretary of the Interior on October 13, 1915, under the authority of the Act of June 30, 1913. The rancheria was set aside for homeless California Indians who had no prior land. The Montgomery Creek Rancheria was named on the original Rancheria Act, but was not terminated.

**Population Profile. 1980:** Indian resident 1; Non-Indian resident 0; Percent Indian of total population 100.0; Total housing units 2; Occupied housing units 1.

**Climate.** The rancheria lies in northern California where the land is irrigable and the climate is generally mild and sunny. Rainfall measures 10 inches annually. Temperatures reach highs of 98 degrees and lows of 22 degrees.

**Transportation.** The rancheria is 34 miles from Redding, the nearest city. Highway No. 299 runs within 1 mile of the rancheria. The road to the rancheria is 3 miles and impassable, except by four-wheel drive vehicles, during the winter. Redding has commercial transportation service by air, train, truck, and bus.

**Community Facilities.** Residents draw water from springs. There are no other utilities available. The county hospital in Redding is the nearest location for medical care. The only house is in poor condition.


MORONGO RESERVATION                    Federal Reservation
Riverside County
Morongo Band of Mission Indians
Tribal Headquarters: Banning, California

**Land Status.** Total area: 32,254.02 acres. The present reservation was patented to the Morongo Band on December 14, 1908, by the Secretary of the Interior under authority of the Act of March 1, 1907.

**Culture.** Traditional religion and kinship trends prevail. Some of the Indian language is spoken.

**Population Profile. 1969:** Tribal enrollment 578; Indian resident 238; Unemployment 20%. **1980:** Indian resident 313; Non-Indian resident 101; Percent Indian of total population 75.6; Total housing units 129; Occupied housing units 119. The average education level attained is 11th grade. Elementary and high school facilities are available.

**Climate.** The temperatures of this geographic location range from a high of 110 degrees to a low of 18 degrees.

**Transportation.** The City of Ontario, 55 miles from the reservation, has the nearest commercial airline facilities. A train depot is available at Colton, 35 miles away. Bus, trucking, and private airport facilities are available in Banning, 5 miles from the reservation.

**Community Facilities.** Water for the reservation is provided by wells. Gas and electricity are provided by Southern California Edison. The sewer system consists of septic tanks. Hospital and dental facilities are available in Banning. Clinic and PHS facilities are provided by the county in Riverside, 25 miles away.

PALA RESERVATION                    Federal Reservation
San Diego County
Pala Band of Mission Indians
Tribal Headquarters: Pala, California

**Land Status.** Tribally-owned land: 6,322 acres. Allotted land: 1,400 acres. Total area: 7,722 acres. An Executive Order of December 27, 1875, set apart lands for this reservation and two orders in 1877 and 1882 restored portions to public domain. An Act of May 27, 1962, appropriated $100,000 for purchase of land in southern California for Mission Indians, part of which was used for removing Indians to the purchased land.

**Culture.** The Pala Reservation is a community built around the famous Pala Mission. The Indians have retained their kinship tradition, some language, and other tribal traditions in spite of the missionaries' efforts to substitute European Christian culture for the Indian.

**Government.** The tribe's Articles of Association were approved in 1960 and amended the following year. The governing body is the general council, composed of all adult members 21 years or older. A five-member executive committee is elected in December for a 1-year term. The committee meets monthly.

**Population Profile. 1969:** Tribal enrollment 447; Indian resident 194, Non-Indian resident 37; Unemployment 28%; Underemployment minority; Median family income $2,500. **1980:** Indian resident 433; Non-Indian resident 126; Percent Indian of total population 77.5; Total housing units 174; Occupied housing units 165. The average education level for the tribe is 10th grade. Two tribal members are college graduates. Students attend schools about 18 miles from their reservation homes.

**Tribal Economy.** The tribal income of $45,000 is almost completely income from San Diego Consolidated Sand and Gravel. This is the only resource on the reservation. The reservation is located in southern California. Part of the land is hilly, and the remainder is suitable for grazing or irrigated agriculture.

**Climate.** Rainfall measures only 3 inches annually. The high temperature is 110 degrees; the low is 28 degrees.

**Transportation.** Fallbrook is the nearest city to the reservation. It lies within 20 miles of Pala. The reservation has a paved access road to State Highway No. 16 to the north, and east-west State Highway No. 76. Bus and trucklines stop in Fallbrook. Oceanside, 25 miles from the reservation, has train service. Residents must travel 55 miles to San Diego, the nearest commercial airport. There is a private airstrip 6 miles from the reservation.

**Community Facilities.** The tribe has its own well and sewer system; however, these are inadequate for future growth. Only bottled gas is available. San Diego Gas and Electric provides the reservation with electricity. There is a private hospital in Fallbrook, and additional medical care is offered through county clinics in Escondido, 25 miles from the reservation. The Mission Hall serves as a community building. The Corpus Christe Fiesta and the Children's Festival are annual events celebrated by tribal members. Of the 80 houses on the reservation, over half are in bad condition.

PAUMA RESERVATION                    Federal Reservation
San Diego County
Pauma Band of Mission Indians
Tribal Headquarters: Pauma Valley, California

**Land Status.** Total area: 250 acres. This reservation was established on August 18, 1892, under authority of the Act of 1891. The reservation is small and only a few residents remain.

**Culture.** The people are motivated towards economic development and community action. On their own incentive, they have started constructing a community building. This reservation has good potential for citrus development and a motel. Very little of the Pauma-Yuma culture is being practiced.

**Population Profile. 1969:** Tribal enrollment 96; Indian resident 50; Unemployment 1%; Median family income $3,500. **1980:** Indian resident 86; Non-Indian resident 3; Percent Indian of total population 96.6; Total housing units 28; Occupied housing units 27. The average educational level attained is 10th grade. Elementary and high schools and college can be attended nearby at Valley Center.

**Climate.** The reservation is located in the southern portion of San Diego County. The climate is moderate and mild, with an average rainfall of about 3 inches per year. Temperatures range from 110 degrees to a low of 28 degrees.

**Transportation.** San Diego, 60 miles away, has the nearest commercial airlines. Oceanside, 25 miles from the reservation, provides train facilities. Escondido, 25 miles away, has bus and truckline facilities. State Highway No. 395 serves the reservation.

**Community Facilities.** A domestic well provides water for the reservation. Gas is provided by a petroleum line from Escondido. Electricity is provided by San Diego Gas and Electric. Septic tanks make up the sewer system. All health facilities (hospital, clinic, and dental) are available in Escondido.

PECHANGA RESERVATION                 Federal Reservation
Riverside County
Pechanga Band of Mission Indians
Tribal Headquarters: Temecula, California

**Land Status.** Total area: 4,097 acres. This reservation was established by Executive Order of June 27, 1882, which set apart certain lands in Riverside County, California, for Indian purposes. The present reservation was selected under authority of the Act of January 12, 1891, and established on August 29, 1893.

**Culture.** Some native language is spoken; traditional language influences remain prevalent.

**Population Profile. 1969:** Tribal enrollment 320; Indian resident 39; Unemployment 30%. **1980:** Indian resident 117; Non-Indian resident 24; Percent Indian of total population 83.0; Total housing units 47; Occupied housing units 39. The average education level attained is

7th grade. Elementary and high school facilities are available at Fallbrook, 15 miles from the reservation. College facilities are available 16 miles away.

**Climate.** The reservation is located in southern California, about 40 miles from the coast in Riverside County, with flat low lands and a climate that is moderate and sunny. The average rainfall is about 3.9 inches per year. Temperatures range from a high of 120 degrees to a low of 22 degrees.

**Transportation.** The nearest commercial airline facilities are located in San Diego, 60 miles away. Train, bus, and trucking facilities are available in Fallbrook, 15 miles from the reservation. Elsinore, 15 miles away, has the nearest private airport facilities. State Highway No. 76 runs east-west 8 miles south of the reservation.

**Community Facilities.** Water for the reservation is provided by wells and springs. Gas and electricity are provided by Pacific Gas and Electric. The sewer system consists of outhouses and septic tanks. Hospitals, clinics, and dental facilities are available in Fallbrook.


RAMONA RESERVATION                       Federal Reservation
Riverside County
Cahuilla Band of Mission Indians              Unoccupied

**Land Status.** Total area: 560 acres. This reservation was established on February 10, 1893, under authority of the Act of 1891. The reservation is a mountainous area and good only for grazing. There are no allotments or assignments or records of any members at Ramona. The reservation has been unoccupied for many years.

**Population Profile.** None.

**Climate.** The reservation is a mountainous area where the average rainfall per year is about 7.8 inches. The temperature ranges from a high of 107 degrees to a low of 17 degrees.

**Transportation.** All commercial transportation facilities can be obtained at Hemet, 21 miles away. The reservation is located 5 miles off State Highway No. 71.

**Community Facilities.** Hospital and clinic facilities are available at Hemet. There is no record of a dental facility available in the surrounding area. PHS facilities are available at Riverside, 70 miles away.


RINCON RESERVATION
San Diego County
San Luiseno Band of Mission Indians
Tribal Headquarters: Valley Center, California

**Land Status.** Total area: 3,975 acres. An Executive Order on December 27, 1875, established the Rincon Reservation and an Executive Order of March 2, 1881, increased the size. The present reservation was established on September 13, 1892, under the authority of the

Act of 1891. As for many other reservations, land inheritance is a problem. Most of the land is taken up by hills and mountains; one-third of the land is level.

**Culture.** Presently there is an Indian culture and language study on the reservation. The culture study was funded by the Bureau of Indian Affairs in Fiscal Year 1968. Mainly through the efforts of the leaders of the Rincon Community, one-fourth of the Rincon Band still speak their native language. The way and traditions are all Indian.

**Population Profile.** 1969: Tribal enrollment 345; Indian resident 91; Unemployment 46%; Median family income $1,000. 1980: Indian resident 297; Non-Indian resident 193; Percent Indian of total population 60.6; Total housing units 133; Occupied housing units 121. The average educational level attained is 11.5 grades. The elementary and high schools are 17 miles from the reservation.

**Tribal Economy.** The Rincon, Pauma, and La Jolla Tribes have a joint venture with the Material Systems Corporation to bring industry to the reservations, to improve housing, and to increase employment and revenues. The tribes' share of the venture is 5 percent.

**Climate.** The Luiseno Mission Indians are located in southern California where the land is hilly and brushy and the climate moderate with little temperature change. The average rainfall is 3 inches per year with high temperatures of 108 degrees and lows of 22 degrees.

**Transportation.** The nearest train and airline facilities are in San Diego, 45 miles away. Bus service facilities are available at Escondido, 17 miles away. The nearest private airport is also at Escondido. State Highway No. 76 is nearby.

**Community Facilities.** A water system is provided by the Bureau of Indian Affairs. A hospital is located in San Diego, 45 miles away. Dental clinics are provided by the Rincon Dental Project. Public Health Services are not available. Housing conditions are poor.


ROARING CREEK RANCHERIA                    Federal Reservation
Shasta County
Pitt River Tribe
Tribal Headquarters: Montgomery Creek, California

**Land Status.** Total area: 80 acres. The land was purchased for the landless California Indians who had no prior allotments under authority of the Howard-Wheeler Act of August 31, 1915. There was no designation of occupying tribes.

**Culture.** Very little Indian language is spoken, but some traditional foods are still eaten. There is no formal government. The tribal council is not recognized by the Bureau of Indian Affairs.

**Population Profile.** 1969: Population 7. The rancheria is occupied by one family. 1980: Indian resident 24; Non-Indian resident 1; Percent Indian of total population 96.0; Total housing units 4; Occupied housing units 4.

**Climate.** The 80 acres of irrigable land are located in northern California in a mild and sunny climate. The rainfall averages 10 inches. The high temperature is 98 degrees; the low is 22 degrees.

**Transportation.** An unpaved dirt road runs the 2 miles from the rancheria to Big Bend Road. Highway No. 299 is the nearest major highway. Redding, 43 miles from Roaring Creek, is served by commercial air, train, truck, and buslines.

**Community Facilities.** As there are no pipelines on the rancheria land, the family must carry water from the spring. The only power supply is the electricity purchased from Pacific Gas and Electric. The county hospital in Redding is the closest medical facility. The sole house is in poor condition.


ROUND VALLEY RESERVATION                     Federal Reservation
Mendocino County
Yuki, Pitt River, Little Lake, Konkow, Wylacki
Pomo, Nomalaki, and Wintun Tribes
Tribal Headquarters: Covelo, California

**Land Status.** Tribally-owned land: 12,706 acres. Allotted land: 8,000 acres. Total area: 18,706 acres. An Act of April 8, 1864, authorized the establishment of four Indian reservations in California. An Executive Order of March 30, 1870, enlarged the Round Valley Reservation and the borders were defined by the Executive Order of May 18, 1875. The Camp Wright Military Reserve was added to the reservation in 1876.

**Culture.** Tribal members hunt and fish on the reservation and weave traditional baskets.

**Government.** The tribes' constitution and bylaws, prepared according to the Indian Reorganization Act of 1934, were approved in 1936. The Tribal Charter was ratified in the following year. The governing body is the Covelo Indian Community Council which has seven members. Council members are elected in March to staggered 4-year terms. The officers are elected annually in March.

**Population Profile. 1969:** Tribal enrollment 1,582; Indian resident 369; Unemployment 60%; Underemployment 28 persons. **1980:** Indian resident 528; Non-Indian resident 740; Percent Indian of total population 41.6; Total housing units 478; Occupied housing units 408. The average education level attained is 11th grade. The public schools are 1 mile from the reservation. The nearest college is 150 miles away.

**Tribal Economy.** The tribe earns $2,000 yearly in forestry and an additional $1,500 from other sources. The tribe can cut up to 43 million board feet per year.

**Climate.** The reservation, located on hilly land in northwestern California, has mild winters, rainfall measuring about 35 inches per year. Temperature extremes are a high of 105 degrees and a low of 29 degrees.

**Transportation.** Willits, the nearest city, lies some 45 miles from Round Valley and is served by commercial train and buslines. Truck service is available in Covelo, 1 mile from the reservation. There are a commercial airport in Ukiah, 70 miles from Round Valley, and a private airstrip in Covelo. Paved county roads connect the reservation with U.S. Highway No. 101, a major north-south route.

**Community Facilities.** The water and sewer systems were installed by the Public Health Service. Reservation residents purchase gas from Standard Oil and electricity from Pacific Gas and Electric. The Public Health Service extends medical care to tribal members in Covelo. Private medical and hospital care are available in Willits, 45 miles from Round Valley.

RUMSEY RANCHERIA                          Federal Reservation
Yolo County
Wintun Tribe
Tribal Headquarters: Brooks, California

**Land Status.** Total area: 66 acres. The original purchase of land for the Rumsey Rancheria was in 1907 and 1908. Additional lands were purchased by the Secretary of the Interior on September 24, 1907, and also under the Howard-Wheeler Act. The Rumsey Rancheria is in the process of termination under the authority of the Rancheria Act, P.L. 85-671, as amended by P.L. 18-419.

**Population Profile. 1969:** Population 3. **1980:** Indian resident 11; Non-Indian resident 2; Percent Indian of total population 84.6; Total housing units 5; Occupied housing units 4.

**Climate.** The climate in this geographic location is mild and sunny. The average rainfall is about 15 inches per year with temperatures ranging from a low of 38 degrees to a high of 109 degrees.

SAN MANUEL RESERVATION                    Federal Reservation
San Bernardino County
San Manuel Band
Tribal Headquarters: Highland, California

**Land Status.** Total area: 653.15 acres. This reservation was established on August 31, 1893, and is located northeast of San Bernardino near Patton State Hospital, and is mostly mountain terrain having no value for grazing or agriculture.

**Culture.** Although small in population, language, foods, kinship, and traditions are still used.

**Population Profile. 1969:** Tribal enrollment 50; Indian resident 27; Unemployment 32%. **1980:** Indian resident 24; Non-Indian resident 7; Percent Indian of total population 77.4; Total housing units 11; Occupied housing units 10. The average educational level attained is 9th grade. Elementary, high school, and college facilities are available at San Bernardino, 5 miles from the reservation.

**Climate.** The climate is mild and moderate with an average rainfall of about 4.6 inches per year. Temperatures range from a low of 15 degrees to a high of 110 degrees.

**Transportation.** The City of Ontario, 25 miles from the reservation, has the nearest commercial airline facilities. Train, bus, trucklines, and a private airport are available at San Bernardino. State Highway No. 15 runs north-south by the reservation.

**Community Facilities.** Water is provided by a well which is tribally-owned. Gas is not purchased. Electricity is provided by Southern California Edison Company. The sewer system consists of cesspools. Hospitals, clinics, and dental facilities are available in San Bernardino.

SAN PASQUAL RESERVATION                    Federal Reservation
San Diego County
San Pasqual Band of Mission Indians
Tribal Headquarters: Valley Center, California

**Land Status.** Total area: 1,379 acres. The present reservation was established July, 1910, under authority of the Act of 1891 as amended and supplemented. Executive Order of April 15, 1911, set aside land for a reservation site to be used in connection with irrigation of land on the reservation.

**Population Profile. 1969:** Tribal enrollment 214; Indian resident 45; Non-Indian resident 6; Unemployment 0; Median family income over $3,000. **1980:** Indian resident 133; Non-Indian resident 76; Percent Indian of total population 63.6; Total housing units 68; Occupied housing units 65. The average education level attained is 9th grade. Elementary and high schools are located at Escondido, 10 miles away and the nearest college is located at San Diego, 40 miles away.

**Climate.** San Pasqual Reservation is surrounded by hills which make the climate moderate. Rainfall is 3 inches per year. Temperatures go as high as 110 degrees to a low of 28 degrees.

**Transportation.** Commercial airlines are available at San Diego, 40 miles away. Train and bus facilities are available at Escondido, 10 miles away. A truckline and a private airport are also available at Escondido. A paved county road connects San Pasqual Reservation with State Highway No. 76.

**Community Facilities.** A well provides only an inadequate supply of water to the San Pasqual Reservation. The homes are heated with bottled gas. Electricity is provided by Pacific Gas and Electric. At the present the reservation does not have a sewer system. Health facilities can be obtained at Escondido and include hospitalization, clinics, and dental facilities. Housing facilities are poor. Only 50 percent of the homes have septic tanks; others have outhouses.

SANTA ROSA RANCHERIA                    Federal Reservation
Kings County
Tache Tribe
Tribal Headquarters: Lemoore, California

**Land Status.** Total area: 170 acres. A court decree of the U.S. District Court, Southern California, Northern Division, established the rancheria in February 1921. An additional purchase provided more land in July 1939, under the Howard-Wheeler Act.

**Culture.** The Tache have little remaining culture except language which is spoken mainly by older members of the tribe. Some traditional foods are still used.

**Population Profile.** **1969:** Tribal enrollment 109; Indian resident 149; Unemployment 58%. **1980:** Indian resident 117; Non-Indian resident 52; Percent Indian of total population 69.2; Total housing units 36; Occupied housing units 32. The average educational level attained is 8½ grades. There are no education facilities available on the reservation. The elementary school is 3 miles from the reservation, and the high school is 7 miles from the reservation.

**Climate.** The climate is usually moderate although temperatures reach a high of 110 degrees and a low of 20 degrees. The rainfall averages about 8 inches per year.

**Transportation.** The City of Visalia, 30 miles from the reservation, has commercial airline facilities. Train facilities are available at Hanford, 14 miles from the reservation. The town of Lemoore provides trucking and bus service and also maintains a private airport. The available access routes are Alkali Drive which is paved and State Highway No. 198 which is 5 miles away.

**Community Facilities.** Water is provided by wells. Gas and electricity are provided by Pacific Gas and Electric Company. The sewer system consists of septic tanks and outhouses. Hospital, clinics, and dental facilities are available at Hanford, 14 miles away.


SANTA ROSA RESERVATION                    Federal Reservation
Riverside County
Santa Rosa Band of Mission Indians
Tribal Headquarters: Hemet, California

**Land Status.** Total area: 11,092.62 acres. This reservation was established on February 2, 1907, under authority of the Act of 1891, as amended. An Act of April 17, 1937, authorized the Secretary of the Interior to purchase 640 acres in the name of the U.S. Government in trust for the Santa Rosa Band.

**Culture.** The culture of the Santa Rosa Reservation, with just a few residents, is one of the few remaining cohesive forces preventing total dispersion of the tribe. Religion, language, some foods, kinship, and other tribal traditions still draw the tribe together.

**Population Profile.** **1969:** Tribal enrollment 61; Indian resident 16; Unemployment 50%. **1980:** Indian resident 12; Non-Indian resident 0; Percent Indian of total population 100.0; Total housing units 6; Occupied housing units 6. The average educational level attained is 10th grade. Elementary and high schools are located in Hemet, 38 miles from the reservation. The nearest college is about 60 miles from the reservation.

**Climate.** The reservation is located in southern California with flat desert land and an arid climate. Average rainfall amounts to about

7 inches per year, and temperatures range from 109 degrees to 16 degrees.

**Transportation.** The nearest airline facilities available are at Palm Springs, 50 miles away. Train, bus, and truckline facilities are available 38 miles northwest of the reservation in Hemet. Hemet also maintains a private airport. State Highway No. 74 is nearby.

**Community Facilities.** Water is owned by the tribe. There are no gas, electricity, or sewer system facilities on the reservation. A private hospital in Hemet serves the reservation. Clinics and dental facilities are provided by the county at Riverside, 60 miles away. There is no PHS medical service available to the reservation.

SANTA YNEZ RESERVATION                    Federal Reservation
Santa Barbara County
Santa Ynez Band of Mission Indians
Tribal Headquarters: Sun Valley, California

**Land Status.** Total area: 99.28 acres. The Santa Ynez Reservation is situated in Santa Barbara County approximately 32 miles north of Santa Barbara. The reservation was established on December 27, 1901, under the authority of the Act of 1891.

**Culture.** Religion, language, foods, kinship, and other tribal traditions still exist among these people.

**Population Profile.** **1969:** Tribal enrollment 169; Indian resident 50; Unemployment 50%; Median family income $3,000 to $5,000. **1980:** Indian resident 120; Non-Indian resident 13; Percent Indian of total population 90.2; Total housing units 42; Occupied housing units 40. The average educational level attained is 10th grade. Elementary, high school, and college facilities are available at Santa Barbara.

**Climate.** The topography of the reservation includes rolling hills, trees, and a running stream, all of which help to moderate the climate. Temperatures range from 97 degrees to a low of 47 degrees. The yearly rainfall is about 8 inches.

**Transportation.** Commercial transportation facilities are available in Santa Barbara. The nearest private airport is located in Santa Ynez, 6 miles from the reservation. U.S. Highway No. 101 is 6 miles from the reservation.

**Community Facilities.** Water comes from a well which is provided by the city. Bottled gas is purchased. Electricity is provided by the Santa Barbara Gas and Electric Company. The sewer system consists of three septic tanks and 11 outhouses. Hospitals, clinics, dental and PHS facilities are available at Santa Barbara.

SANTA YSABEL RESERVATION                    Federal Reservation
San Diego County
Santa Ysabel Band of Mission Indians
Tribal Headquarters: Santa Ysabel, California

**Land Status.** Total area: 10,000 acres. The present reservation was established on February 10, 1893, under authority of the Act of 1891. An Act of June 3, 1926, authorized the Secretary of the Interior to purchase 573 acres for the reservation. The isolated location of the reservation causes many of the people to move off the reservation to be closer to their jobs. There is no economic development on the reservation.

**Culture.** Tribal traditions still exist on the Santa Ysabel Reservation.

**Population Profile.** 1969: Tribal enrollment 300; Indian resident 94; Unemployment 31%; Median family income $2,500. 1980: Indian resident 181; Non-Indian 15; Percent Indian of total population 92.3; Total housing units 66; Occupied housing units 61. The average educational level attained is 8th grade. Elementary and high schools are located in Ramona, 16 miles away. A college is located in Escondido, 30 miles from the reservation.

**Climate.** The Santa Ysabel Reservation is located in the southwest portion of California, with lands that are flat and arid and a warm dry climate. Rainfall averages about 15 inches per year. Temperatures reach a high of 100 degrees to a low of 29 degrees.

**Transportation.** Commercial airlines are available at San Diego, 60 miles away. Train service is available in Escondido, 30 miles away. Bus service and a trucking line are available in Ramona, 16 miles from the reservation, and a private airport is also available in Ramona. State Highway No. 78, running north-south, is nearby.

**Community Facilities.** The reservation's water system consists of a spring. Bottled gas is used for heating. No electricity is available. There are no sewer or septic facilities on the reservation. Health facilities are located at Escondido, 30 miles away and include a hospital, clinic, and dental facilities.


SHEEP RANCH RANCHERIA                       Federal Reservation
Calaveras County
Me-Wuk Tribe
Tribal Headquarters: Sheepranch, California

**Land Status.** Total area: 1 acre. This reservation was purchased for homeless California Indians in 1916 without designation of tribe.

**Population Profile.** 1969: Population 2. 1980: Indian resident 2; Non-Indian resident 0; Percent Indian of total population 100.0; Total housing units 1; Occupied housing units 1.

**Climate.** The reservation lies near Highway No. 4, 23 miles from San Andreas. It is located in the Sierra Nevada Mountains in a mild and moderate climate. Rainfall averages 17 inches annually. The temperature reaches a high of 90 degrees and a low of 35 degrees.

**Transportation.** Angel's Camp, 12 miles from Sheepranch, is served by bus and trucklines. The nearest train station is in Sonora, 30 miles from the reservation. Air service is available at Stockton, 65 miles away. There is also a private airstrip in Angel's Camp.


SOBOBA RESERVATION                              Federal Reservation
Riverside County
Soboba Band of Mission Indians
Tribal Headquarters: San Jacinto, California

**Land Status.** Total area: 5,035.68 acres. An Executive Order of June 19, 1883, set apart lands for the Soboba Reservation. The present reservation was established on June 10, 1913, under authority of the Act of 1891.

**Culture.** The culture of the Soboba Indians is very much traditional. Kinship, food, language, and religion have been the basic elements that distinguish this tribe of Indians.

**Population Profile. 1969:** Tribal enrollment 314; Indian resident 223; Unemployment 6 persons. **1980:** Indian resident 230; Non-Indian resident 28; Percent Indian of total population 89.1; Total housing units 78; Occupied housing units 73. Average educational level attained is 11th grade. Elementary and high schools are located at Hemet 7 miles away. Riverside has the nearest college facilities, 47 miles from the reservation.

**Climate.** The reservation is located in southern California which is flat land with a climate that is mild and moderate. The average rainfall is about 4.7 inches per year. Temperatures range from 110 degrees to a low of 26 degrees.

**Transportation.** Hemet, 7 miles away, has airlines, train, and a private airport. Bus and trucking facilities can be obtained in San Jacinto, 1 mile from the reservation. State Highway No. 74 runs east-west through San Jacinto.

**Community Facilities.** Water is furnished by the tribe. Residents purchase bottled gas. Electricity is provided by Southern California Edison. There is no sewer system on the reservation. A private hospital in Hemet serves the reservation. Clinics and dental facilities can be obtained in Riverside, 47 miles from the reservation.


SULPHUR BANK RANCHERIA                          Federal Reservation
(El-Em Indian Colony)
Lake County
Pomo Tribe
Tribal Headquarters: Clearlake Oaks, California

**Land Status.** Total area: 50 acres. The Sulphur Bank Rancheria was established by court decree on January 10, 1949. Title is held by the United States in trust for Sulphur Bank Band of Pomo Indians.

**Culture.** The culture of these people such as burials and foods is still practiced. Some of the Indian language is spoken.

**Population Profile. 1969:** Tribal enrollment 45; Indian resident 30; Unemployment 20%; Median family income $1,500. **1980:** Indian resident 115; Non-Indian resident 0; Percent Indian of total population 100.0; Total housing units 24; Occupied housing units 24. The average educational level attained is 12th grade. Students have to travel 4 miles to elementary school and 13 miles to high school. College facilities are available 50 miles from the rancheria.

**Climate.** The Pomo Rancheria is located in northern California. The topography consists of lakeside and hills. The climate is mild and moderate. The average rainfall is about 17 inches per year, with temperatures ranging from a high of 90 degrees to a low of 30 degrees.

**Transportation.** The town of Ukiah, 45 miles from the reservation has the nearest commercial airline; also train and bus facilities are available here. Trucklines and a private airport are available in Lakeport, 28 miles from the reservation.

**Community Facilities.** There is no water on the reservation. Gas is purchased in butane bottles. Electricity is provided by Pacific Gas and Electric. As there is no sewer system available, outhouses are used. Hospitals, clinics, dental and PHS facilities are available in Lakeport.


SUSANVILLE RANCHERIA                    Federal Reservation
Lassen County
Paiute, Maidu, Pitt River, and Washoe Tribes
Tribal Headquarters: Susanville, California

**Land Status.** Total area: 30 acres. The reservation land was purchased August 15, 1923, for homeless California Indians, without designation of tribe. All the land is tribally owned but for 1/3 acre assigned to an individual.

**Culture.** The Indian language is no longer spoken. Both young and old, however, practice arts and crafts. Indian religion has virtually disappeared, as has the language.

**Government.** The tribe is governed by a business committee elected by the tribal council to serve a 2-year period. The constitution and bylaws were approved by the Secretary of the Interior in February 1969, as amended from the 1935 constitution.

**Population Profile. 1969:** Tribal enrollment 75; Indian resident 75; Non-Indian resident 1; Unemployment 30%; Underemployment 14 persons. **1980:** Indian resident 82; Non-Indian resident 8; Percent Indian of total population 91.1; Total housing units 40; Occupied housing units 23. The average education level is 10th grade. One tribal member is a college graduate. Elementary and high schools are 1 mile from the reservation.

**Climate.** The reservation is about 70 miles from the Nevada border in mountainous foothills where the weather is cold with some winter snows. Rainfall averages 10 inches yearly. Temperatures range from a high of 95 degrees to a low of 22 degrees.

**Transportation.** Highways No. 44 and No. 36 are near the reservation. Reno is approximately 86 miles from the rancheria. Reno is the nearest location for air and train service. Bus and trucklines stop in Susanville, 1 mile from the reservation. An unpaved private airstrip is 5 miles distant.

**Community Facilities.** The rancheria is connected to the city facilities. California Pacific Utility Company provides water and electricity. Gas is sold by a private distributor. Health care is available at the Lassen County Memorial Hospital and the Lassen County Health Clinic.

**Recreation.** The tribe has an Indian Council Lodge, Inc. The annual Bear Dance is held in Janesville, California.


SYCUAN RESERVATION                    Federal Reservation
San Diego County
Sycuan Band of Mission Indians
Tribal Headquarters: El Cajon, California

**Land Status.** Total area: 640 acres. This reservation has been largely neglected and, consequently, there is little ongoing activity. Very little is known of its past, and only a small bit of Sycuan culture remains.

**Population Profile.** **1969:** Tribal enrollment 37; Indian resident 12; Unemployment 2%. **1980:** Indian resident 48; Non-Indian resident 13; Percent Indian of total population 78.7; Total housing units 18; Occupied housing units 17. The average educational level is 6th grade. The elementary and high schools are located in El Cajon, 6 miles from the reservation. The nearest college is located in San Diego, 25 miles away.

**Climate.** The reservation is located in southern San Diego County, with flat land which has a warm and moderate climate. The average rainfall is about 6.5 inches per year. Temperatures range from a high of 90 degrees to a low of 32 degrees.

**Transportation.** The nearest air, train, truck, and busline facilities are located in San Diego. El Cajon, 6 miles away, has a truckline. U.S. Highway No. 80 is 4 miles from the reservation.

**Community Facilities.** Hospital and clinics are available in El Cajon and San Diego. Private dental and PHS facilities are available in El Cajon. Wells provide water for families. Gas and electricity are provided by the San Diego Gas and Electric Company. Housing conditions are very poor.


TORRES MARTINEZ RESERVATION           Federal Reservation
Riverside County
Torres-Martinez Band of Mission Indians
Tribal Headquarters: Mecca, California

**Land Status.** Tribal land: 11,932 acres. Allotted land: 13,473 acres. Non-Indian land: 5,000 acres. Total area: 25,405 acres. About 338 allotments, 40 acres each, have been given to Indians. Only a small portion of land is irrigable. About 9,000 acres are submerged under the rising Salton Sea. An Executive Order of May 15, 1876, set apart lands for this reservation. An Act of February 11, 1903, added 640 acres to the reservation in exchange for lands to be set apart for the Torres Band under the Act of 1891.

**Culture.** A variety of reasons caused the majority of members to move off the reservation; however, the tribal traditions, language, foods, kinship, and religion maintain ties between the resident and non-resident.

**Government.** The governing body is a five-member council elected to a 2-year term. There are four officers: chairman, vice-chairman, secretary-treasurer, a spokesman, and four committee members.

**Population Profile. 1969:** Tribal enrollment 217; Indian resident 65; Non-Indian resident 1; Unemployment 9 persons; Underemployment 0. **1980:** Indian resident 11; Non-Indian resident 267; Percent Indian of total population 4.0; Total housing units 145; Occupied housing units 86. The average education level attained is 10th grade. Although no members have graduated from college, there are scholarships available through the Bureau of Indian Affairs. The elementary and high schools are 9 miles from the reservation. There is also a missile training facility nearby.

**Climate.** The reservation lies in south-central California, having frontage on the Salton Sea which helps moderate the climate. Temperatures range from a high of 120 degrees to a low of 28 degrees. Rainfall averages 3.4 inches per year.

**Transportation.** The reservation is located 9 miles from Indio which is served by commercial air, train, truck, and bus companies. A private airport is located in Thermal, 3 miles distant. U.S. Highway No. 111 runs north-south through Thermal.

**Community Facilities.** The tribe has a water system; however, there are no sewer facilities. Residents purchase bottled gas, and electricity is supplied by the Southern California Edison. The county hospital and clinic in Indio serve the Indian community. Medical and dental care are also available from private doctors. A community building is under construction.

**Recreation.** A marina is being developed on the water frontage.


TULE RIVER RESERVATION                    Federal Reservation
Tulare County
Tule River Tribe
Tribal Headquarters: Porterville, California

**Land Status.** Total area: 54,116 acres. An Act of April 18, 1864, authorized the establishment of Indian reservations in California. An Executive Order of January 9, 1873, established the Tule River Reservation, and an Order of October 3, 1873, cancelled the Order of January 9, and re-established the reservation. An Act of May 17, 1928, changed the boundaries of the Tule River Reservation.

**Culture.** The culture of the Tule River Tribe still remains with these people.

**Population Profile. 1969:** Tribal enrollment 392; Indian resident 283; Unemployment 28%; Median family income $1,500. **1980:** Indian resident 424; Non-Indian resident 29; Percent Indian of total population 93.6; Total housing units 121; Occupied housing units 119. The average educational level attained is 9th grade. The educational facilities available are elementary, high school, and college, 19 miles from the reservation.

**Climate.** In this geographical location the summers are warm, but the average climate is generally mild. The topography is mountainous, with timber, a river, and a small valley. The average rainfall per year is about 10 inches. The temperatures range from a low of 26 degrees to a high of 90 degrees.

**Transportation.** Porterville has the nearest commercial airlines, bus, and truck service. Tulare, 45 miles away, has train facilities. A county road serves the reservation.

**Community Facilities.** A tribal water system provides the reservation with water. Gas is not used on the reservation. Electricity is provided by Southern California Edison. Indoor plumbing, septic tanks, and outhouses make up the sewer system. Hospital, clinic, and dental facilities are available in Porterville, 21 miles from the reservation.


TUOLUMNE RANCHERIA                    Federal Reservation
Tuolumne County
Tuolumne Band of Me-Wuk Indians
Tribal Headquarters: Tuolumne, California

**Land Status.** Total area: 323 acres. All the land is allotted. The land was purchased in October 1910, and additional land set aside in April of 1912. The deed is in the name of the United States.

**Culture.** The Round House is the culture center where Indian games and dances are held. Although the language is not spoken by many, the dances are still taught to the young people. Traditional native foods such as acorns and pine nuts are still gathered and eaten.

**Government.** The tribe has an Indian Reorganization Act constitution and bylaws which were approved in 1936 and amended in 1940. The governing body, community council, is composed of all qualified voters. A four-member business committee is elected at the November election for a 1-year term. Regular meetings are held in November and April.

**Population Profile. 1969:** Tribal enrollment 62; Indian resident 62; Non-Indian resident 14; Unemployment 36%; Underemployment 2 persons. **1980:** Indian resident 73; Non-Indian resident 20; Percent Indian of total population 78.5; Total housing units 32; Occupied housing units 27. The average education level for the tribe is 10th grade. The elementary and high schools are 4 miles from the reservation. One tribal member is a college graduate.

**Climate.** The seasons are generally mild with some winter snow. The rainfall averages 32 inches per year. Temperatures vary from highs of 93 degrees to lows of 33 degrees.

**Transportation.** The rancheria is 4 miles from Tuolumne. The Twin Hard Road, in need of repair, provides access to the rancheria. State Highway No. 108 is 11 miles away. A busline stops in Tuolumne. Sonora, 10 miles from the rancheria, has train and truck service. The nearest airport having commercial service is in Stockton, 60 miles away. There is a private airport 15 miles from the rancheria at Columbia.

**Community Facilities.** The Pacific Gas and Electric provides the rancheria with water and electricity. Only bottled gas is available. Hospital and other medical services are available in Sonora. The Indian Health Service has a branch at the rancheria. There are roundhouses and a community building on the rancheria. The tribe holds an annual Acorn Festival in September. The 16 houses on the reservation are in poor condition.

TWENTY-NINE PALMS RESERVATION          Federal Reservation
San Bernardino County
Twenty-Nine Palms Band of Indians
Tribal Headquarters: North Palm Springs, California

**Land Status.** Total area: 162.3 acres. This reservation was established on November 11, 1895, under authority of the Act of 1891. At the present time the reservation is uninhabited. The reservation is all desert.

**Population Profile. 1969:** Tribal enrollment 2; Indian resident 0.

VIEJAS RANCHERIA          Federal Reservation
San Diego County
Viejas Group of Capitan Grande Band of Mission Indians
Tribal Headquarters: Alpine, California

**Land Status.** Total area: 1,609 acres. This reservation of the Capitan Grande Band of Mission Indians is comprised of Indians of the Barona Reservation, Viejas (Baron Long) Reservation, and an off-reservation group. An Executive Order of December 27, 1875, established the reservation and an Executive Order of May 3, 1877, restored a portion to public domain.

**Culture.** Very little of the Indian language is spoken, but the traditional practices are still favored among these people.

**Population Profile. 1969:** Tribal enrollment 127; Indian resident 96; Unemployment 5%. **1980:** Indian resident 142; Non-Indian resident 67; Percent Indian of total population 67.9; Total housing units 77; Occupied housing units 67. The average educational level attained is 8th grade. Elementary education can be obtained in Alpine, 6 miles away. The high school is located in El Cajon, 18 miles from the reservation. The city of San Diego has the nearest college facilities, 33 miles from the reservation.

**Climate.** The reservation is located in southern San Diego County where the land is flat and the climate is warm and moderate, with an average rainfall of about 6.3 inches per year. The temperatures range as high as 105 degrees and as low as 26 degrees.

**Transportation.** Airline and train facilities are available 33 miles west of the reservation. Bus and trucklines are available at Alpine and El Cajon.

**Community Facilities.** Wells provide water for the people, and gas and electricity are provided by the San Diego Gas and Electric Company. There are no sewer systems for the reservation. Hospitals, clinics, dental and PHS medical care are available at El Cajon and San Diego.


XL RANCH RESERVATION                          Federal Reservation
Modoc County
Pitt River-Paiute Tribe
Tribal Headquarters: Alturas, California

**Land Status.** Total area: 9,242 acres. All land is tribally-owned. The reservation was established on October 13, 1938, for such bands of the Pitt River Indians of the State of California as designated by the Secretary of the Interior in accordance with the Act of 1934. The deed is held in trust by the Federal Government.

**Government.** The tribe is organized under Articles of Association approved in 1960 as the Pitt River Home and Agriculture Association. The Board of Directors has five members. Elections are held each December for 1-year terms.

**Culture.** The elders of both tribes speak their Indian language. An arts and crafts project has begun in Alturas. The people practice their Indian religion.

**Population Profile. 1969:** Tribal enrollment 39; Indian resident 29; Unemployment 50%; Underemployment 0%. **1980:** Indian resident 24; Non-Indian resident 0; Percent Indian of total population 100.0; Total housing units 12; Occupied housing units 9. The average education achievement level is 10th grade. The Alturas elementary and high schools are 6 miles from the reservation. One tribal member is a college graduate.

**Economy.** The tribal members have formed the Indian Cattlemen Association and operate the tribal cattle herd. There is no other economic activity on the reservation.

**Climate.** The reservation is in northeastern California where the topography is sometimes mountainous and the climate is mild and moderate. Rainfall averages 12 inches per year. The temperature varies from a high of 85 degrees to a low of -29 degrees.

**Transportation.** Alturas, 6 miles from the reservation, is served by bus and trucklines. There is also a private airport; however the nearest commercial service is in Redding, 145 miles distant. The nearest train service is in Redding although the track passes through the reservation.

**Community Facilities.** The water and septic tanks were installed by the PHS. Only bottled gas is available. Electricity is provided by Pacific Gas and Electric. Hospital and other medical care are available in Alturas at the Modoc Medical Center. There is one Modoc Arts and Crafts center. Tribal members meet weekly for Indian dances.

# COLORADO

SOUTHERN UTE RESERVATION                    Federal Reservation
La Plata, Archuleta, and Montezuma Counties
Mouache and Capote Ute Tribes
Tribal Headquarters: Ignacio, Colorado

**Land Status.** Tribally-owned land: 301,867 acres. Allotted land: 4,966 acres. Government land: 277 acres. Total area: 307,110 acres. The reservation was opened years ago to homesteading by non-Indians. The reservation is thus now "checker-boarded" with Indian and non-Indian land holdings. Indian lands within the reservation total less than half of the 818,000 acres enclosed by the original reservation boundaries. Today more non-Indians than Indians live within boundaries of the reservation.

**History.** Originally the Southern Ute, composed of the Mouache, Capote, and Wiminuche bands, were settled on a reservation in southwestern Colorado under a treaty negotiated in 1873. The reservation as first established was 15 miles wide and about 125 miles long. In the years after the reservation was established one group of Utes, the Wiminuche band, separated from the original tribe and moved to the western end of the reservation. The reservation was divided, and the Wiminuche became today's Ute Mountain Tribe with a reservation and tribal organization separate from the original reservation.

**Culture.** The Ute Tribes displayed some Plains Indian characteristics and often appeared on the plains to hunt buffalo. In their early history, they traveled by foot in small bands of 25 to 30 people. Leadership of these bands was very informal. The scant resources required that people exploit all edible resources, be highly mobile, and have efficient food-gathering techniques. The Ute usually wintered with several other Ute bands, but there was no real tribal unity. By 1740, the Utes had acquired and adapted to horses. With this animal they had greatly increased food supply, mobility, and leisure. The present reservation has a tri-cultural base from the Spanish-Americans and Anglos living there.

**Government.** The tribal constitution authorizes a tribal council of six members elected by popular vote of the general tribe to be the governing body of the tribe. The tribal council, subject to any restrictions contained in the tribal constitution and United States law, has the rights and powers to: manage tribal real and personal property, make and perform contracts and agreements, engage in business, enact and enforce ordinances to promote public peace, safety and welfare, and negotiate and assign tribal security for loans. The tribe is organized as a Federal corporation for business purposes.

**Population Profile. 1969:** Tribal enrollment 727; Indian resident 596; Non-Indian resident 7,300; Unemployment 52%; Underemployment 35%; Median family income $4,500. **1980:** Indian resident 855; Non-Indian resident 4,884; Percent Indian of total population 14.9; Total housing units 2,257; Occupied housing units 1,839. The average education level for the reservation is 10th grade. Children attend the elementary and secondary schools in Ignacio. There is also a 4-year college in Durango, Colorado.

**Tribal Economy.** The Southern Ute Reservation lies in the southwestern portion of Colorado and borders on the Ute Mountain Reservation. The tribe is currently exploiting the mineral deposits on the reservation which include oil and gas, coal, and sand and gravel. The tribe has an annual income of $448,800, and employs 22 persons. There are many commercial establishments in Durango and Cortez; however, most of them are owned by non-Indians.

**Climate.** The rainfall averages 15 inches per year. The temperature ranges from a high of 100 degrees to a low of –38 degrees.

**Transportation.** U.S. Route No. 550 runs north-south through the reservation; U.S. Highway No. 160 runs east-west through Durango and Cortez. Durango is 25 miles northeast of the reservation and is served by commercial air and train companies; Ignacio, on the reservation, has bus and truck service.

**Community Facilities.** Ignacio has a municipal water and sewer system. The Southern Union Gas Company supplies gas to the reservation area. Western Colorado Power Company and La Plata Electric Association provide the electricity. The Public Health Service maintains a hospital for tribal members in Ignacio. There is also a private hospital in Durango. Tribal offices are located in Ignacio.

**Recreation.** Theaters are located in Ignacio and Durango. The annual Southern Ute Bear Dance and the Southern Ute Sun Dance attract many visitors. The Southern Ute also hold an annual Tribal Fair.


UTE MOUNTAIN RESERVATION                     Federal Reservation
Montezuma and La Plata Counties, Colorado
San Juan County, New Mexico
San Juan County, Utah
Wiminuche Ute Tribe
Tribal Headquarters: Towaoc, Colorado

**Land Status.** Tribally-owned land: 57,878 acres in Colorado. Allotted land: 9,459 acres in Utah. Government land: 40 acres. Tribal fee patent land: 24,292 acres. Total area: 567,377 acres.

**History.** The Ute were Shoshonean Indians who occupied a territory ranging from southern Wyoming to Taos Pueblo, New Mexico. At the peak of their power, seven main bands were knit into a powerful confederacy under the chief, Taiwi. Their best known chief, Ouray, came into prominence in the early years of westward settlement. Ouray was an able diplomat who spoke Spanish and English as well as several Indian languages. The first treaty between the Confederate Tribes of Utes and the United States was negotiated with Ouray. Today the descendants of the Ute Confederacy live on three major reservations: The Uintah and Ouray, the Southern Ute, and Ute Mountain.

**Culture.** The Ute Tribes displayed some Plains Indians' characteristics, and often appeared on the plains to hunt buffalo. In their early history, they traveled by foot in small, loosely-governed bands of 25 to 30 people. The scant resources required that people exploit all edible resources, be highly mobile, and have efficient food-gathering techniques. They usually wintered with several other groups, but there was no real tribal unity. The Ute had obtained and adapted to horses by 1740. With this animal, they became more mobile, had access to a much greater food supply, and had more leisure.

**Government.** Ute Mountain Reservation operates under a constitution which provides for government by vice-chairman, secretary-treasurer, and seven council members elected for 3-year terms.

**Population Profile.** 1969: Tribal enrollment 1,190; Indian resident 1,143; Non-Indian resident 47; Unemployment 84%; Underemployment 18%; Median family income $4,500. 1980: Indian resident 1,111; Non-Indian resident 27; Percent Indian of total population 97.6; Total housing units 367; Occupied housing units 300. The average education level for the tribe is 6th grade. Ute Mountain children attend public school in Cortez. Vocational training is available in Durango.

**Tribal Economy.** The reservation lies in the southwestern corner of Colorado bordering on the Navajo Reservation. Gas and oil and sand and gravel deposits exist in great quantities and are being exploited. There are also deposits of coal, titanium, selenium, uranium, and bentonite on the reservation. The annual tribal income of over $1 million comes largely from gas and oil. The tribe employs close to 50 people full time. A development committee, associated with the government, has been organized to develop and execute a plan for the reservation's development. There are presently three trading posts, a cafe, and a service station in business on the reservation. The tribe plans to construct a service station at a highway junction.

**Climate.** The rainfall averages 19 inches annually. Temperatures range from a high of 101 degrees to a low of -38 degrees.

**Transportation.** U.S. Route No. 666 runs through the reservation north-south. U.S. Highway No. 164 runs through the Four Corners in the southwestern portion of the reservation to junction with Route No. 666 on the reservation. A busline stops in Towaoc on the reservation. Cortez, 16 miles from the reservation, has regularly-scheduled air and truck service. The nearest commercial train is in Durango, Colorado, 60 miles from Southern Ute.

**Community Facilities.** The water and sewer system was installed by the Bureau of Indian Affairs and Public Health Service. Gas is supplied by the Southern Union Gas Company. The Western Colorado Power Company and the Empire Electric Association supply electricity to the reservation. The PHS hospital is located in Towaoc. There is also a private hospital in Cortez.

CONNECTICUT

PEQUOT RESERVATION                          State Reservation
Fairfield and New London Counties
Pequot and Mohegan Tribes
Tribal Headquarters: Uncasville, Connecticut

**Land Status.** The tribal land includes areas in Trumbell, North Stonington, Kent, and Ledyard.

**History.** The Pequot, or "Invader," arrived in Connecticut in the early 1600's. Following a rebellion by Uncas against the Pequot Chief Sassacus, the tribe split into two factions, one of which followed Uncas and was called the Mohegan, or "Wolf" tribe. In 1637, as part of the colonial settlers' policy to exterminate the Pequot, their fort on the Mystic River was attacked and over 600 men, women, and children were killed when the dwellings were set on fire. Following this disaster, the few Pequot remaining in Connecticut joined the Mohegan. Most of the tribe died, fled to the Mohawk, or were taken into slavery in New England or the West Indies. A few were resettled on the Mystic River in 1655. Following King Philip's War, the Mohegan were the only southern New England tribe of significance.

**Culture.** The Mohegan and Pequot both spoke related dialects of the Algonquian language.

**Population Profile.** In 1910, the census reported 49 persons of Pequot descent and 22 Mohegan in Connecticut. **1969:** The tribe now estimates there are approximately 200 members, but only about 35 actively connected with the reservation. **1980:** Indian resident 16; Non-Indian resident 13; Percent Indian of total population 55.2%; Total housing units 16; Occupied housing units 13.

**Community Facilities.** The descendants of Uncas today maintain a museum which displays the arts and crafts of the Pequot and Mohegan and other aspects of the life of Connecticut Indians. The museum also includes displays of Southwestern and Plains tribes.

FLORIDA

BIG CYPRESS RESERVATION                     Federal Reservation
Hendry County
Seminole Indian Tribe
Tribal Headquarters: Hollywood, Florida

**Land Status.** Total area: 42,700 acres (swamp). All land is tribally owned. There have been no individual allotments. In addition to the reservation, the State of Florida has set aside approximately 104,000 acres adjoining the Big Cypress Reservation called the Florida State Indian Reservation, jointly administered by the Seminole Tribe (northern portion) and the Miccosukee Tribe (southern portion). The Seminoles enjoy hunting and fishing rights on this land.

**History.** The people who came to be known as "Seminoles" (the name means "runaways") were Yamasee, driven from the Carolinas in 1715, Hitchiti-speaking Oconee from the Apalachicola River, and Creek fleeing Georgia after the Creek War, all of whom were fugitives from whites. Their ranks were swelled by fugitive slaves who found refuge and freedom among the Indians. Attempts by owners to recover the slaves led to Andrew Jackson's campaigns in 1814 and 1818. The Seminole were united by hostility and fear they felt toward the young U.S. In 1821, Florida was annexed by the U.S., and pressure by white settlers for Seminole lands and farms led to the attempt in 1832 to remove Indians west of the Mississippi by force. The wife of the chief, Osceola, was seized as a fugitive and bloody warfare followed as the Seminole under Osceola fought bitterly. When Osceola was captured under a flag of truce, some of his warriors fled into the Everglades. Later part of the tribe was transported to Oklahoma where they formed one of the Five Civilized Tribes. A truce with the U.S. was finally signed in 1934, bringing to an end the longest war in history.

**Culture.** With the withdrawal of troops, the Seminole lived in scattered locations and pursued a nomadic existence mostly by hunting and fishing. They now live in small houses built with cypress poles and thatched with palmetto leaves. Their clothing is colorful and elaborate, deer-skinned leggings gradually being replaced by cloth pants. The tunics and overblouses are laboriously fashioned from small strips of different-colored material all sewed into long rows and then stitched together. Seminole folk arts, including doll making, are still followed. The turban, once the headdress of every Seminole brave, has been replaced by the "10-gallon" hat. Seasonal Green Corn and Hunting Dances are still performed and are occasions for meetings and festivals.

**Government.** The Seminole tribal constitution was ratified in 1957. The tribe has an elected five-member tribal council as its governing body. All problems relating to government, law and order, education, welfare, and recreation are handled through standing committees. Authority for the development and management of tribal resources has been delegated to the Seminole Tribe, Inc., a Federally-chartered corporation. Non-Indian committeemen are appointed by the board of directors to act as honorary consultants for development.

**Population Profile.** **1969:** Tribal enrollment 956; Indian resident 315; Unemployment 8 persons; Underemployment 95 persons. **1980:** Indian resident 351; Non-Indian resident 36; Percent Indian of total population 90.7; Total housing units 102; Occupied housing units 101. The average education level attained by tribal members is 7th grade. There are no college graduates on the reservation.

**Tribal Economy.** The annual tribal income for all three Seminole Reservations is $500,000. This is derived 10 percent from forestry, 25 percent from farming, 30 percent from business, and 35 percent from other sources. There are 180 tribal employees including 64 Community Action Program employees. The Seminole Tribe has a housing authority, a development company, a village and crafts enterprise, land development, recreation, and cattle improvement enterprises. In addition, the tribe raises mink.

**Climate.** Annual rainfall is 62 inches. The summer high averages 82 degrees, the winter low averages 68 degrees.

**Transportation.** State roads No. 832 and No. 846 service the reservation north-south. The nearest airport is in Miami, 90 miles away. Trains serve Hollywood, 65 miles away and bus and trucklines serve Clewiston, 30 miles distant.

**Community Facilities.** Water is obtained from wells and canals. There is running water in the Indian housing projects. Gas is not used. Electricity is provided by the Glades Cooperative (REA) and PHS has put in a central sewer system for the new housing units. Hospitals are in Clewiston and Hendry County, and care is provided through the USPHS. There is a clinic on the reservation. One theater, the Okeechobee, and a reservation community center serve recreational needs.


BRIGHTON RESERVATION                    Federal Reservation
Glade County
Seminole Indian Tribe
Tribal Headquarters: Hollywood, Florida

**Land Status.** Total area: 35,805 acres. All land is tribally-owned. In addition to the three Seminole Federal Reservations, the State of Florida has set aside approximately 108,000 acres adjoining the Big Cypress Reservation called the Florida State Indian Reservation, jointly administered by the Seminole Tribe (northern portion) and the Miccosukee Tribe (southern portion). The Seminoles enjoy hunting and fishing rights on this land, most of which is swamp.

**History.** The peoples who came to be known as "Seminole" (the name means "runaways") were Yamasee, driven from the Carolinas in 1715, Hitchiti-speaking Oconee from the Apalachicola River, and Creeks from the Chattahoochee River area, all of whom moved into Florida to escape the whites. Their ranks were swelled by fugitive slaves who found refuge and freedom among the Indians. Attempts by owners to recover these fugitives led to Andrew Jackson's campaigns in 1814 and 1818. The Seminoles were united by the hostility and fear they felt toward their common foe, the young United States. In 1821, Florida was annexed by the U.S. and pressure by white settlers for the Seminole lands and farms led to the attempt in 1832 to remove the Indians west of the Mississippi by force. The wife of their leader, Osceola, was seized as a fugitive and bloody warfare followed as the Seminoles under Osceola fought bitterly. When Osceola was captured under a flag of truce, some of his warriors fled into the Everglades. Later a portion of the tribe was transported to Oklahoma where they formed one of the Five Civilized Tribes. A truce between the Florida Seminoles and the United States was finally signed in 1934, and another such treaty was concluded in 1937.

**Culture.** After the troops were withdrawn, the Seminole continued to fear being captured and sent west. They lived in scattered locations and pursued a nomadic existence, mostly by hunting and fishing. They now live in small houses built with cypress poles and thatched with palmetto leaves. On the Hollywood Reservation, however, modern dwellings have replaced the old shelters. Deerskin leggings have been replaced by cloth trousers. The clothing is colorful and difficult to make. Tunics and overblouses are laboriously sewn of different strips of colored cloth sewed into long rows and stitched together. Seminole folk arts, including dollmaking are an important source of income. The turban, once the headdress of every Seminole brave, has been replaced by the 10-gallon hat. Seasonal Green Corn and Hunting Dances are still performed and are occasions for meetings and festivities.

**Government.** The Seminole Tribe constitution was ratified in 1957. The tribe has an elected five-member tribal council as its governing body. All problems relating to government, law and order, education, welfare, and recreation, are handled through standing committees. Authority for the development and management of tribal resources has been delegated to the Seminole Tribe, Inc., a Federally-chartered corporation. Non-Indian committeemen are appointed by the board of directors to act as honorary consultants for development.

**Population Profile. 1969:** Tribal enrollment 956; Indian resident 272; Non-Indian resident unknown; Unemployment 1; Underemployment 69. **1980:** Indian resident 323; Non-Indian resident 15; Percent Indian of total population 95.6; Total housing units 86; Occupied housing units 77. Education level achieved by the average Seminole Indian is 7th grade. There are no college graduates living on the reservation.

**Tribal Economy.** The annual tribal income is $500,000 (total for all three Seminole Reservations). This is derived 10 percent from forestry, 25 percent from farming, 30 percent from business, and 35 percent from other sources. There are 180 tribal employees including 64 Community Action Program employees. The Seminole Tribe has a housing authority, a tribal development company, a village and crafts enterprise, land development, recreation, and cattle improvement enterprise. In addition, the tribe raises mink. The major mineral resources are phosphates.

**Climate.** Annual rainfall is 62 inches. The average temperature in the summer is 82 degrees and the average in winter is 68 degrees.

**Transportation.** State Route No. 721 runs through the reservation north-south. The nearest commercial airline and train service are at Fort Pierce, 75 miles from the reservation. Buses serve Brighton, 8 miles away. Commercial trucklines serve Fort Pierce.

**Community Facilities.** Water is available from artesian wells or through a central water system operated by PHS to the new housing units. Irrigation ditches provide water for crops. Gas is not used. Electricity is provided through the Glades Cooperative, and PHS provides sewer service for the new housing units. The nearest hospital is at Okeechobee and care is provided by PHS. A health clinic exists on Brighton Reservation. There are a theater and a community center on the reservation.


FLORIDA STATE INDIAN RESERVATION          State Reservation
Broward County
Miccosukee and Seminole Indian Tribes
Tribal Headquarters: None designated for reservation

**Land Status.** 104,000 acres. The State of Florida has set aside an approximate 104,000 acres, some 60 rented from Miami, for the use and benefit of the Seminole and Miccosukee Indians of Florida. These lands are administered jointly by the Seminole Tribe of Florida (northern third of area) and the Miccosukee Tribe (southern two-thirds of area). Although much of the land on the State Reservation may not be developed, all Seminole enjoy hunting and fishing rights there. The land on the State Reservation, outside the conservation area of the Central and Southern Florida Flood Control District, will, in time, be developed and utilized by the Indians of Florida. There are no houses or commercial buildings on the State reservation now. One or two members of the Seminole Tribe may have permits to run small numbers of cattle on limited acreage. However, much of this land is under water most of the year.

**Transportation.** The reservation land can be reached by State Highway No. 84 or the Big Cypress Cross Road maintained by the Bureau of Indian Affairs.


HOLLYWOOD RESERVATION                    Federal Reservation
Broward County
Seminole Indian Tribe
Tribal Headquarters: Hollywood, Florida

**Land Status.** Total area: 480.87 acres. All land is tribally-owned. In addition to the three Seminole Federal Reservations, the State of Florida has set aside approximately 104,000 acres adjoining the Big Cypress Reservation called the Florida State Indian Reservation, jointly administered by the Seminole Tribe (northern portion) and the Miccosukee Tribe (southern portion). The Seminoles enjoy hunting and fishing rights on this land, most of which is swamp.

**History.** The people who came to be known as "Seminole" (the name means "runaways") were Yamasee, driven from the Carolinas in 1715, Hitchiti-speaking Oconee from the Apalachicola River, and Creeks from the Chattahoochee River area, all of whom moved into Florida to escape the whites. Their ranks were swelled by fugitive slaves who found refuge and freedom among the Indians. Attempts by owners to recover these fugitives led to Andrew Jackson's campaigns in 1814 and 1818. The Seminole were united by the hostility and fear they felt toward their common foe, the young United States. In 1821, Florida was annexed by the United States, and pressure by white settlers for the Seminole lands and farms led to an attempt in 1832 to remove the Indians west of the Mississippi by force. Chief Osceola's wife was seized as a fugitive, and bloody warfare followed as the Seminoles, under the leadership of Osceola, fought bitterly. When Osceola was captured under a flag of truce, some of his warriors fled into the Everglades. Later a portion of the tribe was transported to Oklahoma where they formed one of the Five Civilized Tribes. A truce between the Florida Seminoles and the United States was finally concluded in 1934, and another such treaty in 1937.

**Culture.** With the withdrawal of troops, yet in constant fear of being captured and sent west, the Seminole lived in scattered locations and pursued a nomadic existence mostly by hunting and fishing. They lived in small houses built with cypress poles and thatched with palmetto leaves. On the Hollywood Reservation, however, modern dwellings have replaced the old shelters. Deerskin leggings have been replaced by cloth trousers. The clothing is colorful and difficult to make. Tunics and overblouses are laboriously made of different strips of colored cloth sewed into long rows and stitched together. Seminole folk arts, including dollmaking, are an important source of income. The turban, once the headdress of every Seminole brave, has been replaced by the 10-gallon hat. Seasonal Green Corn and Hunting Dances are still performed and are occasions for meetings and festivities.

**Government.** The Seminole Tribe's constitution was ratified in 1957. The tribe has an elected five-member tribal council as its governing body. All problems relating to government, law and order, education, welfare, and recreation are handled through standing committees. Authority for the development and management of tribal resources has been delegated to the Seminole Tribe, Inc., a Federally-chartered corporation. Non-Indian committeemen are appointed by the board of directors to act as honorary consultants for development.

**Population Profile. 1969:** Tribal enrollment 369; Indian resident 369; Unemployment 16; Underemployment 78. **1980:** Indian resident 416; Non-Indian resident 2,176; Percent Indian of total population 16.0; Total housing units 1,346; Occupied housing units 1,198. Education level achieved by the average Seminole Indian is 7th grade. There are two college graduates living on the Hollywood Reservation.

**Tribal Economy.** The annual tribal income is $500,000 (total for all three Seminole Reservations). This is derived 10 percent from forestry, 25 percent from farming, 30 percent from business, and 35 percent from other sources. There are 180 tribal employees including 64 Community Action Program employees. The Seminole Tribe has a housing authority, a tribal development, a village and crafts enterprise, land development, recreation, and cattle improvement enterprises. In addition, the tribe raises mink. Bunker-Ramo Corporation and Okalee Village are located on the reservation. Mineral resources are dolomite, high quality sand, and oil.

**Climate.** Annual rainfall is 62 inches. The average temperature in the summer is 82 degrees, and the average in winter is 68 degrees.

**Transportation.** State roads and the Florida Turnpike service the reservation. The nearest airport is located in Miami, 25 miles away. Train, bus, and trucklines serve Hollywood, a distance of 3 miles.

**Community Facilities.** Water is provided by the City of Hollywood. Gas is not used. Florida Power and Light Company provides electricity and individual septic tanks provide for sewage disposal. Broward General Hospital at Dania provides care through PHS. There is a PHS clinic in Hollywood. There are two drive-in theaters on the reservation, a community center, the Indian Village, and the Craft Shop.

MICCOSUKEE RESERVATION                Federal Reservation
Dade County
Miccosukee (Seminole) Indian Tribe
Tribal Headquarters:  Homestead, Florida (BIA)
Miccosukee Settlement

**Land Status.** Total area: 333 acres. The tribe holds, on a 50-year permit from the Bureau of Indian Affairs and the National Park Service, a strip of land 5½ miles by 500 feet, containing 333.3 acres. This land, known as the Tamiami Trail, is not available for industrial or commercial development. Three tracts of land 600 feet by 65 feet were dedicated in perpetuity by the State of Florida for the sole use and benefit of the tribe. This land is similar to trust land and is available for industrial and commercial development. Presently being developed are a grocery store, service station, and a restaurant. The State Reservation containing 76,000 acres, also dedicated in perpetuity to the tribe by the State, is uninhabited. A court decision recently placed the land in a trust status. Future plans call for a camp site in this area.

**History.** The Miccosukee Tribe is politically but not linguistically or ethnically separate from the Seminole Tribe of Florida. Their history is the same as that for the Seminole Tribe. The Seminole were originally Creek immigrants from Georgia who moved across the border into Florida to escape the clash of Spanish and British interests. Their ranks were swelled by fugitive slaves who found refuge and freedom among the Indians. Friction over recovery of these fugitives led to Andrew Jackson's campaigns of 1814 and 1818. The U.S. Government in 1832, in possession of Florida, attempted to remove the Seminole west of the Mississippi by force. The seizure of Chief Osceola's wife precipitated war, during which Osceola, the spirited war chief of the Seminoles, was captured. Later, a portion of the Seminole were removed to Oklahoma, but about 150 fled into the Everglades. In 1957, when a treaty was signed between the Seminole and the United States, the Miccosukee did not join. Most of the Miccosukee have retained their Indian religion, whereas the Seminole are largely Christian.

**Culture.** The Miccosukee, formerly Seminole, led a nomadic life hiding out from U.S. troops for long periods in their history. They survived by hunting and fishing, building small shelters with wooden frames and palmetto-leaf roofs. Their homes today are being replaced with more modern units. Their dress is both colorful and difficult to make, being made from many strips of different-colored material. Folk arts still exist, and the seasonal Green Corn and Hunting Dances are performed.

**Government.** The Miccosukee Tribe was officially organized on January 11, 1962, with the adoption of a constitution and bylaws pursuant to the Indian Reorganization Act. There is no direct connection with the Seminole Tribe organization, although blood relationships exist. The governing body of the tribe is the general tribal council in which all adult members have a vote. Daily business is conducted by the business committee of the tribe. The tribe is composed of four matrilineal clans, and the business committee is composed of one member from each clan elected for a 3-year period of office. Membership in the tribe is open to Indians of Florida Seminole blood who make formal application for membership.

**Population Profile. 1969:** Tribal enrollment 230; Indian resident 200; Non-Indian resident 10; Unemployment 15% est.; Underemployment 75% est. **1980:** Indian resident 213; Non-Indian resident 63; Percent Indian of total population 77.2; Total housing units 74; Occupied housing units 74. Average educational level attained by the Miccosukee is 4th grade. There is a Federally-run elementary school on the reservation.

**Tribal Economy.** The income of the tribe averages $4,300 per year, 95 percent from grazing and right-of-way leases and 5 percent from business. There are four full-time tribal employees. The tribe owns and operates the Miccosukee Restaurant and Tiger's Indian Village. There is a Community Action Program organization on the reservation.

**Climate.** Rainfall averages 62 inches per year. The average mean temperature in the summer is 82 degrees; in winter 68 degrees.

**Transportation.** U.S. Highway No. 41 runs through the reservation east-west. The nearest airline is in Miami, 40 miles from the reservation. Train and trucklines are available in Miami. Commercial buslines pass through and stop on the reservation.

**Community Facilities.** There is a community water system for the new housing units. Bottled gas is obtainable. Florida Power and Light Company provides electricity. PHS has installed sewer disposal facilities for the new housing. There is PHS contract care hospitalization available in Miami. The Miccosukee Tribal Settlement has a PHS-operated clinic. The Green Corn Ceremony is held every year in addition to Indian religious ceremonies.

# IDAHO

COEUR D'ALENE RESERVATION                    Federal Reservation
Benewah and Kootenai Counties
Coeur d'Alene Tribe
Tribal Headquarters: Plummer, Idaho

**Land Status.** Tribal land: 16,236 acres. Allotted land: 53,063 acres. Total area: 69,299 acres.

**History.** The Coeur d'Alene Tribe was one of 25 of the seminomadic Plateau Indian Tribes. They were known as a peaceful group, but were dissatisfied with treaties being negotiated for their lands. In 1858, the Coeur d'Alene and Spokane, who had long declared with truth that they had never shed the blood of a white man, united with the Palouse and Yakima to defeat the United States forces near Rosalia, Washington. The following year a punitive expedition overwhelmed the tribes, forcing their surrender and destroying their horses. The tribes were then placed on reservations, ceding vast areas of their lands.

**Culture.** The Coeur d'Alene Indians ranged over the dry uplands of Idaho, eastern Oregon, and eastern Washington. All Plateau tribes were traditionally fishermen and hunters who wandered over the country in small, loosely-organized bands searching for game, wild seeds, berries, and roots of camas. With basketry techniques that ranked among the best in North America, they wove the grasses and scrubby brush of the plateau into almost everything they used, including portable summer shelters, clothing, and watertight cooking pots. Having no clans, Plateau Indians counted descent on both sides of the family. There was little formal organization. The few tribal ceremonies centered around the food supply. In the early 1700's, horses were introduced among the tribesmen, and they became highly skilled horsemen who counted their wealth in terms of the new animal.

**Government.** The tribe is organized under a constitution approved on September 2, 1949, and amended in 1961. This constitution provides for a general council form of government. The seven-member tribal council is elected to a 3-year term to administer the tribal business activities.

**Population Profile.** **1969:** Indian resident 523; Unemployment 49%; Median family income $9,200. **1980:** Indian resident 538; Non-Indian resident 4,373; Percent Indian of total population 11.0; Total housing units 2,818; Occupied housing units 1,763.

**Tribal Economy.** The tribe has an annual income of approximately $30,000. An investment fund of $150,000 is available for scholarships for students continuing their education beyond high school.

**Climate.** The rainfall averages 14 inches per year. The temperature varies from a high of 85 degrees to a low of 0 degrees.

**Transportation.** U.S. Highway No. 95 is the major north-south route through the reservation connecting with Interstate 90 to the north to Spokane, Washington. The nearest commercial airline service is located in Spokane, 30 miles from the reservation. Train, bus, and trucklines have regular stops in Coeur d'Alene 25 miles north of the Coeur d'Alene Reservation.

**Community Facilities.** The Washington Power Company provides electricity to the reservation. Medical care for the tribe is available in a private hospital in Spokane.

**Recreation.** Coeur d'Alene Lake, with a shoreline of 125 miles, extends along the eastern boundary of the reservation and offers excellent water sports. Big game hunting, as well as upland bird and waterfowl hunting, is also available in the area.


FORT HALL RESERVATION                    Federal Reservation
Bannock, Bingham, Caribou, and Power Counties
Shoshone and Bannock Tribes
Tribal Headquarters: Fort Hall, Idaho

**Land Status.** Tribal land: 215,558 acres. Government land: 41,343 acres. Allotted land: 266,508 acres. Total area: 523,409 acres.

**History.** In the late 1700's, 10 Bannocks under their chief, Buffalo Horn, continued to wander over southern Idaho, fighting for their fields of camas. They had been ostensibly assigned to the Fort Hall Reservation. A series of murders and raids ended with the death of Buffalo Horn. The Bannocks, disorganized, were eventually assembled and returned to the Fort Hall Reservation.

**Culture.** The Shoshone and Bannock Indians were of seminomadic Plateau Indian culture ranging over the dry uplands of Idaho, eastern Oregon and eastern Washington. All Plateau tribes were traditionally fishermen and hunters who wandered over the country in small, loosely-organized bands searching for game, wild seeds, berries, and roots of camas. With basketry techniques that ranked among the best in North America, they wove the grasses and scrubby brush of the plateau into almost everything they used, including portable summer shelter, clothing, and watertight cooking pots. Having no clans, Plateau Indians counted descent on both sides of the family. There was little formal organization. The few tribal ceremonies centered around the food supply. In the early 1700's, horses were introduced among the tribesmen, and they became highly skilled horsemen who counted their wealth in terms of the new animal.

**Government.** The tribe is organized under the Indian Reorganization Act of 1934, operating under a constitution approved on April 30, 1936, and a charter ratified on April 17, 1937. The Fort Hall Business Council is the tribal governing body. The business council consists of seven persons elected from the five districts on the reservation to 2-year terms. The council has authority over purchases, borrowing, engaging in business, performing contracts, and other normal business procedures.

**Population Profile. 1969:** Tribal enrollment 2,675; Indian resident 3,038; Unemployment 52%; Underemployment 19%; Median family income $5,300. **1980:** Indian resident 2,542; Non-Indian resident 2,241; Percent Indian of total population 53.1; Total housing units 1,496; Occupied housing units 1,330.

**Tribal Economy.** The tribe has an annual income of approximately $400,000. The tribe provides $13,500 annually for student scholarships based on need. The Land Purchase Enterprise is a tribal organization to increase the amount of tribally-owned land. Two industries are located on the reservation: The Food Machinery Chemical Corporation and the J.R. Simplot Company. Both are privately owned. Deposits of phosphate on the reservation are being extracted.

**Climate.** The reservation is located in the southeastern segment of Idaho where the rainfall averages 12 inches annually. The temperature varies from a high of 90 degrees to a low of 13 degrees.

**Transportation.** Interstate 15 and Federal Highway No. 91 are north-south traffic arteries while Federal Highway No. 30 runs east-west through the reservation. The nearest town where commercial transportation is available is Pocatello, Idaho, 5 miles from the reservation. Transportation by air, bus, train, and truck is available here.

**Community Facilities.** The Fort Hall Reservation is served by the City of Pocatello water system. The sewer system on the reservation was installed by the Public Health Service. The Intermountain Gas Company provides gas fuel for the area. Electricity is supplied by the Idaho Power Company. Medical care is available to tribal members at a private hospital in Pocatello.

**Recreation.** The tribe operates a Tribal Arts and Crafts Shop,

Timbee Hall, at Fort Hall, Idaho. It also holds two or three Sun Dances each summer during July and August.


KOOTENAI RESERVATION                    Federal Reservation
Boundary County
Kootenai Tribe
Tribal Headquarters: Bonners Ferry, Idaho

**Land Status.** Government land: 12 acres. Allotted land: 2,683 acres. Total area: 2,695 acres.

**History.** The Kootenai Tribe is one of the seminomadic Plateau Indian tribes whose livelihood was centered around a natural abundance of fish and forests. These people acquired horses in the early 1700's and rapidly became excellent horsemen, widely known for breeding and horse dealing. They bred the well known Appaloosa. In the spring of 1855, the Kootenai and other "horse" tribes were called together for a treaty-making. After expressing dissatisfaction with lands offered, the Kootenai and 16 other tribes were established on reservations and ceded vast areas of land in Idaho, Oregon, and Washington Territories.

**Culture.** The Kootenai Indians ranged over the dry uplands of Idaho, eastern Oregon, and eastern Washington. All Plateau tribes were traditionally fishermen and hunters who wandered over the country in small, loosely-organized bands searching for game, wild seeds, berries, and roots of camas. With basketry techniques that ranked among the best in North America, they wove the grasses and scrubby brush of the plateau into almost everything they used, including portable summer shelters, clothing, and watertight cooking pots. Having no clans, Plateau Indians counted descent on both sides of the family. There was little formal organization. The few tribal ceremonies centered around the food supply. In the early 1700's, horses were introduced among the tribesmen, and they became highly skilled horsemen who counted their wealth in terms of the new animal.

**Government.** The tribe is not organized under the Indian Reorganization Act of 1934, but operates under a constitution which was approved on June 16, 1947. The tribal council is the administrative operating head of the tribe and consists of five members, one being a chief with life tenure.

**Population Profile. 1969:** Tribal enrollment 67; Indian resident 60. **1980:** Indian resident 40; Non-Indian resident 0; Percent Indian of total population 100.0; Total housing units 11; Occupied housing units 10.

**Climate.** This reservation lies in the very northernmost part of Idaho, near the Canadian Border. The temperatures here vary with the seasons, reaching an average high of 80 degrees in the summer and falling to an average low of -10 degrees in the winter. Precipitation measures 14 inches per year.

**Transportation.** U.S. Highway No. 95 runs north-south just west of the reservation. Commercial bus and trucklines serve Bonners Ferry,

10 miles from Kootenai. The nearest commercial train stops in Coeur d'Alene, Idaho, 85 miles south of the reservation. Spokane, Washington, which is located 115 miles southwest of the reservation, is served by commercial airlines.

**Community Facilities.** A hospital in Coeur d'Alene ministers to the medical needs of the Kootenai Tribe.


NEZ PERCE RESERVATION                    Federal Reservation
Nez Perce, Lewis, Clearwater, and Idaho Counties
Nez Perce Tribe
Tribal Headquarters: Lapwai, Idaho

**Land Status.** Tribally-owned land: 33,642 acres. Allotted land: 54,237 acres. Total area: 87,879 acres.

**History.** The Nez Perce have always made their home in the northwestern part of the United States where the Lewis and Clark Expedition met them. Under the 1855 treaty, the tribe ceded most of its territory and settled on lands in Idaho and Oregon. With discovery of gold in the early 1860's, the area was overrun by prospectors. To Nez Perce demands for enforcement of treaty terms, the Indian Commissioners responded by calling another treaty council in 1863 to persuade the Nez Perce to "adjust the boundaries of the reservation." Subsequent negotiations divided the tribe into three factions. As none of the faction leaders would yield, the tribe decided to disband, leaving each leader free to negotiate treaties. One group signed an agreement reducing the size of the reservation by three-fourths in return for cash and new buildings, believing that those who did not sign would not be bound. White officials maintained that the treaty bound the entire Nez Perce Nation. In 1877, the Indians, under Chief Joseph the Young, were ordered to leave the Wallowa Valley; however, a small group rebelled and killed some settlers. The resulting Nez Perce War included some 18 encounters with U.S. troops as the Indians managed to outmaneuver them. This earned the Nez Perce fame in battle, and, as a result, Chief Joseph was the second American Indian to be placed in the National Hall of Fame of American Indians. Eventually defeated by superior numbers, the tribe settled on the present reservation.

**Culture.** The Nez Perce Indians were of seminomadic Plateau Indian culture ranging over the dry uplands of Idaho, eastern Oregon, and eastern Washington. All Plateau tribes were traditionally fishermen and hunters who wandered over the country in small, loosely-organized bands searching for game, wild seeds, berries, and roots of camas. With basketry techniques that ranked among the best in North America, they wove the grasses and scrubby brush of the plateau into almost everything they used, including portable summer shelters, clothing, and watertight cooking pots. Having no clans, Plateau Indians counted descent on both sides of the family. There was little formal organization. The few tribal ceremonies centered around the food supply. In the early 1700's, horses were introduced among the tribesmen, and they became highly skilled horsemen who counted their wealth in terms of the new animal.

**Government.** The tribe is not organized under the Indian Redevelopment Act of 1934 but operates under a constitution which was approved in 1958 and revised in 1961. The Nez Perce Tribal Executive Committee is the official governing body of the tribe, as authorized by the revised tribal constitution. The committee has a membership of nine persons who are elected at large, but distributed geographically to give the reservation wide representation.

**Population Profile.** 1969: Tribal enrollment 2,251; Indian resident 1,463; Unemployment 18%; Underemployment 52%. **1980:** Indian resident 1,463; Non-Indian resident 16,343; Percent Indian of total population 8.2; Total housing units 7,071; Occupied housing units 6,214.

**Tribal Economy.** The tribe has an annual income of $180,000. It operates the Nez Perce Tribal Credit Union and the Tribal Lease Management Enterprise. The only mineral present in large quantities is limestone, but it is not presently being quarried.

**Climate.** The reservation is located in the northwestern portion of Idaho near the Washington-Oregon border where the rainfall averages 15 inches. Temperature varies from a summer high of 85 degrees to a winter low of 0 degrees.

**Transportation.** Federal Highway No. 95 crosses the reservation north-south. Federal Highway No. 12 runs east-west through the reservation. Train, bus, and trucklines have stops on the reservation. Lewiston, 11 miles from the reservation, is served by commercial airlines.

**Community Facilities.** Reservation residents draw their water from wells. Gas is provided by the Washington Water Power Company. The same company and the Clearwater Power Company provide electricity to the reservation. Pacific Northwest Bell serves the area's telephones. Health care is extended to the tribe at the Lewiston Community Hospital. The tribe has two community buildings for use by the residents.

**Recreation.** The U.S. Park Service is now developing the Nez Perce Historical Park which is a scenic area including historical sites of early day Nez Perce Indians and the Lewis and Clark Expedition.


IOWA


SAC AND FOX RESERVATION                Federal Reservation
Tama County
Sac and Fox (Mesquakie) Tribes
Tribal Headquarters: BIA Indian School, Tama, Iowa

**Land Status.** Tribal land in trust: 3,476 acres. Total area: 3,476 acres. This settlement was established by the tribal leaders in 1856. They bought 80 acres in Tama County and placed them in trust with the Governor of Iowa. The tribe pays annual taxes to the State. Additional land purchases increased the total acreage to 3,400. Jurisdiction over the tribe was resumed by the Bureau of Indian Affairs in 1896, and the land is now held in trust for the tribe by the U.S. Government. There have been no individual allotments. The people live scattered throughout the reservation area; there are no communities.

**History.** The Mesquakie probably once lived in the New England area and migrated west. They first encountered Europeans, the French, near Green Bay, Wisconsin in 1636. Although frequently at war with other Indian tribes, the Mesquakie maintained relatively peaceful relations with the whites. The Sac and Fox joined together in a political alliance in 1734. Pressured by settlement in the east, they continued to move south and west. Chief Black Hawk, a Sac, led the tribes in a war to preserve the tribes' land in Illinois; however, they were ultimately driven across the Mississippi River into Iowa. Removed against their will to Kansas, and faced with another removal to Oklahoma, Maminiwaige and other chiefs purchased land in Iowa with money saved, supplemented by the sale of their ponies. The tribe returned to Iowa, and settled.

**Culture.** The Fox call themselves "Mesquakie" or "Red Earth People"; the Sacs call themselves "Osa Kiwag" or "People of the Outlet." Both are woodland tribes closely related to the Chippewa. They lived in permanent villages of rectangular houses and raised crops in the summers. In winter, they followed the herds and lived in portable wigwams. The Sac and Fox, unlike other woodland tribes, are patrilineal. Artwork includes ribbon applique in stylized designs, beadwork, silverwork, and weaving. The tribe value their traditions. They speak their own language and learn English as a second language.

**Government.** Tribal politics are polarized along the issue of Indian or white practices. The traditional party prefers to retain much of their culture, own the land corporately, and reinstate the hereditary chief, while the other party opts for changing the reservation to more nearly resemble the surrounding towns. At present, the tribal council, composed of a chief, assistant chief, secretary, treasurer, and three additional members meets at least monthly. Elections are held every 2 years, and council membership is staggered. Members all live on the reservation and are elected at large.

**Population Profile. 1969:** Tribal enrollment 795; Indian resident 446; Unemployment 19%; Underemployment 35%. **1980:** Indian resident 492; Non-Indian resident 17; Percent Indian of total population 96.7; Total housing units 113; Occupied housing units 106. The education level for those 18 to 25 years of age is between 10th and 11th grades; for those 46 and over it is between 5th and 6th grades. The school on the reservation includes grades 1 through 4. There are currently six tribal members in junior colleges and nine in college. All students have scholarships from the Bureau of Indian Affairs and private sources. Vocational training is available in Des Moines. For more advanced training, one must go out of the State.

**Tribal Economy.** Tribal average income: $10,000. Source: Two leases to non-Indian farmers. Tribal employees: There are no full-time employees. Time is contributed to the tribe by members. Tribal associations, cooperatives, etc.: None. Commercial/industrial establishments on the reservations: Tamacraft, a part-time enterprise owned and operated by a tribal member, employs two. There are no minerals on reservation land; however, the soil is rich for farming.

**Climate.** Rainfall is approximately 31 inches per year. The average temperature is 50 degrees. There are four full seasons.

**Transportation.** U.S. Highway No. 30 passes east-west in the northern part of the reservation. U.S. Highway No. 63 is a north-south highway to the east of the reservation. U.S. Highway No. 180 is 21 miles to the south. Commercial airlines are in Cedar Rapids, 48 miles east, and in Waterloo and Des Moines. Two railroads have tracks running through the reservation but the nearest freight siding is in Tama, 3 miles east. Bus and trucklines serve Tama and Toledo.

**Utilities.** Water for residents comes from wells and springs. No gas is presently available to the reservation. REA and the Iowa Power Company provide electricity. Septic tanks are the only provisions for sewage. A community hospital in Marshalltown, and the University of Iowa Hospital in Iowa City provide care for the tribe. PHS operates a clinic in Tama and contracts with local doctors.

**Recreation.** A variety of recreation programs are organized and held in the Bureau of Indian Affairs community building each year. The annual tribal pow-wow, planned and managed by tribal members, is held in August and includes Indian dancing representing the tribe's history and traditions.

## KANSAS

IOWA RESERVATION                      Federal Reservation
Richardson County, Nebraska and Brown County, Kansas
Iowa Tribe
Tribal Headquarters: Horton, Kansas

**Land Status.** Tribal land: 714 acres. Allotted land: 654 acres. Total area: 1,378 acres. The original reservation area included 11,770 acres allotted to 143 individuals. Under current assignment agreements, the assignees are required to pay 4 percent of the appraised value of the improvements to their assignments annually to the tribe; however, very little has been paid over the years. Of the tribally-owned land, 634 acres are assigned to 12 individual Indian farmers.

**History.** The original Iowa Reservation was established by the treaty of 1836 and was reduced by the Treaty of May 17, 1854 and March 6, 1861. The Iowa were closely related to the Winnebago, Oto, and Missouri Tribes. They are first thought to have lived on the Mississippi along the Upper Iowa River, moving later into northwestern Iowa and southwestern Minnesota. They later moved to Council Bluffs and about 1760 moved east and settled along the Mississippi between the Iowa and Des Moines Rivers. They encountered difficulties with the Sioux and were defeated by Black Hawk in 1821. In 1814, they were allotted lands in what was known as the Platte Purchase. In treaties signed in 1824, 1830, 1836, and 1837, they ceded all their claims to lands in Missouri and Iowa. In the Prairie du Chien Treaty in 1825, they surrendered all claims to lands in Minnesota.

**Culture.** The Iowa were of the Siouan linguistic stock and of the Chiwere subdivision which also included the Oto and Missouri. The people today in Kansas have intermarried with Caucasians for many years, and few appear to be Indian. As a result, they have intermingled with non-Indians in nearby towns and encounter little discrimination.

**Government.** The tribe adopted a constitution and bylaws in 1937 under the 1934 Indian Reorganization Act. The charter was also adopted in 1937. The governing body is the executive committee formed by a chairman, vice-chairman, secretary, treasurer, and one additional member. Elections are held each July. The executive committee has been delegated broad powers and can act in all matters except tribal claims.

**Population Profile.** **1969:** Tribal enrollment 1,437; Indian resident 144; Unemployment 0; Underemployment 9%. **1980:** Indian resident 26; Non-Indian resident 86; Percent Indian of total population 23.2; Total housing units 50; Occupied housing units 38. The Indians work primarily in agriculture and unskilled trades. The average family income is $3,800. The educational attainment level for the tribe is 10th grade. Children attend public schools in nearby towns. There are few adult education programs.

**Tribal Economy.** This part of Kansas and Nebraska is approximately 1,000 feet above sea level. The reservation is in an area which has a primarily agricultural economy. The growing season extends from early May to early October. Both the nearby towns, Falls City, Nebraska, and Hiawatha, Kansas, are dependent on agriculture but also have small industries that support only a small percentage of the population. The one tract of tribal land not in the assignment program is leased to a member of the tribe to produce income for the expenses of the tribal government. The reservation resources produce income only from agriculture. Total income from leases is $1,042 annually.

**Climate.** The rainfall averages 32 inches per year. The temperature averages 52 degrees to 54 degrees, and reaches a high of 110 degrees and a low of -20 degrees.

**Transportation.** All roads on the reservation are constructed and maintained by the counties. There is no problem in obtaining adequate transportation. Horton, Kansas, near the reservation, has both bus and truck service. The nearest airport is in Topeka, Kansas.

**Community Facilities.** Water and sanitary facilities are available to all homes on the reservation; however, several homes have no bathrooms. This is true also of homes in the surrounding area outside the reservation. All homes have electricity. The U.S. Public Health Service maintains an Indian Clinic in Holton, Kansas, providing a wide range of health care services to Indians in the area. The facilities are used by the population to the fullest extent possible.

# KICKAPOO RESERVATION
Brown County
Kickapoo Tribe
Tribal Headquarters: Horton, Kansas

**Land Status.** Tribal land: 980 acres. Allotted land: 3,930 acres. Total area: 4,910 acres. The original reservation was an area of 19,200 acres allotted to 237 individuals. The Kickapoo ceded their lands in Missouri for 768,000 acres in northeastern Kansas in 1832. In 1854, 618,000 acres were ceded to the United States for $300,000. Allotments to 351 individuals took place under the treaty of June 28, 1862. The Indian land is checkerboarded by non-Indian land.

**History.** The Kickapoo and the related Sac and Fox moved into the Wisconsin area, pushed there by the Iroquois in the early 17th Century. By 1720, the Kickapoo ranged as far south as the Illinois River. About 1765, the Sac and Fox and Kickapoo partitioned the conquered area of southern Wisconsin. During this period, the Kickapoo band settled around Peoria, others moved east, and a third group emigrated to Texas. The Illinois Kickapoo sided with the British in the War of 1812. During the Illinois period, the leader, Kanakuk, emerged. The Kickapoo were moved from Illinois to Missouri between 1819 and 1824. Due to difficulties with other tribes and squatters in Missouri, the Kickapoo petitioned for a new reservation in Kansas. This transaction was finalized in 1832 under Kanakuk. The Texas Kickapoo were moved both to Oklahoma and to the reservation in Kansas in 1873.

**Culture.** The Kickapoo are culturally and linguistically related to the Sac and Fox Tribes. The Kickapoo actively participate in several religious organizations. The Drum Religion, entirely Indian, is most active. The Kanakuk Religion is also active, although not as traditional as the Drum Religion. Also included are the Native American Church and several Christian missions. There is a noticeable separateness between the Indian people and the larger community.

**Government.** The Kickapoo Tribe is organized under the Indian Reorganization Act of 1934 and has a constitution and bylaws approved in February 1937, with subsequent amendments, and a corporate charter ratified on June 9, 1937. The tribal council is composed of seven members. Council members are elected by the tribe and, in turn, elect four officers from their own membership for 2-year terms. Matters pertaining to tribal claims and to the approval of membership applications can be acted upon only by the general council.

**Population Profile. 1969:** Tribal enrollment 750 est.; Indian resident 350. **1980:** Indian resident 356; Non-Indian resident 105; Percent Indian of total population 77.2; Total housing units 173; Occupied housing units 129. Children attend schools 1½ miles from the reservation in Powhattan. The average education level for members between 18 and 25 is almost 12 years. For persons over 40, the average is about 8.5 years.

**Tribal Economy.** The area is approximately 1,000 feet above sea level. The growing season is a full 5 months. The tribal income is about $7,400 annually. Most of this is lease payments from agricultural leases to non-Indians. The economy of the reservation is largely agricultural as the soil is excellent and grazing compares to that in northeast Kansas.

The only employment opportunities on the reservation are seasonal farm jobs. Residents generally find employment in the mill towns nearby, while some commute to Topeka, Atchison, and the larger towns. There are three garment factories and a foundry in the area. There are no commercial establishments on the reservation.

**Climate.** The average rainfall is 34 inches. The mean temperature is 53 degrees, with highs of 110 degrees and lows of -20 degrees.

**Transportation.** State Highway No. 20 passes through the reservation running east-west. U.S. Highway No. 75 is 1 mile from the reservation's western border, connecting the reservation with Topeka, Kansas and Omaha, Nebraska. Railheads are located in Horton, Hiawatha, Powhattan, and Netawaka, Kansas, only short distances from the reservation. The nearest commercial airports are in Topeka, Kansas and St. Joseph, Missouri, from 50 to 60 miles away.

**Community Facilities.** By mid-1969, approximately one-half of the homes on the reservation had running water, through the Bureau of Indian Affairs Housing Improvement Program and the USPHS. All homes have electricity, and nine have telephones. In some of the small towns, sewer facilities are not available. The Public Health Service operates an Indian Health Clinic in Holton, Kansas, providing a wide range of health services.

**Recreation.** Tourism in this area is mostly limited to "passers through" during the summer months. The tribe has several powwows during the year, and many members participate in powwows in Kansas and the surrounding states.


POTAWATOMI RESERVATION                    Federal Reservation
Jackson County
Potawatomi Tribe
Tribal Headquarters:  Horton, Kansas

**Land Status.** Tribal land: 90 acres. Allotted land: 20,607 acres. Total area: 20,697 acres. The original reservation covered 77,440 acres which were allotted to 812 individuals. Through sales, fee patents, and inheritance by non-Indians the area has been reduced to its present size.

**History.** The Potawatomi's ancient home is southern Michigan. By 1670, they were driven west of Lake Michigan into the Green Bay area of Wisconsin. They then moved slowly south reaching the Chicago area by the end of the century. After about 1765, they took possession of northern Illinois and expanded into southern Michigan and Lake Erie. During the struggles of the new United States with Britain the Potawatomi sided first with the French against the English and with the English against the Americans until a general peace was achieved about 1815. The Potawatomi gradually moved to the west as settlers pressed in on their eastern side. The greatest land concessions were made between 1836 and 1841 when most of the tribe moved west of the Mississippi. Some of the bands moved to Wisconsin and Michigan, and some to Canada. The Prairie Band in Wisconsin sold their lands and moved to Iowa and then to Kansas. A few Potawatomi accompanied the Kickapoo to Mexico.

**Culture.** The name Potawatomi means "People of the Place of Fire," and they are also known as the Fire Nation. They belonged to the Algonquian linguistic family and were most closely related to the Chippewa and Ottawa, both woodland tribes.

**Government.** The constitution and bylaws were adopted by the tribe in 1961. The governing body, the Business Committee, includes a chairman, vice-chairman, secretary-treasurer, and four additional members serving 2-year staggered terms. The committee meets at the discretion of the chairman.

**Population Profile. 1969:** Tribal enrollment 2,128; Indian resident 610. **1980:** Indian resident 331; Non-Indian resident 654; Percent Indian of total population 33.6; Total housing units 313; Occupied housing units 299.

**Tribal Economy.** The Potawatomi Reservation is located just north of Topeka, Kansas. The land is gently rolling and well suited to agriculture. The altitude of the area is about 1,000 feet above sea level.

**Climate.** The climate favors agriculture with rainfall averaging between 32 and 34 inches yearly and an average temperature in the low 50's. Temperature extremes are a high of 110 degrees and a low of −20 degrees.

**Transportation.** The reservation is conveniently located along U.S. Highway No. 75, a north-south route connecting with two Interstate Highways, Nos. 75 and 35, in Topeka. The nearest commercial airport is in Topeka, and the same city is served by bus, rail, and trucking companies.

**Community Facilities.** The Indian houses in Kansas compare favorably with those of non-Indians. Utilities are connected to most homes. Where sanitation facilities are inadequate, the U.S. Public Health Service (PHS) assists the tribe in installing new facilities. Health care is made available by the PHS at Horton, Kansas, and the same agency also provides for private contract health care.

SAC AND FOX RESERVATION                    Federal Reservation
Brown County, Kansas and
Richardson County, Nebraska
Sac and Fox Tribes
Tribal Headquarters: Horton, Kansas

**Land Status.** Allotted land: 80 acres. Total area: 80 acres. The reservation originally contained 7,924 acres in 131 allotments. However, most of the area has been lost to non-Indians since that time. The Indian lands are now scattered throughout the non-Indian community of the area.

**History.** The Sac and Fox of Missouri Reservation was established in accordance with the Treaty of 1861 and was originally a part of the Iowa Reservation purchased by the Federal Government as a permanent home for the Sac and Fox. The Sac and Fox probably once lived in the New England area and migrated west to Green Bay, Wisconsin, where they were first encountered by the French in 1635. Although frequently at war with other Indian tribes, the Sac and Fox maintained relatively peaceful relations with the whites. The two tribes joined together in a political alliance in 1734. Pressured by eastern settlements, they continued to move south and west. The Sac Chief, Black Hawk, led the tribes in a war to preserve the tribal land in Illinois. However, they were ultimately driven across the Mississippi River into Iowa. In 1842, the Sac and Fox ceded their lands in Iowa for a tract in Kansas. By 1867, most of the Kansas land had been ceded and the tribes moved to Indian territory and also returned to Iowa. In 1889, they took up land in severalty and sold surplus territories to the Government.

**Culture.** Both the Sac and Fox are woodland tribes closely related to the Chippewa and speak an Algonquian language. They lived in permanent villages of rectangular houses and raised crops in the summers. In winter they followed the herds and lived in portable wigwams. The Sac and Fox, unlike other woodland tribes, are patrilineal. Artwork includes ribbon applique in stylized designs, beadwork, silverwork, and weaving.

**Government.** The governing body is a tribal council consisting of five members elected on a staggered-term basis annually. Three members of the tribal council constitute a quorum. Due to the fact that the tribe has difficulty in securing a quorum of the general council at meetings, about 30 eligible voters, a hold-over tribal council has been serving since 1954 and also for periods prior to that time. The council has a long history of self-succession. The tribe adopted a constitution and bylaws in 1937 and ratified their charter in the same year. The constitution was written under the authority of the 1934 Indian Reorganization Act.

**Population Profile. 1969:** Tribal enrollment 250 est; Unemployment 0. **1980:** Indian resident 13; Non-Indian resident 824; Percent Indian of total population 1.6; Total housing units 323; Occupied housing units 296. The average education level is about 11th grade, slightly below the State average. Children attend public schools and the Haskell Institute in Lawrence, Kansas.

**Tribal Economy.** The reservation lies in northeastern Kansas about 1,000 feet above sea level. Most of the land is used for agriculture. There are no other significant resources. The growing season lasts from early May through early October.

**Climate.** The temperature, which averages about 53 degrees, reaches a high of 110 degrees and a low of -20 degrees. Rainfall measures 32 inches per year.

**Transportation.** Roads are constructed and maintained by the counties. The nearest airport is in Topeka, Kansas. Bus and truck service are available in Horton, Kansas.

**Community Facilities.** Water and sanitary facilities are available to residents equal to those of non-reservation families in the surrounding area. The homes of residents are fully modern. Contract hospital and medical care are provided to eligible residents along with a wide range of other services normally supplied by the USPHS.

# LOUISIANA

CHITIMACHA RESERVATION                    Federal Reservation
Saint Mary Parish
Chitimacha Indian Tribe
Tribal Headquarters: Charenton, Louisiana

**Land Status.** Total area: 262.23 acres. The Chitimacha obtained title to their land about 1830 and later divided the land among individuals, many of whom were unable to pay the taxes which were assessed. A friend of the tribe bought up the land when it was placed in a sheriff's sale, and the Federal Government then took over the mortgage and put the land in trust at the request of the tribe in 1935.

**History.** Indian settlement at Chitimacha dates back at least 6,000 years based on artifacts found in the area. About 800 B.C., the people were living in large villages of over 500 inhabitants with a well-developed political system. When the French arrived in Louisiana in the early 1700's, the Chitimacha were a peaceful people. However, when they were attacked by a band of Mississippi Indians, in whose company was a French priest, they repelled the attack and killed the priest, St. Cosme. French reprisals followed under the governor of New Orleans, Bienville, and protracted war continued for many years thereafter. With the help of Indian allies, the French nearly succeeded in decimating the Chitimacha Tribe. The settlement has survived in its present location since 1764 and has recently begun to grow.

**Culture.** The Chitimacha Indians lived by fishing and agriculture and were the most advanced of the Louisiana Indians in the arts of basket-making and metal-work. They raised beans, pumpkins, melons, maize and constructed houses of wooden frames with roofs of mud and palmetto leaves. Community granaries protected the grain from mice. Chitimacha baskets, particularly the "double" basket where both the inside and the outside are intricately woven, are considered to be the finest ever produced. Unfortunately, the art was both time-consuming and difficult and is no longer practiced. The early Indians buried their dead in large mounds, some in the shape of flying birds and placed food beside the graves for the ancestors to use. They have legends of men hunting with dogs and of a young man who was lost in the sky while hunting and still wanders there. Their women had a strong voice in tribal affairs and were even elevated to the status of Chief, an honor rare among American Indians.

**Government.** The Chitimacha Tribe is governed by a council of two members, a chairman, a vice-chairman, and a secretary, all elected for 2-year terms. They are presently preparing a constitution which will enable the tribe to function as a legal entity and to be so recognized by the Federal Government.

**Population Profile. 1969:** Tribal enrollment 600 est.; Indian resident 260; Non-Indian resident 20; Unemployment 0; Underemployment 0; Median family income $5,000 (not including those on pensions or Social Security). **1980:** Indian resident 185; Non-Indian resident 1,115; Percent Indian of total population 14.2; Total housing units 411; Occupied housing units 382. The average educational level achieved by adults is 8th grade. However, the tribe has an adult education program in operation and two young people are now in college. There is an elementary school on the reservation, run by the Bureau of Indian Affairs through its Philadelphia, Mississippi, agency, and established in 1935.

**Tribal Economy.** Tribal income has been $40,000 over a 30-year period from land leases. This is approximately $1,200 a year. Most of the members of the tribe work in the oil fields, as workers, drillers and foremen. On the reservation there are a gas station, a mechanic shop, and garbage pick-up service, all Indian owned. The women's cooperative, the Chitimacha Bead Association, has a small capital investment in bead work and is planning to set up a trading post to sell crafts and to revive some of the traditional arts.

**Climate.** Average annual rainfall is 58 inches. The average July temperature is 82 degrees and the average January temperature is 54 degrees. The first frost comes in late December.

**Transportation.** U.S. Highway No. 90 runs northwest-southeast south of the reservation about 10 miles. State Highway No. 19 runs southwest-northeast through the reservation. The nearest commercial airline is at Patterson, a distance of 40 miles, and the nearest train runs through Berwick, 45 miles distant. Bus and trucklines serve Franklin, 10 miles away.

**Community Facilities.** Water is provided both by wells and from a county water line. Gas is available from the Clayco Company, and electricity is provided by Central Louisiana Electric. Sewage is treated in septic tanks. There are a private hospital and clinic services in Franklin. The only community building is the school. The tribe is now planning to set up an historical pageant some time in the future.


MAINE


PENOBSCOT RESERVATION                    State Reservation
Penobscot County
Penobscot Tribe
Tribal Headquarters: Indian Island, Old Town, Maine

**Land Status.** Total area: 4,446 acres. All the land is tribally-owned. None of the land is allotted although land-use assignments have been made to individuals. The reservation consists of some 146 islands in the Penobscot River. These islands were included in the tribe's domain from pre-colonial times and today are the only lands within the State remaining to the tribe. Twenty-one of the islands were divided into individual lots in the mid-19th Century. Only members of the tribe may legally hold interest in any of the reservation lands. At the present, only Indian Island is inhabited year-round although previously, schools and farms were located on some of the larger upstream islands.

**History.** Early treaties affecting the Maine Indians were made between the various colonial governments and the "Eastern Tribes" and between the tribes and the Commonwealth of Massachusetts. Upon achieving statehood in 1820, Maine agreed to assume these treaty obligations either through renegotiations with the tribes or through provisions in the Compact of Separation between Massachusetts and Maine. For some 30 years prior to 1966, the administration of programs for the Indians of Maine was the responsibility of the State Department of Health and Welfare. Maine's tribes, in common with some 100,000 other Indians in 22 states, have never had a relationship with the Federal Government as the original treaties, from which such relationships normally developed, were negotiated between the tribes and the original colonies prior to the existence of the Federal Government. Maine established a State Department of Indian Affairs in 1966. Prior to that time, Indians had been the responsibility of the Department of Health and Welfare.

**Culture.** The Maine Indians speak a coastal branch of the Algonquian language stock. Indian bands in Maine moved several times each year following available food supplies. They developed skills in hunting, stalking, trapping, fishing, and canoeing. They frequently traveled by canoe. Hides were tanned, the meat dried and cured. They sewed, made fish nets, spears, bows and arrows, wampum, and carved pipes. They also did beadwork and quillwork. The Maine Indians were not excessively warlike, but instead had a peaceful and friendly disposition.

**Government.** The Penobscot Tribe is governed by a governor, lieutenant governor, and a 12-member council which is elected biennially by the tribe.

**Population Profile. 1969:** Tribal enrollment 840; Indian resident 400; Non-Indian resident 10; Unemployment 12%; Underemployment 20%. **1980:** Indian resident 398; Non-Indian resident 60; Percent Indian of total population 86.9; Total housing units 168; Occupied housing units 147. The average education level for the reservation is 10th grade. Five tribal members are college graduates. There are tuition scholarships available from the State which must be used in State institutions. Education and training facilities are available on the reservation at the elementary school and the tribal hall.

**Tribal Economy.** The annual tribal income of $1,000 is completely acquired from excise taxes. The revenue acquired from the sale of two townships is held in a trust fund by the State. The reservation has a Reservation Housing Authority, a Planning Committee, Women's Club, and Girl Scouts. Commercial establishments on the reservation include two arts and crafts shops, a small grocery store, and a snack shop, all privately owned by Indians.

**Climate.** This area averages 43 inches of rainfall each year and 92 inches of snowfall. The average high temperature is 68 degrees; the average low is 20 degrees. Temperatures reach extremes of 100 degrees and -35 degrees.

**Transportation.** Interstate 95 is a major north-south highway. U.S. Highway No. 2 also crosses the reservation east-west. Bangor, 12 miles from the reservation, is served by commercial air, bus, and trucklines. The nearest available train service is in Boston, Massachusetts, 275 miles distant.

**Community Facilities.** The City of Old Town has adequate public works facilities. As no natural gas is supplied to the reservation, residents purchase bottled gas. The Bangor Hydro-electric Company provides electricity to the area. Health care clinics are held in Old Town and Bangor through the Department of Indian Affairs for low-income people only. Hospital care, under the same provisions, is available in Bangor.

**Recreation.** The reservation community center and parish hall and several theaters are located in Old Town, the center of reservation activities. The tribe holds an annual Indian Pageant in July.

PLEASANT POINT AND INDIAN                State Reservation
  TOWNSHIP RESERVATIONS
Washington County
Passamaquoddy Tribe
Tribal Headquarters:  Peter Dana Point, Maine

**Land Status.** Pleasant Point Reservation: 100 acres. Indian Township Reservation: 23,000 acres. Total area: 23,100 acres. The Passamaquoddy Tribe is geographically and structurally divided into two groups living on separate reservations. The larger reservation, Indian Township, is near Princeton, Maine, and has two communities, one at the Princeton "Strip" and one at Peter Dana Point. The two reservations are 50 miles apart by road, with Calais, Maine, a mid-point economic and service center for the area. On the 23,000-acre Indian Township Reservation, 7,000 acres are alienated from the tribe. These lands are the subject of current litigation between the tribe and the Commonwealth of Massachusetts. None of the tribal land has been allotted, although use assignments have been made.

**History.** Early treaties affecting the Maine Indians were made between the various colonial governments and the "Eastern Tribes" and between the tribes and the Commonwealth of Massachusetts. Upon achieving statehood in 1820, Maine agreed to assume these treaty obligations either through re-negotiations with the tribes or through provisions in the Compact of Separation between Massachusetts and Maine. For some 30 years prior to 1966, the administration of programs for the Indians of Maine was the responsibility of the State Department of Health and Welfare. Maine's tribes, in common with some 100,000 other Indians in 22 states, have never had a relationship with the Federal Government, because the original treaties from which such relationships normally developed were negotiated between the tribes and the original colonies prior to the existence of the Federal Government. Maine established a State Department of Indian Affairs in 1966. Prior to this time, Indians had been the responsiblity of the Department of Health and Welfare.

**Culture.** The Maine Indians speak a coastal branch of the Algonquian language stock. Indian bands in Maine moved several times each year following available food supplies. They developed skills in hunting, stalking, trapping, fishing, and canoeing. They frequently traveled by canoe. Hides were tanned, and the meat dried and cured. They sewed, made fish nets, spears, bows and arrows, wampum, and carved pipes. They also did beadwork and quillwork. The Maine Indians were not excessively warlike, but instead had a peaceful and friendly disposition.

**Government.** Although divided into two geographic areas, there is only one Passamaquoddy Tribe. The two reservations function both individually and jointly as the occasion demands. Each reservation is governed by a biennially-elected governor, lieutenant governor, and a six-member tribal council. At each tribal election, the combined tribal membership elects an Indian legislative representative who serves as a delegate without a seat or vote. Since 1954, members residing on the reservations have been able to vote in Federal, State, and county elections, and since 1967, in district elections for the House of Representatives. Maine was the last state in the nation to enfranchise its Indian citizens. They were given the right to vote through Federal legislation in 1924.

**Population Profile. 1969:** Tribal enrollment 1,057; Indian resident (Pleasant Point) 342; Indian resident (Indian Township) 221; Non-Indian resident 25; Unemployment 60%; Underemployment 30%. **1980:** Indian resident (Pleasant Point) 504; Indian resident (Indian Township) 333; Non-Indian resident (Pleasant Point) 45; Non-Indian resident (Indian Township) 90; Percent Indian of total population (Pleasant Point) 91.8; Percent Indian of total population (Indian Township) 78.7; Total housing units (Pleasant Point) 155; Total housing units (Indian Township) 132; Occupied housing units (Pleasant Point) 144; Occupied housing units (Indian Township) 124. The average education level for the tribe is approximately 7th grade. At present, none of the residents are college graduates although there are 10 scholarships for Indians available from the State each year.

**Tribal Economy.** The tribe's two income sources are an excise tax and timber sales. The tax totals $1,400 annually. The tribe receives as working income 40 percent of the timber sales, or $2,000. The remaining 60 percent is deposited in the tribal trust fund, held in trust by the State. The tribe is not given an accounting, and the interest on the fund accrues to the State. The tribe has organized a housing authority. The Community Action Project for the reservation is funded by OEO which provides jobs for 12 persons. The only natural resource on the reservation is timber which is the basis for the tribe's economy.

**Climate.** The reservations are located in the easternmost county of the United States where the climate is typical of eastern Maine. Temperatures vary with the seasons and reach a high of 90 degrees and a low of -25 degrees.

**Transportation.** U.S. Route No. 1 passes through both reservations. This highway runs east along the southern portion of Maine and then swings north continuing along the Maine-Canada border. A bus stops in Perry just 2 miles from the reservation. Bangor, 125 miles distant, is served by commercial air and trucklines. The nearest train service is located in Boston, Massachusetts.

**Community Facilities.** The water and sewer provisions are individual and local. A commercial water supply is located 7 miles from the reservation. Other water is drawn from lakes. The new housing units have small sewer systems. Electricity is available from the Eastern Maine Electric Coop. and the Bangor Hydro-Electric Company. Only bottled gas is used. Medical care for tribal members is provided through the

State Department of Indian Affairs at the Eastport Community Hospital, and at Calais, Maine. Both reservations have community centers where tribal business is conducted.

**Recreation.** The Calais Drive-in Theater is on Peter Dana Point. This part of Maine has numerous campsites and attracts many visitors during the summer outdoor season. The Passamaquoddy Tribe has an annual Indian Ceremonial Day every August, a tribal powwow in which other Indians and non-Indians are welcome to share in the celebration of the Indian heritage.

# MICHIGAN

BAY MILLS RESERVATION                           Federal Reservation
Chippewa County
Chippewa Tribe
Tribal Headquarters: Brimley, Michigan

**Land Status.** Total area: 2,189 acres. The area comprising the original Bay Mills Reservation was purchased by the Methodist Mission Society for the Indian community. The reservation land was acquired in accordance with the Treaty of July 1, 1855, and the Indian Appropriation Act of June 19, 1850. Additional land was purchased under the Expandable Land Acquisition Project of the Indian Reorganization Act.

**History.** In the early historic period, the Chippewa Tribe, a member of the Algonquian family, was among the largest north of Mexico, with lands extending along both shores of Lake Huron and Lake Superior and westward to the Turtle Mountains of North Dakota. Uniformly friendly with the French, the Chippewa joined in Pontiac's Rebellion which broke out against the British in May 1763. Every British-held post in the West except Fort Pitt and Detroit was overrun. Later, the Chippewa joined Tecumseh along with the Potawatomi, Winnebago, and other tribes. The defeat of Tecumseh and his death in 1813 ended the organized resistance, and the cession by the Indians of their lands quickly followed. In 1815, a treaty of peace was signed with the U.S. Government. The last great Indian battle in Michigan was fought at Ox Bow in 1830 between the Sac and the Chippewa over hunting and fishing grounds. Over 4,000 Sac warriors were defeated by the Chippewa. The failure of the Great Lakes Tribes to band together against the invading settlers meant the loss of their lands and their way of life. By treaties signed in 1855, the present Bay Mills Reservation of Chippewa was organized.

**Culture.** The Chippewa were a hunting and fishing people who practiced some agriculture and gathered fruits and wild rice. Their most important society was the Mide which conducted religious and magico-medical ceremonies in long lodges. The people lived in dome-shaped bark or mat-covered lodges. They buried their dead in mounds and used some copper tools, carrying on a wide-spread trade in copper. Hiawatha was their warrior-hero god, and the gods of thunder and lightning were believed to live in the caverns of the Upper Penninsula. When the white man arrived in the area the fur trade became the main economic base of the Chippewa. Today hunting and fishing are still of importance. Some tribal members prefer to live in wigwams and tepees during the summer months. Sweat baths are still taken.

**Government.** The tribe is organized under the Indian Reorganization Act of 1934. A five-member executive council is elected by the eligible voters of the tribe and holds office for 2-year terms. All eligible members of the tribe constitute the General Tribal Council.

**Population Profile. 1969:** Tribal enrollment 300 est.; Indian resident 300; Non-Indian resident 0; Unemployment 98% est.; Underemployment 10%. **1980:** Indian resident 283; Non-Indian resident 39; Percent Indian of total population 87.9; Total housing units 102; Occupied housing units 79. The average education attained by members of the tribe is 8th grade level. There are Head Start, Neighborhood Youth Corps, and other educational programs on the reservation.

**Tribal Economy.** There is no tribal income.

**Climate.** The average rainfall is 31 inches a year. Temperatures average 49.2 degrees in the summer and 31.9 degrees in the winter.

**Transportation.** State Route No. 129, surfaced with tar and chips, runs on the reservation in a north-south direction. The nearest airport is at Sault Ste. Marie, a distance of 21 miles from the reservation. Sault Ste. Marie is also the terminal for trains, commercial bus and trucklines.

**Community Facilities.** Water comes from artesian wells. Gas for heating is obtainable from local bottled gas companies. Electricity is provided by the Rural Electric Company and septic tanks provide sewage disposal. The nearest hospital is in Sault Ste. Marie and provides medical and social services through contract with the USPHS Indian Division. There are community buildings on the reservation. Local ball games are organized.


HANNAHVILLE COMMUNITY                    Federal Reservation
Menominee County
Potawatomi Indian Tribe
Tribal Headquarters: Wilson, Michigan


**Land Status.** Total area: 3,408 acres. All land is individually held by Indians in allotments. There is no tribally-owned land. The land was purchased by Congress, June 30, 1913, except for 39 acres later added in 1942 with the Indian Reorganization Act funds.

**History.** When the first Europeans arrived in the Upper Great Lakes area, they found the Potawatomi, a numerous and powerful tribe, living along the shore of Lake Michigan. Their Chief, Onanquisee, saved a band of LaSalle's men from starvation in 1680. When the Potawatomi ceded their lands in 1833 and agreed to move to the Iowa Territory, about 400 remained in Wisconsin. After the Black Hawk War in 1833, they lost the Nottawaseepe Reservation which amounted to over 73,000 acres. Several of their chiefs became famous. Chief Simon Pokagon became a lecturer of note in the 1850's. Chief Sawauguette, who sold his tribe's reservation in 1833 for $10,000, was poisoned by his people when he attempted to persuade them to leave for the rich hunting grounds promised in Kansas. For years the survivors led a poverty stricken existence. Their last properly-designated chief died in 1934.

**Culture.** The Potawatomi shared the culture patterns of the Ottawa and Chippewa. They lived in agricultural groups in the summer and traveled in hunting bands in the winter. The bands appear to have been politically independent, each ranging through its own territory. The society was organized according to clans which carried animal names. Clothing was of deerskin and fur. They have continued to be isolated due to lack of transportation routes and facilities and the poor resources of the reservation. Hunting and fishing rights do not exist compared to other Indian reservations.

**Government.** The tribe was organized under the Indian Reorganization Act. A council composed of three council officers and nine council members govern the community. Elections for all members of the governing body are held annually.

**Population Profile. 1969:** Tribal enrollment 200; Indian resident 200; Non-Indian resident 0; Unemployment 16 persons; Underemployment 99%. **1980:** Indian resident 206; Non-Indian resident 5; Percent Indian of total population 97.6; Total housing units 46; Occupied housing units 46.

**Tribal Economy.** There is no tribal income. There are no commercial or industrial establishments on the reservation.

**Climate.** Rainfall averages 30 inches per year. The temperature averages a high of 52 degrees in summer and 32 degrees in winter. Daytime temperatures are higher.

**Transportation.** State road No. 41 services the reservation. The road is hard surfaced with tar and chips and runs north-south. The nearest commercial airline is in Escanaba, Michigan, 17 miles away. Commercial train, bus, and truck lines also service Escanaba.

**Community Facilities.** Water is provided by artesian wells. Local companies supply bottled gas for heating. Electricity is from Rural Electric (REA) and sewage is disposed by septic tanks and outdoor privies. Medical and social services are available in Escanaba. The hospital contracts services through USPHS, Indian Division. There is one community building on the reservation.


ISABELLA RESERVATION                      Federal Reservation
Isabella County
Saginaw Chippewa Tribe
Tribal Headquarters: Mount Pleasant, Michigan

**Land Status.** Tribally-owned land: 506 acres. Allotted land: 678 acres. Total area: 1,184 acres. Isabella Reservation is located in the north central part of the Lower Peninsula 3 miles east of the City of Mount Pleasant, Michigan.

**History.** In the mid-17th century, the Chippewa Tribe, a member of the Algonquian family, was among the largest north of Mexico, with lands extending along both shores of Lake Superior and westward to the Turtle Mountains of North Dakota. Uniformly friendly with the French, the Chippewa utilized French weapons to drive the Sioux further westward. The Chippewa joined in Pontiac's Rebellion which broke out against the British in May 1763. Every British-held post in the West except Fort Pitt and Detroit was overrun. Later, the Chippewa joined Tecumseh along with the Potawatomi, Winnebago, and other tribes. The defeat of Tecumseh and his death in 1813 ended the organized resistance and the cession by the Indians of their lands quickly followed. In 1815, a treaty of peace was signed with the U.S. Government. The last great Indian battle in Michigan was fought at Ox Bow in 1830, between the Sac and the Chippewa over hunting and fishing grounds. Over 4,000 Sac warriors were defeated by the Chippewa. The failure of the Great Lakes Tribes to band together against the invading settlers meant the loss of their lands and their way of life. By treaties signed in 1864 and 1885, the Isabella Reservation was established for the Saginaw, Swan Creek, and Black River bands of Indians.

**Culture.** The Chippewa were a hunting and fishing people who practiced some agriculture, principally the gathering of fruits and wild rice. Their most important society was the Mide or Grand Medicine Society which conducted religious and magico-medical ceremonies in long lodges. The people lived in dome-shaped bark or mat-covered lodges. They buried their dead in mounds and used some copper tools, carrying on a widespread trade in copper. Hiawatha was their warrior-hero god and the gods of thunder and lightning were believed to live in the caverns of the Upper Peninsula. When the white man arrived, the fur trade became the main economic base of the Chippewa. Today hunting and fishing are still of importance. Some tribal members prefer to live in wigwams and tepees during the summer months. Sweat baths are still taken.

**Government.** The governing body of the tribe is a 10-member tribal council elected at large from all eligible voters on the reservation for a 2-year term of office. The members of the tribal council are known as "headmen."

**Population Profile. 1969:** Tribal enrollment 262; Indian resident 250; Non-Indian resident 0; Unemployment 24%; Underemployment 21%. **1980:** Indian resident 517; Non-Indian resident 22,856; Percent Indian of total population 2.2; Total housing units 8,566; Occupied housing units 7,799. The education level of most tribal members is 10th grade. Children attend public schools in Mount Pleasant.

**Tribal Economy.** There is no tribal income. There are no commercial or industrial establishments on the reservation.

**Climate.** Rainfall averages 31 inches a year. Temperatures average 56.6 degrees in the summer and 34.8 degrees in the winter.

**Transportation.** State Highway No. 20 runs east-west and services the reservation. The nearest commercial airline is at Mount Pleasant, 3 miles away. Trains, commercial bus and trucklines also serve Mount Pleasant.

**Community Facilities.** Water is provided by the City of Mount Pleasant. Gas is sold in bottled form by local companies. Electricity is from Rural Electric (REA) and septic tanks handle sewage disposal. Medical and social services are available in Mount Pleasant through contract with the USPHS, Indian Division. There is one community hall in Mount Pleasant.


L'ANSE RESERVATION                    Federal Reservation
Baraga County
Lake Superior Band, Chippewa Tribe
Tribal Headquarters: L'Anse, Michigan

**Land Status.** Total area: 13,750 acres. The tribe owns 1,610 acres and individual allotments account for 8,124 acres. The Farm Security Administration owns 4,016 acres. The L'Anse Reservation was established by a treaty between the Chippewa and the Federal Government, signed at LaPointe, Wisconsin, September 30, 1854.

**History.** In the early historic period, the Chippewa Tribe, a member of the Algonquian family, was among the largest north of Mexico, with lands extending along both shores of Lake Huron and Lake Superior and westward to the Turtle Mountains of North Dakota. Uniformly friendly with the French, the Chippewa utilized French weapons to drive the Sioux further west. The Chippewa joined Pontiac's Rebellion, which broke out against the British in May 1763. Every British-held post in the West except Fort Pitt and Detroit was overrun. Later, the Chippewa joined Tecumseh along with the Potawatomi, Winnebago, and other tribes. The defeat of Tecumseh and his death in 1813 ended the organized resistance and the cession by the Indians of their lands quickly followed. In 1815, a treaty of peace was signed with the U.S. Government. The last great Indian battle in Michigan was fought at Ox Bow in 1830 between the Sac and the Chippewa over hunting and fishing grounds. More than 4,000 Sac warriors were defeated by the Chippewa. The failure of the Great Lakes Tribes to band together against the invading settlers meant the loss of their lands and their way of life. The present reservation site was recognized by the treaty of 1854 between the Chippewa and the U.S.

**Culture.** The Chippewa were hunting and fishing people who prac- ticed some agriculture, principally the gathering of fruits and wild rice. Their most important society was the Mide which conducted religious and magico-medical ceremonies in long lodges. The people lived in dome-shaped bark or mat-covered lodges. They buried their dead in mounds and used some copper tools, carrying on a widespread trade in copper. Hiawatha was their warrior-hero god, and the gods of thunder and lightning were believed to live in the caverns of the Upper Peninsula. When the white man arrived in the area, the fur trade became the main economic base of the Chippewa. Today hunting and fishing are still of importance. Some tribal members prefer to live in wigwams and tepees during the summer months. Sweat baths are still taken.

**Government.** The governing body of the tribe is the tribal council. All 12 members of the council are elected by the eligible voters of the tribe for 3-year terms. The terms of office are staggered.

**Population Profile. 1969:** Tribal enrollment 465; Indian resident 435; Non-Indian resident 30; Unemployment 40%; Underemployment 24%. **1980:** Indian resident 581; Non-Indian resident 2,708, Percent Indian of total population 17.7; Total housing units 1,256; Occupied housing units 1,058. The average education level of tribal members is 9th grade. There are two college graduates living on the reservation.

**Tribal Economy.** There is no tribal income and no commercial or industrial establishments are located on the reservation.

**Climate.** Rainfall averages 32 inches per year. Temperature averages are 50.6 degrees in summer and 30.2 degrees in winter.

**Transportation.** Interstate Highway Route 41 runs north-south through the reservation. The nearest airport is at Houghton, Michigan, a distance of 33 miles from the reservation. The nearest train runs to Marquette, Michigan, 73 miles away. Commercial buslines run into L'Anse, Michigan, 3 miles from the reservation and trucklines serve Marquette.

**Community Facilities.** Water is supplied from artesian wells and bottled gas is sold by local companies for heating purposes. Electricity is provided by Rural Electric (REA), and septic tanks and outdoor privies provide sewage disposal. Hospital and social services provided through PHS are available at L'Anse. There is one community building, Zeba Community Hall. Community ball games are scheduled.

## MINNESOTA

FOND DU LAC RESERVATION                    Federal Reservation
Carlton and Saint Louis Counties
Mississippi Band of Chippewa
Tribal Headquarters: Cloquet, Minnesota

**Land Status.** Tribally-owned land: 4,213 acres. Allotted land: 17,154 acres. Non-Indian land: 78,633 acres. Total area: 21,367 acres. The Fond du Lac Reservation lies immediately adjacent to Cloquet, population 10,000, which is a major trade center in Carlton County. Less than 20 miles from the reservation is Duluth, Minnesota, having a population of over 100,000.

**History.** The Chippewa, or Ojibway, were one of the largest Indian nations north of Mexico and controlled lands extending along both shores of Lakes Huron and Superior and westward into North Dakota. Their migration to this area was instigated by Iroquois pressure from the northeast. Drifting through their native forests, never settling on prized farmlands, the Chippewa were little disturbed by the first onrush of white settlers. They maintained friendly relations with the French and were courageous warriors. In the early 18th Century, the

Chippewa drove the Fox out of northern Wisconsin and then drove the Sioux across the Mississippi and Minnesota Rivers. By this time they were also able to push back the Iroquois whose strength and organization had been undercut by settlers. The Chippewa of the United States have been officially at peace with the Government since 1815 and have experienced less dislocation than many other tribes.

**Culture.** The Chippewa were nomadic timber people traveling in small bands, engaging primarily in hunting and fishing, sometimes settling to carry on a rude form of agriculture. These foods were supplemented by gathering fruits and wild rice. Their wigwams of saplings and birchbark were easily moved and erected. Birchbark canoes were used for journeys, but other travel was usually by foot. The tribe was patrilineal, divided into clans usually bearing animal names. Although their social organization was loose, the powerful Grand Medicine Society controlled the tribe's movements and was a formidable obstacle to Christianizing attempts of missionaries. A mysterious power, or manitou, was believed to live in all animate or inanimate objects. The Chippewa today are largely of mixed blood, mostly French and English.

**Government.** The Fond du Lac Reservation is one of six Chippewa reservations in the state organized as the Minnesota Chippewa Tribe under the Indian Reorganization Act of 1934. The revised constitution of this organization, approved in 1964, provides for a local Reservation Business Committee to be elected at each of the member reservations. The chairman and secretary-treasurer of each elected RBC form the 12-member Tribal Executive Committee of the Minnesota Chippewa Tribe. Elections for the Fond du Lac RBC are held every 2 years to elect members to 4-year terms on a staggered basis.

**Population Profile.** **1969:** Tribal enrollment 1,764; Indian resident 744; Non-Indian resident 200; Unemployment 48; Underemployment 41. **1980:** Indian resident 514; Non-Indian resident 2,339; Percent Indian of total population 18.0; Total housing units 1,159; Occupied housing units 893. The average education level for the reservation is approximately 8th grade. There are currently five college graduates on the reservation.

**Tribal Economy.** The only natural resources occurring on the reservation are sand, gravel, and peat. The forest timber has been overcut. The annual tribal income averages $1,900. Ninety percent of this comes from the forestry industry. Most of the remainder is earned in farming. The tribe has organized a Reservation Housing Authority and has an active Community Action Program. Many different types of commercial and industrial establishments are located in the reservation communities of Brookston, Sawyer, and Paupor, and in the bordering city of Cloquet.

**Climate.** The reservation lies in an area which averages 70 inches of snowfall each year. The annual precipitation measures 22 inches. The average summer high temperature is 66 degrees; the average winter low is 9 degrees.

**Transportation.** U.S. Route No. 2 runs east-west through the reservation. U.S. Highway No. 210 is a second east-west highway. Minnesota Route No. 33 crosses the reservation north-south. Duluth is served by commercial airlines. Railroad and buslines stop on the reservation. Truck companies serve Cloquet.

**Community Facilities.** The communities on the reservation have water and sewer systems. Rural areas use wells and septic tanks. The Northwestern Power and Gas Company sells natural gas to the reservation area. Electricity is provided by the Minnesota Power and Light Company. Tribal members contract for medical care through the U.S. Public Health Service. Hospitals are located in Cloquet and Duluth.

GRAND PORTAGE RESERVATION                    Federal Reservation
Cook County
Chippewa Tribe
Tribal Headquarters: Grand Portage, Minnesota

**Land Status.** Tribally-owned land: 37,390 acres. Allotted land: 7,283 acres. Non-Indian land: 79 acres. Total area: 44,752 acres. This reservation was established in 1854 by treaty with the United States Government.

**History.** The Chippewa, or Ojibway, were one of the largest Indian nations north of Mexico, and controlled lands extending along both shores of Lakes Huron and Superior and westward into North Dakota. Their migration to this area was instigated by Iroquois pressure from the northeast. Drifting through their native forests, never settling on prized farmlands, the Chippewa were little disturbed by the first onrush of white settlers. They maintained friendly relations with the French and were courageous warriors. In the early 18th Century, the Chippewa drove the Fox out of northern Wisconsin, and then drove the Sioux across the Mississippi and Minnesota Rivers. By this time they were also able to push back the Iroquois whose strength and organization had been undercut by settlers. The Chippewa of the United States have been officially at peace with the Government since 1815 and have experienced less dislocation than many other tribes.

**Culture.** The Chippewa were nomadic timber people traveling in small bands engaging primarily in hunting and fishing, sometimes settling to carry on a rude form of agriculture. These foods were supplemented by gathering fruits and wild rice. Their wigwams of saplings and birchbark were easily moved and erected. Birchbark canoes were used for journeys but other travel was usually by foot. The tribe was patrilineal, divided into clans usually bearing animal names. Although their social organization was loose, the powerful Grand Medicine Society controlled the tribe's movements and was a formidable obstacle to Christianizing attempts of missionaries. A mysterious power, or manitou, was believed to live in all animate or inanimate objects. The Chippewa today are largely of mixed blood, mostly French and English.

**Government.** The governing body is the Reservation Business Committee. The committee has five members elected to 4-year terms. Elections are held every 2 years on a staggered basis. The Grand Portage Band is a member of the Minnesota Chippewa Tribe which is organized under the 1934 Indian Reorganization Act. The tribe's constitution and bylaws were approved in 1936 and revised in 1964. The governing body of the tribe is the Tribal Executive Committee which is composed of the chairman and secretary-treasurer of each of the six member bands' Reservation Business Committees.

**Population Profile. 1969:** Tribal enrollment 460; Indian resident 212; Non-Indian resident 40; Unemployment 42%; Underemployment 1%. Median family income $4,300. **1980:** Indian resident 187; Non-Indian resident 94; Percent Indian of total population 66.5; Total housing units 142; Occupied housing units 104. The average education level for the reservation is 8th grade. No college graduates are living on the reservation. There is a grade school through the 6th grade. The Minnesota Chippewa Tribe offers scholarship money toward college education.

**Tribal Economy.** The only natural resources on the reservation are timber and a small amount of gravel. The tribe's income in 1968 was $18,000. Two-thirds of this was earned in forestry, the remainder in tribal businesses and hunting and fishing permits. The tribe operates a trading post under the Grand Portage Trading Post Association. A cafe, tavern, shopping center and service station located on the reservation are privately owned.

**Climate.** The reservation lies in the extreme northeast corner of Minnesota approximately 150 miles northeast of Duluth, where the average annual precipitation measures 37 inches. The July high is 83 degrees; the February low is -14 degrees.

**Transportation.** U.S. Highway No. 61 runs through the reservation along the north shore of Lake Superior. The nearest commercial air and train transportation are located in Duluth. Bus and truck service are available 35 miles from the reservation in Grand Marais. Rail, bus, trucking, and shipping facilities also are available at Canadian cities of Port Arthur and Fort William, 35 miles distant.

**Community Facilities.** Sanitary facilities on the reservation are minimal. Water is drawn from both individual and community wells. Electricity is provided by REA. Pickens Gas Service supplies the area with gas. A Public Health Service nurse is located in Grand Portage. The nearest hospital facility is the community hospital at Grand Marais. The school district community building serves as a center for tribal business.

**Recreation.** The reservation is located in one of the most scenic settings of the Lake Superior shoreline. The Grand Portage National Monument, established by Congress, is being developed. Headquarters are located in Grand Portage where visitors may obtain trips to Isle Royale National Park. The tribe holds Summer Rendezvous Days annually, a two-day celebration in the Indian style.


LEECH LAKE RESERVATION                    Federal Reservation
Beltrami, Cass, Hubbard, and Itasca Counties
Chippewa Tribe
Tribal Headquarters: Ball Club, Minnesota

**Land Status.** Tribally-owned land: 14,069 acres. Allotted land:

12,693 acres. Non-Indian land: 4 acres. Total area: 26,766 acres. The reservation was ceded by treaty to the Chippewa nation in 1854. Though originally encompassing almost a million acres, the area was gradually reduced in size by Congressional Acts, including the Allotment Act of 1921, and by Presidential Orders so that today it is one-fourth of its original size.

**History.** The Chippewa Tribe was among the largest north of Mexico, with lands extending along both shores of Lake Huron and Lake Superior and westward through Minnesota to the Turtle Mountains of North Dakota. They migrated to this area in the mid-17th Century, having been driven by the Iroquois from an area further to the northeast. The Chippewa, in turn, pushed the Sioux west, forcing their adaptation from woodland people to the dominant tribe of the plains. The Chippewa in the United States have been at peace with the Government since 1815 and have experienced less dislocation than many other tribes. Their reservations are parts of their traditional homelands.

**Culture.** The Chippewa were timber people of the Algonquian family who engaged primarily in hunting and fishing. They supplemented these occupations with the gathering of fruits, wild rice, and practicing some simple agriculture. They lived in conical wigwams and traveled in birchbark canoes and on foot. Living in family groups and small bands, the Grand Medicine Society controlled the tribe's movements and deterred efforts to Christianize the Chippewa. Today, many Chippewa are of mixed blood, mostly French and English.

**Government.** The Leech Lake Business Committee has five members elected for 4 years each. The chairman, who heads the tribal government is elected at large.

**Population Profile. 1969:** Tribal enrollment 3,499; Indian resident 2,795; non-Indian resident 5,600; Unemployment 37%; Underemployment 23%; Median family income $2,200. **1980:** Indian resident 2,759; Non-Indian resident 5,682; Percent Indian of total population 32.7; Total housing units 5,951; Occupied housing units 2,778. There are presently 30 tribal members in college. The average education level for the tribe is 8th grade. Both the Bureau of Indian Affairs and the tribe provide scholarship money.

**Tribal Economy.** The tribe has an annual income of close to $15,000. Several businesses on the reservation are Indian owned. These include a cab company, a few retail and service stores, and a small resort. A variety of small resorts are owned by non-Indians, as are several small sawmills and a pre-fab housing firm.

**Climate.** Leech Lake is in the lakes area of Minnesota, a very popular vacation area. There are four distinct seasons, and rainfall averages 25 inches per year.

**Transportation.** U.S. Highway No. 2 and State Highway No. 34 cross the reservation east-west. Train, bus, and trucklines serve Cass Lake on the reservation. The nearest air service is located in Bemidji, 17 miles from Leech Lake.

**Community Facilities.** Some areas of the reservation have municipal water and sewer systems. Only bottled gas is available. Electricity is supplied by the Ottertail Power Company. The U.S. Public Health Service operates a hospital at Cass Lake for tribal members. The tribe is building a HUD community facility. In addition, there are a Headstart building and two tribal halls.

**Recreation.** Leech Lake is popular for most outdoor activities. Hunting is excellent, and there are numerous lakes and beautiful scenery. Several resorts have already been established. The tribe plans to participate in the tourism business and is planning several resort and recreation facilities. Ball Club is the setting for the annual July powwow.


LOWER SIOUX COMMUNITY                     Federal Reservation
Redwood County
Eastern or Mississippi Sioux Tribe
Tribal Headquarters: Morton, Minnesota

**Land Status.** Total area: 1,743 acres. All the land is tribally-owned. It was never allotted to individual members but is assigned to eligible members for homesites.

**History.** The Sioux and the Chippewa were rivals for the territory now known as Minnesota. Decisive engagements occurred before 1750 in which the Chippewa defeated the Sioux-Fox near St. Croix Falls and then destroyed Sioux villages at Sandy Lake and Mille Lacs. By the Treaty of Washington, 1837, the Sioux began the sale of their Minnesota lands and agreed that the proceeds should go to pay off their debts to the traders. Deprived of hunting grounds and reduced to semistarvation, the Sioux, under Little Crow, staged an uprising in 1862. Congress reacted by abrogating all Minnesota Sioux treaties and declaring their lands and annuities forfeit. Approximately $200,000 of their funds were appropriated to pay off claims by whites. Between 1887 and 1893, Congress moved to alleviate the desperate conditions by appropriating funds to buy back land for the tribe.

**Culture.** The economic life of the Minnesota Sioux was based on hunting and gathering with periodic trips onto the plains to hunt the buffalo. Their society was complex and highly organized with the high level of group loyalty and intelligence characteristic of the Sioux people. Most of the Sioux moved west and obtained horses, but the Minnesota Sioux, after fleeing to Canada in 1862, returned to Minnesota. They have now assimilated to a moderate degree, and their standard of living has improved. Reservation members find employment on farms and construction work, sometimes traveling as far as Duluth.

**Government.** The reservation was organized under the Indian Reorganization Act. The tribal constitution and bylaws were approved in 1936, and the corporate charter was ratified by members in 1937.

**Population Profile. 1969:** Tribal enrollment 500; Indian resident 109; Non-Indian resident None; Unemployment 20; Underemployment 12. **1980:** Indian resident 65; Non-Indian resident 14; Percent Indian of total population 82.3; Total housing units 34; Occupied housing units 28. The average education level for the tribe is 8th grade. There are no schools on the reservation. Students attend grade and high schools in Morton and Redwood Falls.

**Tribal Economy.** The tribal income of $4,000 per year is largely from farm and gravel permits. About one-quarter of the income is profits from farming. Gravel is the only marketable natural resource.

**Climate.** The reservation lies 1 mile south of Morton, Minnesota, near the Minnesota River, where the rainfall averages 24 inches annually. The average July high is 75 degrees; the average January low is 13 degrees.

**Transportation.** U.S., State, and county roads run in all directions. Redwood Falls, which lies 6 miles from the reservation is served by commercial air, train, bus, and trucklines. The bus also stops at Morton.

**Community Facilities.** Sanitary facilities are poor. Water is drawn from private wells. Oil and wood rather than gas are used for fuel. The Northern States Power Company supplies electricity to the reservation. Medical care and hospitalization, either through personal or welfare payments, are available at Redwood Falls. There is one community building on the reservation.


MILLE LACS RESERVATION                    Federal Reservation
Mille Lacs, Aitkin, and Pine Counties
Chippewa Tribe
Tribal Headquarters: Onamia, Minnesota

**Land Status.** Tribally-owned land: 3,552 acres. Allotted land: 68 acres. Total area: 3,620 acres. This reservation was established in 1855 by a treaty with the U.S. Government. Most of the original Indian land has passed from Indian ownership. The major Indian community is at Vineland, Minnesota.

**History.** The Chippewa, or Ojibway, were one of the largest Indian nations north of Mexico and controlled lands extending along both shores of Lakes Huron and Superior westward through Minnesota to the Turtle Mountains of North Dakota. Their migration to this area resulted from Iroquois pressure from the northeast. Drifting through their native forests, never settling on prized farmlands, the Chippewas were little disturbed by the first onrush of white settlers. They maintained friendly relations with the French and were courageous warriors with the Fox and Sioux. In the early 18th Century, the Chippewa drove the Fox out of northern Wisconsin and then forced the Sioux across the Mississippi and Minnesota Rivers. Vineland was the location of the Sioux village of Kathio, the oldest known village name in Minnesota. Kathio was the location of major battles between the resident Sioux and invading Chippewa tribes. By this time they were also able to push back the Iroquois whose strength and organization had deteriorated and had been undercut by the settlers. The Mille Lacs area was the first west of the Great Lakes to be penetrated by white men. The Chippewa of the United States have been officially at peace with the Government since 1815, and have experienced less dislocation than many other tribes.

**Culture.** The Chippewa were nomadic, timber people, traveling in small bands, engaging primarily in hunting and fishing, sometimes settling to carry on a rude form of agriculture. Their foods were supplemented by gathering fruits and wild rice. Their wigwams of saplings and birchbark were easily moved and erected. Birchbark canoes were used for journeys, but other travel was by foot. The tribe was patrilineal, divided into clans usually bearing animal names. Although their social organization was loose, the powerful Grand Medicine Society controlled the tribe's movements and was a formidable obstacle to Christianizing attempts of missionaries. A mysterious power or manitou was believed to live in all animate or inanimate objects. The Chippewa today are largely of mixed blood, primarily French and English.

**Government.** The Mille Lacs Reservation is one of six Chippewa reservations in the State organized as the Minnesota Chippewa Tribe under the 1934 Indian Reorganization Act. The revised constitution provides for a Reservation Business Committee to be elected at each reservation. The chairman and secretary-treasurer of each Reservation Business Committee form the 12-member Tribal Executive Committee of the Minnesota Chippewa Tribe. Members are elected every 2 years on a staggered basis to serve 4-year terms. The Mille Lacs Reservation Business Committee has five members.

**Population Profile.** **1969:** Indian resident 827; Non-Indian resident 0; Unemployment 82 persons, Underemployment 48 persons; Median family income $3,400. **1980:** Indian resident 293; Non-Indian resident 14; Percent Indian of total population 95.4; Total housing units 112; Occupied housing units 72. The average education level for the tribe is 8th grade. Elementary and secondary schools are situated on the reservation. Vocational training is offered in these schools, the community training center, and an industrial building. Three tribal members are college graduates.

**Tribal Economy.** The tribe had no income in 1968 and thus employs no members. Efforts are being made to improve the economy. The tribe has a Community Action Program and has organized the Reservation Business Enterprise which does contract work for IBM in the industrial building. Numerous commercial and industrial enterprises are owned and operated by non-Indians in the communities located in the former reservation area. Deposits of sand are used locally, while the gravel and granite are used commercially. There are also peat logs which are not presently being cut.

**Climate.** This reservation lies in east-central Minnesota approximately 100 miles north of the Minneapolis-St. Paul metropolitan area and enjoys a variable and seasonal climate. Temperatures range from an average summer high of 60 degrees to an average winter low of 12 degrees.

**Transportation.** State Highway No. 169 runs north-south through the reservation. North Central Airlines serves Brainerd, 45 miles from Mille Lacs. The Soo Line Railroad serves Princeton, Minnesota, 30 miles from the reservation. Bus and trucklines schedule stops in towns on the reservation.

**Community Facilities.** The Mille Lacs Water and Sewer Association serves the reservation's infrastructure. The new public housing units all have a central sewer system. Residents purchase bottled gas. Electricity is provided by the Mille Lacs Region Power Coop. Tribal members contract for medical care through the U.S. Public Health Service at the Municipal Hospital in Onamia. The U.S. Public Health Service operates a hospital in Vineland.

**Recreation.** The Mille Lacs Reservation lies in the center of a major outdoor recreational area for the Twin Cities population. Lakes and wild game are abundant in the area. The Chippewa Tribe also holds an annual Fourth of July celebration, an opportunity to see Indian dancing and displays of crafts.

NETT LAKE RESERVATION                        Federal Reservation
Koochiching and Saint Louis Counties
Chippewa Tribe
Tribal Headquarters: Nett Lake, Minnesota

**Land Status.** Tribally-owned land: 30,035 acres. Allotted land: 11,744 acres. Government land: 5 acres. Non-Indian land: 63,500 acres. Total area: 41,784 acres. The reservation area comprises 41,329 contiguous acres of tax-exempt Indian-owned land, and 1,080 acres located on Lake Vermilion, a fishing and resort lake located about 65 miles from the main reservation near Tower, Minnesota. The Lake Vermilion Reservation is a part of the Nett Lake Reservation and the few families who reside there are enrolled in the Nett Lake Band.

**History.** The Chippewa or Ojibway were one of the largest Indian nations north of Mexico and controlled lands extending along both shores of Lakes Huron and Superior westward through Minnesota to the Turtle Mountains of North Dakota. They migrated to this area after having been driven by the Iroquois from land further to the northeast. Drifting through their native forests, never settling on prized farmlands, the Chippewa were little disturbed by the first onrush of white settlers. They maintained friendly relations with the French, and were courageous warriors with the Fox and the Sioux. In the beginning of the 18th Century, the Chippewa drove the Fox out of northern Wisconsin and then moved against the Sioux forcing them across the Mississippi and Minnesota Rivers. By this time they were also able to push back the Iroquois whose strength and organization had deteriorated through confrontation with the settlers. The Chippewa of the United States have been officially at peace with the Government since 1815 and have experienced less dislocation than many other tribes.

**Culture.** The Chippewa were nomadic timber people traveling in small bands, engaging primarily in hunting and fishing. Their foods were supplemented by gathering fruits and wild rice. Occasionally, the Chippewa settled briefly to carry on a rudimentary form of agriculture. Their wigwams, made of saplings and birchbark, were easily moved and erected. Birchbark canoes were used for journeys; otherwise travel was by foot. The tribe was patrilineal and divided into clans usually bearing animal names. Although their social organization was loose, the powerful Grand Medicine Society controlled the tribe's movements and was a formidable obstacle to Christianizing attempts by missionaries. A mysterious power, or manitou, was believed to live in all animate or inanimate objects. The Chippewa today are largely of mixed blood, mostly French and English.

**Government.** The Nett Lake Reservation is one of six Chippewa

Reservations in Minnesota organized as the Minnesota Chippewa Tribe under the 1934 Indian Reorganization Act. The revised constitution and bylaws, approved by the Secretary of the Interior in 1964, provide for a Reservation Business Committee to be elected at each reservation. The chairman and secretary-treasurer of this committee are part of the 12-member Executive Committee of the Minnesota Chippewa Tribe. Committee members are elected every 2 years on a staggered basis to 4-year terms.

**Population Profile. 1969:** Tribal enrollment 805; Indian resident 675; Non-Indian resident 25; Unemployment rate 80%; Underemployment 11%; Median family income $4,500. The educational level on the reservation is 8th grade. There are presently four college graduates in the tribe. The tribe provides $100 per year for students. Additional college scholarships are available from private and Government sources. Vocational training is offered at the community center.

**Tribal Economy.** The Nett Lake is located in a sparsely populated timbered region some 60 miles south of the Canadian border. The land is generally level, and there are numerous swamps and lakes. The area is poorly adapted to agriculture. The tribe had an income of $19,000 in 1968. Three-fourths of this was earned in forestry. Fifteen percent was income from the wild rice crop, and the remainder was lease payments. The tribe has organized a wild rice cooperative to harvest, process, and sell the wild rice which grows abundantly on the reservation.

**Climate.** About two-thirds of the annual rainfall of 22 inches falls between May and September. The area's snowfall averages 50 inches each winter. The average July high is 66 degrees; however, the temperature sometimes reaches 100 degrees. The January average is 15 degrees with temperatures as low as -50 degrees.

**Transportation.** A gravel-surfaced county road, No. 65, crosses the reservation southeast-northwest. International Falls, 80 miles from Nett Lake, is served by North Central Airlines. The city of Orr, 20 miles distant, has commercial train and bus service. The nearest truckline stops in Cook, 36 miles from the reservation.

**Community Facilities.** The Public Health Service provides the reservation's sewer system. Water is drawn from individual wells. Residents purchase bottled gas, and electricity is supplied through REA. The Northwestern Bell and Spring Creek Telephone Company supply telephone service. Tribal members contract for medical care through the PHS at the Cook Community Hospital. The Cook County Public Health Service sponsors a clinic at Nett Lake. Community and tribal affairs are conducted at the community center in Nett Lake.

**Recreation.** The Nett Lake Chippewa hold an annual Fourth of July celebration on the reservation. The harvesting of wild rice, a major event for both employment and recreation, takes place from September through November. Lake Vermilion is a developed resort area. Visitors are attracted to the water recreation and excellent hunting and other outdoor activities.

PRAIRIE ISLAND RESERVATION                Federal Reservation
Goodhue County
Eastern or Mississippi Sioux
Tribal Headquarters: Welch, Minnesota

**Land Status.** Total area: 534 acres. All land is tribally owned.

**History.** The Sioux and Chippewa were rivals for the territory now known as Minnesota. Decisive engagements occurred before 1750 in which the Chippewa defeated the Sioux-Fox near Saint Croix Falls and then destroyed Sioux villages at Sandy Lake and Mille Lacs. By the Treaty of Washington, 1837, the Sioux began the sale of their Minnesota lands and agreed that the proceeds should go to retire debts to traders. Deprived of hunting grounds and reduced to semistarvation, the Sioux, under Little Crow, staged an uprising in 1862. Congress reacted by abrogating all Minnesota Sioux treaties and declaring their lands and annuities forfeit. Approximately $200,000 of their funds were appropriated. Between 1887 and 1893, Congress moved to alleviate the desperate conditions by appropriation of funds to buy back land for the tribe. The land on this reservation has never been allotted.

**Culture.** The economic life of the Minnesota Sioux was based on hunting and gathering food, including wild rice, with periodic trips to the plains to hunt buffalo. Their society was complex and highly organized with the high level of group loyalty and intelligence characteristic of the Sioux. Most of the Sioux moved farther west and obtained horses, but the Minnesota Sioux, after fleeing to Canada in 1862, returned to Minnesota. They have been assimilated to a moderate degree, and their standard of living has improved. Reservation members generally find employment on farms and construction work or in nearby Minneapolis-St. Paul. Residents receive a crop share rental from the farming of their assigned homesites.

**Government.** The reservation was organized under the Reorganization Act of 1934. Its constitution and bylaws were approved by the Secretary of the Interior on June 30, 1936. The corporate charter was ratified on July 23, 1937, by the tribe.

**Population Profile. 1969:** Tribal enrollment 300; Indian resident 86; Non-Indian resident 0; Unemployment 19%; Underemployment 3%. **1980:** Indian resident 80; Non-Indian resident 31; Percent Indian of total population 72.1; Total housing units 27; Occupied housing units 26. The average education level for the tribe is 8th grade. Children attend public schools in surrounding communities.

**Climate.** Precipitation averages 30 inches per year. The high temperature record is 106 degrees with a record low of -36 degrees.

**Transportation.** U.S. Highway No. 61 is $3\frac{1}{2}$ miles to the southwest of the reservation. County roads service the reservation. The nearest airport is in Minneapolis-St. Paul, 50 miles away. Trains and commercial bus and trucklines service Red Wing, 14 miles from the reservation.

**Community Facilities.** Water is provided by individual wells. There are no gas or sewer lines. The Dakota County Electric and Power Company supplies electricity. There are no Government-owned buildings or Federal employees stationed on the reservation. In Red Wing there are a community hospital and a clinic which provide services through the welfare department. There is one community building on the reservation. An annual powwow is held in the area in July.


PRIOR LAKE RESERVATION                    Federal Reservation
Carver County
Shakopee Mdewakanton Sioux
Tribal Headquarters: Prior Lake, Minnesota

**Land Status.** Total area: 258 acres. Reservation lands were acquired pursuant to Acts of Congress approved March 2, 1888, June 29, 1888, and August 19, 1890. All land is tribally-owned.

**History.** The Sioux and Chippewa were rivals for the territory now known as Minnesota, much of the fighting being over who controlled the wild rice beds around Prior Lake and other lakes. By the Treaty of Washington, 1837, the Sioux began the sale of their Minnesota lands and agreed that the proceeds would go to retire debts to the traders. Soon they were reduced to semistarvation and suffered injustices at the hands of both officials and settlers. Under Little Crow, they rose against the whites in 1862 in an uprising which took more than 480 lives. Congress reacted by abrogating all Minnesota Sioux treaties and declaring their lands and annuities forfeit. The Sioux were driven into Canada. Between 1888 and 1890, Congress appropriated new funds to buy back land for the tribe. The Prior Lake Reservation was part of the Lower Sioux Reservation until November 28, 1969, when their constitution was approved by the Secretary of the Interior.

**Culture.** The Minnesota Sioux culture was based on hunting and gathering. The society was complex and highly organized with the high level of group loyalty and intelligence characteristic of the Great Plains Sioux. Most of the Sioux people moved further west but the Minnesota Sioux, after fleeing to Canada following the uprising of 1862, returned to Minnesota. They are now moderately assimilated, and their standard of living has improved. Reservation members generally find employment on farms and construction work, sometimes traveling as far as Duluth.

**Government.** The tribal constitution was approved by the Secretary of the Interior, November 28, 1969. The first election of the business council was held on December 14, 1969. The general council is composed of all persons qualified to vote in community elections. The business council chairman, vice-chairman, and secretary perform duties authorized by the general council. Term of office: 4 years.

**Population Profile.** 1969: Tribal enrollment 33; Indian resident 20; Unemployment 0%; Underemployment 0%.

**Tribal Economy.** There is no tribal income.

**Climate.** The reservation is north of Prior Lake. Precipitation is 37 inches per year. The high temperature is 94 degrees, the low is -22 degrees.

**Transportation.** State Highway No. 13, U.S. Highway No. 169, and County Highway No. 16 serve the reservation. The nearest airline is in Minneapolis-St. Paul, 20 miles from the reservation. The Shakopee and Prior Lake Railway goes through Indian land. There are commercial bus and trucklines at Shakopee and Prior Lake, 3 miles from the reservation.

**Community Facilities.** Water is provided from individual wells and heating is by bottled gas. There is no sewer system. Northern State Power Company supplies electricity. The nearest hospital and clinic, 3 miles away in Shakopee, is a private facility.


RED LAKE RESERVATION                      Federal Reservation
Beltrami and Clearwater Counties
Chippewa Tribe
Tribal Headquarters: Redlake, Minnesota

**Land Status.** Tribally-owned land: 564,426 acres. Non-Indian land: 72,538 acres. Total area: 636,964 acres. Upper and Lower Red Lakes form over one-third of the reservation's surface area. The tribe owns scattered holdings up to the Canadian border totaling 156,690 acres in addition to the reservation area.

**History.** The Chippewa Tribe was among the largest north of Mexico, with lands extending along both shores of Lake Huron and Lake Superior and westward through Minnesota to the Turtle Mountains of North Dakota. They migrated to this area in the mid-17th Century, having been driven by the Iroquois from an area further to the northeast. The Chippewa, in turn, pushed the Sioux west, forcing their adaptation from woodland people to the dominant tribe of the plains. The Chippewa in the United States have been at peace with the Government since 1815 and have experienced less dislocation than many other tribes. Their reservations are parts of their traditional homelands.

**Culture.** The Chippewa were timber people and engaged primarily in hunting and fishing. They supplemented these occupations with gathering of fruits and cultivation of wild rice. They lived in wigwams and traveled in canoes. Although their social organization was loose, the powerful Grand Medicine Society controlled the tribe's movements and was a formidable obstacle to Christianizing attempts by white men. The Chippewa today are largely of mixed blood, mostly French and English.

**Government.** The tribal governing body is the Red Lake Tribal Council consisting of 11 members. This includes a chairman, secretary, and treasurer who are elected at large, and eight councilmen elected, two each, from the four districts.

**Population Profile. 1969:** Tribal enrollment 4,774; Indian resident 2,737; Unemployment 42%; Underemployment 15%; Median family income $4,500. **1980.** Indian resident 2,823; Non-Indian resident 156; Percent Indian of total population 94.8; Total housing units 769; Occupied housing units 728. Education level: 9.0 grades.

**Tribal Economy.** Average annual tribal income: $351,000. Most of the tribal income, over 95 percent, is derived from forestry. Tribal associations: Tribal Fisheries Association. Commercial/industrial establishments: Red Lake Sawmill - tribally owned; Tribal Construction Co. - tribally-owned; Habitant Fence Co. - tribally-owned; Retail businesses - tribally-owned. Timber is the primary natural resource of the reservation. Quantities of ferrous metals, marl, and peat also exist but are not presently being exploited.

**Climate.** Rainfall averages 23 inches annually; snowfall averages 72 inches each winter. The mean high temperature is 67 degrees; the mean low is 15 degrees.

**Transportation.** State Highway No. 1 is the east-west route through the reservation. State Highway No. 89 crosses the reservation north-south. Commercial air, train, bus, and truck service are readily available in Bemidji, 32 miles from Red Lake.

**Utilities.** Wells supply the water for the reservation. Only bottled gas is available to residents. Electricity is provided by the Beltrami Electric Cooperative Association. Hospital care is available to residents. Electricity is provided by the Beltrami Electric Cooperative Association. Hospital care is available in the PHS hospital in Redlake, and at other hospitals in nearby towns.

**Recreation.** Hunting and fishing are excellent over the entire area. Attractions include St. Mary's Mission and Indian handicraft. An annual fair is held on the reservation.


UPPER SIOUX RESERVATION                    Federal Reservation
Yellow Medicine County
Eastern or Mississippi Sioux
Tribal Headquarters: Granite Falls, Minnesota

**Land Status.** Total area: 746 acres. All land is tribally owned.

**History.** The Sioux and Chippewa were rivals for the territory now known as Minnesota. Decisive engagements occurred before 1750 in which the Chippewa, with the help of French arms, defeated the Sioux-Fox at St. Croix Falls and then destroyed Sioux villages at Sandy Lake and Mille Lacs. By the Treaty of Washington, 1837, the Sioux began the sale of their lands and agreed that the proceeds should go to retire debts to traders. Deprived of hunting grounds and reduced to semistarvation, the Sioux, under Little Crow, staged an uprising in 1862. Congress reacted by abrogating all Minnesota Sioux treaties and declaring their lands and annuities forfeit. Approximately $200,000 of their funds were appropriated. In 1938, the Secretary of the Interior proclaimed certain lands purchased for the use and benefit of the Upper Sioux Indian community in Minnesota to be an Indian reservation.

**Culture.** The economic life of the Minnesota Sioux was based on hunting and food gathering, including wild rice, with periodic trips to the plains to hunt buffalo. Their society was complex and highly organized with the high level of group loyalty and intelligence character-istic of the Sioux. Most of the Sioux moved farther west and obtained horses, but the Minnesota Sioux, after fleeing to Canada in 1862, re-turned to Minnesota. There is no employment on the reservation, and residents must find employment in nearby communities, largely in farming or construction work.

**Government.** The reservation has not been formally organized. The community members do, however, elect five of their number to serve as a board of trustees. This board is elected for a 4-year term.

**Population Profile.** **1969:** Tribal enrollment 300; Indian resident 83; Unemployment 14%; Underemployment 5%. **1980:** Indian resident 51; Non-Indian resident 3; Percent Indian of total population 94.4; Total housing units 22; Occupied housing units 20. The education level for members of the tribe is 8th grade. Children attend public shcools in Granite Falls.

**Tribal Economy.** There is no tribal income.

**Climate.** Precipitation is an average of 23 inches per year. The recorded high temperature was 110 degrees, the low was -35 degrees.

**Transportation.** State Highway No. 67 runs through reservation land. There is no nearby airport. Railroad and commercial bus and trucklines service Granite Falls, 3 miles from the reservation.

**Community Facilities.** Water is provided from individual wells and heat from oil, wood, and propane gas. The Minnesota Valley Coop. (REA) provides electricity. There is no sewer system. A hospital in Granite Falls is available through welfare or private payment of fees. One community building is on the reservation.


WHITE EARTH RESERVATION                    Federal Reservation
Mahnomen, Becker and Clearwater Counties
Chippewa Tribe
Tribal Headquarters: None designated

**Land Status.** Tribally-owned land: 25,568 acres. Allotted land: 1,993 acres. Non-Indian land: 779,084 acres. Government land: 28,555 acres. Total area: 56,116 acres. Only 6.7 percent of the original reservation is now tax-exempt Indian land or U.S. Government Farm Security Administration or resettlement land. The fragmented pattern of land ownership poses problems in the best utilization of the land and resources. The FSA-resettlement land was acquired during the 1930's by the U.S. Government for the use of the Indians on the White Earth Reservation. While this Government-owned land was improved to some degree by the Indian people, the tribe is reluctant to invest in the area since they do not have title to the land. Any income derived from the resettlement land is deposited in the U.S. Treasury and does not accrue to the Indian people.

**History.** The Chippewa, or Ojibway, were one of the largest Indian nations north of Mexico and controlled lands extending along both shores of Lakes Huron and Superior and westward into North Dakota. Their migration to this area was instigated by Iroquois pressure from the northeast. Drifting through their native forests, never settling on prized farmlands, the Chippewa were little disturbed by the first onrush of white settlers. They maintained friendly relations with the French and were courageous warriors. In the early 18th Century the Chippewa drove the Fox out of northern Wisconsin; this time they were also able to push back the Iroquois whose strength and organization had been undercut by settlers. The Chippewa of the United States have been officially at peace with the Government since 1815 and have experienced less dislocation than many other tribes.

**Culture.** The Chippewa were nomadic timber people traveling in small bands engaging primarily in hunting and fishing, sometimes settling to carry on a rude form of agriculture. Their foods were supplemented by gathering fruits and wild rice. Their wigwams of saplings and birchbark were easily moved and erected. Birchbark canoes were used for journeys but other travel was usually by foot. The tribe was patrilineal, divided into clans usually bearing animal names. Although their social organization was loose, the powerful Grand Medicine Society controlled the tribe's movements and was a formidable obstacle to Christianizing attempts of missionaries. A mysterious power, or manitou, was believed to live in all animate or inanimate objects. The Chippewa today are largely of mixed blood, mostly French and English.

**Government.** This reservation is one of six Chippewa Reservations in the State which are organized to form the Minnesota Chippewa Tribe under the 1934 Indian Reorganization Act. Each reservation has a local Reservation Business Committee of five members elected on a staggered basis to 4-year terms. The chairman and secretary of the local Reservation Business Committee form the 12-member Tribal Executive Committee of the Minnesota Chippewa Tribe.

**Population Profile. 1969:** Tribal enrollment 15,149; Indian resident 2,600; Non-Indian resident 37,111; Unemployment 43%; Underemployment 90%; Median family income $3,300. **1980:** Indian resident 2,550; Non-Indian resident 6,936; Percent Indian of total population 26.9; Total housing units 4,506; Occupied housing units 2,944. The average education level is 8th grade. There are grade and high schools on the reservation. There are presently 11 college graduates in the tribe.

**Tribal Economy.** Most of the tribal income of $26,800 per year is earned in forestry. One-third is farming profits, and the remainder is business revenues. The tribe runs a small forestry and sawmill operation.

**Climate.** The reservation lies in northwestern Minnesota where precipitation averages 23 inches per year. The annual average temperature is 38.4 degrees, with a July mean high of 68 degrees and a January mean low of 4.5 degrees.

**Transportation.** There are all-weather hard surface roads giving access to all directions. Train, bus, and trucklines have scheduled stops at various towns on the reservation. The nearest airport served by a commercial airline is Detroit Lakes, 12 miles from the reservation.

**Community Facilities.** Each community has a water and sewer system. No natural gas is supplied to the area. Electricity is provided by the Wild Rice Cooperative. The U.S. Public Health Service holds clinics in White Earth, Ponsford, and Naytahwaush. There is a county hospital in Mahnomen. The only community building is located in Rice Lake.

**Recreation.** Theaters provide entertainment in Mahnomen. The tribe and Community Action Program have a swimming program.

MISSISSIPPI

CHOCTAW RESERVATION                    Federal Reservation
Neshoba, Newton, Leake, Scott, Jones, Attala,
Kemper, and Winston Counties
Tribal Headquarters: Pearl River, Neshoba County, Mississippi

**Land Status.** Tribally-owned land: 17,381 acres. Allotted land: 209 acres. Government land: 229 acres. Total area: 17,819 acres. There are no lands owned or occupied by non-Indians on the reservation; however, reservation lands are checker-boarded with non-reservation land. At the time of the 1830 removal of the Choctaw to Oklahoma, 104,320 acres were awarded to those remaining. By 1918, only one of the 163 sections remained in Indian ownership. The U.S. Government sponsored a land-purchase program and acquired 16,805 acres in seven counties. The title is held in trust by the U.S. The tribe is continuing its effort to purchase additional land.

**History.** The Choctaw were one of the most powerful tribes in what is now the Southeastern United States. The first white man to encounter them, Hernando de Soto, fought a fierce battle with the Choctaw in 1540. The Indians, although defeated, terrorized the Spanish. After 1700, the Choctaw Tribe was caught between and cleverly divided by the French and English. After 1780, the tribe was caught in a similar situation between United States and Spanish interests. Between 1763 and 1830, the Choctaw signed a series of eight treaties which gave away most of their land. The Treaty of Dancing Rabbit Creek, in 1830, which provided for the removal of the tribe to Oklahoma, included a provision allowing those so choosing to remain in Mississippi. The last group to move left Mississippi in 1903, and from then until 1916, the remaining Choctaw were largely forgotten. A series of epidemics brought the tribe to the attention of the Senate which prompted an investigation. In response to the dreadful conditions revealed, Federal money was appropriated for schools and services to the tribe.

**Culture.** The tribe is and has been predominantly agricultural, raising crops typical of the area—squashes, beans, corn. The Choctaw dislike war and prefer to settle disputes over the table. Their game of stickball, an often deadly sport, was used to settle differences between tribes. The tribe is democratic and places women in a prominent, rather powerful position. A part of the mound builders' culture, the Choctaw are the builders of the famous Nanih Waiya, or Mother Mound from which the first Choctaw are said to have been born. Choctaw all learn their own language first and English in school so that most of the tribe is at least bilingual.

**Government.** The Choctaw tribe adopted a constitution in 1945 under the Indian Reorganiztion Act. A 16-member council representing the seven major towns on the reservation is elected every other year. This council elects a chairman, and a vice-chairman, not necessarily from its own members. A secretary-treasurer is also elected. The council meets four times annually with additional meetings called when necessary. The chairman is a full-time employee of the tribe.

**Population Profile. 1969:** Tribal enrollment 4,000; Indian resident 3,185; Unemployment 34%; Underemployment 35%. **1980:** Indian resident 2,756; Non-Indian resident 110; Percent Indian of total population 96.2; Total housing units 627; Occupied housing units 604. Education level 4th grade. To date there are about eight college graduates among the Mississippi Choctaw; however, due to recent emphasis on education, increasing numbers are continuing education. In the academic year 1968-69, there were close to 20 Choctaws in college. Bureau of Indian Affairs scholarships are available to students. Other training and vocational education are available through BIA, OEO, and other Federal programs. BIA cooperated with the RCA Corporation to run a training program to include entire families so that they are able to move to an area where jobs are available if they so choose.

**Tribal Economy.** The reservation land is low, rolling sandy hills. Most of the land, 13,900 acres, is forest land. The remainder is used for agriculture and homesites. The tribal income is derived primarily from forestry and usually averages between $40,000 and $50,000 annually. The tribe organized a land enterprise which operated under tribal authority to develop and utilize land. It is now a profit-making organization. Indians go to nearby towns such as Philadelphia for commerce. The Choctaw operate an arts and crafts shop in Philadelphia.

**Climate.** In a mild Mississippi climate the rainfall for the area averages 53 inches per year. The average high temperature is 78 degrees; the average winter low is 51 degrees.

**Transportation.** All local communities are linked by paved roads with some paved and dirt roads extending into the reservation. Interstate 20 runs east-west through Meridian and Jackson. Two other interstates, 55 and 59, run north-south through Jackson and Meridian to New Orleans. State Highway No. 19 connects Meridian and Philadelphia with Pearl River. The nearest adequate air service is located in Meridian or Jackson. Both Meridian and Jackson have regularly scheduled air service. Train, bus, and truck service are all available in Philadelphia with no scheduled service to the reservation.

**Community Facilities.** Gas and electricity are provided to most of the homes for domestic use. The water and sewer infrastructure is inadequate for domestic purposes. PHS maintains a 28-bed hospital in Philadelphia next to the Bureau of Indian Affairs agency. PHS also contracts with the hospital in Philadelphia for additional services. Several doctors, a dentist, and field nurses provide medical care for the Choctaw. The community building at Pearl River is used for the Community Action Program and other educational and recreational activities.

**Recreation.** The school at Pearl River is used for sports and community events. Non-Indians may obtain hunting and fishing permits for the reservation from the tribe. The Choctaw Tribe holds an annual fair each August, providing recreational events and tribal exhibits.

## MONTANA

BLACKFEET INDIAN RESERVATION                Federal Reservation
Glacier and Pondera Counties
Blackfeet Tribe
Tribal Headquarters: Browning, Montana

**Land Status.** Tribal land: 119,805.72 acres. Allotted land: 775,412.52 acres. Government land: 11,223 acres. Non-Indian land: 44,192 acres. Total area: 906,441.24 acres.

**History.** The present day Blackfeet are descendants of a loose confederacy of Piegan, Blood, and Siksika, all of Algonquian stock. Until confined to a reservation in the late 19th Century, Blackfeet held most of the territory from the North Saskatchewan River in Canada to the southern headstreams of the Missouri River in Montana. The first treaty signed between the United States and the Blackfeet set aside a vast area for the Blackfeet, but 4 years later part of the land was designated by the Government as Common Hunting Grounds. These were to be shared by the Blackfeet, Flathead, Gros Ventre, and Assiniboine. In 1888, all U.S. Blackfeet were gathered onto their present reservation.

**Culture.** The seminomadic culture of the Blackfeet was that of the Plains tribes generally. The Sun Dance was important, as was the "Ikununkatsi" or All Comrades, a series of 12 or more war societies in which membership was based on age. The Blackfeet were famous horsemen and hunters, brave and savage warriors who were greatly feared by their enemies.

**Government.** The Blackfeet Tribe is organized under the Indian Reorganization Act with a constitution and bylaws. The governing body is the popularly elected Blackfeet Tribal Business Council consisting of nine members elected for 2-year terms.

**Population Profile. 1969:** Tribal enrollment 10,467; Indian resident 6,220; Unemployment 42%; Underemployment 10%; Median family income $4,500. **1980:** Indian resident 5,525; Non-Indian resident 1,135; Percent Indian of total population 83.0; Total housing units 2,191; Occupied housing units 1,833. Education level: 9 years. Education grants are available to tribal members up to $450.00 annually.

**Tribal Economy.** Average annual tribal income is $500,000. This income is derived 90 percent from minerals and 10 percent from miscellaneous sources.

**Climate.** Rainfall averages about 14 inches per year. The temperature ranges from 85 degrees to -20 degrees.

**Transportation.** U.S. Highway No. 89 runs southeast-northwest and, U.S. Highway No. 2 runs east-west through the reservation. Train, bus, and truck transportation are available on the reservation at Browning, while commercial air service is available at Great Falls, a distance of 125 miles.

**Utilities.** The water system at Browning is municipally owned. Electricity is furnished by Glacier Electric Cooperative and natural gas by Montana Power Company.

**Recreation.** A large community building is available for various tribal activities and a modern library with 3,000 volumes was recently completed. Browning, gateway to Glacier National Park, is the principal reservation shopping center. There is also the site of the Museum of the Plains Indian, a nationally known repository of Indian artifacts. North American Indian Days are celebrated annually with dances, ceremonies, and rodeo. In addition to Glacier National Park, reservation recreation areas include Lower St. Mary's Lake, Duke Lake, and other beautiful lakes.

CROW RESERVATION                    Federal Reservation
Big Horn and Yellowstone Counties
Crow Tribe
Tribal Headquarters: Crow Agency, Montana

**Land Status.** Tribal land: 335,951.66 acres. Government land: 1,400.59 acres. Allotted land: 1,229,628.07 acres. Total area: 1,566,980.32 acres.

**History.** The Crow Tribe, known to other Indians as the Absarokee or Children of the Large-beaked Bird, was formerly a northeastern tribe. Pressures of colonial expansion forced them to move westward where they become nomadic and were affected by the plains culture. The friendliness of the Crow to the white man dates as far back as 1825 when they joined the U.S. soldiers in fighting other Indian tribes with whom the Crow were at war. The treaty signed at Fort Laramie, Wyoming, in 1851, gave the Crows 38.5 million acres in Montana. By 1888, the Crow were confined to their present reservation which is also the site of the Custer battlefield.

**Government.** The Crow Tribe is governed by a general council composed of all male members of the tribe 21 and over and all female members of the tribe 18 and over. The tribal executive committee consists of 17 members and represents all of the districts on the reservation. Administrative officers are selected by the council. Various commissions have been appointed to assist in specific areas of endeavor. These include industrial development, recreation development, water and utilities, and a general advisory group.

**Population Profile. 1969:** Tribal enrollment 4,828; Indian resident 3,842; Unemployment 26%; Underemployment 32%. **1980:** Indian resident 3,953; Non-Indian resident 2,020; Percent Indian of total population 66.2; Total housing units 1,839; Occupied housing units 1,488. Education level: 9.5 grades.

**Tribal Economy.** Annual average tribal income: $1,691,000. Tribal associations, cooperatives, etc.: Land Purchase Enterprise, Housing Authority, Big Horn Development District. Commercial/industrial establishments on reservation: Crow Industries and the Big Horn Carpet Co., a subsidiary of Mohasco, are both privately owned.

**Climate.** Rainfall averages 10 inches per year. The temperature ranges from a high of 95 degrees to a low of -30 degrees.

**Transportation.** U.S. Highway No. 212 passes east-west, and Interstate 90 north-south through the reservation. Train, bus, and trucklines serve Crow Agency while residents must drive 75 miles to Billings for commercial air service.

**Utilities.** The water and sewer systems are provided by USPHS. Gas is available through the Montana-Dakota Utility Company. Electricity is provided by the Big Horn County Electric Cooperative. PHS also operates a hospital at Crow Agency.

**Recreation.** A major tourism complex including a motel, restaurant, and tepee village is under construction. There is also a museum at Crow Agency. Other areas of interest include the Custer Battlefield National Monument, Yellowtail Dam and Bighorn River Canyon, Tribal Sun Dances, Custer Battle Re-enactment, and the Crow Fair and Rodeo.

FLATHEAD RESERVATION                    Federal Reservation
Flathead, Lake, Missoula, and Sanders Counties
Salish and Kootenai Tribes
Tribal Headquarters: Dixon, Montana

**Land Status.** Tribally-owned land: 558,216.44 acres. Allotted land: 56,860.08 acres. Non-Indian land: 723.12 acres. Total area: 616,816.64 acres. The reservaton was established by the Hellgate Treaty of July 16, 1855, which ceded most of Montana to the United States for 1,234,969 acres for a general reservation for the Kootenai and Salish. A succession of Acts followed which dissipated tribal holdings through land allotment and non-Indian homesteading. About one-half the land within the reservation, including almost all of the better agricultural land located in the valley bottoms is non-Indian owned. The mountains, upland range, and valuable forest lands are Indian-owned.

**History.** The Salish and Kootenai people occupied western Montana, eastern Washington, southern British Columbia, and northern Idaho when the Europeans reached the continent. They moved in groups to other areas for visits and usually maintained friendly relations with the tribes to the north, south, and west. However, as the Plains tribes were confined by the westward expansion of the Europeans, conflicts with the neighboring Blackfeet increased.

**Culture.** The two tribes are from different linguistic families, but both are related to the other Pacific Northwest tribes. The Salish were originally fish eaters, but in time acquired houses and many of the characteristics of the Plains Indians.

**Government.** The tribal government consists of a 10-man council elected from five districts. Five members are elected to 4-year terms in biennial elections. Following the election, a chairman and vice chairman are chosen by the council and a secretary and treasurer are selected at large by the council.

**Population Profile.** **1969:** Tribal enrollment 5,296; Indian resident 2,285; Non-Indian resident 14,000 est.; Unemployment 24%; Underemployment 21%. **1980:** Indian resident 3,771; Non-Indian resident 15,857; Percent Indian of total population 19.2; Total housing units 8,761; Occupied housing units 6,815. The average tribal education is 10th grade. There are five public high schools on the reservation, several public elementary schools, and one parochial elementary school. An adult vocational skill center accommodates 100 students. There are currently 25 tribal members in college. The tribe offers scholarships of $1,600, and funds are also available from the Bureau of Indian Affairs.

**Tribal Economy.** The tribe has an annual income of $3 million, almost all of which is earned in the forestry industry. The tribe employs approximately 50 persons in its various tribal enterprises. The tribe owns and operates the Blue Bay Lodge and the Hot Springs Bathhouse. Tribal members own five separate logging operations; 10 or more are owned by non-Indians. A number of retail and service stores on the reservation are owned by non-Indians. There are desposits of silver, iron, potassium, and aluminum. Abundant clear water resources are provided by the lakes and rivers.

**Climate.** Rainfall measures between 8 and 40 inches per year, varying with the elevation. The average high in July is 67 degrees; the average January low is 25 degrees in the valley.

**Transportation.** U.S. Route No. 93 is the major north–south highway passing through the reservation. U.S. Route No. 2 is an east–west highway. Polson, which lies on the reservation, is served by commercial train and buslines. The nearest truck service is located in Kalispell, 15 miles from the reservation. Missoula, which lies 28 miles from the reservation, is served by commercial airlines.

**Community Facilities.** The towns on the reservation have water systems and at least partial sewer systems. Residents buy bottled gas. Electricity is drawn from the Flathead Irrigation Project. The Indian Health Service contracts with the four hospitals located on the reservation to provide health care and hospitalization to tribal members. An old BIA complex is now used as a community center. There are also community centers at Elmo, Arlee, and Saint Ignatius.

**Recreation.** The Flathead Reservation is considered to be one of the most beautiful areas in western Montana, having spectacular mountain and lake scenery. The tribal resort is beautifully situated on a lake offering guests an excellent view. The tribe holds a 4-day powwow during the week of July Fourth.

FORT BELKNAP RESERVATION                    Federal Reservation
Blaine and Phillips Counties
Gros Ventre and Assiniboine Tribes
Tribal Headquarters: Harlem, Montana

**Land Status.** Tribally-owned land: 162,932.63 acres. Allotted land: 427,579.93 acres. Non-Indian land: 25,535.10 acres. Total area: 616,047.66 acres. The Treaty of Fort Laramie ceded a large block of land to the Assiniboine north of the Missouri in the western two-thirds of Montana. This was divided into the Fort Peck and Fort Belknap Military Reservations in 1873. The Fort Belknap Indian Reservation was established in 1888. It was reduced to its present acreage in 1895. Under the Allotment Act in 1921, almost half a million acres were allotted to individuals.

**History.** The Assiniboine originated in the Lake of the Woods and Lake Winnipeg areas of Canada where they early became allied with the Cree. Those that were within the United States when hostilities ended were placed in the Fort Belknap and Fort Peck Reservations during the 1880's. The Atsina (Gros Ventre) probably came west from the Red River country at the eastern edge of the plains. In the 19th Century they lived in the Milk River area across northern Montana. They allied with the Blackfeet against the Crow and then with the Crow against the Blackfeet. In 1867, the Atsina suffered a severe defeat. In the 1880's, those within the United States were placed on the Fort Belknap Reservation.

**Culture.** The Assiniboine speak a Sioux dialect while the Gros Ventre speak a language of the Algonquian family. Despite this basic difference, earliest recorded history indicates that these tribes occupied adjacent hunting grounds and followed a nomadic plains culture centered on the buffalo. Both tribes also performed the Sun Dance.

**Government.** The Fort Belknap Community Council, which is the official governing body for the reservation, is composed of 12 members from four districts. The Gros Ventre and Assiniboine tribes have equal representation.

**Population Profile.** **1969:** Tribal enrollment 3,557; Indian resident 1,688; Non-Indian resident less than 50; Unemployment 67%; Underemployment 7%. **1980:** Indian resident 1,870; Non-Indian resident 190; Percent Indian of total population 90.8; Total housing units 492; Occupied housing units 490. The average education level is slightly over 8th grade. Students attend high school at Harlem and a Catholic school at Hays. There are also public elementary schools at Harlem, Dodson, and Hays. At present 50 tribal members are attending college, 43 of whom are on Bureau of Indian Affairs' grants.

**Tribal Economy.** The tribal income averages about $100,000 each year. A large part of the income is derived from land leases. The tribe employs four people full time. There are two small Indian-owned stores, the Fort Belknap Builders, producing modular homes, and a Utility Commission. The tribe owns the latter and shares ownership of the modular homes factory with the private firm. Gravel is presently being extracted. There are also large deposits of bentonite and gas and oil; however, these have not been extracted commercially.

**Climate.** The climate is semiarid with severe winters and warm summers. The relative humidity is quite low, and precipitation is uncertain.

**Transportation.** A major east-west highway, U.S. Highway No. 2, crosses the reservation, and State Highway No. 376 provides a north-south traffic axis. Harlem, 3 miles off the reservation, has train service. Transportation by air, bus, and truck is available in Havre, 47 miles from the reservation.

**Community Facilities.** The water is piped from the Milk River to the northwest corner of the reservation. Other such facilities are presently inadequate and are being constructed. The Montana Power Company is the chief provider of natural gas and electricity. Also providing electric power are the Bureau of Reclamation and the Big Flat Cooperative. PHS operates a 15-bed hospital on the reservation. There are tribal halls at Fort Belknap, Hays, and Lodgepole.

**Recreation.** There are good fishing for trout and hunting for mule deer, white-tail deer, antelope, and some migratory waterfowl. Two major celebrations are held on the reservation, the Labor Day Indian Celebration and the Mid-Winter Fair in February. There are picnic and camping grounds in some parts of the reservation and overnight accommodations in Havre.


FORT PECK RESERVATION                    Federal Reservation
Valley, Roosevelt, Daniels, and Sheridan Counties
Assiniboine and Sioux Tribes
Tribal Headquarters: Poplar, Montana

**Land Status.** Tribal land: 233,153.17 acres. Allotted land: 645,114.20 acres. Government land: 86,597.38 acres. Total area: 964,864.75 acres. Under the 1908 Allotment Act, each member received 320 acres in addition to 40 acres of irrigable land. Heads of families also received 20 acres of timberland. Remaining lands were opened to homesteading in 1916. In addition to the land held in trust for the tribe, the tribe has control of 85,000 acres of submarginal land through a lease agreement with the Department of the Interior. Title to the Indian-owned land is complicated due to multiple inheritance. Indian lands are checker-boarded by non-Indian lands throughout the reservation.

**History.** The Assiniboine are a Siouan-speaking people who originally lived in northern Minnesota. The Assiniboine and many Sioux tribes moved westward into Montana because of the pressure from the east exerted by the powerful Chippewa and the European settlers. Both tribes adapted to the Plains culture of their new environment. The Assiniboine participated actively in fur trading with both French and British companies. In an 1851 treaty, the Assiniboine in the vicinity of Fort Peck were granted hunting and fishing privileges in common with the Blackfeet, Gros Ventre, and other tribes in the area. By 1871, large bands of Sioux had moved into the area. To accommodate these groups, the Fort Peck Reservation was established in an Executive Order of 1873 as a home for both Assiniboine and Sioux Tribes. The reservation boundaries were set by Congress in 1888.

**Culture.** Approximately one-half the reservation population is Sioux, one-third Assiniboine, and the remainder mixed blood. They live in two distinct tribal groups, the Assiniboine occupying the southwestern and the Sioux occupying the southeastern portions of the reservation. The tribes, once nomadic hunters of the buffalo, still adhere strongly to their Indian customs, although subject to the white man's ways. Family ties are strong and tribal members still practice the Indian custom of sharing whatever they have with relatives and friends. During the summer months, Indian dances and celebrations are held in five different districts on the reservation.

**Government.** The Fort Peck tribes did not accept the 1934 Indian Reorganization Act. The tribe is governed by a 15-man council. Twelve members are elected at large from six geographic districts. The chairman, vice-chairman, and sergeant-at-arms are elected at large.

Each elected executive board member serves a 2-year term. The board operates under a constitution and bylaws revised in 1960. The board is empowered to act on all matters concerning the tribe subject to the powers of the general council. The general council may initiate or reject any action of the executive board as outlined in the constitution and bylaws.

**Population Profile. 1969:** Tribal enrollment 5,674; Indian resident 6,000; Non-Indian resident 11,000; Unemployment 47%; Underemployment 27%. **1980:** Indian resident 4,273; Non-Indian resident 5,648; Percent Indian of total population 43.1; Total housing units 3,546; Occupied housing units 3,072. The average education for adults is close to the 9th-grade level. Sixteen members have been graduated from college since 1965. Fifty-two were enrolled during the 1969-70 semester, including one in medical school. Vocational training through OEO, BIA, Manpower Development and Training Act, and other educational programs such as Headstart, adult education, and special summer programs are available to tribal members.

**Tribal Economy.** Average annual tribal income: $500,000. Tribal income is derived largely from farming (48 percent), supplemented by mineral income (20 percent), and permits and licenses (26 percent). Nineteen persons are employed full-time by the tribe. Tribal associations and cooperatives include Fort Peck Tribal Industries, Inc., employing 123 Indians in all phases, and Fort Peck Planning Board operating the HUD 701 Land Use Plan. Commercial and industrial establishments on the reservation are the C&M Construction Company, owned and operated by a parent company in Billings, Montana, and the Tesoro Petroleum Company, also owned and operated by a parent company in New York, New York. Oil is currently being utilized on the reservation. Deposits of lignite coal, salt, bentonite, gravel, and clay are also known to exist in sizable amounts.

**Climate.** Rainfall averages 13 inches per year, and the climate is rather dry. The temperature averages a summer high of 72 degrees and a winter low of 9 degrees. Snowfall is usually light.

**Transportation.** U.S. Highway No. 2 runs east-west through the reservation. Commercial air, train, and bus service are available at Wolf Point on the reservation. The nearest truckline is located in Glasgow, Montana.

**Utilities.** Water and sewer systems are provided in the communities of Poplar and Wolf Point. Gas and electricity are provided by the Montana-Dakota Utilities. Hospitals are located in Wolf Point and Poplar Community. PHS clinics are held in towns throughout the reservation. Health and home aides are sponsored by the Community Action Program.

**Recreation.** Fort Peck Lake, 10 miles from the reservation, is a large body of water where all types of water recreation can be enjoyed. Hunting in the area is varied and excellent. Poplar, the location of an historical museum, is where the Iron Ring Celebration, Frontier Days, and the Oil Discovery Celebration take place. Other Indian dances and ceremonials occur throughout the year at various locations on the reservation.

NORTHERN CHEYENNE RESERVATION          Federal Reservation
Big Horn and Rosebud Counties
Northern Cheyenne Tribe
Tribal Headquarters: Lame Deer, Montana

**Land Status.** Tribally-owned land: 262,295.63 acres. Allotted land: 171,297.90 acres. Government land: .68 acres. Total area: 433,594.21 acres. The Northern Cheyenne Reservation was established by Executive Order in 1884 with 271,000 acres, and expanded to 440,000 acres in 1900. In recent years the tribe has successfully conducted a program to consolidate allotted holdings, purchase non-Indian holdings, and to discontinue non-Indian leases in favor of leases of family-sized ranch tracts to tribal members.

**History.** Historians believe the Cheyenne moved from Minnesota west to the Cheyenne and upper Missouri watersheds and gradually gave up the growing of corn, beans, and squash and developed a Plains economy based on the buffalo and later the horse. The Cheyenne actively opposed the advance of the frontier and the wholesale destruction of the buffalo and became a special target for U.S. Army violence. Following the decisive defeat of Custer at Little Big Horn in 1874 by the Sioux and Cheyenne, efforts to subjugate the Cheyenne were intensified. Finally subdued, they were taken as prisoners to Fort Reno, Oklahoma, for resettlement. Led by Chiefs Little Wolf and Morning Star, the Northern Cheyenne escaped and, pursued by 10,000 soldiers, made their way back to Montana in the dead of winter with enormous loss of life due to battles and the cold. Refusing to return to Oklahoma, they finally were allowed to remain and were given lands adjacent to the Crow Reservation in 1884. Until post-World War II, the tribe held a deep mistrust of the non-Indian and the neighboring Crow engendered by the bitter experiences associated with their subjugation.

**Culture.** The Cheyenne, who speak an Algonquian language, are believed to have migrated from the Minnesota area where their culture had been forest-oriented and agricultural. Gradually substituting the buffalo hunt and gathering wild fruits and vegetables for growing food crops, the Cheyenne had developed a Plains Indian life style by the time of contact with the Europeans. Life was nomadic, based upon the horse and the buffalo. The Cheyenne religious tradition is distinguished by the Sun Dance and their treasured sacred bundle, their "Ark of the Covenant," which was carefully protected and deeply revered.

**Government.** The tribe is governed by a 10-member council headed by a president who is elected at large. Both members and president serve terms of 4 years, the members being elected on a staggered basis.

**Population Profile. 1969:** Tribal enrollment 2,906; Indian resident 2,487; Non-Indian resident 20; Unemployment 21%; Underemployment 9%; Median family income $4,000. **1980:** Indian resident 3,101; Non-Indian resident 563; Percent Indian of total population 84.6; Total housing units 1,046; Occupied housing units 924. The average education level for tribal members is between 8th and 10th grade. The St. Labre Mission School includes grades 1-12. There are also two BIA day schools, one BIA boarding school, and three public schools on the reservation. Presently 30 Northern Cheyennes are in college. Both the tribe and the BIA offer scholarships.

**Tribal Economy.** Most of the annual tribal income of $300,000 is a product of the reservation's mineral resources. The remainder is earned through farming. The tribe employs over 20 persons in carrying out tribal business. Tribal organizations formed to increase and strengthen reservation resources include the Land Acquisition Enterprise, the Steer Enterprise, the Cheyenne Livestock Association, and the Northern Cheyenne Arts and Crafts Association. The tribe is also a member of the Big Horn Economic Development Corporation which includes the remainder of Big Horn County and the Crow Indian Reservation. Tribal members can find work in a variety of industries on the reservation. Guild Arts and Crafts, Inc., produces plastic jewelry and other items, employing approximately 120 persons. A post and pole company, a gas station, and an eight-unit motel and restaurant are owned by Indians and employ a total of 13. Two other establishments, owned by non-Indians, a branch plant for the Glendive Upholstering Company, and two gas station complexes, employ a total of 20. Many of the higher hills carry Ponderosa Pine. Mineral deposits include coal, which is being mined, and oil and gas, not presently exploited.

**Climate.** The reservation lies near the southern border of Montana in the Big Horn Mountains, where rainfall averages slightly over 12 inches annually. Temperatures reach seasonal extremes of 105 degrees and -40 degrees. Mean temperatures, however, are 74.5 degrees in July and 26 degrees in January.

**Transportation.** U.S. Highway No. 212 runs through the reservation east-west to junction with the soon-to-be completed Interstate 90 at Crow Agency. Billings lies 98 miles to the northwest on Highway No. 212. Truck and air companies serve Billings. Trucks, buses, and freight trains stop in Crow Agency, 18 miles west of the Northern Cheyenne Reservation.

**Community Facilities.** The tribe operates water systems and partial sewer systems in Lame Deer and Busby. Only bottled gas is available. Electricity is supplied by the Tongue River REA. PHS operates a hospital serving both the Crow and Northern Cheyenne Reservations at Crow Agency. Additional clinics are held at Lame Deer on the Northern Cheyenne Reservation. A new HUD community building has recently been completed at Lame Deer. There are also small community buildings at Ashland and Busby, the latter serving also as a factory.

**Recreation.** The reservation lies in a section of Montana known for its outdoor activities such as fishing and hunting. The Custer Battleground is located on the Crow Reservation and attracts many visitors each year. Visitor facilities are generally campgrounds with trailer spaces and picnic areas. Motels are located in nearby towns.


ROCKY BOY'S RESERVATION                    Federal Reservation
Chouteau and Hill Counties
Chippewa-Cree Tribe
Tribal Headquarters: Rocky Boy's, Montana

**Land Status.** Total area: 107,612.76 acres. In April 1916, 56,035 acres were set aside by Congress for the Chippewa and Cree bands of Chief Rocky Boy. Other lands were added later. None of this land has been allotted or sold though individual use assignments have been made.

**History.** A band of Chippewa from Minnesota moved into northern Montana and nearby Canada in the latter part of the 19th Century. During the same period, Cree, led by Chief Little Bear, were in the same area. Having no land base, both bands squatted on the fringes of Montana cities and reservations. They were officially but unsuccessfully deported to Canada in 1896 through action of Congress. In 1916, through the efforts of Chiefs Rocky Boy and Little Bear and prominent citizens, the reservation was established on part of the Fort Assiniboine Military Reserve by Executive Order.

**Culture.** The Chippewa and Cree lived in small bands on both sides of what is now the Canadian border from the Great Lakes as far west as northern Montana and Saskatchewan with the Cree generally living further north. These groups spoke languages of the Algonquian family. The Chippewa Band which settled at Rocky Boy's are reported to have originated in Minnesota though they had adopted a Plains rather than forest-oriented culture in most respects.

**Government.** Organized under the Wheeler-Howard Act of June 1934, the Rocky Boy's adopted a constitution in 1935 and ratified their charter in 1936. The governing body is the nine-member business committee elected by popular vote from the five districts.

**Population Profile. 1969:** Tribal enrollment 1,486; Indian resident 1,510; Non-Indian resident 5; Unemployment 72%; Underemployment 17%. **1980:** Indian resident 1,549; Non-Indian resident 101; Percent Indian of total population 93.9; Total housing units 387; Occupied housing units 347. The average education level for the reservation is 7th grade. Twenty tribal members are college graduates.

**Tribal Economy.** Three-fourths of the tribal income of $42,000 annually is earned through farming. Most of the remainder comes from mineral leases, hunting permits, and forestry. The tribe has organized the Chippewa-Cree Crafts Cooperative to produce the traditional patchwork quilts and beadwork. This organization is assisted by the Rocky Boy's Development Corporation. The only commercial establishment on the reservation is a general store and gas station owned by a non-Indian. Coal is currently being mined. Also existing in large quantities are natural gas, vermiculite, and columbium.

**Climate.** Rainfall in this area averages 15 inches annually. The temperature reaches a high of 100 degrees and a low of -35 degrees.

**Transportation.** Interstate 87 is the major north-south route passing through the reservation. Box Elder lies just one-quarter mile outside the reservation and has commercial train and bus service. The nearest air and trucklines stop in Havre, Montana, 20 miles from Rocky Boy's.

**Community Facilities.** The only public works facilities are in the community of Rocky Boy's. Outlying areas use wells and septic tanks. Gas is not piped into the reservation, but residents have tanks. The Montana Power Company supplies electricity to the reservation. Health care is available at the clinic in Rocky Boy's from the Public Health

Service and at the PHS Hospital in Harlem, Montana, 60 miles distant. There is also a private hospital in Havre. A large community building and training center is being constructed. There is also a small tribal office building.

# NEBRASKA

OMAHA RESERVATION                          Federal Reservation
Thurston County
Omaha Tribe
Tribal Headquarters: Macy, Nebraska

**Land Status.** Tribal land: 8,553 acres. Allotted land: 18,860 acres. Non-Indian land: 67,495 acres. Total area: 27,413 acres. What is now Thurston County was the Omaha Reservation as determined by the treaty finalized in Washington, D.C. on March 16, 1854. However, by a treaty of March 6, 1865, the Omaha sold the northern half to accommodate the Winnebago Tribe. Most allotted and tribal lands are actively farmed by tribal members; however, 71 percent of the land within the reservation is non-Indian owned.

**History.** The traditional home of the Omaha Indians was centered around the confluence of the Big Sioux and Missouri Rivers at present-day Sioux City, Iowa. After the arrival of the Europeans on the continent and before the establishment of the reservation, the tribe was in frequent conflict with the Sioux to the north and west. Their numbers were drastically reduced by smallpox in 1802 from several thousand to 300. The Omaha and Winnebago, with a similar language, were traditional friends.

**Culture.** The Omaha had a culture and lifestyle about midway between the agrarian Mandan and nomadic Sioux. Their homes were of earth construction like the Mandan, though skin tents were used when on the move. They grew corn and made pottery and a variety of household and culinary items. Their language is a Siouan dialect intelligible to the Winnebago. Their social structure called for marriage between two distinct groups of clans and allowed for polygamy. Their most sacred object was a Sacred Pole, though the use is no longer understood.

**Government.** The tribe is organized as a Federal corporation under the Indian Reorganization Act of 1934. The constitution and bylaws were ratified by the tribe and the Secretary of the Interior in early 1936 and revised in 1966. The tribal council is composed of seven members, which includes the chairman, vice-chairman, secretary, and treasurer. They are all elected at large by majority vote to a 3-year term. The council elects its own officers.

**Population Profile. 1969:** Tribal enrollment 2,660; Indian resident 1,367; Non-Indian resident 2,400; Unemployment 44%; Underemployment 41%. **1980:** Indian resident 1,275; Non-Indian resident 4,184; Percent

Indian of total population 23.4; Total housing units 2,018; Occupied housing units 1,826. The education level on the reservation is the 9th grade. Children attend public schools. These schools offer vocational education in shop, agriculture, and home economics. The tribe has a full time OEO Community Action Program. There are currently 17 tribal members in college.

**Tribal Economy.** The tribe earns $40,000 a year from lease income and $80,000 interest on judgment funds. Ten people are full-time employees of the tribe. The tribe operates the Omaha Tribal Farm which raises livestock, and the Chief Big Elk Park, a recreation area. The tribe is also a member of the Nebraska Inter-Tribal Development Corporation together with the Winnebago and the Santee Sioux, and has formed the Omaha Tribal Opportunities Corp. Two industries, owned by non-Indians are located on the reservation: Omahaline and Campbell Manufacturing Company.

**Climate.** Rainfall on the reservation averages just under 29 inches per year. The temperature ranges from an average of 76 degrees to an average low of 19 degrees.

**Transportation.** U.S. Highways Nos. 77 and 73 cross north-south through the reservation, while Nebraska Routes Nos. 51 and 94 run east-west. Bus and trucklines stop in all towns on the reservation. Rail freight service is available in Walthill and Rosalie. The nearest commercial air service is in Sioux City, Iowa, 33 miles from the reservation.

**Community Facilities.** Walthill and Macy have community water and sewer systems. Other areas obtain water from underground wells. Gas is provided by the Iowa Electric Light and Power Company; electricity by the Consumer Public Power District. The USPHS operates a hospital in Winnebago. Tribal members can also secure medical care through PHS contract and private hospitals in Omaha and Sioux City.

**Recreation.** The reservation lies along the Lewis and Clark Trail. All towns have parks. Indian dancing is held weekly in Macy. An annual powwow is held in August at Macy. A county fair takes place in the last week of August. There are good hunting, fishing, and boating along the river.


SANTEE SIOUX RESERVATION                    Federal Reservation
Knox County, Nebraska
Santee Sioux Tribe
Tribal Headquarters: Niobrara, Nebraska

**Land Status.** Tribal land: 3,599 acres. Allotted land: 2,192 acres. Non-Indian land: 75,000 acres. Total area: 5,791 acres. The reservation was established by the Executive Order of February 27, 1866, though several adjustments in its boundary were made so that lands west of the Niobrara River were given up. Under the Allotment Act of 1887, tribal members were given allotments with the remainder of the reservation opened up to settlement by non-Indians.

**History.** The Santee Sioux, unlike their neighbors the Yankton Sioux, were inclined to battle, and in 1862, most of the warriors were killed at the New Ulm Massacre. In 1863, the remaining tribal members, mostly old men, women, and children were moved from Minnesota to Crow Creek from whence they moved in 1866 to the present reservation.

**Culture.** The Santee Sioux, including the Sisseton, Wahpeton, Mdewakanton, and Wahpokoota bands, a relatively small group of the Sioux family, seem to have had the cultural characteristics of the mainstream Sioux. They were migratory, aggressive, and dependent upon wild game and plant life for their sustenance.

**Government.** The Santee Sioux Tribe is organized as a Federal corporation having a constitution and bylaws ratified in 1936. The tribal charter was ratified in August of 1966. The tribe is governed by a council of 12 members. Regularly scheduled meetings are held four times a year. Councilmen are elected to a 3-year term on a staggered basis, four new members elected each year. The council elects a chairman, vice-chairman, secretary, and treasurer from its own membership.

**Population Profile.** 1969: Indian resident 244; Non-Indian resident 2,200; Unemployment 50%; Underemployment 37%. 1980: Indian resident 420; Non-Indian resident 494; Percent Indian of total population 46.0; Total housing units 288; Occupied housing units 254. The average education level for the Indians is 9th grade. All children attend public schools. Two high schools cover the reservation. At present there are five Santee in college.

**Tribal Economy.** The tribal income of less than $3,000 per year comes from leases granted by the tribe. The Santee Tribe is a member of the Nebraska Inter-Tribal Development Corporation together with the Omaha and Winnebago tribes. There are several retail stores, a small resort, and a gas station, all owned by non-Indians. Gravel deposits on the reservation are being used. Sand also exists in large quantities but is not being used at present.

**Climate.** Rainfall averages 23.5 inches per year. The temperature ranges from a high of 95 degrees to a low of 10 degrees.

**Transportation.** Highways Nos. 84 and 12 run east-west; Highway No. 14 runs north-south. Bus and trucklines serve Bloomfield, 4 miles from the reservation. Rail freight service is also available 4 miles from the reservation. The nearest commercial air service is 30 miles distant in Yankton, South Dakota.

**Community Facilities.** Water is obtained from individually dug and artesian wells. Septic tanks are the only provision for sewage. Residents use bottled gas or obtain electricity from the North Central Power District. Hospitalization for the Santee is provided in Creighton, Nebraska. The PHS of Wagner, South Dakota, operates a clinic biweekly at Niobrara. In addition, there is an emergency station at Bloomfield. The community building at Santee houses tribal activities.

**Recreation.** Parks in Niobrara and Bloomfield have facilities for baseball, swimming, and other sports. The Lewis and Clark Lake also offers excellent recreational opportunities.

WINNEBAGO RESERVATION                    Federal Reservation
Thurston County
Winnebago Tribe
Tribal Headquarters: Winnebago, Nebraska

**Land Status.** Tribal land: 3,640 acres. Government land: 14 acres. Allotted land: 24,648 acres. Non-Indian land: 67,243 acres. Total area: 28,302 acres. The northern half of the Omaha Reservation was purchased for the Winnebagos by the Treaty of March 6, 1865. Today, 71 percent of the reservation lands are non-Indian owned. Most tribal and allotted lands are farmed by tribal members.

**History.** The Winnebago Tribe lived in the Lake Winnebago and Green Bay areas of Wisconsin when the Europeans first arrived on this continent. Through smallpox, struggles with the white man, and hostile tribes, the Winnebagos subsequently were decimated. They moved constantly until 1,200 were finally settled near their old friends and allies, the Omahas, in 1865. A smaller group was settled in Wisconsin.

**Culture.** The Winnebago are a timber people with houses, dress, and most crafts similar to the Sauk, Fox, and Menominee. Their language is a Siouan dialect intimately related to the Oto, Iowa, and Missouri groups. The tribe was traditionally divided into four Upper or Air Clans, and eight Lower, or Earth Clans. Marriages between Upper and Lower individuals were required. The Thunderbird and Bear clans were the most prominent, respectively, among the two groups. The two most important religious ceremonies are the Summer Medicine Dance and Winter Feast.

**Government.** The 1936 constitution and bylaws were amended in 1968. The tribe is a Federal corporation. The nine-member council is elected at large by secret ballot from tribal membership. The chairman, vice-chairman, and secretary are elected by the council from its own membership to serve for 1 year. The treasurer and lesser officers are appointed. The council meets monthly.

**Population Profile. 1969:** Tribal enrollment 1,813; Indian resident 745; Non-Indian resident 2,700; Unemployment 29%; Underemployment 29%. **1980:** Indian resident 1,140; Non-Indian resident 1,414; Percent Indian of total population 44.6; Total housing units 854; Occupied housing units 792. The education level for the tribe is between the 9th and 10th grades. There are currently approximately 12 students in college. Their financing is primarily through the Bureau of Indian Affairs. All children attend public schools. Winnebago and Walthill schools offer vocational courses in shop and home economics. The reservation has a complete Community Action Program.

**Tribal Economy.** The tribal annual income of $43,800 is composed entirely of lease rental monies. The tribe is a member of the Nebraska Inter-Tribal Development Corporation together with the Omaha and the Santee Tribes, and is also a member of the Winnebago (village of) Industrial Development Corporation. Winnebago Pet Food, owned by a non-Indian, employs all Indians. There are also two groceries, a feed store, a hardware dealer, and gas stations, all owned by non-Indians. Limestone is being quarried for agricultural use.

**Climate.** Rainfall measures 24 inches annually. Temperatures range from an average July high of 76 degrees to an average January low of 20 degrees.

**Transportation.** U.S. Highways Nos. 77 and 73 and State Highway No. 9 cross north-south through the reservation. Commercial bus and trucklines stop on the reservation. Rail freight service is available in Rosalie and Walthill on the reservation. For air service, Winnebago residents must drive 23 miles to Sioux City, Iowa.

**Utilities.** Winnebago has a community water and sewer system. Other areas on the reservation obtain water from deep wells. The Iowa Electric Light and Power Company provides gas to the area. A 34,500 volt feed of electricity is supplied by the Consumer Public Power District. Hospital care for residents is available at the Winnebago Public Health Hospital in Winnebago and at private hospitals in Omaha and Sioux City through contracts. The tribe has an old community building and a tribal office building.

**Recreation.** Hunting, fishing, and boating along the Missouri River are popular. The Lewis and Clark Trail passes through the reservation. The annual Indian powwow is held in Winnebago. All the towns have parks.

# NEVADA

BATTLE MOUNTAIN COLONY                    Federal Reservation
Lander County
Shoshone Tribe
Tribal Headquarters: Battle Mountain, Nevada

**Land Status.** Tribal land: 680 acres. Total area: 680 acres.

**History.** In 1847, due to a great influx of non-Indians, the food supply on which the Indians depended became scarce. The angered Indians fought with the military forces sent there to maintain peace. Major peace treaties were agreed upon in 1863 and by 1880 the area was generally peaceful. The Battle Mountain Colony was established by Executive Order in 1817 for the Shoshone Indians. This band claims descent from the Western Shoshone Indians as they were closely affiliated with Chief Te-Moak, allegedly the grandson of the Chief Te-Moak who signed the Treaty of 1863 resolving the differences between the Indians and the U.S. military. As part of the peace settlement, qualified Indians could select land for assignment.

**Culture.** The Shoshone, who lived in the Great Basin area, have been called the "Digger Indians" because of the way in which they obtained their food. They gathered nuts and berries, dug for roots and other edibles, and hunted small game in an area offering only sparse subsistence. Because food was difficult to obtain, they traveled in small bands of 25 to 30 persons, usually the extended kin group, moving on when they had gleaned all they could from an area. Only simple social organization and crafts were developed. The Shoshone readily adopted the horse and developed a new lifestyle typical of the Plains Indian hunters. Very few Indian arts and crafts are practiced today. The language is spoken by the majority of the tribe; however, little of the cultural tradition is otherwise practiced.

**Government.** The tribe is informally organized and is governed by the general council and a tribal council of six members.

**Tribal Economy.** The tribe has no income. It is a member of the Inter-Tribal Council of Nevada, an organization formed to promote the development of and opportunities for Nevada reservations.

**Population Profile.** 1969: Tribal enrollment 159; Indian resident 159; Unemployment 35%; Median family income $1,870.

**Climate.** Rainfall in this arid region of Nevada averages only 6 inches per year. The temperature varies from a high of 90 degrees to a low of 15 degrees.

**Transportation.** U.S. Highway No. 40 is an east-west route through the reservation. The nearest commercial air service is in Elko, 60 miles from the colony; however, train, bus, and trucklines serve the town of Battle Mountain, 1 mile from the colony.

**Community Facilities.** The tribe has its own water and sewer system. Electricity can be purchased from the Sierra Pacific Power Company. There is a tribal community building on the reservation. Health care for the tribal members is available in the PHS clinic at Elko, and at the Battle Mountain General Hospital.


CARSON COLONY                          Federal Reservation
Ormsby County
Washoe Tribe
Tribal Headquarters: Carson City, Nevada

**Land Status.** Tribally-owned land: 156 acres. Total area: 156 acres. The land was purchased in 1917 and shortly thereafter with Washoe Tribe funds.

**History.** The Washoe were among the nomadic tribes living in the Nevada area before the arrival of the white man. Traditional enemies of the Paiute and Shoshone, the Washoe regarded the white men as saviors. As a result of skirmishes with the Northern Paiute in the early 1860's, the Washoe lost their lands. They now live primarily in three communities near Reno, Nevada.

**Culture.** Some of the tribal arts and crafts are still practiced and the language is spoken by the elders. For the most part, the Indian heritage of the people is retained, but the lifestyle is necessarily altered from the mobile hunting and gathering economy they once had.

**Government.** Carson Colony is part of the Washoe Tribal Council, a body of nine members governing the three Washoe communities. The constitution and bylaws were written under the Indian Reorganization Act, approved in 1936, and revised in 1966. The Carson Community Council is a sub-council of five members.

**Population Profile.** 1969: Tribal enrollment—included in Washoe

Tribe, enrollment 1,200; Resident population 129; Unemployment 30; Underemployment 80%. **1980:** Indian resident 213; Non-Indian resident 14; Percent Indian of total population 93.8. Total housing units 81; Occupied housing units 65. There are no college graduates in the colony at present.

**Tribal Economy.** Average annual tribal income: None. There are no tribal associations or industries on the colony.

**Climate.** Rainfall averages 7.7 inches per year. The temperature ranges from a high of 100 degrees to a low of 0 degrees.

**Transportation.** U.S. Highway No. 395 runs north–south through the reservation. Commercial train and airlines serve Reno, 34 miles from the colony. Bus and trucklines stop in Carson, 2 miles away.

**Utilities.** Water and sewer disposal are provided by the tribe. Electricity is available from the Sierra Pacific Power Company. Health care service through the Bureau of Indian Affairs is located in Stewart, Nevada.

DRESSLERVILLE COLONY                     Federal Reservation
Douglas County
Washoe Tribe
Tribal Headquarters: Dresslerville, Nevada

**Land Status.** Total area: 39.80 acres. In March 1917, the United States purchased with $10 in gold the 40 acres of land for the use and benefit of the Washoe Indian Tribe with the stipulation that if the lands were not used by the U.S. for the use and benefit of the Washoe Indian Tribe, the land would revert to and become the property of the seller, Mr. and Mrs. W.F. Dressler.

**History.** Before the gold rush days in California and Nevada, the Washoe Indians lived quietly in the valleys and watersheds of the Truckee and Carson Rivers in southwest Nevada, near Lake Tahoe and the Sierra Mountains in California. The advent of the prospectors and settlers diminished the Indians' natural food supply, causing the Indians to expand over a wider area in search of food. In this way, they came to the Washoe Valley in approximately 1860. Land not suitable for agriculture was allotted to them in 1895. A 40-acre tract was purchased for their agricultural use in 1917.

**Culture.** The Washoe Tribe lived in the Nevada and California area, gathering all edible food for subsistence. Their social organization was simple. The scarcity of food and resources forced the people to expend all their energies on survival. Most of their crafts products were designed for practical use, such as the seed-gathering baskets. Today, very few of the people speak their Indian language. Traditional customs and arts and crafts are vitually no longer practiced.

**Government.** The Dresslerville Community Council governs the reservation. It is a sub-council of the Washoe Tribal Council.

**Population Profile. 1969:** Tribal enrollment 153; Indian resident 53; Unemployment 2.4%; Underemployment 60%. **1980:** Indian resident 127; Non-Indian resident 2; Percent Indian of total population 98.4;

Total housing units 57; Occupied housing units 34. Education level: 10 grades. The average education level for this reservation is 10 years of school, an average significantly higher than the State average of 7.7 years. In addition, two members of the tribe are college graduates.

**Tribal Economy.** The tribe has an income of $400 per year which is derived from the interest from the tribal treasury. The tribe owns and operates the ranch, where it grows and harvests hay.

**Climate.** Rainfall averages 7 inches per year. The temperature varies from a high of 95 degrees to a low of 10 degrees.

**Transportation.** Highway No. 395 is a north–south traffic artery through the reservation. Commercial bus and truck service are located in Gardnerville, Nevada, 4 miles from the reservation. To obtain air or train transportation, the residents must drive 60 miles to Reno.

**Community Facilities.** The water and sewer systems on the reservation were installed by the Public Health Service. The reservation is not connected to any commercial gas lines, but electric power is provided by the Sierra Pacific Power Company. Health care for the Washoe Indians is provided in the PHS hospital in Schurz, Nevada, and at a clinic in Gardnerville. Tribal activities are headquartered in two quonset huts used as office space and community center.


DUCK VALLEY RESERVATION                    Federal Reservation
Elko County, Nevada and
Owyhee County, Idaho
Shoshone and Paiute Tribes
Tribal Headquarters: Owyhee, Nevada

**Land Status.** Tribally-owned—Nevada: 144,274 acres. Tribally-owned—Idaho: 145,545 acres. Total area: 289,819 acres. An additional 3,855 acres are Government owned. The reservation is held in tribal trust status. The land is tribally-owned and was never allotted. It may be assigned to members of the Shoshone-Paiute Tribe.

**History.** The Duck Valley Reservation was established by Executive Order in 1877 for the Western Shoshone. In 1886, a group of Paiute, by Governor's order, settled the north side of Duck Valley Reservation. These two groups were combined and organized into one tribe in 1938 under the Indian Reorganization Act. The reservation today, by subsequent Executive Orders, is larger than originally.

**Culture.** There is no group according to cultures, but rather a grouping according to standards of the community. There is a marked difference in home environment, ranging from the poorest to the very well off. Because of mixed marriages, the public school system, and overall acceptance of the non-Indian student, the Indian culture is slowly disappearing and is now almost non-existent.

**Government.** The tribal constitution and bylaws were prepared under the Indian Reorganization Act and approved in April of 1936. The governing body is the business council composed of seven members elected to 3-year terms.

**Population Profile. 1969:** Tribal enrollment 1,200; Indian resident

990. **1980:** Indian resident 932; Non-Indian resident 109; Percent Indian of total population 89.5; Total housing units 354; Occupied housing units 278.

**Tribal Economy.** Average annual tribal income: None. Tribal associations, cooperatives: Cattleman's Association. Commercial/industrial establishments on the reservation: None. There are no minerals on reservation land.

**Climate.** Rainfall averages slightly over 13 inches per year. The temperature ranges from a high of 108 degrees to a low of -34 degrees.

**Transportation.** State Highway Nos. 11 and 51 pass north-south through the reservation. Public transportation and shipping facilities by air, train, truck, and bus are located in Elko, 100 miles from the reservation.

**Utilities.** The water and sewer systems are extended to individuals by the Bureau of Indian Affairs and the Public Health Service. The Idaho Power Company makes electricity available to the reservation. Hospital and health care through PHS can be obtained by the Indians in Owyhee.


DUCKWATER RESERVATION                    Federal Reservation
Nye County
Shoshone Tribe
Tribal Headquarters: Duckwater, Nevada

**Land Status.** Total area: 3,785 acres. A Department of the Interior Proclamation of November 13, 1940, declared the various purchases of 1940 through 1944 to be an Indian reservation for the use and benefit of Shoshone Indians of Duckwater and other Indians of southern Nevada. The land is tribally-owned.

**History.** The original white settlement in the Duckwater Valley was in 1868. The white settlers homesteaded on land which the Shoshone Indians maintained was rightfully theirs. The Shoshone Tribe had lived in this area long before the Europeans settled on the American continent and had developed their own system of recognizing land rights. Most of the Shoshones who lived here are now located in Idaho and the Western Shoshone Duck Valley Reservation in Nevada and Wyoming.

**Culture.** The Shoshone Indians lived in the Great Basin area, traveling in small groups of 25 to 30. Land resources were barely sufficient for the tribes to maintain a subsistence level, while making use of every edible food in the area, such as nuts, roots and berries, and wild game. Social organization was of necessity very simple. The bands were usually an extended kin group led by the oldest able male. Their religion was shamanistic. The majority of the people today still speak their language; however, they retain very little of their traditions.

**Government.** The tribal constitution and bylaws prepared under the authority of the Indian Reorganization Act of 1934 were approved in November 1940. The constitution provides for a governing body, the tribal council composed of five members elected to serve staggered terms.

**Population Profile. 1969:** Tribal enrollment 150. Indian resident 63; Unemployment 18%. **1980:** Indian resident 103; Non-Indian resident 3; Percent Indian of total population 97.2; Total housing units 32; Occupied housing units 29.

**Tribal Economy.** The tribe has no income of its own. It is a member of the Inter-Tribal Council of Nevada, organized by the tribes to promote the development of and opportunities for the reservations in the State. There are no significant resources on the reservation land.

**Climate.** Rainfall averages only 6 inches. The temperature reaches a high of 105 degrees and a low of -10 degrees.

**Transportation.** U.S. Highway No. 20 runs northeast-southwest through the reservation. Ely, some 40 miles from the reservation, is the major location for transportation by air, truck, or bus in the area. The nearest commercial train service is in Elko, 160 miles from the reservation.

**Community Facilities.** All facilities for water supply and waste disposal are individually owned. There are presently no commercial sources of power supplied to the reservation. Health care for the Duckwater Shoshone is provided at the Steptoe Hospital in Ely, Nevada.


ELKO COLONY                                    Federal Reservation
Elko County
Shoshone Tribe
Tribal Headquarters: Elko, Nevada

**Land Status.** Tribal land: 195 acres. Total area: 195 acres. Residents of this colony are the descendants of the Shoshone who selected their allotments near the town of Elko. This reservation was provided for by Executive Order in 1918. As Shoshone Indians, these people may have some right and interest in one or more of the claims filed with the Indian Claims Commission.

**History.** The Indians of Nevada were first encountered by whites in the 1820's. The influx of traders, miners, and settlers began rapidly to restrict the Indians' lifestyle, and by 1850, there was friction between the two groups. After several major battles, the U.S. Government and Nevada tribes signed a series of treaties in 1863. The area was generally peaceful by 1880. Bands of Indians began living near towns such as the group at Elko. The Elko Colony, however, was not established until 1918; an Executive Order designated the land near Elko as an Indian reservation.

**Culture.** These Indians claim to be a segment of Chief Te-Moak's band of Western Shoshone Indians. The Shoshone, who lived in the Great Basin area, have been called the "Digger Indians" because of the way in which they gathered their food. They gathered nuts and berries, dug for roots and other edibles, and hunted small game in an area offering only sparse subsistence. Because food was difficult to obtain, they traveled in small bands of 25 to 30 persons, usually the extended kin group, moving on when they had gleaned all they could from an area. Only simple social organization and basic crafts were developed. Due to the close proximity of the town of Elko, Indian arts and crafts have disappeared. Most Indians still speak their language. The Indians are proud of their heritage although they practice few traditions.

**Government.** Elko Colony is a member of the Te-Moak Western Shoshone Council, a governing body having total jurisdiction over all matters concerning lands of member reservations. The council is an active organization which meets at least monthly. The local councils have retained sovereignty over all matters other than land. The Elko governing body is a council of six members who are elected to 2-year terms.

**Population Profile.** 1969: Indian resident 140.

**Tribal Economy.** The tribe has no income of its own and consequently has no independent projects. The tribe is a member of the Inter-Tribal Council of Nevada, an organization to promote the development of opportunities for Nevada Indian reservations.

**Climate.** The reservation is in an arid climate which averages only 6 inches of rain per year. The temperature ranges from a high of 90 degrees to a low of 10 degrees.

**Transportation.** U.S. Route No. 40 crosses east-west through the reservation. The City of Elko, 2 miles from the colony, is served by commercial, air, train, bus, and trucklines.

**Community Facilities.** The colony is connected with the Elko water and sewer system. The California Pacific Utility Company provides both gas and electricity. Health care for the Indians is available at the Elko General Hospital.


ELY COLONY                                        Federal Reservation
White Pine County
Shoshone Tribe
Tribal Headquarters: Ely, Nevada

**Land Status.** Total area: 9.95 acres. All the land is tribally owned in trust with the U.S. Government. The land was conveyed to the United States in 1931 for the Ely Shoshone Indians. This purchase was made for these Indians since the Indians did not have tribal rights on any established reservation.

**History.** The Shoshone lived as mobile bands in the eastern part of Nevada. When horses became available they adopted a "Plains Indian" lifestyle. The influx of white settlers and prospectors beginning in the 1830's drastically altered their way of life. After some friction with the settlers and the U.S. military, the Shoshone and the U.S. agreed to treaties in 1863, and by 1880, Nevada was peaceful. The Indian bands frequently settled near the new towns and adopted many facets of white culture. Small purchases of land were made for these groups in the late 19th and early 20th Centuries so they could share the Indians' rights to special land privileges and Government services.

**Culture.** The Shoshone were a "Digger Indian" group, traveling in small bands in search of the scarce food in their region, making use of every edible plant and animal. They readily adopted the horse and the Plains culture; they thus had more contact and friction with other tribes than their neighbors, the Paiutes. However, with the settlement of the area, the basis for their living pattern was eliminated, and they were forced to adapt to the new culture. All Indians on this reservation are Shoshone. Most speak the Shoshone language. Some individuals still do traditional craft work.

**Government.** The tribe adopted a constitution and bylaws in 1966 under the Indian Reorganization Act.

**Population Profile.** 1969: Tribal enrollment 150; Indian resident 31; Non-Indian resident 0; Unemployment 16%; Underemployment 16%. 1980: Indian resident 67; Non-Indian resident 11; Percent Indian of total population 85.9; Total housing units 20; Occupied housing units 19.

**Tribal Economy.** The tribe has an annual income of $30.00 from the rental of a building. The tribe is a member of the Inter-Tribal Council of Nevada, an organization formed by the tribes to promote the development of the Nevada reservations.

**Transportation.** Highway No. 50 runs east-west through the reservation. The north-south highway is Nevada No. 6. Commercial air, bus, and truck service are located in Ely, between 1 and 4 miles from residents' homes. Commercial airlines serve Wells, 138 miles from the colony.

**Community Facilities.** The colony is connected with the City of Ely water and sewer system. The city also provides electric power and gas to the colony. The White Pine Hospital in Ely provides medical care for the tribe. The Steptoe Hospital and the Eastern Nevada Medical Center, also in Ely, provide additional medical care. There is a community building on the colony where tribal activities are centered.


FALLON COLONY AND RESERVATION                    Federal Reservation
Churchill County
Paiute-Shoshone Tribe
Tribal Headquarters: Fallon, Nevada

**Land Status.** Tribally owned on reservation: 770 acres. Tribally owned on colony: 60 acres. Allotted on reservation: 4,650 acres. Total area: 5,480 acres. Inheritance to allotted lands is a problem because many heirs may be attached to one lot. As a result, lease, sale, and management of these lands is impeded. The land is held in trust patent for the tribe by the U.S. Government.

**History.** As a result of the General Allotment Act, 196 allotments were made to a band of Paiutes living in the Sink and Stillwater area. In 1906, an agreement was reached between the Bureau of Indian Affairs and the Fallon Indians to trade acreage for water rights. In 1917, 840 acres were added as tribal trust land. After a number of sales and changes, the present reservation acreage was reached. Sixty acres were added in 1917 to establish the Fallon Colony at Rattlesnake Hill.

**Culture.** Before the formation of the reservation, bands of Paiute and Shoshone Indians moved about in small bands utilizing natural foods and game in the area. Crafts that have survived include beadwork, cradleboard making, and some basket weaving. Fishing and hunting are now pursued more for recreation than for necessity.

**Government.** The governing body of the Fallon Paiute-Shoshone Tribe, the Fallon Business Council, consists of five members elected by tribal members. They serve a term of 2 years or until they are replaced. Members elect from within themselves a chairman, vice-chairman, and secretary-treasurer. The constitution and bylaws, approved in 1964, cover the duties and privileges of these members.

**Population Profile.** **1969:** Tribal enrollment 1,200; Indian resident 329; Unemployment 50%; Underemployment 19%. **1980:** Indian resident 304; Non-Indian resident 39; Percent Indian of total population 88.6; Total housing units 154; Occupied housing units 94. The average education level is the 11th grade. There is one college graduate living on the reservation. Adult education classes and training programs sponsored by the Inter-Tribal Council of Nevada offer opportunities to achieve and improve employment.

**Tribal Economy.** The annual average tribal income of $1,000 is derived entirely from lease payments. Tribal associations and cooperatives include Tribal Industries, Inc., Nevada Indian Rodeo Association, and Inter-Tribal Council of Nevada.

**Climate.** Rainfall averages almost 5 inches per year. The temperature varies from a high of 73 degrees to a low of -39 degrees.

**Transportation.** Interstate Highway 80 now crosses east-west through the reservation, and U.S. Highway No. 50 is also an east-west highway. U.S. Highway No. 95 runs north-south. Commercial air and train services are located in Reno, 71 miles from the reservation. Bus and trucklines serve Fallon, 13 miles from the reservation.

**Utilities.** The Sierra Pacific Power Company supplies the water, gas, and electricity to the Fallon Reservation. The sewer system was installed by USPHS. Hospital care is located in Fallon at the Churchill Public Hospital, in Schurz, Nevada, at the Schurz Indian Hospital, and at the Walker River PHS Hospital.

**Recreation.** The tribe's activities such as sports, dances, and dinners are usually held in the community hall or the Senior Citizens Building.


FORT MCDERMITT RESERVATION                Federal Reservation
Humboldt County, Nevada and
Malheur County, Oregon
Paiute and Shoshone Tribes
Tribal Headquarters: McDermitt, Nevada

**Land Status.** Tribally owned—Nevada: 16,381 acres. Tribally owned—Oregon: 18,269 acres. Allotted: 145 acres. Total area: 34,650 acres.

**History.** This reservation was established as a military post in 1867 and abandoned some years later. The site was transferred to the Secretary of the Interior by Executive Order in 1889, making the area public domain land. The Act of August 1, 1890, authorized disposition of this land under the Homestead Law. In 1892, allotments of this land were made to the Indians under the General Allotment Act of 1887.

**Culture.** With the exception of speaking the Paiute language, participation in a distinctly Indian culture is practically non-existent here.

**Government.** The tribe is organized under the Indian Reorganization Act with a constitution and bylaws approved in 1936. The governing body is the tribal council whose eight members are elected to serve 4-year terms.

**Population Profile. 1969:** Enrollment 500; Indian resident 353; Unemployment 43%. **1980:** Indian resident 463; Non-Indian resident 9; Percent Indian of total population 98.1; Total housing units 129; Occupied housing units 95.

**Tribal Economy.** Annual average tribal income: None. The median family income for the reservation is $2,700. There are no tribal associations or industries on the reservation.

**Climate.** Rainfall averages 6 inches per year. The temperature ranges from a July average high of 70 degrees to a January average low of 26 degrees.

**Transportation.** U.S. Highway No. 95 passes in a north-south direction through the reservation. Commercial air and train service are located in Winnemucca, some 75 miles from the reservation. Bus and trucklines serve the reservation.

**Utilities.** The water and sewer systems are tribally operated. Electricity is provided by the Harney Electric Company. The Humboldt General Hospital is located in Winnemucca.

**Recreation.** Tribal activities are held in the reservation community building.


GOSHUTE RESERVATION                          Federal Reservation
White Pine County, Nevada
Juab County, Utah
Goshute Tribe


**Land Status.** Tribal land—Nevada: 70,410.79 acres. Tribal land—Utah: 37,523.52 acres. Allotted land: 80 acres in Utah. Government land: 80 acres in Utah. Total area: 108,094.31 acres. The land for the reservation was acquired by two purchases by the Bureau of Indian Affairs for the tribe.

**Culture.** The population is largely Shoshonean Goshute, however, there are also some Paiute and Bannock living on the reservation. These Indians eked a living from the hostile Great Basin climate by gathering roots and berries and hunting small game. The people traveled in small bands which were usually the extended kin groups as this was all a given area could support. Because of the struggle to survive, the Indians developed only very simple organization and culture.

**Government.** The tribal government is organized according to the Indian Reorganization Act of 1934. The constitution and bylaws were approved in November of 1940 and provide for the Goshute

Business Council to be the governing body. The council's membership is made up of five tribal members who are elected to serve 3-year terms.

**Population Profile. 1969:** Tribal enrollment 200 est.; Indian resident 109; Unemployment 10 persons; Underemployment 20 persons. **1980:** Indian resident 105; Non-Indian resident 0; Percent Indian of total population 100.0; Total housing units 30; Occupied housing units 28. Education level: 7.7 years.

**Tribal Economy.** The tribal income averages $5,500 per year. Much of this income comes from range leases. The topography is typical of the central Nevada and Utah area. The average elevation is 6,000 feet with extremes of 5,400 feet and 11,000 feet. The presence of minerals or other resources on the reservation is unknown.

**Climate.** The climate is moderate here with rainfall averaging 8 inches per year. The temperature varies from a high of 95 degrees to a low of 0 degrees.

**Transportation.** U.S. Highway No. 50 crosses east-west through the reservation. Transportation by train, bus, or truck is available in Wendover, Utah, 75 miles from the reservation. Residents must drive 100 miles to Ely, Nevada, for commercial air transportation.

**Community Facilities.** Water is drawn from individual wells. There are no other utilities on the reservation. For hospital care, residents must go to Ely, Nevada, a drive of 100 miles. There is one community building on the reservation. The tribe schedules an Indian powwow each year.

LAS VEGAS COLONY                          Federal Reservation
Clark County
Paiute Tribe
Tribal Headquarters: Las Vegas, Nevada

**Land Status.** Total area: 10 acres. The land of the colony was purchased in 1911 for the use of the Paiute Indians.

**History.** The Paiute were a peaceful tribe living in Nevada until their way of life was changed by the arrival of the settlers and prospectors during the decades between 1820 and 1850. The Paiute attempted to prevent the influx to retain their old way of life and met with the U.S. military in several battles. By 1880, however, they had recognized the futility of their efforts and tried instead to adapt to the new way of life imposed upon them. Bands of Paiute settled near towns and adopted some of the imported culture. The Government eventually purchased small sections of land for these bands to use as reservations.

**Culture.** The Paiute Indians traveled in small bands, usually the extended kin group. As the food supply was meager, they had to make use of every edible plant and animal, moving on to new areas when one could no longer support them. Because it was necessary to devote almost all their energies to simple survival, the Paiute rarely involved in frictions with other tribes or bands. Their social organization was simple; the bands were led by the oldest able male. Their religion was shamanistic, and the Paiute attributed great importance to dreams and to the powers of the shaman or medicine man. As in most colonies in the State, the manifestations of Indian culture are rarely evident. Arts and crafts are not produced; the traditions are no longer observed. The Paiute have intermarried with Indians of Arizona so very little of the language is spoken.

**Government.** The tribe is organized under their articles of association which were approved in January 1966. The governing body is the colony council formed of three members. The council is supported by the advisory board of four members.

**Population Profile.** **1969:** Tribal enrollment 51; Indian resident 85; Unemployment 19 persons; Underemployment 26 persons. **1980:** Indian resident 106; Non-Indian resident 7; Percent Indian of total population 93.8; Total housing units 25; Occupied housing units 24.

**Tribal Economy.** The tribe as an organization has no income. It is a member of the Inter-Tribal Council of Nevada, an organization formed by the tribes to promote the development of the Nevada reservations. Because of the colony's location in the Las Vegas area, the economic activities of individuals are integrated with the economy of the city.

**Climate.** The Las Vegas area is extremely arid, but popular as a resort and vacation location because of the clear weather it experiences most of the year. The rainfall averages barely over 1 inch per year, and the temperature is usually seasonably warm with extremes of 111 degrees and 15 degrees.

**Transportation.** Interstate 14 and U.S. Highway No. 91 cross Las Vegas northeast-southeast connecting the area with Salt Lake City and Los Angeles. U.S. Highway No. 93 junctions with the Interstate and runs north through Nevada and southeast to Interstate 40 and Phoenix. U.S. Highway No. 95 runs northwest and south of the city. All manner of commercial transportation is available in the City of Las Vegas. Bus, truck, and train stations are no more than 3 miles from the colony, while the airport is 6 miles away.

**Community Facilities.** The colony is connected to the Las Vegas water and sewer infrastructure. The Nevada Power Company provides electricity. Health care for the Paiute of Las Vegas is available at the Southern Nevada Memorial Hospital in Las Vegas and through the District Health Department of Clark County, also in the city. A private doctor runs a clinic in the city which treats the Indian population. The tribe maintains a community building for tribal activities.

**Recreation.** The colony is located in one of the most active cities in the State. Nevada is popular as a resort State, because of the weather and the natural environment and the legalization of gambling.


LOVELOCK COLONY                                    Federal Reservation
Pershing County
Paiute Tribe
Tribal Headquarters: Lovelock, Nevada

**Land Status.** Total area: 20 acres. The entire area of 20 acres is tribal trust land. There are no heirship claims. The entire acreage is used for residential purposes by tribal members.

**History.** The Paiute Tribe was first encountered by white traders in 1825. From that time, whites moved to and through Nevada in increasing numbers until, by the time of the gold rush of 1849 and Nevada's Statehood, the Indian lifestyle was severely inhibited. The Indians expressed their frustration and attempted to regain the past in the Paiute War, which was primarily two battles in 1860-61. This led to a series of treaties with the United States in 1863. The Lovelock Colony was not established until November 1, 1907, when the secretary of the Interior allotted 20 acres for the use of the Lovelock band of Indians.

**Culture.** The Paiute Indians are from the Great Basin cultural group, where the daily life was so taxing that social organization and culture remained simple and uncomplicated. The Indians made use of every edible, including roots, berries, and wild game. They traveled in small bands of about 30 people, moving to new areas when the food where they were became sparse. The strictly Indian culture is no longer extant among them due to their close proximity to the non-Indian community; however, a large portion of the people do speak Paiute.

**Government.** The tribe is organized under the Indian Reorganization Act. The constitution and bylaws were approved in March of 1968. The governing body is the Lovelock Colony Council composed of five members.

**Population Profile. 1969:** Tribal enrollment 150; Indian resident 136; Non-Indian resident 3; Unemployment 35%; Underemployment 20%; Median family income $3,400. **1980:** Indian resident 117; Non-Indian resident 9; Percent Indian of total population 92.9; Total housing units 40; Occupied housing units 37. The average Indian education level for the State is 7.7 years of school. The Lovelock Colony has two graduates.

**Tribal Economy.** The tribe has no income; however, it is a member of the Inter-Tribal Council of Nevada, organized by the tribes to promote the development of the Nevada Indian reservations.

**Climate.** Rainfall averages only 4½ inches per year. The temperature ranges from a high of 68 degrees to a low of 29 degrees.

**Transportation.** A major east-west highway, U.S. No. 40, crosses the reservation. Commercial train, truck, and buslines stop in Lovelock, 1 mile from the colony; however, residents must drive 92 miles to Reno for air transportation.

**Community Facilities.** The colony is a part of the city water and sewer system. Electricity is purchased from the Sierra Pacific Power Company. Health care for tribal members is provided by the Public Health Service in Lovelock. The tribe has a community hall, where sports and social events are scheduled.

MOAPA RESERVATION                          Federal Reservation
Clark County
Paiute Tribe
Tribal Headquarters: Moapa, Nevada

**Land Status.** Total area: 1,174 acres. The present reservation was finalized in 1875 by an Executive Order for the Paiute Indians. Approximately 616 acres were allotted to Indian residents; however, in 1941 all allotted lands were restored to tribal status through relinquishment by the owners. At present, the 1,174 acres are all tribally owned.

**History.** The Paiute lived in Nevada relatively peacefully until their way of life was altered during the decades between 1820 and 1850 by the arrival of settlers and prospectors in increasing numbers. The Paiute attempted to drive the whites out of their area and met them in several skirmishes or battles known as the "Paiute War". There were several treaties in 1863, and most of the friction had disappeared by 1880. The Paiute then adopted some of the customs of the new settlers, and began to live in permanent settlements and learn new ways to provide food and shelter for themselves.

**Culture.** The Paiute had been a peaceful tribe, traveling in small bands searching for food. Because of the meager food supply they made use of all edible plants and animals. Their total attention was put to survival, and they rarely concerned themselves with war. Social organization was necessarily simple, the leader of the band usually being the eldest able male. Religion was shamanistic, and great emphasis was placed on the importance of dreams and the powers of the shaman or medicine man. Today, the Indians on the Moapa Reservation still observe the Indian wake or burial service in conjunction with church services. They do the traditional bead work. A majority of the tribe speak the Paiute language.

**Government.** The tribe adopted a constitution and bylaws in 1942 under the authorization of the Indian Reorganization Act. The constitution provides for the Moapa Business Council as the governing body. The six council members are elected to 3-year terms.

**Population Profile. 1969:** Tribal enrollment 350; Indian resident 73; Unemployment none; Underemployment 23%. **1980:** Indian resident 182; Non-Indian resident 3; Percent Indian of total population 98.4; Total housing units 48; Occupied housing units 43.

**Tribal Economy.** The tribe's income is $5,000 per year from the farming lease. The tribe has formed a farming cooperative.

**Transportation.** Highways Nos. 7 and 15 and U.S. 93 provide north-south transportation facilities. A trainline stops at Moapa, 3 miles from the reservation. Bus and trucklines service Glendale, 7 miles from the reservation. The nearest commercial airlines are located in Las Vegas, a 55-mile drive from the reservation.

**Community Facilities.** The tribe has its own water supply, the Overton Water Company. The tribe also provides septic tanks. Individuals buy bottled gas and obtain electricity from the Overton Power Company. Health care is available in the Public Health Service Hospital in Schurz, Nevada, and the Memorial Hospital in Las Vegas. Clinics are held in

Phoenix, Arizona, by the Public Health Service and in Las Vegas by the Welfare Department. The tribe has one community building where tribal activities take place.

PYRAMID LAKE RESERVATION        Federal Reservation
Washoe County
Paiute Tribe
Tribal Headquarters: Nixon, Nevada

**Land Status.** Tribally owned: 475,085.55 acres. Total area: 475,085.55 acres. The reservation is in trust status with the U.S. Government. Several lots in the township of Wadsworth and several ranches within the boundaries of the reservation are owned in fee by non-Indians. Pyramid Lake lies in the center of the reservation.

**History.** The reservation was created by Executive Order of 1874 for Paiute and other Indians residing there. The tribe is incorporated and owns the land. The Paiute never signed a treaty with the United States.

**Culture.** As most of the school children attend public schools away from the reservation, there is a resulting drift away from the old Indian culture. About the only remaining facets of Indian culture are the small amount of beadwork being done by a few and the native tongue spoken by the majority of residents.

**Government.** The tribe is organized under the Indian Reorganization Act with a constitution and bylaws approved in 1936. The Pyramid Lake Paiute Tribal Council is the governing body and performs the minor administrative functions of the tribe. It is composed of 10 members.

**Population Profile. 1969:** Tribal enrollment 399; Indian resident 900; Unemployment 24%. Underemployment 74%. **1980:** Indian resident 720; Non-Indian resident 133; Percent Indian of total population 84.4; Total housing units 351; Occupied housing units 251. There are two college graduates on the reservation. Schools on the reservation are for grades one through six. Students must attend schools in nearby cities for junior high and high school.

**Tribal Economy.** Average annual tribal income: $47,700.00. One community developer works for the tribe. Tribal associations, cooperatives, etc.: Cattlemen's Association, General Store, and Pyramid Lake Arts and Crafts. Commercial/industrial establishments on the reservation: One combination trading post and service station is owned by an Indian. No known mineral deposits are to be found on the reservation.

**Climate.** Rainfall averages 7 inches per year. The temperature ranges from a high of 92 degrees to a low of 31 degrees.

**Transportation.** State Highways 33 and 34 run along the west and east sides of the reservation to connect with Interstate 80, a major east-west highway. All kinds of commercial transportation are available in Reno, 40 miles from the reservation.

**Utilities.** The water system is operated by the tribe. Electricity is provided by the Sierra Pacific Power Company. Hospital care is available to Pyramid Lake residents at the USPHS Hospital in Schurz, Nevada. Tribal members may also contract for medical care through the USPHS in Sparks. Monthly clinics are held on the reservation.

**Recreation.** The tribe organizes various sports in the tribal gym and community hall. Pyramid Lake, from which the reservation derives its name, has been a major recreation attraction for tourists; however, the water level is being lowered to supply water to California and Nevada. Unless a pending tribal suit is successful, the lake will be lost as an important resource for the recreation and fishing industries.

RENO-SPARKS INDIAN COLONY                    Federal Reservation
Washoe County
Washoe-Paiute Tribe
Tribal Headquarters: Reno-Sparks, Nevada

**Land Status.** Tribally-owned: 28.8 acres. Total area: 28.8 acres. The entire acreage is pending deed held in trust for the tribe by the U.S. Government. The water rights for the reservation have been lost. The land is divided into small lots assigned to individual members.

**History.** The U.S. Government, through the Bureau of Indian Affairs, set aside this purchased tract for displaced Nevada Indians in 1917. In 1924, an additional 8.8 acres were added to the original 20 acres. The reservation is now almost entirely surrounded by various types of industry.

**Culture.** Indian arts and crafts have diminished to practically nothing. The Indian languages are spoken by a few of the older people; however, most of the younger members speak only English. Customs and traditions have all but vanished.

**Government.** The colony is organized under the Indian Reorganization Act. The constitution and bylaws, approved in 1936, provide for a six-member Reno-Sparks Indian Council. Members serve for a 2-year term.

**Population Profile. 1969:** Tribal enrollment 537; Indian resident 533; Non-Indian resident 4; Unemployment 18%; Underemployment 36%. **1980:** Indian resident 451; Non-Indian resident 12; Percent Indian of total population 97.4; Total housing units 137; Occupied housing units 125. At present, one member is a college graduate. Vocational training is available through Manpower Training and Mutual Self-Help Housing.

**Tribal Economy.** Annual average tribal income: $400.00. This income is derived entirely from rental of office space. Tribal associations, cooperatives: Headstart, Mutual Self-Help Housing, and Park Committee. Commercial/industrial establishments on the reservation: None. No minerals are to be found on the reservation.

**Climate.** Rainfall averages 7.5 inches per year. The temperature ranges from 100 degrees to 0 degrees.

**Transportation.** U.S. Highway No. 40 passes east-west through the colony. U.S. Highway No. 395 is a north-south highway. All means of commercial transportation are readily available in Reno, 1 mile or less from the reservation.

**Utilities.** All public utilities on the reservation are provided by the Sierra Pacific Power Company. Health care for Indian residents is available in the Washoe Medical Center in Reno. Additional contract medical care in Reno is arranged by the USPHS.

**Recreation.** Colony activities are centered in the community building, built under the Community Action Program. Additional recreation is readily at hand in Reno.


SOUTH FORK RESERVATION                    Federal Reservation
Elko County
Shoshone Tribe
Tribal Headquarters: Lee, Nevada

**Land Status.** Total area: 15,156 acres. This reservation was established by Executive Order in 1941 under the Indian Reorganization Act. Approximately 9,500 acres of land purchased in 1938 and 1939 in connection with the land acquisition program were proclaimed as an Indian reservation for the use of the Te-Moak bands of Western Shoshone Indians. Subsequent land purchases have been added to the reservation. All land is tribally owned.

**Culture.** The Shoshone have been called the "Digger Indians" because of the way in which they gathered their food. The Utah and Nevada Great Basin area where they lived offered only a sparse subsistence. The Indians gathered nuts and berries, dug for roots and other edibles, and hunted small game. Because food was difficult to obtain, they traveled in small bands of 25 to 30 people, usually the extended kin group, moving from a new area when they had gleaned all they could where they were. Only simple social organization and basic arts were developed. Very little of the Indian arts and crafts are practiced on the reservation today. The language is, however, still spoken by most.

**Government.** The South Fork Reservation together with the Elko Colony formed the Te-Moak Western Shoshone Council, a governing body for the Te-Moak Western Shoshone bands having total jurisdiction over all matters concerning land. The local councils retain sovereignty over all matters. The Te-Moak Western Shoshone Council is an active organization which meets monthly. The South Fork Community Council, a sub-council of the Te-Moak Western Shoshone Council is the local government for the South Fork Reservation. Six tribal members are elected to serve 2-year terms.

**Population Profile. 1969:** Population 102; Unemployment 12%; Underemployment 42%. Education level: 7.7 years.

**Tribal Economy.** The tribe has no income and, as a result, sponsors no economic activities. It is a member of the Inter-Tribal Council of Nevada and through this organization, is making efforts to improve the economy of the reservation.

**Climate.** The climate in this area is typical of central Nevada and Utah. It is relatively dry, averaging only 6 inches of rain each year. The temperature is usually seasonable with a high of 90 degrees in the summer and a low of 15 degrees in the winter.

**Transportation.** U.S. Highway No. 40 crosses east-west through the reservation. The City of Elko, 28 miles from the reservation, is served by commercial transportation lines by air, bus, train, and truck.

**Community Facilities.** Residents provide their own water and sewer facilities. Health care is available at the Elko General Hospital and at the PHS clinic, also in Elko. There is one community building on the reservation.


SUMMIT LAKE RESERVATION                    Federal Reservation
Humboldt County
Paiute Tribe
Tribal Headquarters: None

**Land Status.** Tribally owned: 9,741.33 acres. Allotted: 764.94 acres. Total area: 10,506.27 acres. All the land is in tribal trust with the exception of three allotments outside of the west boundary of the reservation.

**History.** The old Camp McGarry Military Reserve was a part of this reservation. The land for this reservation was withdrawn from entry, sale, or other disposition by Executive Order in 1913 and set aside for the Paiute, Shoshone, and such other Indians as the Secretary of the Interior might settle thereon. The Paiute Tribe has never concluded a treaty with the U.S. Government.

**Culture.** There is very little, if any, evidence of clinging to, or desire to retain, the Indian culture. At present, as there is only one tribal member living permanently on the reservation, tribal organization and culture can have little function.

**Government.** The tribe is organized under the Indian Reorganization Act. The constitution and bylaws were approved in 1965. These provide for a tribal council of five members elected to serve a 3-year term.

**Population Profile. 1969:** Tribal enrollment 50; Indian resident 1. **1980:** Indian resident 15; Non-Indian resident 0; Percent Indian of total population 100.0; Total housing units 7; Occupied housing units 7.

**Tribal Economy.** Tribal economy is limited to funds received for grazing rights. There are no cooperatives, tribal organizations, or industries on the reservation. There are no exploitable minerals on the reservation.

**Climate.** Rainfall averages 10 inches per year. The temperature ranges from 70 degrees to 25 degrees.

**Transportation.** There are no State or U.S. highways crossing the reservation. Air service is 75 miles from the reservation. Commercial train, truck, and buslines serve Alturas, California, 100 miles from the reservation.

**Utilities.** There are no provisions for water, sewage, or power on the reservation. For health care, the Paiute can go to a hospital in Cedarville, California, a USPHS clinic in Fort McDermitt, or to Winnemucca for individual health care.

WALKER RIVER RESERVATION
Churchill, Lyon, and Mineral Counties
Paiute Tribe
Tribal Headquarters: Schurz, Nevada

Federal Reservation

**Land Status.** Tribally-owned land: 310,757 acres. Allotted land: 8,789.62 acres. Government land: 964.23 acres. Total area: 320,510.85 acres.

**History.** On November 25, 1859, Agent Dodge recommended the establishment of a reservation for the Indians in the vicinity of Walker River. Subsequently, by Executive Order of March 19, 1871, land was set aside for Paiute Indians. Various resolutions following the original Executive Order changed the land status of Walker River to its present area.

**Culture.** The distinctly Indian culture has all but disappeared from the everyday lives of the members of this tribe. They all speak English and very few of the older members cannot read or write. Few among the younger generation speak their Indian language.

**Government.** The tribe drew up a constitution according to the Indian Reorganization Act of 1934. Both constitution and bylaws were approved in March 1937. The constitution established the Walker River Paiute Tribal Council as the governing body for the tribe.

**Population Profile. 1969:** 1,000 est.; Indian resident 375; Unemployment 43 persons; Underemployment 40 persons. **1980:** Indian resident 471; Non-Indian resident 100; Percent Indian of total population 82.5; Total housing units 201; Occupied housing 177. Children attend the public school at Schurz. There is one college graduate in the tribe.

**Tribal Economy.** The tribe has an income of approximately $30,000 per year. Tribal members have formed a Cattlemen's Association. The tribe owns "Clines," a bar, service station, and motel combination. There are large iron ore deposits on the reservation which are not currently being mined.

**Climate.** Walker River lies in the western part of Nevada. Rainfall averages 5.68 inches annually and temperatures reach a high of 100 degrees and a low of -24 degrees.

**Transportation.** The reservation lies along the major north-south highway, U.S. No. 95. Reno, 100 miles from the reservation, is served by commercial train and airline companies. The nearest bus and trucklines stop in Schurz.

**Community Facilities.** The tribe operates a water and sewer system which serves most of the reservation. Those individuals not served by the tribe provide their own facilities. The Walker River Public Health Service extends medical care to tribal members at the hospital in Schurz. The gym and tribal building is the focus of tribal business and recreational activities.

WINNEMUCCA COLONY                              Federal Reservation
Humboldt County
Paiute Tribe
Tribal Headquarters: Winnemucca, Nevada

**Land Status.** Total area: 340 acres. All land is tribal. The title to the land is held by the United States, subject, however, to right-of-way for water supply pipelines and for any and all existing and lawfully established county roads.

**History.** The Indians of Nevada were first encountered by whites in the 1820's. Whites began rapidly to affect the Indians' lifestyle, and by the 1850's, with the gold rush and Statehood, there was a great deal of friction between the two groups. The Paiute War, two battles in the early 1860's, and the extension of United States authority over the land resulted in the treaty settlements of 1863. The Winnemucca colony was not established until 1917 when an Executive Order set aside lands for homeless Shoshone Indians. An Act of May 21, 1928, authorized the purchase of land in the vicinity of Winnemucca to be used as an Indian colony but did not specify a tribe.

**Culture.** The colony originally consisted mainly of Shoshone Indians, but now there are very few. The majority are Paiute from the Fort McDermitt Reservation. Most speak their language, but Indian arts, crafts, and traditions are almost non-existent. These Indians are from the Great Basin cultural group, also known as the "Digger Indians". They were able to live only at a subsistence level, digging for roots and other edibles in an area of scanty food supply. They traveled in small groups as the food supply in a given area was not sufficient to supply more than an extended kin group. Of necessity, social organization and culture were simple.

**Government.** The tribe is informally organized and is governed by a general council and a spokesman. The council meets monthly.

**Population Profile.** **1969:** Tribal enrollment 30; Indian resident 30; Median family income $2,830. **1980:** Indian resident 35; Non-Indian resident 2; Percent Indian of total population 94.6; Total housing units 15; Occupied housing units 11.

**Tribal Economy.** The tribe has no income of its own. It is a member of the Inter-Tribal Council of Nevada, an organization formed by the tribes to promote the development of opportunities for the Indian reservations of Nevada.

**Climate.** In this arid region, the rainfall averages 6 inches per year. The temperature ranges from a high of 90 degrees to a low of 15 degrees.

**Transportation.** A major east-west highway, U.S. No. 40, passes through the reservation. Commercial train, bus, and trucklines serve the community of Winnemucca, 1 mile from the colony. The nearest commercial air service is located in Elko, Nevada, 130 miles from the colony.

**Community Facilities.** The colony is a part of the city water and sewer system and purchases electricity from the Winnemucca Light and Power Company. Health care through clinics is available in Winnemucca and at the Elko General Hospital.

YERINGTON RESERVATION AND COLONY          Federal Reservation
Lyon County
Paiute Tribe
Tribal Headquarters: Campbell Ranch, Nevada

**Land Status.** Reservation land: 1,156 acres. Colony area: 10 acres. Total area: 1,166 acres. All this land is tribally owned. Assignments are made on the reservation. Land purchases for the reservation were made in 1936 and 1941. The reservation land was originally a part of the Campbell Ranch. Land within the city limits of Yerington was purchased for non-reservation Indians in 1917 and is now the Yerington Colony. The colony was recently placed in trust status.

**History.** The Paiute bands had been living in the Nevada area long before America was "discovered" by Columbus. Their way of life, very basic in adjustment to the harsh environment, was not interrupted until the decades between 1820 and 1850 when white settlers and prospectors came to Nevada in great numbers. White settlers began using the land for agriculture, eliminating a large part of the scanty food supply for the Paiute, and owning it in a manner completely foreign to the Paiute system of land "ownership." The Paiute Wars, climaxing in 1860 and 1861, were the Indians' attempt to protest the change and regain their former lifestyle. The treaty agreements in 1863 eventually brought peace as the Paiute recognized they could not keep whites out. By 1880, the entire State was in relative peace.

**Culture.** Because of the scarcity of food, the Paiute traveled in small bands gathering every edible food available such as roots, nuts and berries, and wild game. Social organization was, of necessity, simple, the group usually being an extended kin group led by the oldest able male. Few Paiute on the Yerington Reservation speak their language today, and very little of the Indian heritage and arts and crafts is retained.

**Government.** The    constitution and bylaws for the tribe were approved in 1937. The constitution provides for a Yerington Paiute Tribal Council of seven members which governs the tribe.

**Population Profile. 1969:** Tribal enrollment 196; Indian resident 198; Non-Indian resident 3; Unemployment 18%; Underemployment 50%. **1980:** Indian resident 105; Non-Indian resident 316; Percent Indian of total population 24.9. Total housing units 155; Occupied housing units 146.

**Tribal Economy.** The tribe has no income of its own. It is a member of the Inter-Tribal Council of Nevada, an organization formed by the tribes to promote the development of the reservations in the State.

**Climate.** Rainfall measures about 7 inches annually. The average high temperature is 70.5 degrees, and the average low is 30 degrees.

**Transportation.** U.S. alternate route 95 with access to U.S. Highways Nos. 95 and 50 and Nevada Route No. 3 provides highway transportation in all directions. Commercial bus and trucklines stop in Yerington, 3 miles from the reservation. For commercial air and train service, residents must drive 82 miles to Reno, Nevada.

**Community Facilities.** The colony is connected to the city water and sewer systems while the Campbell Ranch has a local water system.

The Sierra Pacific Power Company provides electricity to both the colony and ranch. Individuals provide their own gas. Health care for the Indians is available through the Public Health Service at Schurz, Nevada, and at the Lyon Health Center in Schurz by contract with private doctors.

YOMBA RESERVATION                          Federal Reservation
Lander County
Shoshone Tribe
Tribal Headquarters: Austin, Nevada

**Land Status.** Total area: 4,682 acres. The reservation is composed of several old ranches and interspersed with non-Indian ranches. A dam constructed by the Bureau of Indian Affairs is a water source for irrigation. The lands are good for hay and grazing.

**History.** The Western Shoshone Indians originally roamed over parts of Idaho, Utah, Nevada, and California, constantly searching for food. With the coming of prospectors and settlers, trouble broke out among the Indians and whites. Military forces were sent to restore peace and order. Several Shoshone groups of Indians refused to move to lands set aside for them in the peace treaties of 1863. One of these groups was still living in the headwaters of the Reese River when lands in that area were purchased for their use in 1937.

**Culture.** The Shoshone Tribes lived in the Great Basin area where they eked out a living from scanty resources. They traveled in small bands and gathered as food every available edible, moving on to new areas when food was too scarce. Social organization was, of necessity, simple, the group being led usually by the oldest able male. Though the Indians on the reservation still retain their Indian heritage and speak their language, Indian arts and crafts are not practiced to any great extent today.

**Government.** The tribe's constitution and bylaws were approved December 20, 1939, under the authority of the Indian Reorganization Act. The Yomba Tribal Council, the governing body, has a membership of six, two members elected each year to serve 3-year terms.

**Population Profile. 1969:** Tribal enrollment 100 est.; Indian resident 61; Unemployment 36%; Underemployment seasonal. **1980:** Indian resident 57; Non-Indian resident 3; Percent Indian of total population 95.0; Total housing units 29; Occupied housing units 15. The average Indian education level for the State as a whole is 7.7 years of school. There are two college graduates in the tribe.

**Tribal Economy.** The tribe has no income of its own. It is a member of the Inter-Tribal Council of Nevada, an organization formed by the tribes to promote the development of the Nevada Indian reservations.

**Transportation.** U.S. Highway No. 50 is the major transportation artery for the reservation, running east-west. Commercial air and train service are available in Reno, 180 miles from Yomba. Bus and trucklines are more conveniently located in Austin, 35 miles from the reservation.

**Community Facilities.** There are no community facilities for water and waste disposal. Residents must provide their own water and septic tanks. Health care for tribal members is available in Fallon at the Fallon Clinic and the Churchill Public Hospital. There is a community building on the reservation.

# NEW MEXICO

ACOMA PUEBLO                                    Federal Reservation
Valencia County
Keresan Tribe
Tribal Headquarters: Acoma Pueblo, New Mexico

**Land Status.** Tribal land: 245,346 acres. Allotted land: 320 acres. Non-Indian land: 5.29 acres. Total area: 245,672 acres. The original Spanish land grant to the Pueblo of Acoma was made on September 20, 1689. Upon the recommendations of the Surveyor General, in his report of September 30, 1856, the Congress of the U.S. confirmed the grant to the Pueblo by the Act of December 22, 1858. A patent covering this grant was issued to the Pueblo by President Hayes on November 19, 1877.

**History.** The Acomas originally inhabited the "Enchanted Mesa"; however, during a storm the only access path was destroyed. Tribal members who were not on the mesa at the time settled on a neighboring mesa. The Acoma Pueblo is regularly referred to as the "Sky City," because of its location on top of a 350-foot-high mesa. Acoma vies with Oraibi, a Hopi village for the title of oldest continually inhabited city in the U.S. From pottery shards found at Acoma, it has been determined that this site has been occupied for at least 1,000 years. It is mentioned as early as 1539 by Fray Marcos de Niza and was first visited by Coronado's army in 1540. The Acoma, together with most of the Pueblos, joined in the Pueblo Revolt of 1680. Because of the inaccessibility of Acoma, the residents were not severely dealt with by the Spaniards. The principal feast day is September 2 in honor of St. Stephen.

**Culture.** The native religion is still very influential and powerful and continues to play a significant role in the overall behavior of the Acoma Indians. Acoma are members of the western group of Keresan linguistic stock. The Keresan language is still widely spoken; however, English is becoming more common, especially among the younger generation. The Acoma, like other Pueblo, are strongly communal; however, with increasing exposure to the white man's world, some of them are beginning to move away from the village to the outskirts.

**Government.** Originally, the government of Acoma was controlled by the caciques. The various functions of government, such as war and peace, witchcraft, hunting, husbandry, and the like, were regulated by representatives of the societies that pertained to that particular activity. However, with the advent of Spanish influence, the form of government was changed by establishment of a kind of elective system, and the control of strictly civil affairs was put in the hands of a governor, one or more lieutenant governors and a council.

**Population Profile.** 1969: Tribal enrollment 2,512; Indian resident 1,920; Unemployment 28%. **1980:** Indian resident 2,268; Non-Indian resident 91; Percent Indian of total population 96.1; Total housing units 763; Occupied housing units 480. The local school system includes two Federally-supported schools in Acomita and McCartys. Pupils in junior and senior high attend the school on the adjoining Laguna Reservation or the Santa Fe or Albuquerque Indian Schools. The education level for the reservation as a whole is 5th grade. There are six college graduates in the tribe.

**Reservation Economy.** There are three small grocery–confectionery commercial establishments on the reservation owned and operated by the Acoma. There are also small roadside businesses along U.S. Highway No. 66. Major shopping centers are located in Grants, 15 miles west, and Albuquerque, 65 miles east. Deposits of clay, obsidian, and coal on the reservation are being exploited. Additional mineral deposits include building stone, lava, and limestone, but these are not presently quarried.

**Climate.** Rainfall averages 10 to 12 inches annually. The temperature ranges from a high of 97 degrees to a low of 0 degrees.

**Transportation.** Interstate 40–U.S. Route No. 66 passes through the reservation as the major east-west highway connecting the reservation with Albuquerque, Grants, and Gallup, N.M. The nearest regularly scheduled commercial airlines and trucklines serve Albuquerque, 65 miles from Acoma. Several bus, truck, and trainlines serve the reservation directly.

**Community Facilities.** The tribe's only water supply is from wells at Acomita and McCartys. Bottled gas is available. Electricity is purchased from the Continental Divide Cooperative Association. Hospital care for the Acomas is provided at the Bernalillo County Indian Hospital in Albuquerque and at a weekly PHS clinic at the Laguna Pueblo. The community building is used for OEO–Community Action Program offices and council meetings, and the second community building is used for religious activities only.

**Recreation.** Acoma is a popular tourist attraction. The pueblo itself, one of the two oldest in this country, is beautifully situated on the mesa overlooking the fields surrounding it. The very old Spanish mission is widely known for its beauty and historic interest. Tribal members guide visitors on a tour of the pueblo.

ALAMO RESERVATION                    Federal Reservation
McKinley and Valencia Counties
Navajo Tribe
Tribal Headquarters: Window Rock, Arizona

**Land Status.** Tribal land: 43,335 acres. Allotted land: 19,774 acres. Total area: 63,109 acres.

**History.** The Navajo migrated to the southwest in wandering bands and settled in northern New Mexico during the 1500's. Within two centuries, they had spread over a large part of the Plateau country. From the time the United States acquired this country in 1848, there was a great deal of friction between the Navajo and the U.S. Army. Because they lived in small bands in isolated areas and were relatively nomadic, the Navajo were difficult to subdue; however, in 1863, they were rounded up and sent to Fort Sumner. Here they were to be taught the skills and advantages of sedentary life. In 1868, recognizing the failure of this experiment, the Government concluded a treaty with the tribe which established the Navajo Reservation. The present Alamo Reservation was founded by Navajo who settled there rather than continue the march to the main reservation.

**Culture.** The Navajo are members of the Athapascan linguistic family. They call themselves "Dineh," or "The People." The Navajo, always quick to adopt from other cultures, learned many new ways from the Pueblos among whom they lived. They learned to grow cotton, adopted the Pueblo loom, and developed a distinctive weaving technique. From the Spanish they acquired horses, sheep and wool, and, later, silversmithing. Navajo religion, always primarily concerned with maintaining harmony with nature, includes many adaptations of Pueblo ceremonials and rituals.

**Government.** The Navajo Tribe is governed by a council consisting of 74 members representing the 96 chapters which make up the reservation. This includes the Alamo, Canoncito, and Ramah Reservations as well as the Eastern Administrative Area. All programs and projects are processed through the advisory committee before being submitted to the council. Chapter approval is required before the tribe can utilize any land within the chapter's boundaries. The popularly elected tribal chairman is the administrative head of the tribe.

**Population Profile.** **1969:** Indian resident 1,030;  Unemployment 60%. **1980:** Indian resident 1,062; Non–Indian resident 10; Percent Indian of total population 99.1; Total housing units 214; Occupied housing units 211. The tribal enrollment and many of the population statistics are included with the Navajo tribal statistics and are not separate for this reservation.

**Tribal Economy.** The tribal income for this reservation alone is minimal; however, it is included as a part of the main Navajo Reservation and has access to that treasury. Alamo's economy is much like that of any other chapter within the Navajo Reservation.

**Transportation.** The Alamo Reservation lies just north of U.S. Highway No. 60, which runs in an east-west direction. Socorro, 30 miles from Alamo, is the nearest commercial center. Bus and trucklines service are available here. For air and train service, the Alamo residents must travel 110 miles to Albuquerque, New Mexico.

**Community Facilities.** The Public Health Service has provided for the wells from which the residents obtain their water. Septic tanks are the only provision for waste disposal. The PHS Hospital in Albuquerque provides medical care for these Navajo. There is also a private hospital in Socorro.

CANONCITO RESERVATION                    Federal Reservation
Bernalillo and Valencia Counties
Navajo Tribe
Tribal Headquarters: Canoncito, New Mexico

**Land Status.** Tribal land: 68,144 acres. Government land: 40 acres. Allotted land: 8,629 acres. Total area: 76,813 acres.

**History.** The Navajo migrated to the southwest in wandering bands and settled in northern New Mexico during the 1500's. Within two centuries they had spread over a large part of the Plateau country. From the time the United States acquired this area in 1848, there was a great deal of friction between the Navajo and the U.S. Army. Because they lived in small bands in isolated areas and were relatively nomadic, the Navajo were difficult to subdue. However, they were rounded up in 1863 and sent to Fort Sumner where they would be taught the skills and advantages of sedentary agricultural life. In 1868, recognizing the failure of this experiment, the government concluded a treaty with the tribe which established the Navajo Reservation. The present Canoncito Reservation was founded by Navajo who settled there rather than continue the march to the Navajo Reservation.

**Culture.** The Navajo are members of the Athapascan linguistic family. They call themselves "Dineh" or "The People." The Navajo, always quick to adopt from other cultures, learned many new customs from the Pueblo Indians, among whom they lived. They learned to grow cotton, adopted the Pueblo loom, and developed a distinctive weaving technique. From the Spanish they acquired horses, sheep and wool, and, later, silversmithing. Navajo religion, always primarily concerned with maintaining harmony with nature, includes many adaptations of Pueblo ceremonials and rituals.

**Government.** The Navajo Tribe is governed by a council consisting of 74 members representing the 96 chapters which make up the reservation in New Mexico as well as the Eastern Administrative Advisory Area. All programs and projects are processed through the advisory committee before submission to the Council. The popularly elected tribal chairman is administrative head of the tribe. District approval is required before the tribe can utilize any land within the chapter boundaries.

**Population Profile.** **1969:** Indian resident 740; Unemployment 50%. **1980:** Indian resident 969; Non-Indian resident 9; Percent Indian of total population 99.1; Total housing units 219; Occupied housing units 218. The tribal enrollment and most of the population statistics are not separate for the Canoncito Reservation but are included with those for Navajo.

**Tribal Economy.** The Canoncito chapter annual income is $1,500, which is the revenue from a land lease. This represents the income for this area only. As part of the Navajo tribe, the Canoncito area shares the Navajo tribal income, which is largely the revenue from resource sales. Although physically separate, Canoncito economy is much like that of any other chapter within the Navajo Reservation.

**Transportation.** The Canoncito Reservation lies just north of Interstate 40, which runs west to Grants and Gallup and east to Albuquerque.

Albuquerque, which lies 30 miles east of Canoncito, is a major transportation hub for central New Mexico. All forms of commercial transportation are available there.
**Community Facilities.** Water for the reservation residents is drawn from wells. The Southern Union Gas provides gas and the New Mexico Public Service Company provides electricity to the reservation. The PHS hospital in Albuquerque provides medical care and hospitalization to tribal members.


COCHITI PUEBLO                                    Federal Reservation
Sandoval County
Keresan Tribe
Tribal Headquarters: Cochiti Pueblo, New Mexico

**Land Status.** Tribally-owned land: 28,776 acres. Government land: 3 acres. Total area: 28,779 acres. There is no individually-owned land; however, the Cochiti members are permitted use of land for residential and agricultural purposes as long as the land is used productively.
**History.** The Cochiti moved to the present location from areas generally north of the village including Frijoles Canyon, which is now Bandelier National Monument. Ruins of Cochiti villages can be found in nearby areas including the top of the Cochiti Mesa, an area accessible only by foot. Spanish explorers first visited the Pueblo in 1540 and named it Mediana de Torre. Because Cochiti lay west of the Rio Grande away from the main routes, it was not visited often by the Spanish until after 1581.
**Culture.** Cochiti culture is presently a mixture of Spanish, Anglo, and Cochiti. The traditional culture continues to be predominant although increasingly affected by the Anglo culture. Most of the Indians are tri-lingual, speaking their native Keresan, Spanish, and English. Traditional daily attire is worn primarily by the older people; however, there is a strong current of revival of the old ways, which includes wearing traditional cloth, practicing the native religion, and participating in the "secret dances" and the activities of the medicine men.
**Government.** Cochiti has two forms of government, the traditional Indian form, and the system as introduced by the white man. The dual form of government has continued to the present day. A governor, who is appointed to his office by the traditional leader, heads the civil government. The traditional government continues to dominate in power and influence while the secular offices are primarily perfunctory.
**Population Profile.** 1969: Tribal enrollment 700; Indian resident 490; Non-Indian resident 60; Unemployment 30%; Underemployment 40%. **1980:** Indian resident 613; Non-Indian resident 226; Percent Indian of total population 73.1; Total housing units 319; Occupied housing units 254. The average tribal education level is 9th grade. The new Cochiti Elementary School is a part of the Sandoval County School System. There are no other educational or vocational training facilities on the reservation. Thirteen tribal members are college graduates.
**Tribal Economy.** The tribal annual income of $10,000 is largely

lease monies. The remaining 10 percent is earned through farming. The tribe has formed both a farm cooperative and a ranching cooperative. Cochiti has also formed a development committee. Until recently there were two grocery stores in the village, both owned by Spaniards. One closed at the death of the owner. The $30 million dam currently under construction 2 miles north of the village should attract and support a much greater level of economic activity. The Cochiti Development Company is actively working to take full advantage of this opportunity. Minerals currently being mined include turquois, gypsum, and clay. There are also pumice deposits on the reservation.

**Climate.** Chochiti is set in the mountains west of the Rio Grande. Temperatures vary with the seasons, reaching a high of 98 degrees in the summer and a low of -12 degrees in the winter.

**Transportation.** State Highway No. 22 crosses the southeast corner of the reservation. A train stops in Domingo, 7 miles from Cochiti. Santa Fe, which lies 30 miles to the north, is served by commercial air, bus, and trucklines.

**Community Facilities.** Cochiti has its own water system and sewage facilities provided by PHS. Gas is available from the Cotton Butane Company of Santa Fe. Electricity is supplied by the New Mexico Public Service Company. Hospitalization and medical care are offered at the PHS hospital in Santa Fe and the Bernalillo County Indian Hospital in Albuquerque. A clinic sponsored by PHS is held at the Santo Domingo Pueblo. Two community buildings are used for meetings and court proceedings. Two kivas are used for ceremonial purposes, one being for each clan.

**Recreation.** The tribe's annual fiesta on July 14 is open to the public. There are many community events, especially during the Christmas holidays. In addition to these, there are numerous activities which are kept closed to and secret from non-Indians.


ISLETA PUEBLO                              Federal Reservation
Bernalillo and Valencia Counties
Isleta Tribe
Tribal Headquarters: Isleta, New Mexico

**Land Status.** Tribally-owned land: 210,937 acres. Non-Indian land: 11 acres. Total area: 210,948 acres. The U.S. Congress, recognizing the Spanish land grant to Isleta, confirmed the grant in 1858. President Lincoln issued a patent covering the grant of 109,464 acres in 1864. Further grants, purchases, exchanges, and awards have increased the reservation to its present area. The governor assigns land to individuals or families for use. Disputes are settled in tribal court.

**History.** The original pueblo was located at the site of the present pueblo when Coronado visited the area in 1540. The Spanish established the Mission of San Antonio de Isleta by 1613. Plains Indian raids caused the Pueblo Indians living east of the Manzano Mountains to move to Isleta around 1675. The Isleta Pueblo did not actively participate in the Pueblo Revolt against the Spanish in 1680 and became a refuge for Spanish settlers. In spite of this, Governor Otermin captured the Pueblo in 1681 and took four or five hundred prisoners with him to El Paso where they settled at Ysleta. The remaining population abandoned Isleta and fled to Hopi country. They returned in 1716 bringing their Hopi relatives with them. The present pueblo was built around 1709 by scattered Tigua families. Most of the Hopi later returned to Arizona but have retained their ties to the Isleta. Acoma and Laguna migrated to Isleta in the early 1800's becaue of drought and religious differences at their home pueblos. Isleta has incorporated a variety of pueblo people.

**Culture.** Isleta is one of the New Mexico pueblos and demonstrates many similarities to the others. Their contacts with Acoma, Laguna, and Hopi maximize these similarities. Agriculture was the primary means of livelihood. The Isleta irrigated their fields with water from the Rio Grande centuries before the arrival of the Spanish. The principal crop was corn. They lived in adobe houses of square architecture complementing the natural setting. These houses were grouped around the central plaza. The kiva, near the plaza, was the ceremonial building. The tribal clans, divided into the summer and winter moeties, are matrilineal and exogamous. The Spanish influenced the Isleta lifestyle, and the new religion was in some ways incorporated into the traditional religion. The native tongue and religion continue to shape behavior and philosophy. Many traditional activities remain an integral part of Isleta life. Isleta are known for the excellent pottery and cloth they produce.

**Government.** The Isleta Tribe's sovereignty was recognized by President Lincoln who presented the governor with a silver-headed cane in 1863 as a symbol of the tribe's power of self-government. The Indian Reorganization Act of 1934 gave Indian tribes the opportunity to organize themselves into the tribal government led by a governor. The registered voters of the pueblo annually elect a governor, a council president, and two runners-up. The governor appoints the first and second lieutenant governors, sheriff, secretary, and treasurer. The three elected officers appoint the 12 council members.

**Population Profile. 1969:** Tribal enrollment 2,356; Indian resident 2,030; Unemployment 26%; Underemployment 19%; Median family income $2,200. **1980:** Indian resident 2,289; Non-Indian resident 123; Percent Indian of total population 94.9; Total housing units 901. Occupied housing units 709. The reservation education level is 5th grade. Four tribal members are college graduates. The Federal Government operates an elementary day school at Isleta. High school students attend public schools in Los Lunas and Albuquerque.

**Tribal Economy.** The tribe has an annual income of $27,000. The C.& S. Packing Company is located on the reservation. Two small grocery stores are situated in the Pueblo. The tribe operates a concession stand. Minerals currently being used include volcanic ash and sand and gravel. Other minerals present include copper, silver, lead, zinc, tungsten, quartzite, and limnite.

**Climate.** Rainfall averages only 8 inches per year. The temperature ranges from a high of 100 degrees to a low of of 0 degrees.

**Transportation.** State Highways Nos. 45, 47, and 85 run through

the reservation. Albuquerque lies just 15 miles north of Isleta and is a major transportation and commercial center for the area.
**Community Facilities.** The Public Health Service has installed a water and sewer system for the reservation. Natural gas is provided by the Southern Union Gas Company. The Southwest Public Service Company supplies electricity to the area. The telephone system is operated by the Mountain States Telephone Company. A clinic on the reservation is operated by the PHS. Hospital care is available in Albuquerque at the Bernalillo County Indian Hospital. Many of the men obtain health care from the Veterans Administration.


JEMEZ PUEBLO                              Federal Reservation
Sandoval County
Jemez Tribe
Tribal Headquarters: Jemez Pueblo, New Mexico

**Land Status.** Tribal land: 88,680 acres. Non-Indian land: 6.71 acres. Total area: 88,867 acres. The original Spanish land grant to the Pueblo was made on September 20, 1689. Upon the recommendation of the Surveyor General, in his report of September 30, 1856, the Congress of the United States confirmed the grant to the Pueblo of Jemez by the Act of December 22, 1858. A patent covering this grant was issued to the Pueblo by President Lincoln on November 1, 1864. The present gross area of the grant is 17,331 acres. The pueblo has purchased, with its compensation funds, three parcels of non-Indian land totalling 4.09 acres. In 1878, a Presbyterian Mission School was established on a small parcel of land at Jemez Pueblo. Within the grant, the U.S. owns 2.06 acres used for a day school for the Jemez children. The net Indian land within the original Jemez Pueblo grant is 17,313.85 acres.
**History.** According to history and legends of the Jemez people, the lands bordering the Jemez River and its tributaries have been their home for centuries. The Jemez's first encounter with the white man, in this case the Spanish explorers, came circa 1540. Although relations seemed amiable at first, the establishment of missions and the resultant efforts to suppress the Indian religion, together with the encroachment on Indian land, caused the relationship to deteriorate rapidly. The Indians were forced to concentrate in fewer villages for defense, and by 1622, Jemez and Jemez Springs were the only inhabited pueblos in the area. One of these was abandoned prior to the Pueblo Revolt of 1680. Jemez took a prominent part in the Pueblo Revolt, attacking the Spanish again and again. They tell the story of a secret meeting attended by representatives of all 19 pueblos, at which they agreed to fight the Spanish on a certain day. The Spanish were driven to retreat to El Paso, and the Pueblos were free of Spanish domination for the next 12 years. From 1680 to 1695, the Jemez fled to the nearby mesas several times for protection against the Spanish, and against the Navajo and Utes who were on the warpath during this period.
**Culture.** The Jemez Pueblo Indians are strongly communal. The

native language and the native religion continue to play a vital role in the total behavior and attitudes of these people. The Catholic and Protestant churches had and are continuing to have a strong influence on the Pueblo Indians of Jemez. In the past, each head of the family was dependent upon the tribal caciques for their assignments of land for either homesites or agricultural lands. However, in recent years, Pueblo members have received their lands through inheritance or by sale between themselves. There are still many activities, traditional in nature, which are a part of everyday life.

**Government.** Originally the government of the Pueblos, including Jemez, was controlled by the caciques. Another important personage in the Pueblo government was the war chief, who held his position for life, and was responsible for overseeing the religious life of the Pueblo. The various functions of government, such as war and peace, witchcraft, hunting, husbandry, and the like, were regulated by representatives of the societies that pertained to the particular activity. With the advent of the Spanish, the outward form of the government of most of the Pueblos was changed, and the control of strictly civil affairs was put in the hands of a governor, two lieutenant governors, and a council of 12. At Jemez the council members are all former governors of the Pueblo. Religious and ceremonial affairs are controlled by the caciques.

**Population Profile. 1969:** Tribal enrollment 1,528; Indian resident 1,380; Unemployment 58%. Underemployment 14%. **1980:** Indian resident 1,504; Non-Indian resident 11; Percent Indian of total population 99.3; Total housing units 417; Occupied housing units 306. The average education level for the reservation is 7th grade. The local schools provide instruction for grades one through six. The Catholic Parochial School teaches grades one through eight. The Jemez Springs Consolidated School provides instruction for the 12th grade. There are seven college graduates in the tribe.

**Reservation Economy.** Local business establishments are limited to three small grocery-confectionery combinations, owned and operated by individual tribal members, and serve, primarily, as local conveniences. The major shopping center for the pueblo is located in Albuquerque, some 45 miles to the southeast. A small toy manufacturing plant was established recently on the reservation. Deposits of sand and gravel, clay, and building stone are being quarried. Uranium and copper also exist in relatively large quantities but are not yet exploited.

**Climate.** Rainfall averages between 11 and 13 inches at Jemez. It is located in the Jemez Mountains well above the level of Santa Fe and Albuquerque. Temperatures range from a high of 97 degrees to a low of 0 degrees, although generally cooler than the valley land.

**Transportation.** State Highway No. 44 connects the reservation with Albuquerque and Interstate 25 to the southeast, and to Farmington to the northwest. State Highway No. 4 is a mountainous route to Los Alamos. Reservation residents pick up a busline in San Ysidro, 15 miles from the reservation. Commercial trainlines serve Bernalillo, 35 miles from Jemez. For air and truck service, the Jemez residents must drive 45 miles to Albuquerque.

**Community Facilities.** The Jemez water system was installed by PHS, and sewer and electricity are provided by the Jemez REA Coop. Residents also use bottled gas. Jemez Pueblo is served by the Indian Division of the U.S. Public Health Service insofar as the people's health needs are concerned. One registered nurse serves the entire pueblo. A weekly visitation is made by a doctor from the Public Health Service, and dental services are also available weekly. The nearest hospital is located in the City of Albuquerque. Modern medical assistance is minimal locally and limited to clinic services.

**Recreation.** The tribal buildings are all used for traditional activities. An annual fiesta and other dances are held regularly, attracting tourists and visitors from other pueblos.

JICARILLA RESERVATION                      Federal Reservation
Rio Arriba and Sandoval Counties
Jicarilla Apache Tribe
Tribal Headquarters: Dulce, New Mexico

**Land Status.** Tribally-owned land: 742,315 acres. Total area: 742,315 acres. The Jicarilla Apache Reservation was established in 1887 by Executive Order. Amendments in 1907 and 1908 adjusted the western border which adjoins the Carson National Forest.

**History.** Long before the Spanish arrived in the Southwest, related Navajo and Apache tribes had made their way south to New Mexico and had begun to drift apart culturally. The wandering Apache bands were divided into sub-tribes, sub-tribes into bands, and bands into groups made up of families related through the mother with weak overall tribal linkages. The "small basket" or Jicarilla Apaches lived in northern New Mexico, though their ancient lands included parts of Colorado and Oklahoma. Driven from this area in 1716 by the Comanches, they made new homes in northeast New Mexico. Though they began farming, the Apaches held to their tradition as great hunters and fighters until captured and subdued by the U.S. Army in 1880 in a policy of virtual extermination. After several years of administrative bungling which involved imprisonment and several relocations, the Jicarilla Apache group were settled on their existing reservation.

**Culture.** The Apache were nomadic raiders closely related to the Navajo. Location among different environments and tribes resulted in some variations from band to band. Children were trained to be hunters and fighters. The Apache usually lived in wickiups, easily constructed and easily moved. In cold weather, skins were laid over the walls to provide added protection. Apache clothing was also made out of skins. Jicarilla means "small basket", referring to the pitch-sealed small baskets used by the Jicarilla as drinking cups. Apache religion was shamanistic, and the tribe also developed a rich mythology. Mountain spirits were believed to possess great powers of good and evil over people. The Apache feared both witches and the dead, who, they believed, could influence the living.

**Government.** The tribe is governed by a president, vice-president, and eight councilmen serving 4-year terms. The councilmen serve staggered terms. The tribal constitution has provisions for Federal relationships, territorial boundaries, tribal membership, civil rights, elected tribal government, the powers of the tribal council, an executive department, and law and order.

**Population Profile.** 1969: Tribal enrollment 1,625; Indian resident 1,497; Non-Indian resident 1,250. Unemployment 42%; Underemployment 28%; Median family income $4,500. 1980: Indian resident 1,715; Non-Indian resident 281; Percent Indian of total population 85.9; Total housing units 719; Occupied housing units 517. The education level of the tribe is 7 years of schooling. Tribal members attend public schools. The high school is located in Dulce. There are presently 20 tribal members in college. Tribal scholarship funds are supplemented by the BIA.

**Tribal Economy.** The tribal income, which averages $800,000 annually, is largely composed of revenues from mineral leases let by the tribe. The remainder, between 20 and 30 percent, is provided through tribal businesses. Fifty people are employed in tribal activities. The tribe owns and operates the Jicarilla Apache Tribal Industries for which a plant is being constructed, a leathercraft shop, cattle sales barn, the Stone Lake Liquor Store, and a tourism enterprise which includes store and camp grounds. Tribal members own a laundromat and garage. The tribe has formed the Jicarilla Arts and Crafts, Jicarilla Buckskin and Leathercraft, and land and forestry improvements organizations. There are a variety of commercial establishments in Dulce, including a bank, post office, beauty shop, motel, and restaurant which are privately owned. Minerals existing on the reservation include natural gas, oil, and timber. Coal deposits, although sizable, are not being mined.

**Climate.** The reservation lies along the Continental Divide where the elevation is 7,000 feet. The climate is cool and pleasant, the temperature averaging between 42 degrees and 48 degrees. The summer median temperature is 60 degrees, the winter median is 32 degrees. Rainfall measures 19 inches per year; snowfall measures 2 feet each winter.

**Transportation.** New Mexico Route 44 crosses north–south through the reservation. New Mexico Route 17 is an east–west highway passing through the reservation. The only commercial transportation serving the reservation is a busline which takes passengers to Chama, 28 miles away, for connections to other areas. Truck service is available in Pagosa Springs, nearly 50 miles from Jicarilla. The nearest commercial air service is located in Farmington, New Mexico, 86 miles from the reservation, or in Durango, Colorado, 109 miles distant.

**Community Facilities.** The Jicarilla Reservation draws water from the Navajo River for industrial, domestic, and agricultural use. This is also the major source of electricity, together with the Utah Construction and Mining Company. Natural gas, a resource of the reservation, is purchased through the Southern Union Gas Company or drawn from wells. Health care and clinics are offered through the PHS at Dulce; however, the nearest hospital facilities for the tribe are at the PHS Hospital in Santa Fe, New Mexico, 125 miles from the reservation. The tribe has both a tribal office building and a community building.

**Recreation.** Much of the land in the reservation and in the adjoining Carson National Forest has been preserved in its natural, healthy state.

Having an abundant supply of game, this is one of the best hunting areas in the State. Mule deer are especially abundant. There are three annual deer hunts, a three-day Little Beaver Roundup celebration in mid-July, a three-day tribal feast at Stone Lake in September, and an annual rodeo. Numerous fishing and camping areas throughout the reservation attract many campers; however, there are overnight facilities in Dulce for non-campers.

LAGUNA PUEBLO                                        Federal Reservation
Valencia, Bernalillo, and Sandoval Counties
Keresan Tribe
Tribal Headquarters: Laguna, New Mexico

**Land Status.** Tribal land: 412,211.50 acres. Allotted land: 41,225.55 acres. Non-Indian land: 1,016.73 acres. Total area: 417,453.78 acres. The Laguna Indian Reservation is located in west-central New Mexico between the cities of Albuquerque and Grants. The reservation lands are in three locations and total some 418,000 acres. The two smaller portions of Laguna land lie southwest and northeast of the main reservation area. The northeastern part is separated from the main reservation area by the Canoncito Reservation. The main reservation area adjoins Acoma Pueblo on the west and Isleta Pueblo on the east. The original Spanish Land Grant to the Laguna consisted of New Mexico; the Laguna purchased several large areas from the Spanish or Mexican holders. Twice, Presidents of the United States had granted the use and occupancy of additional tracts.

**History.** According to history, the Pueblo of Laguna is the youngest of the Keresan villages, and the last of the present 19 pueblos to be established. However, Laguna legends describe migration from the north from whence the Laguna people trace their beginning. People of the Pueblo believe that it was founded many years before Cubero found it in 1689, the Pueblo having been bypassed by earlier Spanish expeditions. History tells us that Laguna was founded between 1697 and 1699 by people from Acoma, Zuni, Zia, Oraibi, and, according to tradition, from San Felipe, Sandia and Jemez. There is much speculation about the original population, but it was not from any unified tribal group and is presumed to be most closely related to the Acoma tribe.

**Culture.** The Pueblo Indians were named so by the Spanish because they lived in permanent villages. The Laguna Pueblo Indians have strong communal bands. In addition to tribal bands, the Laguna maintain close ties and friendships with other Pueblo tribes. The tribal members still live in small communities, much as when first encountered by the Spanish, the main settlement being Old Laguna. The other communities are Casa Blanca, Encinal, Paraje, Mesita, Paguate, and Seama. The native language and the native religion continue to play a significant and vital role in the total behavior and outlook on life. The Catholic Church, as well as other non-Indian religions, has and is continuing to have a strong influence on the Pueblo Indians of Laguna. There are still many activities, communal and traditional in nature, which play an integral part in the everyday life of the Laguna Indians.

**Government.** The Tribal Council of Laguna derives its legal authority from the Amended Constitution of the Pueblo of Laguna, which went into effect on November 10, 1958. The amended constitution was adopted pursuant to the provisions of the Act of June 18, 1934, and approved by the Secretary of the Interior. The tribal council has a total membership of 21, made up of 12 representatives elected from the individual villages, and nine staff officers, elected at large. Three of the members of the council, namely, the governor, the treasurer and the secretary, serve in their positions full-time.

**Population Profile.** **1969:** Tribal enrollment 4,432; Indian resident 2,880; Education level 8th grade; Unemployment 47%; Underemployment 10%. **1980:** Indian resident 3,564; Non-Indian resident 227; Percent Indian of total population 94.0; Total housing units 1,319; Occupied housing units 1,025. There are five Federally-operated schools on the reservation and plans underway for the construction of a Laguna Consolidated High School to accommodate approximately 480 children. There are at present 25 college graduates in the tribe.

**Tribal Economy.** The tribal income averages $1,175,400 yearly and is almost totally derived from mineral resources. Tribal business and recreation fees form a small part of the tribal income. The tribe employs 12 persons full time. There are approximately 15 individually-owned Indian enterprises at Laguna Pueblo. The major industrial activity includes Burnell-Nytronics, Inc. and the Anaconda Mining Corp. (Jackpile Open Pit Uranium Mine). The Santa Fe Railroad operates a section on tribal lands and also employs Laguna Indians. Deposits of uranium, clay, and sand and gravel on the reservation are currently being utilized. Marble is also present in large quantities but is not being quarried.

**Climate.** Rainfall averages almost 10 inches yearly in this arid region of New Mexico. The average high temperature is 91 degrees; the average low is 40 degrees.

**Transportation.** Interstate 40-Route 66 crosses east-west through the reservation, providing easy access to Albuquerque, New Mexico. Secondary roads on the reservation are maintained by the Bureau of Indian Affairs. Commercial air, bus, and truck service are readily available in Albuquerque, 40 miles from Laguna. Train service is offered on the reservation.

**Community Facilities.** The tribe owns and operates its own water and sewer system, with no user charge for the sewer system. Residents purchase bottled gas or pipe gas from the Union Gas Company. Electricity is provided by the Continental Divide Electric Cooperative in Grants, New Mexico. The reservation is connected to the Mountain States Telephone Company. A part-time medical officer, a dental officer and dental assistant, Public Health nurse and sanitarian aide are stationed at the Public Health Service Indian Health Center at Laguna. Hospital care is available at the 215-bed Bernalillo County Indian Hospital and the PHS Indian Sanatorium, both in Albuquerque. OEO-Community Action Program offices are located in the tribal community building, where council meetings are also held.

**Recreation.** In keeping with its traditions, the Laguna tribe holds an annual fiesta. A more recent addition to tribal activities is the baseball tournament.


MESCALERO RESERVATION                    Federal Reservation
Otero County
Apache Tribe
Tribal Headquarters: Mescalero, New Mexico

**Land Status.** Tribally-owned land: 460,384 acres. Total area: 460,384 acres.

**History.** Before 1500, fierce nomadic bands of Athapascan Indians came from the north to roam the area which is now Arizona and New Mexico. When the Spanish arrived, they used the Zuni word "Apache" meaning "Enemy". Wandering Apache bands trained to be hunters and fighters were met by Coronado. The Mescalero Apaches, called "Mescal People" from the custom of eating parts of the mescal cactus, are related to the Lipan Apache of Texas and the Eastern Chiricahua. The Apache terrorized American settlers until 1880 when the Indians were located on the reservation.

**Culture.** The Apache were nomadic raiders who never fully adopted the use of the horse except as meat. Each band's culture was affected by the area in which it located. The Apache lived in thatched wickiups which were covered with hide in the winter for greater protection. Clothing was made out of skins. They were skilled in basketry, sealing some baskets with pitch to be watertight. Religion was shamanistic, and the tribe developed a rich mythology. Mountain spirits were believed to possess great powers of both good and evil over people. These spirits are impersonated in the Mountain Spirit Dances.

**Government.** The popularly-elected tribal business committee includes 10 members who are responsible for conducting all municipal functions with support of other governmental agencies. The authority of the tribal council is derived from the constitution and bylaws approved under the Indian Reorganization Act of 1934.

**Population Profile. 1969:** Tribal enrollment 1,624; Indian resident 1,676; Unemployment 69%; Underemployment 11%. **1980:** Indian resident 1,922; Non-Indian resident 179; Percent Indian of total population 91.5; Total housing units 549; Occupied housing units 481.

**Tribal Economy.** The average annual tribal income is $570,000, 85 percent of which is derived from the forest industry. Tribal associations and cooperatives include the Apache Summer Christmas Tree Enterprise, Heavy Equipment Enterprise, and the Cattle Growers Association. Commercial/industrial establishments include the Sierra Blanca Ski Resort—tribally owned and operated, Tribal General Store—tribally owned and operated, and various retail businesses—privately owned.

**Climate.** Rainfall averages 20 inches per year. The mean temperature is 50 degrees.

**Transportation.** U.S. Highway No. 70 crosses the reservation northeast-southwest. The nearest commercial airlines and trains are located in Alamogordo, 30 miles from the reservation. Bus and trucklines serve Mescalero.

**Utilities.** Water is obtained from wells. Electricity is available through the Otero County Electric Company. The USPHS operates a hospital in Mescalero.

**Recreation.** The major tourist attraction on the reservation is the Sierra Blanca Ski Resort which has five lifts. The gondola lift operates during the summer also. Fishing and hunting are popular here. St. Joseph's Catholic Mission, constructed over a period of 30 years by the parish priest and volunteer assistants, is a point of major interest. The tribe operates a neighborhood facility which includes a library, indoor swimming pool, and bowling alleys.


NAMBE PUEBLO                                    Federal Reservation
Santa Fe County
Tano-Tewa Tribe
Tribal Headquarters: Nambe Pueblo, New Mexico

**Land Status.** Tribally-owned land 19,073 acres. Government land: 2 acres. Total area: 19,075 acres. Nambe has no documentary evidence of its land grant from the Spanish government. After testimony from the elders of the tribe, the U.S. Surveyor General confirmed the grant in 1858. It was patented in 1864.

**History.** The Nambe Indians have lived for centuries in the area north of Santa Fe, farming the land. They participated in the Pueblo Revolt of 1682 to drive out the Spanish. The Pueblo Indians maintained independence from Spain for 12 years. The Nambe were declared citizens of Mexico when that country won its independence from Spain. Their rights were confirmed in the treaty of Hidalgo signed by Mexico and the United States in 1848.

**Culture.** The people of Nambe belong to the Tanoan linguistic group and speak Tewa. Nambe is surrounded by many Spanish settlements and has lost many of its ceremonial traditions and most of the arts and crafts once practiced here. Only one woman at Nambe still knows how to make good pottery, but rarely does. Woven cotton belts, used in the dress, which were once produced in excellent quality are similarly disappearing. In recent years, Nambe has held a festival on July Fourth at Nambe Falls.

**Government.** The tribal council, the governing body of the Pueblo, is comprised of a governor, lieutenant governor, secretary-treasurer, and six members. They are all appointed annually by the cacique, or traditional tribal leader, and receive no compensation.

**Population Profile. 1969:** Tribal enrollment 257; Indian resident 136; Non-Indian resident 94; Unemployment 32%; Underemployment 13%; Median family income $3,200. **1980:** Indian resident 188; Non-Indian resident 909; Percent Indian of total population 17.1; Total housing units 394; Occupied housing units 345. The average education level for the tribe is 4th grade. There are presently two college graduates on the reservation. Students attend Pojoaque High School and will soon be able to obtain vocational training in Espanola.

**Tribal Economy.** Tribal revenues measure about $1,300 yearly.

The tribe is a member of the All Pueblos Council for New Mexico and the Eight Northern Pueblos Community Action Project. The only commercial development on the reservation is the limited recreation facilities at Nambe Falls. There are no significant mineral deposits on the reservation, the major natural resource being the scenic beauty of Nambe Creek and Falls.

**Climate.** Rainfall averages between 10 and 11 inches on the reservation. The temperature varies from a high of 98 degrees to a low of 0 degrees.

**Transportation.** U.S. Highway No. 64 runs north–south through the reservation. New Mexico Route 84-285 is also a north–south highway. Santa Fe, which lies 17 miles out of the reservation, is served by commercial air, bus, and trucklines. A train stops at Lamy.

**Community Facilities.** The water for residents is drawn from wells. Butane gas can be purchased, and electricity is provided by the Jemez Mountain Cooperative. The Public Health Service operates a hospital in Santa Fe. Medical and hospital care are also available at the Bernalillo County Indian Hospital in Albuquerque, New Mexico.

**Recreation.** Some hiking and picnicking facilities are developed for the Nambe Creek and Falls. These are still not fully developed and are somewhat inaccessible.


PICURIS PUEBLO                           Federal Reservation
Taos County
Tewa Tribe
Tribal Headquarters: Picuris Pueblo, New Mexico

**Land Status.** Total area: 14,947 acres. All the land is tribally owned. The Spanish Land Grant of 1689 was confirmed by the U.S. Congress in 1858 and patented in 1864. No additions have been made to the reservation since then.

**History.** The Picuris Pueblo is located in a mountainous and remote section of New Mexico south of Taos. Recent archeological excavations revealed that Picuris was founded between 1250 and 1300 by Indians who moved from a large pueblo near Talpa on New Mexico Route 3, now known as Pot Creek Ruin. The Picuris Indians were declared citizens of Mexico when that country won its independence from Spain. Their rights were reaffirmed by the United States in the 1848 Treaty of Hidalgo with Mexico.

**Culture.** The people of Picuris are of Tanoan linguistic stock and most of the tribe still speak Tigua. The tribe is closely knit, and family ties are strong. The group is considered to be of greater importance than the individual. They want to maintain their identity as an Indian group and their traditional culture. The Picuris make gold-flecked cooking ware out of the micaceous clay found in that area.

**Government.** Although the Pueblo of Picuris recognized the Indian Reorganization Act of 1934, they have not yet adopted a constitution. The tribe is governed by four elected officers, the governor, lieutenant-governor, war captain, and sheriff, who are elected annually by a tribal council of all-male tribal members over 15 years of age.

**Population Profile. 1969:** Tribal enrollment 165; Indian resident 102; Non-Indian resident 100; Education level 4th grade; Unemployment 40%; Underemployment 15%. **1980:** Indian resident 125; Non-Indian resident 1,414; Percent Indian of total population 8.1; Total housing units 599; Occupied housing units 475.

**Tribal Economy.** The tribe has only a minimal income and must obtain outside sources of funds to carry on tribal activities and projects. The several commercial establishments on the reservation are owned by non-Indians. The tribe is a member of the Eight Northern Pueblos Community Action Program. A livestock sales facility has been constructed by the tribe with funding assistance and is in operation. The tribe are using the sand and gravel deposits on their land. Also present are copper, lithium, and mica.

**Climate.** The reservation is situated in mountainous country in northern New Mexico. Rainfall averages between 10 and 13 inches each year. Temperatures range from a high of 100 degrees to a low of 0 degrees.

**Transportation.** New Mexico Highways Nos. 3 and 75 junction near the pueblo. Santa Fe, located 40 miles to the south, is served by air, bus, and trucklines. The nearest train stop is at Lamy, 60 miles to the south.

**Community Facilities.** Water is drawn from wells. Electricity is supplied by the Kit Carson Electric Cooperative. Only bottled gas is available. Hospital facilities are located at the PHS Indian Hospital in Santa Fe and at the Bernalillo Indian Hospital in Albuquerque.

**Recreation.** The tribe recently completed the community building which is used for tribal arts and crafts and traditional meetings. The tribal museum, depicting the history and lifestyle of the tribe, is housed in this building, and is an excellent demonstration of Picuris and Pueblo culture. The tribe holds an annual fiesta here, which is also of great interest to visitors.


POJOAQUE PUEBLO                            Federal Reservation
Santa Fe County
Tano-Tewa Tribe
Tribal Headquarters: Pojoaque Pueblo, New Mexico

**Land Status.** Total area: 11,599 acres. All the reservation land is tribally owned. The reservation grant was confirmed in 1858 and patented in 1865.

**History.** The Pojoaque Tewa Indians settled in the Rio Grande Valley and established their pueblo village. Except for raids from other tribes their life was relatively peaceful until the Spanish exerted control over the land. For 12 years following the Pueblo Revolt of 1682, the Pueblos maintained their independence. Spain then reasserted control until Mexico won independence. The 1848 Treaty of Hidalgo between the U.S. and Mexico confirmed the rights of the Pueblo Indians of Pojoaque.

**Culture.** The people of Pojoaque belong to the Tanoan linguistic family and speak Tewa. They inherited the Pueblo culture and the settled, agricultural way of life. Despite their small population, the people are trying to maintain their identity. The surrounding Spanish population has had a profound influence on these people. Complete freedom of religion is practiced, and the tribal religion is virtually extinct.

**Government.** Tribal officials include a governor, lieutenant governor, secretary, treasurer, and councilmen. The traditional form of government, appointed by the religious leaders, has been changed to conform with the Indian Reorganization Act of 1934.

**Population Profile.** 1969: Tribal enrollment 60; Indian resident 44; Non-Indian resident 20; Education level 8th grade; Unemployment 15%. **1980:** Indian resident 94; Non-Indian resident 1,049; Percent Indian of total population 8.2; Total housing units 425; Occupied housing units 379.

**Tribal Economy.** The tribe has an annual income of approximately $4,000. It is a member of the Eight Northern Pueblos Community Action Program. With this organization, Pojoaque is planning construction of a Pueblo Plaza which will be a tribal enterprise. Part of it is already occupied. Sand and gravel deposits on the reservation are being used. There is also a deposit of silicate.

**Climate.** Rainfall in this area near Santa Fe averages between 10 and 13 inches each year. The temperature high is 100 degrees; the low is 0 degrees.

**Transportation.** New Mexico Route 285 runs north–south through the reservation and provides direct access to Santa Fe and Albuquerque. Santa Fe, 16 miles to the south, is served by commercial air, bus, and trucklines. Lamy, 30 miles from Pojoaque, is the nearest train depot.

**Community Facilities.** The water and sewer system on the reservation were installed by the Public Health Service. Natural gas is piped to the Southern Union Gas Company. Jemez Mountain Coop. provides electricity. The Public Health Service maintains a hospital in Santa Fe for the northern Pueblos. There is also a Bernalillo County Indian Hospital in Albuquerque. The offices of the Eight Northern Pueblos Community Action Program are located on Pojoaque.


RAMAH RESERVATION                          Federal Reservation
McKinley and Valencia Counties
Navajo Tribe
Tribal Headquarters: Ramah, New Mexico

**Land Status.** Tribal area: 85,961 acres. Government land: 13,402 acres. Allotted land: 47,633 acres. Total area: 146,996 acres.

**History.** The Navajo migrated to the Southwest in wandering bands and settled in northern New Mexico during the 1500's. Within two centuries they had spread over a large part of the Plateau country. From the time the United States acquired this area in 1848, there was a great deal of friction between the Navajo and the U.S. Army. Because they lived in small bands in isolated communities and were relatively nomadic, the Navajo were difficult to subdue. They were rounded up in 1863 and sent to Fort Sumner where they would be taught the skills and advantages of a sedentary agriculture life. In 1868, recognizing the failure of this experiment, the Government concluded a treaty with the tribe which established the Navajo Reservation. The present Ramah Reservation was founded by Navajo who settled there rather than continue the march to the Navajo Reservation.

**Culture.** The Navajos are members of the Athapascan linguistic family. They call themselves "Dineh" or "The People." The Navajos, always quick to adopt from other cultures, learned many new customs from the Pueblo Indians among whom they lived. They learned to grow cotton and adopted the Pueblo loom and developed a distinctive weaving technique. From the Spanish they acquired horses, sheep and wool, and, later, silversmithing. Navajo religion, always primarily concerned with maintaining harmony with nature, includes many adaptations of Pueblo ceremonials and rituals.

**Government.** The Navajo Tribe is governed by a council consisting of 74 members representing the 96 chapters which make up the reservation. This includes the Alamo, Canoncito, and Ramah Reservations in New Mexico as well as the Eastern Administrative Area. All programs and projects are processed through the advisory committee before submission to the council. Chapter approval is required before the tribe can utilize any land within the chapter's boundaries. The popularly elected tribal chairman is the administrative head of the tribe.

**Population Profile. 1969:** Indian resident 1,060; Unemployment 60%. **1980:** Indian resident 1,163; Non-Indian resident 74; Percent Indian of total population 94.0; Total housing units 434; Occupied housing units 337. The tribal enrollment and most of the population statistics are not separate for the Ramah Reservation but are included with those for the Navajo.

**Tribal Economy.** The Ramah Chapter has a minimal income. As part of the Navajo Tribe, the Ramah area shares the Navajo tribal income, largely revenues from mining and mineral sales. Although physically separate, Ramah's economy is much like that of any other chapter within the Navajo Reservation.

**Transportation.** State Highway No. 53 passes east-west through the reservation. Transportation by air, bus, train, or truck is available in Gallup, New Mexico, which lies 45 miles north of Ramah.

**Community Facilities.** Community wells provide the water for the reservation. Electricity is available through the Continental Divide Coop. The reservation also has a community sewer system. The Public Health Service operates a hospital at Black Rock on the Zuni Reservation which serves the Navajo living on Ramah.

**Recreation.** Tourist interest is centered around the El Morro National Monument, the rock which bears non-Indian inscriptions dating back to 1603. The Indian inscriptions, of course, antedate those of the Spanish. There are also numerous cliff dwellings here and an ancient pueblo ruin. Immediately west of Ramah is the Zuni Pueblo. The pueblo itself attracts many visitors and outdoor recreation facilities are being developed.

SANDIA PUEBLO                              Federal Reservation
Sandoval County
Tano-Tigua Tribe
Tribal Headquarters:  Sandia Pueblo, New Mexico

**Land Status.** Tribal land: 22,884.45 acres. Total area: 22,884.45 acres. The original grant from the King of Spain was confirmed by Congress in 1858 and patented in 1864.

**History.** Sandia was established around 1300. It was one of the pueblos visited by Coronado in 1540-1541 when he headquartered his troops at nearby Pueblo of Mohi (Tiquex), now a ruin. Some Sandia lived at Kuana. Sandia was deserted at the time of the Pueblo Revolt and its residents fled to Hopi country. They remained until 1742.

**Culture.** The Sandia Pueblo Indians are strongly communal oriented. The native tongue and the native religion continue to play a vital role in the total behavior and outlook on life. The Catholic Church, as well as other non-Indian religions, continues to have a strong influence on the Pueblo Indians of Sandia. There are still many activities, communal and traditional in nature, which are an integral part of everyday life of the Sandia Indians. Increasing exposure to the white man's culture, as through education, is producing some profound changes.

**Government.** The tribal council of Sandia Pueblo represents the Sandia Pueblo tribal members. The powers and rights of the Sandia tribal council are based primarily on their original status of sovereignty which has been recognized by the Governments of Spain, Mexico, and the United States. Under President Lincoln in 1864, Sandia and other pueblos were presented confirmation of their land grants; silver-headed canes were presented to the assembled tribal governors at that time. Traditionally these canes are kept by the governors of the pueblos as symbols of their authority during their terms of office.

**Population Profile. 1969:** Tribal enrollment 211; Indian resident 180; Non-Indian resident 4; Unemployment 40%; Underemployment 50%. **1980:** Indian resident 227; Non-Indian resident 2,282; Percent Indian of total population 9.0; Total housing units 855; Occupied housing units 752. The average education level for the tribe is 5th grade. At present there is one college graduate in the tribe. Children attend the Bernalillo Public School System.

**Tribal Economy.** The tribe employs two people full time. It is a member of the All-Pueblo Council, an organization to promote the interests of the Pueblo tribes. The two grocery stores on the reservation are owned by Indians. Sand and gravel deposits are being quarried. These are the only mineral resources for the reservation.

**Climate.** The climate on the reservation is typical for this area of central New Mexico, averaging between 8 and 11 inches of rainfall each year, and having temperatures ranging from 100 degrees to 0 degrees.

**Transportation.** Interstate No. 25 and U.S. Highway No. 85 are two major north-south routes passing through the reservation. Commercial transportation by air, train, and truck is available in Albuquerque, 15 miles from Sandia. Buslines also serve Bernalillo, 6 miles from the pueblo.

**Community Facilities.** The reservation water and sewer system was installed by the Public Health Service. Gas fuel is supplied by the Southern Union Gas Company, and residents also buy bottled gas. The Public Service Company of New Mexico supplies electricity to the reservation. Health care for the Sandia Indians is available at the Bernalillo County Indian Hospital and the PHS Indian Sanatorium, both in Albuquerque. The community building in Sandia is used for traditional meetings.

**Recreation.** Located near Albuquerque between the Rio Grande and the Sandia Mountains, the area proves to be an excellent tourist attraction. The Indian people, having maintained their colorful culture, are a strong attraction by themselves. They are generally eager to share their traditions with visitors. The Sandia Pueblo holds a fiesta annually in addition to smaller celebrations.


SAN FELIPE PUEBLO                                        Federal Reservation
Sandoval County
Keresan Tribe
Tribal Headquarters: San Felipe Pueblo, New Mexico

**Land Status.** Tribal land: 48,852.76 acres. Allotted land: 71.04 acres. Non-Indian land: 6.10 acres. Total area: 48,929.90 acres. The original grant from the King of Spain in 1689 was confirmed by Congress and patented in 1864 for an area of over 30,000 acres. Additional grants brought the acreage to its present total.

**History.** According to San Felipe tradition, they were driven from their home on the Pajorito Plateau by enemy peoples and established a pueblo on the mesa overlooking the Rio Grande. The present pueblo on the west bank of the river was founded during the first half of the 18th century. Like other Pueblo Indians, the San Felipe were declared citizens of Mexico when that republic won its independence from Spain. Their rights were confirmed by the treaty of Hidalgo signed by government agents of Mexico and the U.S. on February 2, 1848, and ratified shortly thereafter.

**Culture.** The San Felipe Pueblo Indians have strong communal ties. The native tongue and the native religion continue to play a vital role in the total behavior and outlook on life. The Catholic Church as well as other non-Indian religions continue to have a strong influence on the Pueblo Indians of San Felipe. There are presently many activities, communal and traditional in nature, which are an integral part of everyday life of the San Felipe Indians. Increasing exposure to the white man's society, as through education and jobs, is producing some profound changes in the overall attitudes. The older people still wear their traditional attire daily whereas the younger people do not.

**Government.** The tribal council of San Felipe Pueblo represents the San Felipe tribal members. The powers and rights of the San Felipe Tribal Council are based primarily on their original status of sovereignty, which has been recognized by the Governments of Spain, Mexico, and the United States. Under President Lincoln in 1864, San Felipe and other pueblos were presented confirmation of their land grant. Silver-headed canes were presented to the pueblo governors by the President and are kept by the governors as symbols of their authority during their terms of office. The caciques continue to have power over traditional affairs.

**Population Profile. 1969:** Tribal enrollment 1,340; Indian resident 1,060; Non-Indian resident 0; Unemployment 52%; Underemployment 40%. **1980:** Indian resident 1,789; Non-Indian resident 477; Percent Indian of total population 78.9; Total housing units 498; Occupied housing units 418. The educational level averages 3 grades for the tribe as a whole. At present one tribal member is a college graduate. Students attend the Bureau of Indian Affairs elementary school for grades one through six and the Bernalillo Public School System.

**Tribal Economy.** The tribal council is responsible for the business affairs of the tribe. It is a member of the All Pueblo Council, an organization which represents the interest of all the Pueblo tribes. Commercial establishments on the reservation include a cabinet shop, sponsored by OEO, and a snack shop. Sand and gravel deposits on the reservation are being quarried.

**Climate.** Rainfall averages between 11 and 13 inches annually. The temperature, like that of central New Mexico, varies from a high of 100 degrees to a low of 0 degrees.

**Transportation.** Interstate No. 25 is the major north–south highway for the area, providing easy and rapid access to Santa Fe some 30 miles to the north, and to Albuquerque some 25 miles to the south of the reservation. Train and bus transportation are available in Bernalillo, 13 miles from the pueblo.

**Community Facilities.** The water and sewer system were installed by the PHS. Residents purchase bottled gas and obtain electricity from the Public Service Company of New Mexico. Health care for tribal members is provided at the Bernalillo County Indian hospital and the PHS Indian Sanatorium, both in Albuquerque, and at weekly PHS clinics held at the pueblo.

**Recreation.** A tribal building is used for traditional activities. An annual fiesta is held at the pueblo. Dances are held throughout the year to celebrate traditional religious holidays. These dances, very intricate and colorful, are usually open to the public.


SAN ILDEFONSO PUEBLO                          Federal Reservation
Santa Fe County
Tewa Tribe
Tribal Headquarters: San Ildefonso Pueblo, New Mexico

**Land Status.** Total area: 26,192 acres. The Surveyor General for the United States confirmed the grant of 17,292 acres in 1858. The grant was patented in 1864. Since that time, additions to the reservation have been made by congressional acts. All the land is tribally owned.

**History.** The Tewa Indians settled at San Ildefonso and have lived there continuously for almost 700 years. The Spanish capital was established in Santa Fe in 1610. From then on, the Pueblos were forced to adopt the Spanish serfdom system and Roman Catholicism. Conditions worsened throughout the 17th Century when the Pueblos turned back to their own culture and religion. Pope, who came from a neighboring pueblo, San Juan, led the Pueblo Revolt in 1680. The Indians found, however, that they could not defend themselves from Apache and Navajo raids. Following an epidemic, the Spanish began attempts to reconquer the area. In 1692, Santa Fe was re-entered and established as the capital. Some of the Pueblo Indians fled north to live with the Navajo and other tribes, teaching them many customs of the Pueblos. Spanish rule never extended beyond this valley. With Mexico's independence, the San Ildefonso Indians became citizens of that nation. Their rights were confirmed by the 1848 Treaty of Hidalgo between the U.S. and Mexico. Since then, the Pueblo Indians have lived quietly and tried to maintain their culture.

**Culture.** Pueblo people depended primarily on intensive agriculture, corn being the principal crop. Men did field work, irrigated the fields, and hunted to supplement crops. Women did all the cooking, maintained the houses, and crafted excellent pottery. The Indians lived in adobe or mud houses which were replastered each year. These houses, sometimes built into one or two vast buildings, were constructed around the village plaza, the center of community activity. The people here still speak Tewa, their native language. Family organization is patriarchal, and the sense of community and group responsibility is strong. San Ildefonso is famous for its black-on-black pottery, the most famous artists being Maria and her son, Popovi Da.

**Government.** The civil government of the pueblo is directed by a governor and a tribal council. Until recently, the governor served for 1 year only; however, the pueblo set a precedent by voting for a 2-year term of office. Tribal ceremonies are conducted by the cacique, or traditional leader of the pueblo.

**Population Profile. 1969:** Tribal enrollment 319; Indian resident 218; Unemployment 73%; Underemployment 20%; Median family income $1,800. **1980:** Indian resident 488; Non-Indian resident 1,003; Percent Indian of total population 32.7; Total housing units 528; Occupied housing units 470. The education level for the tribe is 4th grade. There is one college graduate. Students attend the Pojoaque High School system. The community building is open for studying every week night.

**Tribal Economy.** The tribal annual income is $17,000. Part of this is used to pay the salaries of the four tribal government employees. Some reservation land is leased to White Rock, a community and commercial establishment near Los Alamos. The artists, Maria and Popovi-Da, have a shop in the pueblo where their products as well as those of other Indians are sold. They also sell crafts from other reservations and books pertaining to Indians and the Southwest. Some sand and gravel and pumice deposits are on the reservation land.

**Climate.** The reservation is located near Espanola and Los Alamos. The rainfall averages between 10 and 13 inches annually. The temperatures range from a summer high of 100 degrees to a winter low of 0 degrees.

**Transportation.** New Mexico Highway No. 4 runs east-west through the reservation. U.S. Highway No. 84 runs northwest-southeast. U.S.

Highway No. 64 comes from the northeast to junction with Highway
No. 84 and U.S. Highway No. 285, a major north–south corridor. Santa
Fe, 18 miles to the south on Highway No. 285, is served by commercial
air, bus, and trucklines. The Santa Fe Railroad serves the entire area.
**Community Facilities.** Water is drawn from wells. PHS provides
septic tanks to the reservation. The Southern Union Gas Company
supplies the area with natural gas. Electricity is available from the
Jemez Mountain Coop. Hospital care for tribal members is provided
at the PHS hospital in Santa Fe and the Bernalillo County Indian Hospital
in Albuquerque. Tribal affairs are carried out in the several community
and office buildings which were constructed by the tribe.
**Recreation.** Traditional dances and ceremonials are held at San
Ildefonso and are open to the public. The annual San Ildefonso Fiesta
is held on January 23.


SAN JUAN PUEBLO                                  Federal Reservation
Rio Arriba County
Tano-Tewa Tribe
Tribal Headquarters: San Juan, New Mexico

**Land Status.** Tribally-owned land: 12,232 acres. Non-Indian land:
2 acres. Total area: 12,235 acres. The original Spanish Land Grant
to the Pueblo of Santa Clara was confirmed in 1689. The United States
reconfirmed this grant, an area of 16,174 acres, in 1858 and patented
it in 1864.
**History.** The Spaniards, led by Don Juan de Onate, founded their
first capital in New Mexico in July of 1598 at the Indian pueblo of
Oke near the present San Juan Pueblo. The capital was moved to Santa
Fe in 1610. The Spanish serf system was imposed upon the Indians
in the area, a way of life which was so restrictive that the Pueblos,
led by Pope, a native of San Juan, united and drove the Spanish out
in 1680. Independence was maintained for 12 years although other
tribes increased without Spanish protection. The Spanish re-entered
Santa Fe in 1692, and, within 4 years, regained control of the area.
The San Juan area fell under Mexican control when that country gained
independence from Spain. In 1848, under the Treaty of Hidalgo, the
Indians were transferred to the United States.
**Culture.** The Indians of San Juan speak English and Spanish as
well as Tewa, their native language. They have intermarried with the
Spanish more than any other pueblo; however, much of the Tewa culture
and social organization is retained. The women of the pueblo still produce the excellent pottery for which the pueblos are known.
**Government.** The pueblo is governed in the traditional manner
by a governor, his staff officers, and the tribal council. They are responsible for the civil matters concerning the reservation. The cacique,
a traditional tribal religious and cultural leader, is responsible for
the native religious observances.
**Population Profile. 1969:** Tribal enrollment 1,255; Indian resident
653; Non-Indian resident 1,000; Unemployment 58%; Underemployment

20%; Median family income $2,500. **1980:** Indian resident 851; Non-Indian resident 3,298; Percent Indian of total population 20.5; Total housing units 1,536; Occupied housing units 1,303. The reservation population's education level is 6th grade. Seven tribal members are college graduates. The San Juan children attend the Espanola school system.

**Tribal Economy.** The San Juan tribal income averages $7,300 per year. There are numerous general merchandise stores and several service stations on reservation land; none are owned by Indians. The San Juan Mercantile, a trading post providing food, hardware, and Indian arts and crafts, is located at the center of the pueblo. Sand and gravel deposits are the only salable resources on the reservation.

**Climate.** The rainfall averages between 10 and 13 inches per year. Temperatures vary with the seasons, reaching a high of 100 degrees in the summer and a low of 0 degrees in the winter.

**Transportation.** U.S. Highway No. 64 runs through the reservation to the northeast. U.S. Highway No. 84 junctions with No. 64 and continues to the northwest. U.S. Highway No. 285 is a major north-south highway for the area. Santa Fe, which lies 24 miles to the south, has air, bus, and truck service. The Santa Fe Railroad serves the entire area.

**Community Facilities.** The Public Health Service has provided the reservation with a water and sewer system. Electricity is available from the Jemez Mountain Coop. Health care for the residents is available in Santa Fe at the Public Health Service Hospital. Medical care is also extended through the Bernalillo County Indian Hospital in Albuquerque.


SANTA ANA PUEBLO                              Federal Reservation
Sandoval County
Keresan Tribe
Tribal Headquarters: Santa Ana Pueblo, New Mexico

**Land Status.** Tribal land: 42,527.50 acres. Non-Indian land: 2.81 acres. Total area: 42,527.50 acres. The original grant from the King of Spain included an area of over 15,400 acres and was confirmed by Congress in 1869 and patented in 1883. Additional grants brought the reservation to its present area of 42,527 acres.

**History.** The Mother Pueblo of Santa Ana was established around 1700. Some of the Santa Ana people state that their former ancestors dwelt at Kuana and spoke a Keresan tongue. Like other Pueblo Indians, the Santa Ana people were declared citizens of Mexico when that republic won its independence from Spain. Their rights were confirmed by the Treaty of Hidalgo, signed by government agents of Mexico and the U.S., February 2, 1848, and duly ratified shortly thereafter.

**Culture.** The Santa Ana Pueblo Indians continue to have a strong sense of community. The native tongue (Keresan) and the native religion continue to play vital roles in the total behavior and outlook on life, although the Catholic Church as well as other non-Indian religions have a strong influence on the Pueblo Indians of Santa Ana. There are still many activities, tribal and traditional in nature, which are an integral part of everyday life of the Santa Ana Indians. Increasing exposure to the white man's culture, as through education, is producing some profound changes in the overall attitudes.

**Government.** The tribal council of Santa Ana Pueblo represents the Santa Ana Pueblo tribal members. The powers and rights of the Santa Ana tribal council are based primarily on their original status of sovereignty, which has been recognized by the governments of Spain, Mexico, and the United States. Under President Lincoln in 1864, Santa Ana and other pueblos were presented confirmation of their land grant; silver-headed canes were presented to the assembled tribal governors at that time. Traditionally, these canes are kept by the governors of the pueblos as the symbol of their authority during their terms of office. The Indian Reorganization Act of 1934 gave Indian tribes the opportunity to organize themselves into corporate bodies.

**Population Profile. 1969:** Tribal enrollment 422; Indian resident 400; Non-Indian resident 0; Unemployment 51%; Underemployment 30%. **1980:** Indian resident 407; Non-Indian resident 2; Percent Indian of total population 99.5; Total housing units 181; Occupied housing units 99. The average education level for the reservation is the 3rd grade. Students attend the Bernalillo Public School system.

**Transportation.** Interstate Highway No. 25 is the major north-south highway for the Rio Grande Valley. The pueblo is connected to this by State Highway No. 44. Bernalillo, 6 miles away at the intersection of Highway Nos. 44 and 25, offers both train and bus transportation. The nearest commercial truck and air transportation are available in Albuquerque, 23 miles from Santa Ana.

**Community Facilities.** The reservation's water and sewer systems are installed by the USPHS. Residents can buy bottled gas or utilize the electricity made available by the Public Service Company of New Mexico. Health care for the tribal members is available at the Bernalillo County Indian Hospital and the PHS Indian Sanatorium, both in Albuquerque. The PHS also holds weekly clinics on the reservation. The community building includes office space for the Community Action Program and meeting rooms for the pueblo council.

**Recreation.** The annual fiesta illustrates the vibrant culture of the Santa Ana Pueblo Indians. The festival is an occasion for the entire pueblo and friends and relatives from other pueblos to gather and celebrate with traditional dances and music. In addition, there are numerous tribal events which serve to maintain the community ties and tribal traditions.


SANTA CLARA PUEBLO                          Federal Reservation
Rio Arriba and Sandoval Counties
Tano-Tewa Tribe
Tribal Headquarters: Santa Clara Pueblo, New Mexico

**Land Status.** Tribally-owned land: 45,744 acres. Non-Indian land: 4 acres. Total area: 45,748 acres. The Santa Clara Grant was confirmed in 1858 and patented in 1909 for 12,220 acres. A subsequent grant and Executive Order brought the reservation to its present acreage.

**History.** The Santa Clara originally lived in the Puye Cliffs and in pueblos built along the slopes and on mesa tops, but in the late 11th Century were forced by drought conditions to move into the Espanola Valley on the Rio Grande. The ruins were last occupied around 1680. After that the whole tribe moved to the present location near Espanola.

**Culture.** The people of Santa Clara are members of the Tanoan linguistic family and speak Tewa. Social organization still recognizes the extended kin group and maintains strong kinship ties. They shared the traits of Pueblo culture, living in permanent villages, and lived principally through intensive agriculture. The pueblo's women are masters at shaping their famous black pottery without a wheel. Other handicrafts include beadwork, painting, and cloth embroidery. The pueblo has produced several significant modern artists.

**Government.** Santa Clara, organized under the Indian Reorganization Act of 1934, has a constitution and bylaws which provide for the election of the governor, his officers, and the tribal council. There are presently four political parties in the tribe. The cacique, the traditional leader, still oversees the tribe's religious activities.

**Population Profile. 1969:** Tribal enrollment 916; Indian resident 493; Non-Indian resident 10 families; Unemployment 53%; Underemployment 20%; Median family income $1,600. **1980:** Indian resident 1,839; Non-Indian resident 6,819; Percent Indian of total population 21.2; Total housing units 3,202; Occupied housing units 2,837. The education level for the reservation is 7th grade. There are presently seven college graduates in the tribe.

**Tribal Economy.** Santa Clara's tribal income of approximately $35,000 annually is primarily revenue from the tourism program they have developed. The Santa Clara Canyon area provides campsites and various types of outdoor activities. The Puye Cliff Ruins have also been opened to visitors. Considerable commercial activitiy is carried on near Espanola. Mineral resources on the reservation are limited to sand, gravel, and pumice deposits.

**Climate.** Rainfall averages between 11 and 14 inches per year. The temperatures are seasonal but usually stay between 100 degrees and 0 degrees.

**Transportation.** U.S. Highway No. 84 runs northwest-southeast; U.S. Highway No. 64 runs northeast-southwest. U.S. Highway No. 285 joins them and continues south to Santa Fe, 22 miles distant, and, via U.S. Highway No. 85 and Interstate 25, to Albuquerque. Commercial transportation by air, bus, and truck is available at Santa Fe. The Santa Fe Railroad serves the entire area, the nearest siding being at Lamy, 40 miles from the reservation.

**Community Facilities.** There is no reservation-wide water and sewer system. Residents using gas purchase bottled gas. Electricity is available from the Jemez Mountain Coop. Hospitalization and medical services are provided for the Indians of this area at the PHS Hospital in Santa Fe. There is also a larger hospital, the Bernalillo County Indian Hospital, in Albuquerque. The tribe has a community building and several traditional meeting places.

**Recreation.** The Santa Clara Tribe has opened the ruins of the homes of its ancestors to the public. Tourists can now see the Puye Cliff dwellings and the ruins of the ancient pueblo built on the mesa top. Facilities for hunting, camping, picnicking, and fishing are located in the very beautiful Santa Clara Canyon. The tribe's annual fiesta is held each July. This is an opportunity for visitors to observe traditional pueblo dances, sample the foods, and meet the people.

SANTO DOMINGO PUEBLO                    Federal Reservation
Sandoval County
Keresan Tribe
Tribal Headquarters: Santo Domingo Pueblo, New Mexico

**Land Status.** Total area: 69,259.82 acres. All the land is tribally owned. The original 1689 Spanish Land Grant was confirmed by Congress in 1858. A patent covering the grant was issued to the pueblo by President Lincoln on November 1, 1864. This grant was in conflict with another claim, and the Pueblo Land Boards, established in 1924, found that the conflicting claim predated that of the pueblos. Of the present total Santo Domingo acreage, 150 acres are in conflict with the Cochiti Grant.

**History.** The Santo Domingos, an eastern Keresan Tribe, were first known to live at a site 12 miles west of Cochiti. According to Indian history, their next home site, Guipuy on the Galisteo Creek, was partially destroyed by the flooding Galisteo, and the Santo Domingos then moved to Huashpatzona. The Pueblo Revolt of 1680 caused other moves as the tribe sought protection from the Spanish and from raiding tribes. They settled finally on the Jemez Mesa in 1692. The present pueblo was established about 1700. The name Santo Domingo was first used by Gaspar Castano de Sosa in 1591. Onate established a monastery there as head mission for the Province of the Keres Pueblos. The first church was built in 1605. Following the establishment of the village in its present site, Santo Domingo became the chief mission of the region.

**Culture.** The Santo Domingo Pueblo Indians appear to be the most conservative of all 19 pueblos in retaining their lifestyle and culture in spite of continuous contact with the non-Indian culture. The native tongue and religion play vital roles in the community's behavior and outlook, although the Catholic Church and other non-Indian religions have had a strong influence on the tribe. The community has maintained a closely knit structure, and continues many traditional activities as an integral part of everyday life. Many Santo Domingo Indians continue to wear their native attire daily. The Santo Domingo are known for their skill in jewelry making and other forms of Pueblo Indian arts. They sell their craft in Santa Fe and other nearby markets and are widely known for their skill in market bargaining.

**Government.** The tribe is governed by the Council of the Pueblo of Santo Domingo, a representative body whose original status of sovereignty was recognized by Spain, Mexico, and the United States.

President Lincoln presented Santo Domingo and several other pueblos with silver-headed canes in confirmation of their land grant. These canes are traditionally kept by the governors in office as symbols of their office. The tribe has accepted the 1934 Indian Reorganization Act but has not yet adopted a constitution or a charter.

**Population Profile.** **1969:** Tribal enrollment 2,058; Indian resident 1,940; Non-Indian resident 0; Unemployment 45%; Underemployment 13%; Median family income $1,900. **1980:** Indian resident 2,139; Non-Indian resident 23; Percent Indian of total population 98.9; Total housing units 436; Occupied housing units 347. The average education level for the tribe is 5th grade. The children attend the Santo Domingo Elementary School, 5 miles from the pueblo. High school students attend schools in Bernalillo, Santa Fe, and Albuquerque. There are two college graduates in the tribe.

**Tribal Economy.** Three small community stores are the only commercial ventures owned and operated by Indians for all of the reservation area. The large trading post located near the pueblo is owned and operated by a non-Indian. Industrial activitiy has been limited to a wood products firm. Sand and gravel are the only exploitable natural resources on the reservation.

**Climate.** Rainfall measures between 11 and 13 inches annually. Temperatures reach a high of 100 degrees and a low of 0 degrees.

**Transportation.** State Highways Nos. 22 and 25 and Interstate 25 serve the reservation. Trains stop at the railroad siding at Domingo, 1½ miles from the pueblo. Bus service is available in Bernalillo, 25 miles from Santo Domingo. Tribal members must travel 40 miles to either Albuquerque or Santa Fe for truck or air transportation.

**Community Facilities.** The Santo Domingo Tribal Utility Authority, with the assistance of USPHS, provides water and sewage infrastructure to the reservation. Gas is supplied by the Southern Union Gas Company. The Public Service Company of New Mexico provides electricity. Extensive medical care and hospitalization are available in Albuquerque at the Bernalillo County Indian Hospital and at the PHS Hospital in Santa Fe. A community building in the pueblo houses the Community Action Program.


TAOS PUEBLO                                    Federal Reservation
Taos County
Tano-Tigua Tribe
Tribal Headquarters: Taos Pueblo, New Mexico

**Land Status.** Total area: 47,341 acres. All land is tribally owned which is presently acknowledged to belong to the tribe. The tribe has sought unsuccessfully for over 20 years to regain possession of the Blue Lake Mountain area which is a religious area of sacred significance. Congress at this writing has two proposals before it concerning this dispute. The present land grant was confirmed December 22, 1858.

**History.** The Spanish discovered Taos Pueblo in 1540 under Hernando de Alverado much as it is today, with two large communal houses facing each other across Taos Creek. Colonists from Onate's community soon settled nearby. A series of Indian revolts against the settlers caused by exploitation, by imposed labor and whipping, and imprisonment for refusing religious conversion culminated in the successful Pueblo Revolt of 1680 spearheaded from Taos and led by Pope, a San Juan Indian. The Spaniards were driven from Mexico not to return for 13 years. The Indians celebrated their victory and washed off converted "Christians" with amole (soapweed) in the Santa Fe River. The Spanish returned in 1693 and in 1696, with the order by de Vargas that all pueblo governors be shot; resistance effectively ceased. The ruins of the mission, built in 1704, with walls four feet thick, still stand. After the conquest of New Mexico by the United States in 1847, Taos again revolted against the occupation troops and murdered the American governor, Charles Bent, among others. The revolt was crushed and the leaders hanged.

**Culture.** The Indians of Taos have an ancient and rich cultural past, much of which continues to survive. They live in large communal houses, the upper stories of which are reached by ladders. Round outdoor baking ovens and strings of chili drying in the sun are typical. The underground kivas serve as meeting places for the men, with women admitted only on certain occasions. The Deer, Turtle, and Sun-Down Dances are unique and noted for their beauty and precision. The latter, given on September 30th yearly, is the most important ceremony and expresses thanksgiving for the harvest. The Taos people are handsome, distinguished, and independent. Most are farmers, many are artists, and others find employment in the nearby town of Taos. The Taos are the least typical of the Pueblo Indians for they share many characteristics with the Plains Indians, particularly the Kiowa with whom they have linguistic relationship.

**Government.** Taos has a tribal council as the governing body. The governor is appointed by the cacique. Other selected officers are the lieutenant governor, sheriffs, fiscales, and war chiefs. The government of Taos is a strong one, especially with regard to village concerns. Observance of the native religion and participation in community work are universally required of residents. The Taos people have little concept of individual property rights and have a strong sense of community property.

**Population Profile. 1969:** Tribal enrollment 1,470; Indian resident 859; Non-Indian resident 0; Unemployment 65; Underemployment 20%; Median family income $1,900. **1980:** Indian resident 1,034; Non-Indian resident 3,193; Percent Indian of total population 24.5; Total housing units 2,074; Occupied housing units 1,526. The education level average is 7th grade. There are ten college graduates living in the pueblo. Children attend school in Taos municipal schools or at parochial schools.

**Tribal Economy.** Tribal income is $39,500.

**Climate.** The average rainfall is 14 to 16 inches yearly. Temperature high is 100 degrees in July; it sometimes drops as low as -10 degrees in January. The pueblo's elevation is over a mile above sea level.

**Transportation.** U.S. Highway No. 64 comes within a few miles of the pueblo, and New Mexico Route 3 serves the settlement. The nearest airport is in Santa Fe, 60 miles from the pueblo, and the nearest train is at Lamy, 80 miles distant. Commercial bus and trucklines serve Santa Fe.

**Community Facilities.** Water comes from Taos Creek. There are no gas, electric, or sewer facilities. Hospitals are located in Santa Fe and operated by the U.S. Public Health Service. Taos is provided with weekly clinic visitation services. The annual fiesta is held September 29.

TESUQUE PUEBLO                          Federal Reservation
Santa Fe County
Tano-Tewa Tribe
Tribal Headquarters: Tesuque Pueblo, New Mexico

**Land Status.** Tribally-owned land: 16,810.66 acres. Non-Indian owned: 3 acres. Total area: 16,813.16 acres. The reservation grant of 16,708 acres was confirmed in 1858 and patented in 1864. A subsequent tribal purchase brought the reservation acreage to its present total.

**History.** The Tesuque Pueblo was established around 1250. Like other Pueblo Indians, the Tesuque Indians were declared citizens of Mexico when that nation gained independence from Spain. The tribe's rights were confirmed by the U.S. in the 1848 Treaty of Hidalgo between the U.S. and Mexico.

**Culture.** The family organization is patriarchal, with strong family and clan kinship patterns. The people are Roman Catholics, but the native religion is still strong. The Tewa language is still used widely; however, Spanish and English are also spoken. The Indians of Tesuque have maintained the vibrancy of their native dances and perform them regularly throughout the year. The best known of these are the Eagle and the Deer Dances. Pottery and jewelry, for which Pueblo Indians are known, are made by some of the members.

**Government.** Tesuque's civil government is managed by a governor, other officers, and a council. The officers are appointed in the traditional manner by the cacique who directs the native religious observances and tribal mores. Many of the younger men have influence and serve in important positions. Both old and young tend to listen to and respect the opinions and ideas of the other.

**Population Profile. 1969:** Tribal enrollment 231; Indian resident 135; Non-Indian resident 0; Education level 4th grade. Unemployment 46%; Underemployment 18%; Median family income $1,600. **1980:** Indian resident 236; Non-Indian resident 133; Percent Indian of total population 64.0; Total housing units 158; Occupied housing units 118.

**Tribal Economy.** The reservation is a member of the Eight Northern Pueblos Community Action Program. The only commercial establishments on the reservation are a cafe and two service stations which lease land from the tribe. Minerals present on the reservation include sand, gravel, and mica.

**Climate.** Rainfall averages between 10 and 13 inches yearly. The temperature varies with the seasons, reaching a high of 100 degrees in the summer and a low of 0 degrees in the winter.

**Transportation.** U.S. Highways Nos. 64, 84, and 285 provide arteries to the east, west, north, and south. Santa Fe, 10 miles south of Tesuque, is served by commercial air, bus, and trucklines. The nearest railroad stop is at Lamy, 30 miles from Tesuque.

**Community Facilities.** The water and sewer system for the reservation was installed by the Public Health Service. The Jemez Mountain Cooperative provides electricity to the reservation. Residents also purchase bottled gas. Hospital facilities for tribal members are available at the PHS Hospital in Santa Fe and the Bernalillo County Indian Hospital in Albuquerque. One community building on the reservation is used for meetings and OEO activities. Other buildings are used for traditional ceremonies.

**Recreation.** There is an annual fiesta at Tesuque Pueblo. Nearby pueblos offer other attractions, such as the Santa Clara Canyon and cliff dwellings. The Bandelier National Monument lies north of Tesuque near White Rock. Santa Fe, to the south, is the old Spanish capital and the present capital of New Mexico.

ZIA PUEBLO                                        Federal Reservation
Sandoval County
Keresan Tribe
Tribal Headquarters: Zia Pueblo, New Mexico

**Land Status.** Total area: 112,511.12 acres. The Pueblo grant acquired in 1689 from the King of Spain was confirmed by the U.S. Congress in 1858. The land has been enlarged since by both purchase and grant to its present size. The tribe owns 111,360.07 acres and non-Indians own 428.61 acres. There have been no allotments.

**History.** Zia was established around 1300 A.D. when Zia Indians moved from a site farther up the Jemez. The Zia, who are related to the Jemez Indians, participated in the Pueblo Revolt of 1680 in which the Spanish were driven from New Mexico. In 1687, during re-conquest a bloody battle was fought in which 600 Indians died and 70 were taken into slavery. The old men were executed. The present mission structure, built in 1692, still stands and is in use. President Lincoln in 1864 presented the pueblo governors silver-headed canes in confirmation of their land grants. Traditionally, these canes are kept by the governors of the pueblos as the symbol of their authority during their terms of office.

**Culture.** The Zia Indians are strongly communal in orientation. The native tongue (Keresan) and the native religion continue to play a vital role in their outlook on life. The Catholic Church, as well as other non-Indian religions, has a continuing influence on the Zia people. There are still many activities of a communal and traditional nature which are an integral part of everyday life. Increasing exposure to the white man's culture is producing some profound changes in overall attitudes. Zia is known for its fine distinctive pottery, unique in color and design.

**Government.** The Tribal Council of Zia Pueblo represents the Zia

Tribe. The powers and rights of the Zia Tribal Council are based primarily on their original status of sovereignty, which has been recognized by the governments of Spain, Mexico, and the United States. The Indian Reorganization Act of 1934 gave Indian tribes the right to organize themselves into corporate bodies.

**Population Profile.** 1969: Tribal enrollment 479; Indian resident 380; Non-Indian resident 0; Unemployment 52%; Underemployment 45%; Median family income $1,400. **1980:** Indian resident 524; Non-Indian resident 0; Percent Indian of total population 100.0; Total housing units 132; Occupied housing units 103. The education level average is 4th grade. One college graduate lives in the pueblo, and two are now in college. Children attend school in the Jemez Springs Consolidated School System.

**Climate.** Rainfall averages 8-13 inches yearly. Temperature high in July is 100 degrees with a low of 0 degrees in January.

**Transportation.** New Mexico Highway No. 44 runs by Zia Pueblo in a northwest-southeastern direction. The nearest airport is in Albuquerque, a distance of 40 miles. Commercial train and bus service are available in Bernalillo, 20 miles away. Trucklines serve Albuquerque as the nearest stop.

**Community Facilities.** Water is supplied by wells and heating by liquid propane gas. Public Service Company of New Mexico supplies electricity. Sewer needs are served by septic tanks. Hospital facilities are at the Bernalillo County Medical Center in Albuquerque, a PHS Hospital. The annual fiesta is held August 15.


ZUNI PUEBLO                                        Federal Reservation
McKinley and Ramah Counties
Zuni Tribe
Tribal Headquarters: Zuni, New Mexico

**Land Status.** Tribal land: 405,034 acres. Allotted land: 2,213 acres. Total area: 407,247 acres.

**History.** Zuni is the popular name of a Pueblo (village dweller) tribe of the Zunian linguistic family. Soon after the Spanish conquest of Mexico the white man heard rumors of the Zunis and their "Seven Cities of Cibola" of which Hawikuh was the capital. Coronado met the first Zunis in his expedition in 1540 and invaded the city of Hawikuh, where the first mission was established in 1629. In 1672, the Apaches raided Hawikuh and burned the mission which was never re-established. One of the "Seven Cities" was Halona which stood on the site of present-day Zuni. Zuni people have occupied this site since 1692.

**Culture.** In character and customs the Zunis resemble other Pueblo tribes, being quiet, good tempered, and industrious. They are expert agriculturists and have highly developed arts and crafts. Zuni silver and turquoise work ranks with the finest of Indian jewelry. Basketry and textiles are meticulously handcrafted. The Zuni women still bake bread in their outdoor adobe ovens. Religious ceremonies are observed and practiced today as they have been for centuries. Zuni men have become famous as fire fighters.

**Government.** The tribal council, with the governor as its administrative head, is the final decision-making body on the reservation. The council manages financial affairs, can establish business enterprises, levy and collect taxes, and execute contracts. The Zuni government is quasi-religious and, in most cases, decisions are unanimously accepted.

**Population Profile. 1969:** Tribal enrollment 5,352; Unemployment 56%; Indian resident 5,128; Underemployment 12%. **1980:** Indian resident 5,988; Non-Indian resident 303; Percent Indian of total population 95.2; Total housing units 1,445; Occupied housing units 1,228.

**Tribal Economy.** Annual average tribal income: $39,000. Tribal cooperatives: Zuni Craftsman Cooperative. Commercial/industrial establishments: Ami-Zuni Corporation—private ownership; Dittmore-Freimuth, Inc.—private ownership; Ken's Eat-and-Go Restaurant—private ownership.

**Transportation.** State Highway No. 53 passes from east-west through the reservation, and State Highway No. 32 runs north-south. Buslines stop on the reservation. For air, train, and truck transportation, the residents must go to Gallup, some 40 miles from Zuni.

**Utilities.** The Zuni Domestic Water and Sewage Association operates the water and sewage system for the reservation. Electricity is provided to the area by the Continental Divide Coop. Hospital care is available in Blackrock, at the PHS Hospital, and in nearby towns.

**Recreation.** Zuni is the only surviving community of Coronado's famed "Seven Cities of Cibola." The physical setting is beautiful, including several lakes, and is good for both fishing and hunting. Religious ceremonies are carried on virtually unchanged since ancient days. Of special interest is the Shalako Kachina Dance, most spectacular of the Pueblo Kachina dances. It is one of the few which may be witnessed by non-Indians.

# NEW YORK

ALLEGANY RESERVATION                    Restricted Reservation
Cattaraugus County
Seneca Tribe
Tribal Headquarters: Saylor Building, Irving, New York

**Land Status.** Total area: 30,469 acres. All land is tribally owned. The 1794 Pickering Treaty established the boundaries of the Seneca Nation of which the Allegany Reservation is a part. As agreed in the treaty, the State continues to pay the tribe an annual payment of cloth and a small amount of cash. The reservation land is owned by the Seneca Nation and may not be sold without consent of the United States. By custom the Seneca Nation grants assignments or surface rights to individual members of the tribe. Nearly 10,000 acres, or 32 percent of the reservation, are leased on a 99-year basis to the villages of Salamanca, Kill Buck, Vandalia, and Carrollton. These leases will expire in 1991. Salamanca leases a total of 3,774 acres. An estimated 2,000 acres have been taken from the reservation for rights-of-ways for utilities, highways, and railroads. Over 10,000 acres were taken on permanent easement for the Kinzua Dam and Reservoir built for flood control purposes.

**History.** The Iroquois Tribes of central, northern, and western New York were nine members of the Six Nations of the Iroquois League of Confederacy which was founded by the leaders De Kanawida and Hiawatha in the mid-16th Century. The league was originally formed by five tribes, the related Tuscaroras not joining until 1716 when they moved to the area from the Carolinas. Although formed originally for mutual defense, the league became a powerful Indian empire, the force behind much of the inter-tribal pressures in the West and Midwest. The league evolved into a federated government and was an important model for the crafters of the American Constitution. The league's decline after two centuries of prominence was largely the result of involvement in the disputes between the entering European powers and their participation in the Revolutionary War. Most of the members of the league supported the British as they had in the French and Indian wars. Their alliance gave Britain the necessary advantage over France but proved fatal to the league's negotiating base following the victory of the Colonies. The two Seneca reservations, Allegany and Cattaraugus, were established permanently in 1784. The State of New York had responsibility for Indian education, health, welfare, and legal protection.

**Culture.** The Indian name of the Iroquois confederacy described a people dwelling in longhouses, the characteristic structures of Iroquois bark assembly halls, council houses, and composite family dwellings. Several families, usually matrilineally related, lived in a longhouse, each occupying a specified place. All property was owned and inherited by the women. Their economy was based on hunting and a single form of agriculture. The tribes were skilled in framing log cabins and tilling the soil as well as military enterprise. Although they were the military masters of most of the eastern United States, the Iroquois preferred to use diplomacy in settling differences. They are most widely acclaimed, however, for their moral caliber and the effectiveness of their socio-political organization. Through the last two centuries, Seneca culture has become submerged in the culture of the white man just as cultures of other ethnic groups in the United States.

**Government.** The Seneca Nation adopted a constitution in 1848 which abolished the position of chiefs and provided for executive, legislative, and judicial branches of government. Enrolled members of the Seneca Nation, both male and female, who are 21 years of age and over are eligible to vote and hold office. Tribal membership is based on matrilineal lines so that only children of women who are members of the Seneca Nation are permitted to inherit or acquire allotment rights. The Seneca National Tribal Council is made up of 16 members elected biennially, eight each from the Allegany and Cattaraugus Reservations.

**Population Profile. 1969:** Seneca Nation Enrollment 4,600; Indian resident, Allegany 1,200; Non-Indian resident, Allegany 8,480; Unemployment 35%; Median family income $1,500. **1980:** Indian resident 925;

Non-Indian resident 6,756; Percent Indian of total population 12.0; Total housing units 3,060; Occupied housing units 2,832. Education level 11th grade. Four public elementary schools, a public high school, two Catholic schools, and a Seventh Day Adventist School are located in Salamanca. The tribe has a fund of $1.8 million drawing interest which is used for scholarships for students continuing their education.

**Tribal Economy.** The bulk of the tribal income, which has averaged $114,000 over the last five years, was from sand and gravel sales during peak construction for new highways. As the road is nearing completion, this source of income will be greatly reduced. The Seneca Nation employs 11 persons in its Housing Authority, Educational Foundation, and Community Action Program. A number of industries are located in Salamanca. These include two furniture plants, a plastic works, two milling plants, electronic plants, a lumber mill, and two railroad shops. The city has all of the business and commercial facilities and shops that any community of 8,000 to 10,000 normally has.

**Climate.** The reservation lies in western New York State, south of Buffalo and just north of the Pennsylvania border. Rainfall here averages 44 inches annually. Temperatures reach an average high of 57 degrees and an average low of 25 degrees. The area has four distinct seasons.

**Transportation.** Route 17, a major east-west highway, runs through the reservation. U.S. Route 219 is a north-south highway. Salamanca has regular train, bus, and truck service; however, the nearest commercial air service is located in Bradford, Pennsylvania, 35 miles distant.

**Community Facilities.** The reservation has a common water system, and septic tanks. Gas is supplied by the Iroquois Gas Company. The Niagara Mohawk Electric Company provides electricity to the area. The Salamanca District Hospital serves Salamanca and the districts. A number of private practitioners are also located in Salamanca. The Kinzua Dam was completed in 1967 creating a lake of 35 miles. The Seneca Nation was awarded rehabilitation funds in the amount of $12,128,917 in 1964 for the land taken for the dam. The tribe used these funds for housing for displaced families, two community buildings, one on each reservation, and investment of $750,000 with interest to be used for building maintenance. A fund has also been reserved for education purposes.

CATTARAUGUS RESERVATION                    Restricted Reservation
Cattaraugus, Erie, and Chautauqua Counties
Seneca Tribe
Tribal Headquarters: Irving, New York

**Land Status.** Total area: 21,680 acres. All the reservation land is tribally owned. The reservation was established in the Pickering Treaty of 1794. As provided in this treaty, the State continues the annual payment of cloth and a small amount of cash. The land is owned by the Seneca Nation and may not be sold without consent of the United States. According to custom, the Seneca Nation grants assignments or surface-use rights to individual members of the tribe.

**History, Culture, and Government.** Residents of the Cattaraugus Reservation are members of the Seneca Nation. This reservation, together with the Allegany Reservation, is jointly governed by the Seneca Nation. For information on Seneca history and culture and the government structure, refer to the Allegany Reservation.

**Population Profile. 1969:** Seneca Nation enrollment 4,600; Indian resident, Cattaraugus 2,400; Unemployment rate 35%; Median family income 1,500. **1980:** Indian resident 1,855; Non-Indian resident 139; Percent Indian of total population 93.0; Total housing units 898; Occupied housing units 566. The education level for the tribe is 11th grade. Elementary and secondary schools in Gowanda and Silver Creek, both off-reservation communities, serve the reservation residents. The tribe provides scholarships for students continuing their education.

**Tribal Economy.** The tribal income has averaged $114,000 over the last five years. Ninety-three percent of this is from sand and gravel sales; however, as the roads being supplied are near completion, this portion of tribal income will be greatly reduced. The Seneca Nation Industrial Park is located on this reservation because of its proximity to the Buffalo area. It is complete with water, sewer, gas, and electric facilities and access roads and railroad siding. Located in this park is the First Seneca Corporation which manufactures pillows and bedding. The nearby town of Gowanda serves as the shipping center of the reservation residents.

**Climate.** This reservation lies in the New York State "snowbelt" area in the extreme western part of the State, near Buffalo. Winds coming east from the Great Lakes carry heavy amounts of snow and rain. The reservation averages 43 inches of rainfall per year. There are four distinct seasons.

**Transportation.** The reservation lies along the New York State Thruway, or Interstate 90 and U.S. Highway No. 20, both of which run parallel to the shore of Lake Erie. State Highway No. 62 runs north-south just to the east of the reservation. State Highway No. 432 passes through the reservation from southeast to northwest. Commercial bus and trucklines stop on the reservation. Train service is available in Brockton, 15 miles from the reservation. Residents must travel 30 miles to Buffalo to obtain commercial air transportation.

**Community Facilities.** The Silver Creek Municipal Water Supply pipes water to residents. Others draw water from wells. Gas is supplied by the Iroquois Gas Company, electricity by the Niagara Mohawk Electric Company. Hospital care is available at the Tri-County Hospital in Gowanda and at the Brooks Memorial Hospital in Dunkirk. The New York State Public Health Department holds a clinic at the former Thomas Indian School. The Seneca Nation constructed a community building, the Saylor Center, from rehabilitation funds, on the Cattaraugus Reservation.

ONONDAGA RESERVATION                    State Reservation
Onondaga County
Onondaga and Oneida Tribes
Tribal Headquarters: Nedrow, New York

**Land Status.** Total area: 7,300 acres. All the land is tribally owned. The Onondaga have retained approximately one-fourth of the land owned by them at the close of the Revolutionary War. This area, which included the present city of Syracuse, was sold by 1822. Some 450 Oneidas have moved to this reservation and have intermarried with the Onondagas. Fee title to the land is held by the State of New York, having equitable title with the Indians. New York State has jurisdiction over all criminal and civil disputes occurring on the reservation within the State. New York State is unique in the responsibilities it has assumed toward the Indians. Following the adoption of the Constitution, the State never ceded any land or territory to the Federal Government, and the Indian lands have, therefore, never at any time been Federal territory. Rather than cede lands to the Federal Government or wait for Congress to negotiate a peace settlement with the New York State Indians, the State Governor, DeWitt Clinton, took the initiative to arrive at treaties with the Indians and New York State. Since that time, New York State has implemented programs for the reservation, assuming major responsibility for the welfare of the tribes. When living on tribal lands, the Indian is an owner of tax-free property.

**History.** The Iroquois Tribes of central, northern, and western New York were members of the Six Nations of the Iroquois League of Confederacy which was founded by the leaders De Kanawida and Hiawatha in the mid-16th Century. The league was originally formed by five tribes, the related Tuscaroras not joining until 1716 when they moved to the area from the Carolinas. Although formed originally for mutual defense, the league became a powerful Indian empire, the force behind much of the inter-tribal pressures in the West and Midwest. As the central tribe in the founding of the league, the Onondagas were "Keepers of the Council Fires." The league evolved into a federated government and was an important model for the crafters of the American Constitution. The league's decline after two centuries of prominence was largely the result of involvement in the disputes between the entering European powers and their participation in the Revolutionary War. Most of the members of the league supported the British as they had in the French and Indian Wars. Their alliance gave Britain the necessary advantage over France, but proved fatal to the league's negotiating base following the victory of the Colonies.

**Culture.** The Indian name of the Iroquois confederacy described a people dwelling in longhouses, the characteristic structure of Iroquois bark assembly halls, council houses, and composite family dwellings. Several families, usually matrilineally related, lived in a longhouse, each occupying a specified place. All property was owned and inherited by the women. The tribes were skilled in framing log cabins and tilling the soil as well as military enterprise. Although they were the military masters of most of the eastern United States, the Iroquois preferred to use diplomacy in settling differences. They are most widely acclaimed, however, for their moral caliber and the effectiveness of their socio-political organization.

**Government.** The Onondaga, most conservative of the Iroquois tribes, are organized around the Longhouse religion. There are several other churches on the reservation, but only Longhorn members can vote in tribal elections. A council of 12 is elected for 2-year terms and meets monthly. As required by tradition, the chief of the entire Iroquois Nation must be an Onondaga. He is the Tadodaho, and only he can summon the Six Nation Council. The Onondaga Reservation remains the capital of the confederacy. The Onondaga tribe maintains that as a foreign nation, it has a different relationship to both Federal and State governments. The tribe has continually challenged the Selective Service laws and State taxation.

**Population Profile.** 1969: Tribal enrollment 1,132; Indian resident 1,550; Non-Indian resident 12; Unemployment 10%; Underemployment 25%. 1980: Indian resident 592; Non-Indian resident 4; Percent Indian of total population 99.3; Total housing units 212; Occupied housing units 168. The tribe has an average education level of 10th grade. Children attend public schools in nearby towns. Five tribal members are college graduates.

**Tribal Economy.** The reservation is located in rich bottomlands of an empty lake; however, little agriculture is carried out. The tribe has a small income of under $3,000 from annuities. It is one of the poorer reservations in New York State. There are several small family-owned grocery stores and service stations which are owned by both Indian and non-Indian families.

**Climate.** The reservation lies in the New York State snowbelt just south of Syracuse, New York. The climate is temperate, having four distinct seasons.

**Transportation.** State Highway No. 11-A and U.S. Highway No. 11 run through the reservation north-south. Interstate 81 has interchanges in La Fayette and Nedrow just off the reservation. Syracuse lies 6 miles north of Onondaga and has ample transportation service by bus, rail, truck, and air. It is a major transportation hub for this upstate area.

**Community Facilities.** There is no public infrastructure on the reservation. Water is drawn from wells, and individual dwellings have either septic tanks or outhouses. Only bottled gas is available. The Syracuse Electric Company supplies the reservation with electricity. Medical care is financed through the State Health Department at hospitals in Syracuse. The Health Department also sponsors a clinic in Nedrow. The Iroquois Longhouse, the nation's traditional meeting place, is located in the reservation.

**Recreation.** Religious services and celebrations including the Green Corn Dance are held according to the Longhouse religion. The reservation is situated in a beautiful empty lake basin, formed along with the Finger Lakes, by the glaciers. There are no facilities for non-Indians, however, as the Onondagas treasure this as the only remainder of their home and heritage. Syracuse offers much in the way of lodging and entertainment.

POOSPATUCK RESERVATION                    State Reservation
Suffolk County, Long Island, New York
Poospatuck Tribe
Tribal Headquarters: None

**Land Status.** Tribally-owned land: 60 acres. Total area: 60 acres. This reservation was granted to the Poospatucks by the colonial government in the name of the King. New York State recognizes the land as a tax-free reservation and extends services to the tribe, which include health, education, and social services.

**History.** The Poospatuck were part of the Long Island tribes' Montauk Confederacy. Their economy was based primarily on fishing and whaling, and it is believed that early in the 18th Century most of the men in the tribe were lost in a whaling expedition. The necessity for marriage outside the tribe could account for the present tri-racial appearance of the tribe. The tribe was never permitted to vote on the Indian Reorganization Act, primarily because of its mixed ancestry.

**Culture.** The Poospatuck are believed to have had tribal and commercial relationships with the Algonquian Indians of Connecticut. They were primarily a fishing and whaling people. At present, they are the smallest tribe on the smallest reservation in New York State, and although their problems are numerous, they receive little assistance from the State.

**Government.** The governing body of the tribe is elected in compliance with Book 25 of the New York State Indian Law. Three land trustees are elected every 2 years; one is designated president, one secretary, and the third as treasurer.

**Population Profile. 1969:** Tribal enrollment 100; Indian resident 75; Unemployment N.A.; Underemployment N.A. **1980:** Indian resident 94; Non-Indian resident 109; Percent Indian of total population 46.3; Total housing units 59; Occupied housing units 52. The education level of the tribe is unknown. Scholarship money is available from the State in the amount of $1,000 per student per year.

**Climate.** Located on Long Island, the reservation has the same climate as the area around it. Temperatures range from the 90's to 0 degrees.

**Transportation.** Highway No. 25 passes east-west along the reservation. Airlines are located in New York City, 50 miles from the reservation. Trains and trucklines stop in Riverhead, 10 miles away. A bus stops in Brookhaven, 5 miles from the reservation.

**Utilities.** Water is obtained from individual wells. Septic tanks are the only provision for sewage. Health care through the State social services is available to the Indians in Riverhead and Brookhaven.

**Recreation.** An annual powwow is held on Labor Day.


SHINNECOCK RESERVATION                    State Reservation
Suffolk County
Shinnecock Tribe
Tribal Headquarters: Southhampton, Long Island, New York

**Land Status.** Tribal land: 300 acres. Total area: 300 acres. The Shinnecock Tribe have retained this land since it was first reserved for them by the colonial government in the name of the King. It is a State reservation, receiving social services from New York State. The reservation is tax-free and valued at $45 million.

**History.** The Shinnecock, part of the Montauk Confederacy, were largely a fishing and whaling tribe. They had contact with the Algonquin tribes in Connecticut, travelling the Long Island Sound. They are now a responsibility of the State rather than the Federal Government.

**Culture.** The Shinnecock today appear tri-racial, a probable result of intermarriage following the loss of men in whaling. Little of their former culture is evident now. Tribal members participate fairly successfully in the economy of the area around them.

**Government.** The governing body of the reservation is elected in compliance with Book 25 of the New York State Indian Law. Three land trustees are elected every 2 years, one as president, one as secretary, and one as treasurer.

**Population Profile. 1969:** Tribal enrollment 300; Indian resident N.A. **1980:** Indian resident 194; Non-Indian resident 103; Percent Indian of total population 65.3; Total housing units 104; Occupied housing units 104. Much of the employment is seasonal, resulting in a high unemployment rate during the winter months.

**Tribal Economy.** Average annual tribal income: None. Tribal employees: None. Tribal associations, cooperatives, and related organizations: None. Commercial/industrial establishments on the reservation: None.

**Climate.** The temperature varies through the four seasons from a high in the 90's to a low near 0 degrees.

**Transportation.** Highway No. 27-A passes east-west through the reservation. Commercial airlines serve New York City some 60 miles from the reservation. A train station is located 20 miles away at Riverhead. Bus and trucklines are available in Southhampton on the reservation.

**Utilities.** There are no provisions for public utilities on the reservation. Individual wells and septic tanks meet basic needs. Health care in Southhampton is provided through the State social services.

**Recreation.** The tribe holds an annual Labor Day powwow.


ST. REGIS MOHAWK RESERVATION                    State Reservation
Franklin County
St. Regis Mohawk Tribe
Tribal Headquarters: Hogansburg, New York

**Land Status.** Tribal land: 14,640 acres. Total area: 14,640 acres. The reservation lies in the northernmost part of New York State along the St. Lawrence River and is divided from the Canadian portion of the reservation, the Caughnawaga Reserve, by the 45th Parallel, the international boundary. The Canadian Caughnawaga Reserve encompasses 23,750 acres. Because the State of New York never ceded any land to the Federal Government following ratification of the

Constitution, the Mohawk Reservation has never been Federal territory. The Indians recently demanded recognition of the duty-free passage rights as guaranteeed to them in the Jay Treaty of 1794. This has frequently been violated by Canadian customs officers.

**History.** An Iroquois tribe of central New York State, the Mohawk were the keepers of the Eastern Gate for the Iroquois League or Confederacy. The league, originally formed by five tribes, added a sixth in the early 1700's and was known as the Six Nations. Formed in the early 16th Century for mutual defense, the league became a powerful Indian confederacy and ultimately a model for the United States Government. Pressure from the Iroquois was largely responsible for the westward movement of other Indian tribes. The Iroquois fought with the British during the American Revolution and consequently lost a great deal of land to the new State government. The American Revolution marked the end of Iroquois power, as the league's organization and population fell away.

**Culture.** The St. Regis Mohawks were of the Eastern Woodland cultural group. They lived in permanent villages in multi-family buildings called longhouses and supported themselves through hunting and agriculture. The tribe was matrilineal, with chiefs inheriting office through their mothers. Property was owned by the women. Mohawk men have become widely known as excellent high-steel workers. Although in the past the Canadian and U.S. Mohawks have been divided politically with much confusion concerning citizenship, recent events have resulted in an upsurge of tribalism and the native religion which centers around the longhouse.

**Government.** Three chiefs and three sub-chiefs are elected every 2 years to staggered terms of office.

**Population Profile. 1969:** Tribal enrollment 2,222; Unemployment rate 5%; Underemployment 24%. **1980:** Indian resident 1,763; Non-Indian resident 39; Percent Indian of total population 97.8; Total housing units 576; Occupied housing units 516.

**Tribal Economy.** Average annual tribal income: None. Tribal employees: None. Tribal associations, cooperatives, and related organizations: The People's Committee was formed in 1968 to promote interest of the communities on both reservations. Commercial/industrial establishments on reservations: The four such establishments are all under private Indian ownership—Mohawk Indian Village, marina and restaurant, trailer court and marina, and the Mohawk Construction Company.

**Climate.** The temperature varies from a high of 90 degrees to a low of 20 degrees.

**Transportation.** Route 37 is an east-west highway serving the reservation. Commercial airlines and trains are available 5 miles from the reservation in Massena, New York. Truck and buslines serve the reservation.

**Utilities.** Water and sewer are provided by the individual, with wells and septic tanks. Electricity is available through the Mohawk REA. Hospital and other health care is available in Massena and Hogansburg through the State social services.

**Recreation.** Tribal activities are held in the tribal community center and the American Legion hall. The Green Corn Ceremony is held annually.

TONAWANDA RESERVATION State Reservation
Niagara, Erie, and Genesee Counties
Tonawanda Band of Seneca Tribe
Tribal Headquarters: Tonawanda Indian Community, New York

**Land Status.** Tribally-owned land: 7,549 acres. Total area: 7,549 acres. From proceeds realized by the relinquishment of the land west of the Missouri, the tribe purchased 7,549 acres of their original 12,000-acre reservation. The deed was taken in trust in the name of the Secretary of the Interior. In 1863, the Secretary conveyed these lands to the Comptroller of the State of New York in trust for the Tonawanda Band of Seneca Indians. Most of the land is allotted by the tribe to its members. Leasing and mortgaging laws generally follow those regulations applicable to Federal reservations. Land cannot be alienated without the permission of the Secretary of the Interior.

**History.** Under a treaty negotiated in 1838 between the Seneca and the United States, the Seneca supposedly agreed to relinquish the Allegany, Cattaraugus, and Tonawanda Reservations in exchange, among other considerations, for land west of the Missouri. The Indians objected to the treaty, and negotiations were renewed. In 1842, a compromise treaty was negotiated by which the Seneca were allowed to retain the Cattaraugus and Allegany Reservations, but the Tonawanda Reservation was to be relinquished to a land company. Disgruntled over the treaty, the Seneca split as a tribe and became two entities. Those from the Tonawanda group refused to move from their reservation, and, in 1857, another compromise treaty relinquished their land west of the Missouri. From the proceeds they purchased 7,549 acres of the original 12,000-acre reservation.

**Culture.** With exception of the annual celebrations and the practices of the Handsome Lake religion now carried on by an increasing number of people, the Indian culture of the Tonawanda Seneca is nil. On special occasions even the clothing and beadwork that was once quite common must now be borrowed by the Seneca from museums. In recent years there has been a revival of lacrosse, but other sports in which the Indians participated are being largely ignored.

**Government.** The governing body of the reservation is elected in compliance with the New York State Indian Law (written by Eli S. Parker, a Tonawanda Seneca, who was Commissioner of Indian Affairs during Grant's presidency). A president, clerk, treasurer, marshal, and three peacemakers are elected annually. The peacemakers are chosen from among the chiefs for a 1-year term. Every enrolled male Indian of full age whose name is on the preceding annuity roll is eligible to vote. The council is composed of chiefs who are elected by the clan mothers and serve for life or good behavior.

**Population Profile. 1969:** Tribal enrollment 803; Indian resident 586; Non-Indian resident 8; Unemployment unknown; Underemployment unknown. **1980:** Indian resident 438; Non-Indian resident 29; Percent Indian of total population 93.8; Total housing units 150; Occupied housing units 141. The education level among the adults of the reservation is at the 8th grade. Scholarship funds are available from the tribe and the State. Vocational education programs are held in the Tonawanda Community Building.

**Tribal Economy.** There is no tribal income. Tribal associations and cooperatives include the Tonawanda Community Association. There are no commercial or industrial establishments on the reservation.

**Climate.** The area lies in a moderate, four seasonal climate zone. The temperature ranges from a high of 90 degrees to a low of 10 degrees.

**Transportation.** Route 267 passes east-west through the reservation. Commercial airlines and trains are available in Buffalo, 25 miles from the reservation. A busline stops in Batavia, 16 miles away, and truck service is available in Akron, 4 miles from the reservation.

**Utilities.** The only water for the reservation comes from individual wells; there is no waste disposal system. Electricity is available from Niagara Mohawk. Hospital care is available to the Indians in the Genessee Memorial Hospital in Batavia through State social services. Clinics are held in the Tonawanda Community Hall, and health care is also available through the State social services in Buffalo.

**Recreation.** Tribal activities center in the Tonawanda Indian Community Building. Dances are held at several dates during the year, such as at Indian New Year, five days after the January new moon. A traditional Indian convention is held in August.


TUSCARORA RESERVATION                    State Reservation
Niagara County
Tuscarora Tribe
Tribal Headquarters: Tuscarora Rural Community,
                    Niagara County, New York


**Land Status.** Tribal land: 5,700 acres. The Tuscarora Reservation is located 9 miles northeast of Niagara Falls. Slightly more than one-third of this area was acquired by gifts of 640 acres from the Senecas and of 1,280 acres from the Holland Land Company. The remainder was purchased from the latter company with money received for the release of their lands in North Carolina. Recently, approximately 550 acres were taken by the State Power Authority for use as a reservoir with approximately $850,000 as compensation. The entire area is collectively owned by the tribe, which rents to its individual members.

**History.** Although of the Iroquois linguistic group, the Tuscarora are indigenous to North Carolina. Continual pressure for land from white settlers forced the Tuscarora to western New York, and, in 1718, they were admitted as the sixth Nation in the Iroquois Confederacy. For remaining neutral during the Revolutionary War, the Treaty of 1784 secured for them the possession of the land upon which they were living.

**Culture.** The Tuscarora, like the majority of tribes in New York, rule and share through a system of matriarchy. There are nine clans within the Iroquois group, and the oldest mother in each clan chooses its chief. The chiefs govern for the remainder of their lifetime or until removed from their positions for misbehavior. Only those individuals born of an Iroquois mother are considered as members of the tribe, eligible to share in its resources and privileges. English is, today, the principal language of the tribe. Life on the reservation is, with some exceptions, much as it is in any relatively poor rural community. Few traditions are practiced.

**Government.** The tribe voted against the Indian Reorganization Act. It has a council composed of the chiefs and headmen of the Tuscarora nation. The council's power lies mainly in the areas of land and resources. The council can allot land to individual Indians, who in turn, may sell for their own benefit any timber on that portion which they clear for cultivation.

**Population Profile. 1969:** Indian resident 650. **1980:** Indian resident 873; Non-Indian resident 48; Percent Indian of total population 94.8; Total housing units 388; Occupied housing units 318. At present there are 15 college graduates in the tribe. Educational facilities to supplement the school system are available in the Tuscarora School and the Council House.

**Tribal Economy.** Tribal associations and cooperatives include a PTA for the Tuscarora School which serves grades 1-4, a farming cooperative formed by several individuals, and Tuscarora Roofing. The five trailer courts, four car-wrecking yards, two small auto repair garages, and one grocery store and soda fountain on the reservation are all Indian owned.

**Transportation.** U.S. Highway Nos. 104 and 31 pass east-west through the reservation. The nearest commercial airlines and trains are located in Buffalo, 29 miles away. A busline stops in Pekin, 6 miles from the reservation, and commercial trucking lines serve Niagara Falls, 12 miles away.

**Utilities.** Water is obtained from individual wells. Residents must provide their own septic tanks. Electricity is offered by the Niagara Mohawk Company. Several hospitals are available in Ransomville, Buffalo, and Niagara Falls. The Niagara Mental Health Clinic in Niagara Falls and a health clinic on the reservation offer health care. TB and psychiatric treatment are available in Lockport.

**Recreation.** Tribal activities are held in the Tuscarora School and the Council House. Regular events are the National Outing and the Community Fair.

# NORTH CAROLINA

CHEROKEE RESERVATION                              Federal Reservation
Cherokee, Graham, Jackson,
    Macon and Swain Counties
Eastern Band of Cherokee
Tribal Headquarters: Cherokee, North Carolina

**Land Status.** Tribal land in trust: 56,573 acres. Total area: 56,573 acres. The U.S. Congress transferred Cherokee lands to Federal Government trust in 1925 at the petition of the tribe. Conflicting possessory titles to land holdings interfere with efficient land use and management.

The bank is currently working to simplify titles with the assistance of a HUD grant.

**History.** The Cherokee, a powerful Iroquoian Tribe, once held all of the southwest Allegheny Mountain region in Virginia, Tennessee, the Carolinas, and Georgia. The U.S. Government waged war on the Cherokee from about 1820, resulting in the removal of the tribe by U.S. forces in 1835. The march to the new land in Oklahoma resulted in the death of many members and is known to the tribe as the "Trail of Tears." A number of the survivors of the wars refused to move west of the Mississippi. Since 1889, the Eastern Band of Cherokees has operated as a recognized tribe under a North Carolina State Charter.

**Culture.** Evidence indicates that the Cherokee originated north of where they were first encountered by De Soto in 1540 in the south Allegheny region. The tribe adopted a form of government in 1820 modeled on that of the United States. Several years later, Sequoyah, a mixed blood, invented the Cherokee alphabet, enabling the Cherokee to read and write their language. The Cherokee nation was divided into two factions, one favoring and one opposing the Treaty of Removal of 1835.

**Government.** The Cherokee Band is governed by the Principal Chief and his assistant, each elected for 4 years, and a 12-member council elected for a term of 2 years. The Tribal Business and Credit Committees form the executive branch of the tribal government.

**Population Profile. 1969:** Tribal enrollment 4,641; Indian resident 4,641; Non-Indian resident 1,859; Unemployment 31%; Underemployment 11%. **1980:** Indian resident 4,844; Non-Indian resident 873; Percent Indian of total population 84.7; Total housing units 1,868; Occupied housing units 1,647. The education level for the tribe is the 8th grade. At present there are nine college graduates living on the reservation. Scholarships are available from the tribe, the Historical Society, and from Federal agencies. The Cherokee Boys Club and the High School both offer vocational education.

**Tribal Economy.** The average tribal income is $400,000 per year. Fifty percent of this is derived from tax. The remainder comes from forestry and business. The tribe employs 22 permanent and 19 seasonal workers. Tribal associations and cooperatives include the Cherokee Boys Club, Cherokee Planning Board, Cherokee Tribal Water and Sewer Enterprise, Fish Management and Wildlife Enterprise, Qualla Housing Authority, and Community Club Council. Commercial/industrial establishments on the reservation include the Boundary Tree Lodge and Motel which is tribally owned. The Oconaluftee Indian Village and Historical Pageant is owned and operated by the Cherokee Historical Association. Three private companies, White Shield of North Carolina, Saddlecraft, Inc., and Vassar Corporation, are also on the reservation. There are numerous tourist businesses in Cherokee.

**Climate.** Rainfall averages 47.25 inches per year. Temperature ranges from 95 degrees to 10 degrees.

**Transportation.** Highways Nos. 19 and 40 pass east-west through the reservation. Highway No. 441 is a north-south route. The nearest commercial airline is in Asheville, 56 miles from the reservation. Commercial trains are available in Whittier and Bryson City, 10 miles away. Bus and truck services are available on the reservation.

**Utilities.** Water for residents is provided by the Tribal Water and Sewer Enterprise; the Nantahala Electric Company provides electric power, which together with the Soco Valley Water Users Association, also provides sewage service. A hospital operated by the PHS Indian Division is located on the reservation.

**Recreation.** Activities are held in the Cherokee Tribal Community Center. Also on the reservation are a museum of the Cherokee and the Cherokee Fair. "Unto These Hills," a historical pageant dramatizing the tribe's history at the time of the removal, is held throughout each summer.

## NORTH DAKOTA

FORT BERTHOLD RESERVATION                    Federal Reservation
Dunn, McLean, McKenzie, Mountrail,
and Mercer Counties
Mandan, Hidatsa, and Arikara Tribes
Tribal Headquarters: New Town, North Dakota

**Land Status.** Tribally-owned land: 41,237.03 acres. Government land: 174 acres. Allotted land: 376,590.89 acres. Non-Indian land: 2,720 acres. Total area: 418,002.01 acres.

**History.** Long before the Sioux migrated into the Dakotas from the East, three sedentary tribes had settled along the Missouri River which bisects the two states. Of these, the Mandan are believed to have arrived first. They once occupied several villages of semisubterranean earth lodges in what is now South Dakota, but then moved farther north. Another agricultural tribe, the Arikara, were also settling along the river, occupying three villages of earth lodges between the Grand and Cannonball Rivers. The Hidatsa established an agricultural life near Devil's Lake but were pushed west by the Sioux and settled at the junction of the Heart and Missouri Rivers. All these groups were greatly reduced in number by the smallpox epidemic of 1837. Survivors were placed on the reservation established by Executive Order in 1871.

**Culture.** The Three Affiliated tribes have always been involved in agricultural activities. The remains of their original semisubterranean homes are objects of interest today. The Mandan and Hidatsa speak a Sioux language while the Arikara speak a Caddoan language. These tribes traded widely with other tribes as far away as Mexico.

**Population Profile. 1969:** Tribal enrollment 3,709; Indian resident 2,677; Unemployment 80%; Underemployment 9%. **1980:** Indian resident 2,640; Non-Indian resident 2,937; Percent Indian of total population 47.3; Total housing units 2,163; Occupied housing units 1,658.

**Tribal Economy.** Average annual tribal income: $95,000. Thirty percent of the tribal income comes from grazing permits. Tribal associations, cooperatives: Soil Conservation Enterprise. Commercial/industrial establishments: Three Tribes Stoneware—privately owned. The growing season is 109 days. Oil deposits are currently being exploited. Clay and lignite exist in large quantities on the reservation but are not currently being extracted.

**Climate.** Rainfall averages 16 inches per year. The temperature ranges from a high of 95 degrees to a low near 0 degrees.

**Transportation.** Three State Highways cross the reservation: Route 37 runs northwest-southeast, Route 23 runs east-west, and Route 8 runs north-south. Commercial airlines, bus, and trucklines serve Minot, North Dakota, 80 miles from the reservation. Train service is available in New Town on the reservation.

**Utilities.** Water is obtained from municipal wells, and additional water could be drawn from the Garrison Reservoir. The Montana-Dakota Utility Company provides electricity to the area. A private hospital is located in Garrison, 20 miles east of the reservation boundary.

**Recreation.** There are excellent hunting and fishing as well as boating on the Garrison Reservoir. Parks, playgrounds, campgrounds, bowling, and golf facilities are available. The Four Bears Park on the Garrison Reservoir is being developed to include lodging and eating facilities. A museum is already operative.


FORT TOTTEN RESERVATION                    Federal Reservation
Benson, Nelson, and Eddy Counties
Devils Lake Sioux
Tribal Headquarters:  Fort Totten, North Dakota

**Land Status.** Total area: 50,154.00 acres. The reservation land is mostly allotted. Allotments account for 47,958.38 acres. The tribe owns 473.24 acres, non-Indians own 194,315 acres, and 1,800 acres are Government owned. Fort Totten was built in 1867. The reservation was originally 360 square miles.

**History.** The Sioux were not native to the Great Plains area but migrated from their traditional homeland in the Great Lakes region near Lake Superior. The Teton Sioux were the largest of the seven Council Fires Divisions, and the first to wander onto the Plains. They were first encountered by French explorers in the middle of the 17th Century. As the 19th Century began, they were the dominant tribe of the Northern Plains. Although habitually at war with other tribes, the Sioux did not actively resist white immigration until the whites began to intrude in great numbers and violated treaties. After the Minnesota Sioux uprising, General Sibley was sent to punish the Sioux and pursued them from Devils Lake southward. Battles followed at Whitestone Hill and Killdeer Mountain. The treaty signed in 1868 granted the Sioux freedom between the North Platte, Missouri, and Yellowstone Rivers. When discovery of gold in the Black Hills brought hordes of gold seekers into Sioux country in violation of that treaty, war was inevitable. Custer was defeated in 1876 at the Little Bighorn by the summer encampment of the Teton Sioux. The Wounded Knee massacre wiped out many of the Sioux people, mostly women and children, in the winter of 1890 and marked the end of Sioux resistance.

**Culture.** When the Sioux arrived on the Plains their culture changed from that of a forest and lake people to that of mounted horsemen whose primary source of livelihood was the buffalo. The Sioux Plains culture was one of the most highly developed both socially and politically of all the North American Indian tribes. Their sense of honor was strong, as was their sense of loyalty to the group. Greater praise was accorded a warrior who touched the enemy first without killing him than for enemy slain in battle. The ingenuity of the Sioux people with the products of the buffalo was unique and creative. All items of food, clothing, housing, utensils for water carrying, tools for sewing and digging, and ceremonial dress, were fashioned from parts of that animal. The Sioux political organization and military strategy were both well developed, particularly as evidenced by the great summer encampments. Distinctive foods were corn balls, butter made from marrow, sausage, red bean, and tipsin roots. The tribe still dances the Omaha Grass Dances, the Rabbit, and the Hoop Dances.

**Government.** The Devils Lake Sioux are governed by a tribal council composed of a chairman, four councilmen, a vice-chairman, and an acting secretary. The councilmen are elected from their districts for a term of 4 years. The chairman and the secretary are elected by popular vote of all members of the tribe. The vice-chairman is appointed from among the council membership. Their constitution is non-Indian Reorganization Act and was established in 1946, revised in 1960.

**Population Profile.** **1969:** Tribal enrollment 1,629; Indian resident 1,746; Non-Indian resident 1,379; Unemployment 58%; Underemployment 95%; Median family income $3,200. **1980:** Indian resident 2,261; Non-Indian resident 1,052; Percent Indian of total population 68.2; Total housing units 1,030; Occupied housing units 852. Education level achieved overall for adult members of the tribe is 8th grade. However, for adults 18 to 25 years of age, the average school years completed is 10.5 years. There are four schools on the reservation, including one high school.

**Tribal Economy.** The tribal income is $3,400 yearly. There are three full-time tribal employees. There are a few stores on the reservation, including grocery stores and a gas station. All are non-Indian owned. There is also a small concrete culvert plant, also non-Indian owned. Sand and gravel are the primary mineral resources.

**Climate.** The average rainfall is 18 inches yearly. Temperature averages are 66 degrees in summer, 8 degrees in winter.

**Transportation.** Four highways service the reservation: U.S. Routes 2 (east-west), 281 (north-south), and State Highways Nos. 20, 57, and 19. Commercial airline service is available at Devils Lake. There are freight depots and sidings on the reservation. The nearest bus service is at Fort Totten itself and St. Michael. Trucking lines serve Devils Lake.

**Community Facilities.** Water comes from wells. Gas is not available. Electricity is provided by three different sources: Baker Electric Coop., Cheyenne Valley Electric Coop., and Otter Tail Power Company. There are a PHS Hospital in Devils Lake and a clinic at Fort Totten. State musicals are performed during the summer at Fort Totten Little Theatre. There is a tribal hall with offices and meeting room in Fort Totten. The Catholic Youth Club maintains a building for basketball games. Rodeos, horse-racing, and powwows are regular features of the year.

TURTLE MOUNTAIN RESERVATION Federal Reservation
Rolette County
Chippewa Tribe
Tribal Headquarters: Belcourt, North Dakota

**Land Status.** Tribally-owned land: 35,579 acres. Allotted land: 34,144 acres. Non-Indian land: 517 acres. Total area: 70,240 acres. The Turtle Mountain Band of Chippewa entered into a treaty on October 2, 1892, ratified by Congress in 1904, which exchanged their claim to 9 million acres for $1 million, a reservation of 72,000 acres in North Dakota, and allotments elsewhere for families that could not be accommodated on the reservation. Approximately 35,000 acres of trust land are held by the Chippewa in various parts of Montana, North Dakota, and South Dakota under this latter provision.

**History.** The Chippewa, or Ojibway, were one of the largest tribes in North America. Originally believed to have been confederated with the Ottawa and Potawatomies in the Three Fires Confederacy, they were driven west by expanding Iroquois to the Great Lakes area. The confederacy was disbanded by the time the tribes reached Mackinaw. The Chippewa were friendly with the French, with whom they had a good amount of contact. With the availability of French weapons, the Chippewa were able to drive the Sioux and Fox west. Possession and use of wild rice fields was a major cause of war and rivalry with the Sioux, Fox, and other tribes. In the 18th Century, the stronger Chippewa were able to force the now weakening Iroquois east. Because of their location away from the Anglo frontier, the Chippewa had little contact with settlers. The tribes have been at peace with the United States since the treaty was signed in 1815.

**Culture.** The Chippewa were woodland Indians who lived primarily by hunting the abundant game, fishing, and gathering fruits and wild rice in an area rich in natural food resources. They lived in wigwams and traveled by canoe. Chippewa social organization was loose, the tribe being dominated by the Grand Medicine Society which had strong influence over the people. They believed that a power dwelt in all objects, animate and inanimate. These powers, or manitous, were wakeful in summer, but dormant in cold weather. The calumet was a ceremonial object, carved and decorated, usually a pipestem or long-stemmed pipe. The Chippewa demi-God, Manibozo, was the model for Longfellow's poem, "Hiawatha."

**Government.** The tribal chairman is elected at large to a 2-year term. Eight council members are elected from districts to a 2-year term. The tribe is unincorporated and has a constitution and bylaws approved in 1959. The Turtle Mountain Band of Chippewa have also joined in the United Tribes of North Dakota Development Corporation.

**Population Profile. 1969:** Tribal enrollment 11,311; Indian resident 7,037; Non-Indian resident few; Unemployment 52%; Underemployment 12%. **1980:** Indian resident 4,021; Non-Indian resident 290; Percent Indian of total population 93.3; Total housing units 1,216; Occupied housing units 1,095. The average education level for tribal members is 8th grade. There are four public and one parochial elementary schools on the reservation and a public high school at Belcourt. There are presently about 60 tribal members in college. A goodly portion of their support is provided by the Bureau of Indian Affairs.

**Tribal Economy.** The reservation lies near the Canadian border in North Dakota. The land is generally low, rolling, or turtle-backed hills from which the reservation derives its name. Sand and gravel deposits are used locally. The annual tribal income of $10,000 is earned almost completely through agricultural land lease payments. The tribe employs one person full time. The major employer on the reservation is the William Langer Jewel Bearing Plant at Rolla, North Dakota, which is non-Indian owned. There are 15 small retail and service stores in Belcourt, which are owned by Indians.

**Climate.** The rainfall averages 17 inches per year. The July average high temperature is 66 degrees; the January average low is 2 degrees.

**Transportation.** U.S. Highway No. 281 and North Dakota Highway No. 5 pass through the reservation east-west. The north-south route through the reservation is North Dakota Route 3. Trucklines stop on the reservation. Rolla, 6 miles outside the reservation, is served by commercial trains. The nearest air and buslines serve Devils Lake, 85 miles from Turtle Mountain.

**Community Facilities.** The BIA has installed water and sewer facilities in Belcourt which serve some homes. Gas is piped to the area by the Midwest Natural Gas Company. Electricity is supplied by the REA Co-ops and private companies. A 50-bed hospital is located in Belcourt, which is operated by the Public Health Service. Medical facilities are also located in Rolette and Rolla. A multi-purpose building has been constructed at Belcourt, and an old frame building is used as the tribal office.

**Recreation.** The Turtle Mountains offer beautiful scenery, with numerous lakes for boating and trailer sites. Other attractions include the tribally-operated authentic Indian Village. Nearby attractions include the International Peace Gardens.


## OKLAHOMA


**Note:** The Indian land status in Oklahoma is unique in comparison with Indian lands elsewhere. Because of special laws related to Indian-owned land in Oklahoma, there is only one reservation in that State—the Osage—insofar as the term generally applies to Indian lands in other parts of the United States.

The members of the 32 tribes mentioned herein have been assimilated to such a degree that any statement made in reference to tribal economy, transportation, climate, community facilities, and recreation would reflect the status of the non-Indian community. Therefore, these headings have been omitted from the Oklahoma portion of this handbook.

Most population figures used herein are taken from the BIA Labor Force Report dated January 1985, which reflect BIA data as of December 1984 and refer basically to the resident Indian population. Total tribal enrollment figures, however, are usually taken from individual tribal profiles based on their specific rules of membership, which may include Indian members wherever they may be living. Land Status figures are taken from the BIA's annual land status report as of September 1984.

ABSENTEE-SHAWNEE TRIBE OF OKLAHOMA          Federal Trust Area
Cleveland, Oklahoma, and Pottawatomi Counties
Tribal Headquarters: Shawnee, Oklahoma

**Land Status.** Tribally owned land: 89.25 acres. Allotted land: 12,119.47 acres. Government owned land: 10.00 acres. Total area: 12,218.72 acres.

**History.** The Shawnee were formerly a leading tribe with settlements in South Carolina, Tennessee, Pennsylvania, and Ohio. Because of both their interior position away from the traveled routes of early days and their migratory habits, little is known of their origin. Delaware Indian tradition claims that the Shawnee and the Nanticoke were originally one people; and, while this may or may not be true, Shawnee today refer to the Delaware as their "grandfathers."

Historically, the Shawnee became known around 1670. At that time they lived in two main bodies at a considerable distance from each other—one in the Cumberland region of Tennessee and the other on the Savannah River in South Carolina. During the late 18th Century, the two main bodies united in Ohio. For about 40 years, until the Treaty of Greenville in 1795, the Shawnee were almost constantly at war with the English and the Anglo-Americans. After the death of Tecumseh, their most famous war chief, they lost their taste for war and began to move to their present locations. One group settled on a reservation in Kansas, another went to Texas to join a band of Cherokee. A third group settled on the Canadian River in the Indian Territory of Oklahoma, just south of the Quapaw Reserve, and are today known as the Absentee-Shawnee Tribe of Oklahoma. Another band, which also settled in eastern Oklahoma, is today known as the Eastern Shawnee Tribe of Oklahoma.

**Culture.** Linguistically, the Absentee-Shawnee Tribe belongs to the Central Algonquian dialect group and were the southern advance guard of the Algonquian stock, closely related to the Sac and Fox. The name "Shawnee" derives from an Algonquian word, Shawunog, meaning "Southerners." The majority of the tribe have accepted modern life. However, many older members cling to tribal traditions as evidenced by religion, arts and crafts, powwows, and speaking the native language in the home.

**Government.** The tribe is organized under the Oklahoma Indian Welfare Act of 1936. In accordance with its constitution and bylaws, ratified in 1938 and amended and approved in 1977, the tribe is governed by an executive committee consisting of a governor, lieutenant governor, secretary, treasurer, and representative. Elections, held in June, are by referendum to staggered 2-year terms.

**Population Profile. 1984:** Tribal enrollment 2,297; Indian resident 1,340; Total labor force 564; Unemployed 113; Unemployment rate

20%. There are no boarding schools in the immediate area, although there are two in the Anadarko area. However, most children attend public schools. At least 40 students attend some type of higher education each year through the Bureau of Indian Affairs Scholarship Program.

APACHE TRIBE OF OKLAHOMA                    Federal Trust Area
Caddo, Comanche, Cotton and
  Kiowa Counties
Tribal Headquarters: Anadarko, Oklahoma

**Land Status.** Tribally owned land: 7,045.80 acres. Allotted land: 201,350.17 acres. Government owned land: 1.00 acre. Total area: 208,396.97 acres. Land is owned jointly with the Comanche and Kiowa Tribes of Oklahoma. Acreage totals include all three tribes; acreage by individual tribes is not available. This land is held in trust by the United States under the Act of June 24, 1946.

**History and Culture.** The name "Apache" is said to be a Zuni Indian word meaning "enemy." The Apache of Oklahoma are also called the Prairie Apache, a name applied to them through error, on the assumption that they were the same as the Apache people of Arizona. They are of the Athapascan linguistic family, but have had no political connection with the Apache Tribes of the Southwest. They came from the North as a component part of the Kiowa. More recent authorities, however, believe that the Apache did divide somewhere in Montana, the main body going southward on the west side of the mountains and a smaller body going northward to become allied on the east side of the mountains with the Kiowa. Whichever theory of their origin is correct, the Apache have a distinct language and called themselves "Nadiishdewa," or "our people." The Pawnee and early French explorers and settlers called them "Gattacka" or "Gataka," and these names appeared on the first treaty they signed with the United States in 1897. Perhaps 1847 marked the beginning of the Apache being identified with the Kiowa, and the two tribes, for the most part, have had a common history.

**Government.** The tribe is not organized under the Oklahoma Indian Welfare Act. From 1936 through 1963, the Apache Tribe was governed by a joint constitution with the Comanche and Kiowa Tribes. In accordance with its current constitution and bylaws, adopted and approved by the Bureau of Indian Affairs in 1971 and ratified in 1972, the tribe is governed by a tribal business committee, which meets once each month. The committee consists of a chairman, vice chairman, secretary-treasurer, and two committee members, who are elected to 2-year concurrent terms.

**Population Profile. 1984:** Total enrollment 891; Indian resident 485; Total labor force 182; Unemployed 96; Unemployment rate 53%. Most Apache children attend public schools in their home communities. During the 1982-83 school year, 16 tribal members attended colleges and universities with assistance from Bureau of Indian Affairs grant funds, and 10 students attended vocational schools. In addition, many Apache adults are attending the various adult education programs.

CADDO TRIBE OF OKLAHOMA                          Federal Trust Area
Caddo County
Tribal Headquarters: Binger, Oklahoma

**Land Status.** Tribally owned land: 2,602.64 acres. Allotted land: 55,599.92 acres. Government owned land: 129.83 acres. Total area: 58,332.39 acres. Land is owned jointly with the Wichita and Delaware Tribes of Oklahoma. Acreage totals include all three tribes. Acreage by individual tribes is not available. This land was ceded by the Caddo, Delaware, and Wichita to the United States pursuant to agreement with the United States on June 4, 1891, and ratified by the Act of May 2, 1895. The land was restored to the tribes by order of the Secretary of the Interior on September 11, 1963.

**History and Culture.** The Caddo belong to the Caddoan linguistic family. They were first known to have been in the Louisiana Territory and were referred to in the chronicles of the DeSoto expedition in 1541. Soon after the United States purchased the Louisiana Territory, a peace treaty was made in which the Caddo ceded all their Louisiana lands and agreed to move. They moved to Texas, and from there on August 1, 1859, they moved to the Indian Territory of Oklahoma and settled on the Washita River in what is now Caddo County, Oklahoma. The present Caddo Tribe also includes the remnants of the Anadarko Tribe.

The Caddo were affiliated with the Wichita and Delaware Tribes after the three tribes were settled north of the Washita River, and their dealings have been relatively friendly ever since. Their affiliation, however, is only in their social activities and their joint landholdings; all three tribes have separate governing bodies.

The Caddo have retained most of their tribal songs and dances, and they conduct dances throughout the year, especially during the spring and summer. They are one of the few tribes that have certain Indian songs they sing in harmony.

**Government.** The tribe is organized under the Oklahoma Indian Welfare Act of 1936. In accordance with its constitution and bylaws, adopted and approved by the Department of the Interior in 1938 and amended in 1976, the tribe is governed by a tribal council, which meets quarterly. The council consists of a chairman, vice chairman, secretary, treasurer, and from four to 15 elected district representatives, all of whom are elected to no more than three consecutive 2-year terms, and elections are staggered. The tribe has a Federal Corporate Charter, which was ratified on November 15, 1938.

**Population Profile. 1984:** Total enrollment 2,947; Indian resident 1,218; Total labor force 509; Unemployed 159; Unemployment rate 31%. Almost all Caddo children attend public schools in their home communities. During the 1984-85 school year, 64 tribal members were attending colleges and universities with assistance from Bureau of Indian Affairs grant funds. In addition, many Caddo adults are attending the various adult education programs. The estimated average education level of Caddo tribal members is 11.5 years.

CHEROKEE NATION OF OKLAHOMA                    Federal Trust Area
Adair, Cherokee, Craig, Delaware, Mayes,
McIntosh, Muskogee, Nowata, Ottawa,
Rogers, Sequoyah, Tulsa, Wagoner, and
Washington Counties
Tribal Headquarters: Tahlequah, Oklahoma

**Land Status.** Tribally owned land: 41,451.35 acres. Allotted land: 50,227.18 acres. Government owned land: 727.44 acres. Total area: 92,405.97 acres. This land is held in trust by the United States for the tribe under the Acts of June 26, 1936 and October 9, 1936.

**History.** The Cherokee originally occupied vast areas in what are now the states of North and South Carolina, Virginia, Tennessee, Georgia, and Alabama. Under the removal policy of the United States Government, the 1835 Treaty of New Echota provided for the forcible relocation of the entire tribe to Indian Territory. There followed a tragic time in Cherokee history, which even today they remember as "The Trail of Tears." About 14,000 Cherokee began the 800-mile journey on foot to what is now Oklahoma. At the time of the exodus, about 1,000 Cherokee, resisting removal, hid in the mountains. After a long struggle, they won recognition as a tribe, since known as the Eastern Band of Cherokee, and were allocated lands that today make up the Cherokee Reservation of North Carolina.

**Culture.** The earliest Cherokee were farmers, artists, hunters, fishers, traders, and warriors. Land-hungry settlers, war, and disease took a heavy toll after the coming of the white man; but by 1820, the tribe had embarked on a period of recovery and rebuilding that led them to rank first among American Indians in progress and prosperity. In 1821, Sequoyah, son of a Cherokee woman and a white trader, invented a Cherokee alphabet with which the tribe learned to read and write in their own language.

**Government.** The Cherokee Nation is not organized under the Oklahoma Indian Welfare Act of 1936. Prior to statehood, the Cherokee Nation had its own tribal government. After statehood (1907), the principal officers of the Five Civilized Tribes of Oklahoma were appointed by the President of the United States under authority of the 1906 Act. The 1970 Act, Public Law 91-495, authorized the Five Civilized Tribes to select their principal officers by popular election. The Cherokee Nation of Oklahoma now operates under a federally recognized constitution, approved by the Commissioner of Indian Affairs in 1975 and ratified in 1976, which provides for a principal chief, deputy principal chief, and a 15-member legislative Tribal Council. Elections are held every four years.

**Population Profile. 1984:** Total enrollment 67,000 (approximate); Indian resident 42,992; Total labor force 21,190; Unemployed 4,105; Unemployment rate 19%. The Cherokee Nation administers a wide range of educational and vocational programs for children and adults. During the 1984-85 school year, 543 higher education grants were awarded, and 44 grant recipients graduated with certificates, bachelor's, or master's degrees.

CHEYENNE-ARAPAHO TRIBES OF OKLAHOMA          Federal Trust Area
Blaine, Canadian, Custer, Dewey, Kingfisher,
Roger Mills, and Washita Counties
Tribal Headquarters: Concho, Oklahoma

**Land Status.** Tribally owned land: 10,405.19 acres. Allotted land: 74,628.39 acres. Government owned land: 2.74 acres. Total area: 85,036.32 acres. Land is owned jointly by the Cheyenne and Arapaho Tribes. Acreage totals include both tribes; acreage by individual tribe is not available.

**History.** The earliest known evidence dates from 1600 and places the Arapaho east of the headwaters of the Mississippi River in Minnesota and the Cheyenne in southwestern and northern Minnesota. The two tribes have long been associated, having wandered in the same direction and fought jointly for defense; yet, they were tribally separate and politically independent. With the westward push of settlers, the Cheyenne and Arapaho moved west and adopted a life style that evolved into the culture of the Plains Indians. Their wandering led them to North and South Dakota, Wyoming, Montana, Nebraska, Kansas, and Colorado. In about 1835, portions separated from the main body became known as the Southern Cheyenne and Southern Arapaho. In 1869, the Cheyenne and Arapaho were assigned a reservation in Oklahoma, and the Darlington Agency was established in 1870 to serve them.

**Culture.** The Cheyenne-Arapaho Tribes speak Algonquian languages. The culture of these tribes evolved from that of a secondary people living in bark houses, growing corn, and making pottery, to the nomadic horsemen of the plains as typified by the standard American version of the Indian clothed in fringed buckskin and full warbonnet and living in a tepee made of buffalo skins. The heritage of the Plains Indian is an established life style based on a pastoral and hunting economy that uses time in line with the season of the year and the habits of the animals that were his lifeblood.

**Government.** The Cheyenne-Arapaho Tribes are organized under the Oklahoma Indian Welfare Act of 1936. In accordance with their constitution and bylaws, adopted in 1937 and amended in 1975, the tribes are governed by the Cheyenne-Arapaho Business Committee consisting of a chairman, vice-chairman, secretary, treasurer, sergeant-at-arms, business manager, and two other elected representatives. Although committee members are elected for 4 years, the chairman, vice chairman, secretary, and treasurer are subject to 2-year terms following each 2-year election.

**Population Profile. 1984:** Total enrollment 8,581; Indian resident 5,220; Total labor force 3,078; Unemployed 1,910; Unemployment rate 62%. Although there is one boarding school located in Anadarko, Oklahoma, and one Indian Junior College located in Lawrence, Kansas, most school-age students attend public schools. At the end of the school semester in 1984, 130 students were enrolled in 12 different colleges with assistance from Bureau of Indian Affairs Higher Education Grant program funds, and six students graduated. Also, there were 130 high school graduates and/or GED-certified students.

CHICKASAW NATION OF OKLAHOMA                Federal Trust Area
Atoka, Bryan, Carter, Garvin, Grady,
Jefferson, Johnston, Love, Marshall,
McClain, Murray, Pontotoc, and
Stephens Counties
Tribal Headquarters:  Ada, Oklahoma

**Land Status.** Tribally owned land: 1,358.28 acres. Allotted land: 76,242.96 acres. Total area: 77,601.24 acres. This land is held in trust by the United States under the Act of July 26, 1936.

**History.** According to the DeSoto narratives of 1540, the earliest habitat traceable for the Chickasaw is northern Mississippi. In addition, they claimed other territory far beyond the narrow limits of their villages. Noted for their warlike disposition, they constantly fought with the neighboring tribes—sometimes with the Choctaw and Creek, sometimes with the Cherokee, Illinois, Kickapoo, Shawnee, Mobilians, Osage, and Quapaw. They were constant enemies of the French, a feeling intensified by the intrigues of British traders and their hatred of the Choctaw, who had entered into friendly relations with the French colonists. Their relations with the United States began with the Hopewell Treaty in 1786, when their northern boundary was fixed at the Ohio River. They began to emigrate west of the Mississippi as early as 1822; in 1832, they signed a treaty yielding their lands in Mississippi in return for a promise by the Government to find them a home west of the Mississippi River. By 1837, most Chickasaw had migrated west to Indian Territory, and in the treaty of 1855, their lands in Indian Territory were definitely separated from those of the Choctaw, with which they had been included.

**Culture.** The Chickasaw are of the Muskogean linguistic family and are one of the Five Civilized Tribes of Oklahoma. Their native written language is the same as that of the Choctaw Nation; their speech is also identical except for some dialectal expressions. At one time, the Chickasaw language served as a medium of commercial and tribal intercourse for all the tribes along the lower Mississippi. In manners and customs they differed little from the Choctaw, although they were less sedentary and agriculturally minded and more turbulent, restless, and warlike in disposition. Their traditional origin is the same as that of the Creek and Choctaw and is given in the so-called "Creek migration legend." The traditional ceremonies, dances, and language of the Chickasaw are still maintained as a matter of pride and historical interest though they are seldom an important part of Chickasaw life. This Indian nation has commingled both culturally and economically with the non-Indian society to a greater degree than many other Oklahoma tribes.

**Government.** The Chickasaw Nation is not organized under the Oklahoma Indian Welfare Act. Prior to statehood, the Chickasaw Nation had its own tribal government. After statehood (1907), the principal officers of the Five Civilized Tribes of Oklahoma were appointed by the President of the United States under authority of the Act of 1906. The 1970 Act, Public Law 91-495, authorized the Five Civilized Tribes of Oklahoma to select their principal officers by popular election. The

Chickasaw Nation of Oklahoma now operates under its constitution of 1979, which was amended, approved by the Bureau of Indian Affairs, and ratified in 1983. This constitution provides for a governor, a lieutenant governor, and a 13-member tribal council. Elections for governor and lieutenant governor are held every 4 years; council members are elected every 3 years.

**Population Profile.** 1984: Total enrollment 11,780 (as of 1980); Indian resident 9,020; Total labor force 3,689; Unemployed 1,107; Unemployment rate 30%. Most Indian children in the Chickasaw Nation attend public schools rather than BIA boarding schools. Effective October 1983, the Higher Education Grant Program was contracted by the Chickasaw Nation, and in 1985, 69 Chickasaws were enrolled in colleges or universities and 7 graduated. In addition, the Chickasaw Nation administers a wide range of educational and vocational programs for children and adults.

CHOCTAW NATION OF OKLAHOMA                    Federal Trust Area
Atoka, Bryan, Choctaw, Coal, Haskell,
  Hughes, Latimer, LeFlore, McCurtain,
  Pittsburg, Pontotoc, and Pushmataha
  Counties
Tribal Headquarters: Durant, Oklahoma

**Land Status.** Tribally owned land: 11,161.27 acres. Allotted land: 121,718.30 acres. Government owned land 297.00 acres. Total area: 133,176.57 acres. This land is held in trust by the United States under the Act of July 26, 1936.

**History.** According to Choctaw legends, the tribe, which belongs to the Muskogean linguistic family, originated from the sacred hill called "Nanih Waiya" near what is now Noxapater, Mississippi. The first recorded white contact with the tribe was in October 1540, when Choctaw warriors under Tuskalusa fought a 9-hour losing battle to protect their lands near present-day Mobile, Alabama, from attack by DeSoto and his expeditional force. Tribal legend tells that Choctaw survivors hanged themselves rather than surrender. Otherwise, little is known about the early history of the tribe until the 18th Century, when most Choctaw allied with the French, who were fighting the British and their Indian allies, the Chickasaw and Natchez, for colonial territories and trading rights. Later, during the periods of British control (1763-1783) and Spanish control (1783-1819), some Choctaw troops fought under American generals in both the Revolutionary War and the War of 1812. In 1819, Choctaw lands, which once included much of what are now Alabama and Mississippi, came to the United States by a treaty with Spain. Under the 1830 Treaty of Dancing Rabbit Creek, Mississippi, the Choctaw became the first of the five great southern tribes to be forcibly removed to Indian Territory. A small remnant remained, from which today's Mississippi Choctaw descend. The removal, from 1831 to 1834, was full of hardships from beginning to end.

By the time Oklahoma became a state in 1907, the Choctaw Nation had been a party to 16 treaties and agreements with the United States, under which the Government made nominal payments for Choctaw lands, but the Curtis Act of 1898 cleared the way for complete domination by white settlers. Tribal government, however, continued in limited form under Federal supervision until federal relationships with the Choctaw Nation as a separate government within the boundaries of Oklahoma ended in 1950.

**Culture.** The name "Choctaw" is the anglicized form of the tribal name, "Chahta." Choctaw society was a matriarchy organized according to the ancient tribal clan. The Choctaw were pre-eminent among southeastern tribes as agriculturalists raising corn, melons, pumpkins, and sunflowers, and adopting other vegetables and domestic livestock with the advent of the French. They have always been known for patience, diplomacy, and the avoidance of aggressive warfare, though they have been ready to fight bravely and tenaciously in defense of their own territory. Additionally, they are noted for their educational accomplishments, aided by enlightened missionary efforts.

**Government.** The Choctaw Nation is not organized under the Oklahoma Indian Welfare Act of 1936. Prior to statehood, the Choctaw Nation had its own tribal government. After statehood, the principal officers of the Five Civilized Tribes of Oklahoma were appointed by the President of the United States under authority of the 1906 Act. The 1970 Act, Public Law 91-495, authorized the Five Civilized Tribes of Oklahoma to select their principal officers by popular election. The Choctaw Nation of Oklahoma now operates under its constitution of 1979, which was amended, approved by the Bureau of Indian Affairs, and ratified in 1983. This constitution provides for a principal chief, an assistant chief, and a 12-member tribal council, who are elected to 4-year terms.

**Population Profile. 1984:** Total enrollment 90,000; Indian resident 20,054; Total labor force 7,905; Unemployed 1,900; Unemployment rate 24%. The Choctaw Nation was contracted for the operation of the Johnson O'Malley Program, which currently assists 2,440 Indian students and 48 school districts within the counties, in coordination with proposals written by each county's Parent Committee. In addition, 181 students are currently enrolled at Jones Academy in Hartshorne, Oklahoma. The Choctaw Nation also operates an expanding Headstart program and a GED program. Its Higher Education Program awarded 309 grants and scholarships in 1985.


CITIZEN BAND POTAWATOMI TRIBE OF                Federal Trust Area
OKLAHOMA
Cleveland, Oklahoma, and Pottawatomi
Counties
Tribal Headquarters: Shawnee, Oklahoma


**Land Status.** Tribally owned land: 261.34 acres. Allotted land: 3,769.46 acres. Total area: 4,030.80 acres.

**History.** Prior to 1700, the Potawatomi lived near the upper Lake Huron territory and on the islands of Green Bay, Wisconsin. They were later located near what is now Chicago and Milwaukee. During the

French and Indian War, they were close allies of the French until the peace of 1763. They were also allied with Ottawa chief Pontiac against the British and white settlers. During the Revolutionary War, however, they fought with the British against the American colonies; and hostilities continued until the Treaty of Greenville of 1795 brought about peace between the colonies and the Potawatomi.

In 1833, the Potawatomi, together with the Ottawa and Chippewa, signed the Chicago Treaty, ceding all their lands in Illinois and along the western shore of Lake Michigan and agreeing to move to Iowa within 3 years. They were in Iowa only briefly before the Government moved them again, this time to Kansas. Today, in Kansas, the Prairie Band of Potawatomi is descended mainly from Indiana, Illinois, and Michigan Potawatomi.

The Citizen Band Potawatomi Tribe of Oklahoma is so-called because certain Prairie Band members applied for citizenship papers in the 1860's, having been granted this right by treaty. Many sold their fee patent land in Kansas; and, landless and destitute, they were removed to Indian Territory. Reservation land was provided for them there; however, since they were citizens, legal questions arose as to their right to live on it. Today, there is no Potawatomi reservation in Oklahoma, but the band owns 1.25 acres of land; individual band members own land, also.

**Culture.** The Potawatomi Tribe is a member of the Algonquian linguistic group, and its name is derived from the Chippewa (Ojibway) term "Potawatomink," which means "People of the Place of the Fire." Tribal members have been fully integrated in the broader society. However, many individual Indians maintain some semblance of their culture in arts and crafts, dances, and other activities.

**Government.** The tribe is organized under the Oklahoma Indian Welfare Act of 1936. In accordance with its federally approved constitution of 1938, most recently amended in 1985, it is governed by a business committee consisting of a chairman, vice chairman, secretary-treasurer, and two committee members, all of whom are elected to staggered 2-year terms. Regular meetings of the committee are held quarterly.

**Population Profile. 1984:** Total enrollment 11,088; Indian resident 1,910; Total labor force 1,086; Unemployed 188; Unemployment rate 17%. No Citizen Band Potawatomi children are enrolled in either of the two boarding schools in the Anadarko area. Due to a low blood quantum requirement for tribal membership, very few qualify for Bureau of Indian Affairs programs. Only 11 band members were attending college through the BIA Scholarship Program in 1985. The tribe has its own Scholarship Program, however, and 50 members were attending some type of higher education program.


COMANCHE TRIBE                              Federal Trust Area
Caddo, Comanche, Cotton,
   and Kiowa Counties
Tribal Headquarters:  Lawton, Oklahoma

**Land Status.** Tribally owned land: 7,045.80 acres. Allotted land:

201,350.17 acres. Government owned land: 1.00 acre. Total area: 208,396.97 acres. Land is owned jointly with the Apache and Kiowa Tribes of Oklahoma. Total acreage includes all three tribes; acreage by individual tribe is not available. This land is held in trust by the United States under the Act of June 24, 1946.

**History.** The Comanche were one of the southern tribes of the Shoshonean stock and the only one to live entirely on the Plains. They are a comparatively recent offshoot of the Shoshoni of Wyoming and, until recently, kept in continual friendly communication with them.

For nearly 2 centuries they were at war with the Spaniards in Mexico and raided Mexican settlements as far south as Durango and Zacatecas. Generally friendly to the Americans, they were bitter enemies of the Texans, who had dispossessed them of their best hunting grounds, and they waged relentless war against them for almost 40 years. Around 1795, they became close confederates of the Kiowa and also allied themselves with the Apache.

Several treaties were consummated between the United States and the Comanche Tribe between 1834 and 1875. In the Treaty of Medicine Lodge in 1867, the Comanche, Apache, and Kiowa Tribes were assigned a tract of land in Oklahoma between the Washita and Red Rivers in southwestern Oklahoma, which they still share.

**Culture.** The Comanche are of the Shoshonean linguistic group. In 1719, they were mentioned as living in what is now western Kansas. Legends indicate that they may have had horses before the Spanish arrived. Where they obtained them is not known. The horse changed the Comanche's mode of living into a nomadic one. They made little agricultural use of the land and lived in easily transportable tepees. Long known as the finest horsemen of the Plains, they had a reputation for courage in batttle when facing great odds. They were traditionally hunters. Their diet consisted of game meat, berries, and edible roots, but mainly of the buffalo, whose skin was used for clothing, bedding, and shelter. Generally, they are today dedicated to a middle-class agricultural economy.

**Government.** The Comanche Tribe is not organized under the Oklahoma Indian Welfare Act of 1936. From 1936 through 1963, the Comanche Tribe was governed by a joint constitution with the Apache and Kiowa Tribes. In accordance with its current constitution and bylaws, adopted by voters in 1966 and approved by the Bureau of Indian Affairs in 1967, it is governed by a tribal business committee consisting of a chairman, vice chairman, secretary-treasurer, and four committee members, all of whom are elected for 3-year staggered terms. Regular meetings of the business committee are held monthly.

**Population Profile. 1984:** Total enrollment 8,131; Indian resident 3,642; Total labor force 1,492; Unemployed 692; Unemployment rate 46%. Most Comanche children attend public schools in their home communities. During the 1982-83 school year, 123 tribal members were attending colleges and universities with assistance from Bureau of Indian Affairs grant funds. According to the 1970 census, the median education level of tribal members 25 years of age and older was 12 years. In addition, many Comanche adults are participating in the various adult education programs.

DELAWARE TRIBE OF WESTERN OKLAHOMA        Federal Trust Area
Caddo, Oklahoma
Tribal Headquarters:  Anadarko, Oklahoma

**Land Status.** Tribally owned land: 2,602.64 acres. Allotted land: 55,599.92 acres. Government owned land: 129.83 acres. Total area: 58,332.39 acres. Land is owned jointly with the Caddo and Wichita Tribes of Oklahoma. Acreage totals include all three tribes; acreage by individual tribes is not available. This land was ceded by the Caddo, Delaware, and Wichita to the United States pursuant to agreement with the United States on June 4, 1891, and ratified by the Act of May 2, 1895. The land was restored to the tribes by order of the Secretary of the Interior on September 11, 1963.

**History and Culture.** The Delaware call themselves Lenape, meaning "real men," or Leni Lenape, signifying "men of our nation." The English name Delaware was given to the tribe from the river named for Lord De La Warr, the valley of which was the tribal center in earliest colonial times, extending from southeastern New York into eastern Pennsylvania through New Jersey and Delaware. The early traditional history of the Delaware is contained in their national legend, the Walam Olum.

The Delaware are members of the Algonquian linguistic family. They were once one of the larger tribes of the Eastern Woodland people. Gradually they moved west and were located in at least 10 different states during this migration. At present, two groups of Delaware live in Oklahoma. The main part of the tribe, known as "Registered Delaware," came from their reservation in Kansas in 1867 and settled with the Cherokee and were allotted land with them. Their descendants live in Washington, Craig, Nowata, and Delaware Counties. The other group, still a distinct Delaware Tribe, was associated with the Caddo and Wichita Tribes in Texas and came to the Washita River in Indian Territory in 1859. A number of Delaware moved and associated with other tribes in the north and northwestern country. Approximately 750 Delaware are called Absentee Delaware.

**Government.** The tribe is not organized under the Oklahoma Indian Welfare Act of 1936. The tribal executive committee was approved by resolution and adopted by the tribe in 1958; the tribe's constitution and bylaws were approved and ratified in 1973. In accordance with its constitution, the executive committee consists of a president, vice president, secretary, treasurer, and two committee members, who are elected to no more than two consecutive 4-year terms. Elections are staggered.

**Population Profile.** 1984: Total enrollment 989; Indian resident 396; Total labor force 191; Unemployed 86; Unemployment rate 45%. Almost all Delaware children attend public schools in their home communities. During the 1984-85 school year, 18 tribal members were attending colleges and universities with assistance from Bureau of Indian Affairs grant funds. The average education level of Delaware tribal members is quite high; except for the very elderly, very few tribal members have less than a high school education, and an unusually large number have some college or vocational training. In addition, many Delaware adults are participating in the various adult education programs.

**EASTERN SHAWNEE TRIBE OF OKLAHOMA**      Federal Trust Area
Ottawa County
Tribal Headquarters: Quapaw, Oklahoma

**Land Status.** Tribally owned land: 84.48 acres. Allotted land: 708.46 acres. Total area: 792.94 acres. This land was purchased for the Eastern Shawnee under authority found in Section 1 of the Oklahoma Indian Welfare Act of June 26, 1936, with funds made available by the Appropriation Act of August 9, 1937, Public Law 249, 75th Congress.

**History.** The Shawnee were formerly a leading tribe with settlements in South Carolina, Tennessee, Pennsylvania, and Ohio. Because of both their interior position away from the traveled routes of early days and their migratory habits, little is known of their origin. Delaware Indian tradition claims that the Shawnee and Nanticoke were originally one people; and, while this may or may not be true, Shawnee today refer to the Delaware as their "grandfathers."

Historically, the Shawnee became known around 1670. At that time they lived in two main bodies at a considerable distance from each other—one in the Cumberland region of Tennessee and the other on the Savannah River in South Carolina. During the late 18th Century, the two main bodies united in Ohio. For about 40 years, until the Treaty of Greenville in 1795, the Shawnee were almost constantly at war with the English and the Anglo-Americans. After the death of Tecumseh, their most famous war chief, they lost their taste for war and began to move to their present locations. One group settled on a reservation in Kansas; another went to Texas to join a band of Cherokee. A third group settled on the Canadian River in the Indian Territory of Oklahoma, just south of the Quapaw Reserve, and are today known as the Absentee-Shawnee Tribe of Oklahoma. Another band, which also settled in eastern Oklahoma, is today known as the Eastern Shawnee Tribe of Oklahoma.

**Culture.** Linguistically, the Eastern Shawnee Tribe belongs to the Central Algonquian dialect group and were the southern advance guard of the Algonquian stock, closely related to the Sac and Fox. The name "Shawnee" derives from an Algonquian word, <u>Shawunog</u>, meaning "Southerners." The majority of the tribe has accepted modern life. However, many older members cling to tribal traditions as evidenced by religion, arts and crafts, powwows, and speaking the native language in the home.

**Population Profile. 1984:** Total enrollment 1,400 (approximate); Indian resident 377; Total labor force 175; Unemployed 26; Unemployment rate 15%.


**FORT SILL APACHE TRIBE OF OKLAHOMA**      Federal Trust Area
Caddo and Comanche Counties
Tribal Headquarters: Apache, Oklahoma

**Land Status.** Tribally owned land: 38.65 acres. Allotted land: 3,044.25 acres. Total area: 3,082.90 acres.

**History.** The Fort Sill Apache are composed of members of the

Warm Springs Band of Apache and the Chiricahua Apache. This small group of Indians is often referred to as Chief Geronimo's Band of Apache. According to older members of this group, Victorio, chief of the Apache, took a group of 40 warriors on the warpath to protest the tribe's being moved from their New Mexico reservation to one located at San Carlos, Arizona. Upon Victorio's death at the hands of a band of Mexicans in Chihuahua, State of Mexico, Geronimo assumed command of the group. He carried on warfare until August 1886, when Gen. Nelson A. Miles forced him to surrender. Geronimo and all his band were taken as prisoners of war to Fort Marion, Florida, near St. Augustine. Because of many deaths and much sickness in the tribe, the Government removed them to Mount Vernon Barracks, Alabama, where they were kept prisoner for 7 years. On October 4, 1894, Geronimo and the remnants of his band, now about 296 in all, were brought from Alabama to Fort Sill, Oklahoma. They remained at the Fort Sill Military Reservation as nominal prisoners of war until 1913, when the Government arranged to allot an 80-acre tract of land to each member who desired to remain in Oklahoma. Those who wished to move to the Mescalero Reservation in New Mexico could do so, and only 87 stayed in Oklahoma and were given allotments of land in or near what is now the town of Apache.

**Government.** The tribe is not organized under the Oklahoma Indian Welfare Act of 1936. In accordance with its 1976 constitution and bylaws, approved by the Bureau of Indian Affairs, it is governed by a tribal business committee consisting of a chairman, vice chairman, secretary-treasurer, and three committee members. Elections are staggered and held every 2 years.

**Population Profile. 1984:** Total enrollment 306; Indian resident 70; Total labor force 38; Unemployed 18; Unemployment rate 47%. Almost all Fort Sill Apache children attend public schools in their home communities. During the 1984-85 school year, seven were attending colleges and universities with assistance from Bureau of Indian Affairs grant funds. The average education level of Fort Sill Apache tribal members is quite high; except for the elderly, very few members have less than a high school education. In addition, many Fort Sill Apache adults are participating in the various adult education programs.


IOWA TRIBE OF OKLAHOMA                    Federal Trust Area
Lincoln, Logan, Oklahoma, and
  Payne Counties
Tribal Headquarters: Perkins, Oklahoma

**Land Status.** Tribally owned land: 20.50 acres. Allotted land: 1,297.77 acres. Total area: 1,318.27 acres.

**History.** The earliest known Iowa settlement is believed to have been along the Upper Iowa River. Later they moved into the north-western part of the present State of Iowa. In the latter part of the 18th Century, the Iowa moved to the Missouri River and settled south of the spot where Council Bluffs, Iowa, now stands on the east side of the river. About 1760, they moved east and came to live along the Mississippi between the Iowa and Des Moines Rivers. Early in the 19th

Century, part of the tribe moved further up the Des Moines River, while others established themselves on the Grand and Platte Rivers, Missouri. In 1814, they were allotted lands in what was known as "The Platte Purchase," extending from the Platte River of Missouri through western Iowa to the Dakota country. By treaties signed August 4, 1824; July 15, 1930; September 17, 1836; and November 23, 1867, they ceded all their lands in Missouri and Iowa to the United States. On August 19, 1825, they also ceded lands in Minnesota. The Treaty of 1836 assigned part of the tribe to a reservation along the Great Nemaha River, in present-day Richardson County, Nebraska, and Brown County, Kansas. The remainder were moved to central Oklahoma in 1883.

**Culture.** The people have, for the most part, adopted modern ways; however, they still cling to some aspects of their tribal culture as revealed in arts and crafts, funeral customs, adoptions to replace deceased members of the family, feasts, and annual powwows.

**Government.** The tribe is organized under the Oklahoma Indian Welfare Act of 1936. In accordance with its recent constitution, approved and ratified in 1977 and superseding that of 1937, the tribe is governed by a business committee consisting of a chairperson, vice chairperson, secretary, treasurer, and one council member, all of whom are elected to staggered 2-year terms. Regular meetings of the business committee are held quarterly.

**Population Profile. 1984:** Total enrollment 280; Indian resident 155; Total labor force 63; Unemployed 17; Unemployment rate 27%. Although a few Iowa children attend the two boarding schools in the Anadarko area, most attend public schools. Usually 5 to 10 attend some type of higher education program each year through the Bureau of Indian Affairs Scholarship Program.

KAW TRIBE OF OKLAHOMA     Federal Trust Area
Kay County
Tribal Headquarters: Kaw City, Oklahoma

**Land Status.** Tribally owned land: 183.50 acres. Total area: 183.50 acres.

**History.** The Kaw or Kansa are one of five tribes in the Dhegiha group of the Siouan linguistic family. According to tradition, the five tribes—Kaw, Osage, Ponca, Omaha, and Quapaw—were one people and lived along the Wabash River and far up the Ohio. Pushed westward by the encroachment of superior forces, they split at the mouth of the Ohio River. Those going down the Mississippi River took the name "Quapaw" or "Downstream People." The latter afterward divided into four tribes—the Kaw, Osage, Ponca, and Omaha. By terms of the treaties with the United States from 1820 to 1846, the Kaw relinquished their claims to several million acres in Kansas and Nebraska. A new reservation was assigned them in 1846 at Council Grove on the Neosho River, Kansas. These lands were finally overrun by white settlers. In 1872, the tract was sold, and a new reserve was purchased for the tribe near the Osage, in Indian Territory. In 1902, that reservation was allotted under law to the tribal membership; and today there is no tribal member who still owns any of the trust land.

**Culture.** For the most part, the Kaw have been assimilated with the surrounding non-Indian community and carry on their everyday activities in the same manner as their non-Indian neighbors.

**Government.** The tribe is organized under a governing resolution adopted in 1958 and approved by the Secretary of the Interior in 1959. This resolution provides for a business committee consisting of a chairman, vice chairman, secretary-treasurer, and three committee members, all elected to 4-year terms. Regular meetings of the business committee are held monthly.

**Population Profile. 1984:** Total enrollment 1,064; Indian resident 543; Total labor force 289; Unemployed 72; Unemployment rate 25%. Tribal members reside throughout the area both on farms and in local communities. Some of the school systems support Title IV-A Indian Education programs. While the Kaw Tribe does not sponsor any of these educational programs, tribal members are eligible for benefits under them. A Tribal Higher Education program operates from tribal headquarters, administering BIA Higher Education funds, and in 1985, six Higher Education and five Adult Vocational Training students received benefits under this program.


KICKAPOO TRIBE OF OKLAHOMA                    Federal Trust Area
Lincoln, Oklahoma, and Pottawatomi Counties
Tribal Headquarters: McLoud, Oklahoma

**Land Status.** Tribally owned land: 173.23 acres. Allotted land: 5,260.53 acres. Total area: 5,433.76 acres.

**History.** The Kickapoo moved into the Wisconsin area in the early part of the 17th Century. They later moved into Illinois, near the present-day city of Peoria. During the War of 1812, they were allies of Tecumseh, a Shawnee chief against the United States. In 1809 and 1819, the Kickapoo ceded their lands in Illinois to the United States and moved to Missouri and then Kansas. About 1852, a large part of Kickapoo, along with some Potawatomi, went to Texas and then to Mexico, where they became known as "Mexican Kickapoo." In 1863, another dissatisfied band joined them. Ten years later, part of this band was induced to return to Indian Territory. Those who chose to remain in Mexico were granted a reservation on the Sabinas River about 12 to 15 miles from the town of Musquiz, State of Coahuila.

**Culture.** The Kickapoo belong to the Algonquian linguistic family and are closely related to the Sac and Fox. Most tribal members still adhere to tribal custom and tradition in religion, arts and crafts, funerals, and other such activities.

**Government.** The tribe is organized under the Oklahoma Indian Welfare Act of 1936. In accordance with its constitution, ratified in 1937 and amended in 1977, the tribe is governed by a business committee consisting of a chairman, vice chairman, secretary, treasurer, and councilman. Elections are staggered; all members are elected every 3 years and councilmen are limited to 2 consecutive terms. Regular meetings of the business committee are held quarterly. A Federal Charter was adopted in 1938.

**Population Profile. 1984:** Total enrollment 1,757; Indian resident 1,001; Total labor force 381; Unemployed 85; Unemployment rate 22%. Although there are two boarding schools in the Anadarko area, few Kickapoo children attend them, and most attend public schools. Only about 16 attend some type of higher education each year, through the Bureau of Indian Affairs Scholarship Program.


KIOWA TRIBE OF OKLAHOMA                    Federal Trust Area
Caddo, Comanche, Cotton,
  and Kiowa Counties
Tribal Headquarters: Carnegie, Oklahoma

**Land Status.** Tribally owned land: 7,045.80 acres. Allotted land: 201,350.17 acres. Government owned land: 1.00 acre. Total area: 208,396.97 acres. Land is owned jointly with the Apache and Comanche Tribes of Oklahoma. Acreage totals include all three tribes; acreage by individual tribes is not available. This land is held in trust by the United States under the Act of June 24, 1946.

**History.** The Kiowa were believed to have migrated from the mountain regions at the source of the Yellowstone and Missouri Rivers in what is now western Montana. According to tradition, they left this region because of a dispute with another tribe over hunting spoils, and they moved to the Black Hills in present-day South Dakota. Toward the end of the 18th Century, the Kiowa were driven south by the Sioux, finally settling in the area of present western Oklahoma and the Panhandle of north Texas, and west into a part of New Mexico.

Early in their history, they formed an alliance with a small band of Apache, which continues today in Oklahoma. And in 1790, having made peace with their one-time enemies, the Comanche, they established control of the area from the Arkansas River to the headwaters of the Red River and the two tribes became masters of the southern Plains. This alliance appears to be the basis for both the Kiowa-Apache-Comanche alliance of today and also the Kiowa-Comanche Reservation in Oklahoma, where the two tribes were settled by the United States. In 1840, the Kiowa made a permanent peace with the Cheyenne and their allies, the Arapaho, and became friendly with the Wichita. However, they were enemies with the Caddo as well as with the Navajo and the Ute and some western Apache groups.

Throughout the 19th Century they continually resisted white immigration along the overland trails. With the Comanche, they attacked Texas frontier settlements, extending their raids far south into Mexico. Treaties with the United States Government beginning in 1837 had little effect, and the tribe continued fighting. After the Battle of Washita in 1868, the Kiowa, Apache, and Comanche were forced onto a reservation near Fort Sill, Oklahoma. Their defiance continued, however, and only military defeats and the disappearance of the buffalo ended their resistance.

**Culture.** The name "Kiowa" comes from the tribe's own word, "Gaigwu" (or "Kaigwu"), signifying "principal people." It was also the name of one of the six divisions that made up the tribal camp circle when they came eastward to the Plains from their original home in the Rocky Mountains. Only the Kiowa Tribe is classed in the Kiowan linguistic family.

When they came to South Dakota in the early 18th Century, they formed a permanent alliance with the Crow, which contributed to their change from small game hunters using the dog and travois to buffalo hunters with large herds of horses. They became a typical Plains tribe, adopting the buffalo-skin tepee, the annual summer Sun Dance, and medicine bundles, and establishing soldier societies such as the "Koitsenko." Among Indian tribes north of Mexico, the Kiowa are distinguished for their pictographic records in the form of calendar histories.

They are regarded as one of the great Plains tribes, reputedly very brave and courageous and the most warlike and defiant of the tribes in the Southwest. In their raids, which ended less than a hundred years ago, they are said to have killed more white men than any other tribe. Today they are considered one of the more progressive Indian groups in southwestern Oklahoma.

**Government.** The tribe is not organized under the Oklahoma Indian Welfare Act of 1936. From 1936 through 1963, the Kiowa Tribe was governed by a joint constitution with the Apache and Comanche Tribes. In accordance with its current constitution and bylaws, adopted and approved by the Bureau of Indian Affairs in 1970, the tribe is governed by a tribal business committee consisting of a chairman, vice chairman, secretary, treasurer, and four committee members. Elections are staggered, and members are limited to two consecutive 2-year terms. Regular meetings of the business committee are held monthly.

**Population Profile. 1984:** Total enrollment 8,602; Total labor force 1,638; Indian resident 3,999; Unemployment 771; Unemployment rate 47%. Most Kiowa children attend public schools in their home communities. During the 1982-83 school year, 173 tribal members attended colleges and universities with assistance from Bureau of Indian Affairs grant funds. According to the 1970 census, the median education level of Kiowa tribal members 25 years of age and over was 12.1 years. In addition, many Kiowa adults are participating in the various adult education programs.


MIAMI TRIBE OF OKLAHOMA                    Federal Trust Area
Ottawa County
Tribal Headquarters: Miami, Oklahoma

**Land Status.** Tribally owned land: 57.93 acres. Total area: 57.93 acres.

**History.** The Miami are an Algonquian tribe, the earliest recorded notice of which is from information furnished in 1658 by Gabriel Druillette, who called them the Oumanik. Then living about the mouth of Green Bay, Wisconsin, they withdrew into the Mississippi Valley 60 leagues away and were established there from 1657 to 1676. The first time the French came into actual contact with them was in 1668. In about 1671, the Miami formed new settlements at the south end of Lake Michigan, where missions were established late in the 17th Century, and on the Kalamazoo River in Michigan. The extent of territory they occupied a few years later suggests that when the whites first heard of them, the Miami Indians in Wisconsin formed but a part of the tribe, with other bodies already established in northeast Illinois and Indiana. Encroachments by the Potawatomi, Kickapoo, and other northern tribes drove the Miami out to the east, and they formed settlements on the Miami River in Ohio. They held this country until the peace of 1763, when they retired to Indiana. They played a permanent role in all the Indian wars in the Ohio Valley until the close of the War of 1812. Soon after, they began to sell their lands; and by 1827, they had disposed of most of their holdings in Indiana and had agreed to move to Kansas. They later moved to Indian Territory, where the remnant still resides.

**Government.** The tribe is organized under the Oklahoma Indian Welfare Act of 1936. In accordance with its constitution of 1939, the tribe is governed by a business committee consisting of a chief, second chief, secretary-treasurer, and two councilmen, all of whom are elected to 3-year terms. Regular meetings of the business committee are held monthly. A Federal Charter was ratified in 1940.

**Population Profile.** 1984: Total enrollment 1,900 (approximate); Indian resident 393; Total labor force 161; Unemployment 24; Unemployment rate 15%.

MODOC TRIBE OF OKLAHOMA                    Federal Trust Area
Ottawa County
Tribal Headquarters: 74355

**Land Status.** Tribally owned land: 9.34 acres. Total area: 9.34 acres.

**History.** Before the advent of the white man, Modoc territory extended from southwestern Oregon into northwestern California as far east as Goose Lake. In 1864, the Modoc entered into a treaty with the United States, ceding their California lands to the Government and agreeing to reside with the Klamath on their reservation in Oregon. However, the Modoc were held in disregard by the Klamath and grew restless and discontented, both with their lot and with the fact that confirmation of the treaty was delayed from year to year. In 1870, a group of Modoc under the leadership of "Captain Jack" (Kintpuash) left the Klamath Reservation, determined to obtain a reservation on their former lands in California. Attempts to force them to return to the Klamath Reservation resulted in the Modoc War of 1872-73. After resisting for months, Captain Jack surrendered, was tried by court martial at Fort Klamath and was hanged, together with three of his warriors. The remaining rebels were exiled to the Oklahoma Indian Territory until an act of Congress restored them to the Klamath Reservation in Oregon in the early 20th Century. Some opted to remain in Oklahoma, where their descendants live today; but descendants of the largest surviving group live on the Klamath Reservation in southwest Oregon.

The Act of August 1, 1956, terminating Federal supervision over the property of the Modoc Tribe, was repealed by the Act of May 15, 1978, which reinstated the Modoc as a federally recognized tribe.

**Culture.** The Modoc are related to the Klamath Indians, both tribes belonging to the Lupuamian linguistic family living in southeastern Oregon. The name "Modoc" is from the Indian word "Moatokni," meaning "Southerners." Conflicts with early white settlers in the West won the Modoc a reputation of being warlike and ferocious.

**Government.** The tribe is not organized under the Oklahoma Indian Welfare Act of 1936. Although the Modoc do not at present have a constitution, a Self-Determination grant has been awarded to the tribe for the purpose of developing one. The tribe has a chief, an historian and a grants coordinator.

**Population Profile.** 1984: Total enrollment 200 (approximate); Indian resident 133; Total labor force 63; Unemployed 10; Unemployment rate 16%.


MUSCOGEE (CREEK) NATION                    Federal Trust Area
Creek, Hughes, Mayes, McIntosh,
  Muskogee, Okfuskee, Okmulgee,
  Rogers, Seminole, Tulsa, and
  Wagoner Counties
Tribal Headquarters: Okmulgee, Oklahoma

**Land Status.** Tribally owned land: 5,943.34 acres. Allotted land: 137,437.64 acres. Government owned land: 3.20 acres. Total area: 143,384.18 acres. This land is held in trust by the United States under the Act of July 26, 1936.

**History.** The Muscogee (Creek) Nation, one of Oklahoma's Five Civilized Tribes, was so named by the English because of the large number of watercourses in its country. During early times, they occupied most of Alabama and Georgia, living along the Coosa and Tallapoosa Rivers and along the Flint and Chattahoochee Rivers. When discovered by DeSoto in 1540, they had already formed the Creek Confederacy to resist attack from powerful northern tribes; and they were successful.

Between 1836 and 1840, approximately 20,000 Muscogee (Creek) were removed to Oklahoma, where they established their seat of government at Okmulgee, consisting of a principal chief, judicial department, and legislature. Impoverished first by the removal and later by the Civil War, their resourcefulness is evidenced by the swiftness with which they recovered from disaster and prospered.

Today there are four main groups of Muscogee (Creek) in Oklahoma—the Creek Nation, the Alabama-Quassarte (Coushatta), the Kialegee, and the Thlopthlocco Creek, each with a tribal council and all of whom form today's Creek Confederacy, with its seat of government still at Okmulgee in eastern Oklahoma.

**Culture.** The Creek Confederacy of the 16th Century was dominated by the Abihka, Kusa, Kashita, Kawita, Wakokai, Hilibi, and Huhliwahli, each with its own language and communities. Each town or small tribe was under an elected chief, who was advised by the town council on all important matters. Though the chief had great authority and kingly attributes, he was king only by the will of the people, since high rank was not hereditary and could only be gained by proving superior fitness. The Creek early conceived the idea of subordinating the military to civilian authority. War chiefs merely led the fighting, with governing left to rulers chosen for their wisdom and general ability.

The Muscogee (Creek) society was orginally matriarchal, and the effects of this are still evident among present-day Muscogee (Creek). While property is no longer owned in total by the female, the concept of joint ownership of property is not willingly assumed by the Muscogee (Creek). Early recognizing the need for education, the Muscogee (Creek) today are considered among the most advanced Indians in the country and have contributed their industry and skills to every major contemporary occupation.

**Government.** The Muscogee (Creek) Nation is organized under the Oklahoma Indian Welfare Act of 1936. Prior to statehood, the Muscogee (Creek) Nation had its own tribal government. After statehood (1907), the principal officers of the Five Civilized Tribes were appointed by the President of the United States under authority of the 1906 Act. The 1970 Act, Public Law 91-495, authorized the Five Civilized Tribes of Oklahoma to select their principal officers by popular election. The Muscogee (Creek) Nation of Oklahoma now operates under its constitution, approved by the Bureau of Indian Affairs and ratified in 1979, which provides for a principal chief, a second chief, and a national council. Officers are elected for 4-year terms; council members are elected for 2-year terms.

**Population Profile. 1984:** Total enrollment 50,000 (approximate); Indian resident 42,519; Total labor force 16,393; Unemployed 3,311; Unemployment rate 20%. There are no reservation schools with the exception of a Bureau of Indian Affairs boarding school at Eufaula, Okla., located within the boundaries of the Muscogee (Creek) Nation. At present, the tribe is conducting both Head Start Programs and an Adult Education Program. According to the 1975 Socio-Economic Census, the tribe estimates the dropout rate for secondary school students within a given academic year to be about 4.5 percent per year. There are approximately 72 different public school districts either wholly or partially within the tribal boundaries, making public school attendance accessible to tribal children. During the 1980-81 school year, 268 tribal members were attending 61 different colleges with assistance from Bureau of Indian Affairs grant funds.


OSAGE TRIBE                                        Federal Trust Area
Osage County
Tribal Headquarters: Pawhuska, Oklahoma

**Land Status.** Tribally owned land: 674.80 acres. Allotted land: 170,307.18 acres. Total area: 170,981.98 acres. This land is reserved for allotment by Section 2 of the Act of June 28, 1906. In addition, the Osage Tribe is in the process of having beneficial ownership returned to it for approximately 730 acres of former railroad right-of-way.

**History.** The first historical notice taken of the Osage appears to have been by the French explorer Marquette, who located them on his map of 1673 on the Osage River. They were a warlike people, held in terror by the surrounding tribes, especially the Caddoans.

Under treaties of 1808, 1818, and 1825, the Osage ceded to the Government much of their land in Arkansas and all lands west of the Missouri River. Subsequent treaties further reduced their lands until their present reservation was established in the northeastern part of Oklahoma in 1870. At the turn of the 20th Century, the Osage were considered to be the wealthiest tribe in the United States because oil was discovered on Osage land. However, every oil-rich Osage has a score of contemporaries without oil who continue to farm their lands in Oklahoma as did their grandfathers.

**Culture.** The Osage were the most important southern Siouan tribe of the western division. They are classed in a linguistic group with the Omaha, Ponca, Kansa (Kaw), and Quapaw; supposedly, at one time, they were a single group living along the Ohio River. Their tribal life centered about their religious rites and ceremonials that included a highly developed symbolism. Among friends and tribal members, they have always been generous and hospitable. They were greatly respected for their courage and prowess in battle.

The Osage culture is slowly being revived by the tribe. Several programs are aimed at accomplishing this. There has been active participation in the arts and crafts classes, which include ribbonwork, leatherwork, and Osage fingerweave. Osage language classes are well attended. Each summer, normally in June, the Osage Ceremonials are held at each of the three Osage villages.

**Government.** The Osage Tribe of Oklahoma is not organized under the Oklahoma Indian Welfare Act of 1936. The tribe does not have a constitution. It operates under the 1960 Act, Public Law 321, which provides for the division of lands and funds of the Osage Indians in Oklahoma Territory, and for other purposes. It also provides for the election of a principal chief, assistant principal chief, and eight members of the Osage tribal council. Elections are held every 4 years.

**Population Profile.** 1984: Total enrollment 2,229; Indian resident 6,743; Total labor force 2,775; Unemployed 472; Unemployment rate 17%. During the 1983-84 school year, 25 Osage students were awarded Higher Education Scholarships. During the 1985 Fiscal Year, 32 students were funded through the Osage Agency Vocational Development Program for technical training, while 12 clients were assisted through the Direct Employment Program. Descendants of original Osage allottees have the proceeds of interest generated from a million dollar judgment fund set aside for educational purposes by the Act of October 27, 1972 (Public Law 92-586), to be administered by an Osage Tribal Education Committee under rules and regulations of the Secretary of the Interior. During the 1984-85 school year, 451 of these awards were made.

OTOE-MISSOURIA TRIBE                    Federal Trust Area
Noble County
Tribal Headquarters: Red Rock, Oklahoma

**Land Status.** Tribally owned land: 1,680.00 acres. Allotted land: 18,931.31 acres. Total area: 20,611.31 acres. This land is held in trust by the United States under the Act of February 28, 1891.

**History.** According to tradition, the people later known as the Otoe, along with their relatives the Winnebago and the Iowa, once lived in the Great Lakes region. In a prehistoric migration southwest in search of buffalo, they separated. The division that reached the mouth of the Grand River, a branch of the Missouri, called themselves Niutachi, or "those that arrive at the mouth," and soon separated into two bands because of a quarrel between two of their chiefs. One band went up the Missouri and became known as the Otoe, and the other band stayed near their first settlement and were called the Missouria. From 1817 to 1841, the Otoe lived near the mouth of the Platte River. Since 1829, the Missouria have been absorbed by the Otoe, so that the two are now indistinguishable.

On March 15, 1854, the Otoe-Missouria signed a treaty ceding all their lands except a strip 10 miles wide and 25 miles long on the waters of Big Blue River, but when it was found that there was no timber on this tract, it was exchanged for another tract taken from the Kaw (Kansa). In a treaty signed August 15, 1876, and amended March 3, 1879, they agreed to sell 120,000 acres of the western end of the reserve. Finally, a treaty signed on March 3, 1881, provided for the sale of all the rest of their lands in Kansas and Nebraska and for the selection of a new reservation. Consent to the treaty was recorded May 4, and the tribe moved the following year to the new reservation which was in Indian Territory.

**Culture.** The Otoe-Missouria belong to the Siouan linguistic family. All the old ways have passed on with the older people.

**Government.** The tribe operated traditionally until 1984, when they organized under the Oklahoma Indian Welfare Act of 1936. Their constitution, ratified in 1984, provides for government by a tribal council consisting of a chairman, vice chairman, secretary, treasurer, and three council members, all of whom are elected to staggered 3-year terms. Regular meetings of the tribal council are held monthly.

**Population Profile. 1984:** Total enrollment 1,422; Indian resident 1,231; Total labor force 655; Unemployed 164; Unemployment rate 25%. The Red Rock Public School System has approximately 70 percent Indian student enrollment. Thus, the tribe has contracted the Johnson O'Malley Program to aid the eligible Indian students of the school system. At present, the Otoe-Missouria Tribe is developing an Education Department, which will be comprised of the following Bureau of Indian Affairs education programs: Higher Education, Adult Vocational Training, and Johnson O'Malley.

OTTAWA TRIBE OF OKLAHOMA                    Federal Trust Area
Ottawa County
Tribal Headquarters: Miami, Oklahoma

**Land Status.** Tribally owned land: 40.28 acres. Total area: 40.28 acres.

**History.** A large party of Ottawa was first met by Champlain in 1615 near the mouth of the French River, Georgian Bay Region, Canada, which seems to have been the original location of the tribe in the historic period. They were generally counted as allies of the Huron and the French during the French and Indian War. As a result of conflicts with the Iroquois in the 17th Century, the Ottawa emigrated westward and southwest, their location being on Lake Huron between Detroit and Saginaw Bay from about 1700.

Between 1785 and 1862, the Ottawa signed 23 different treaties with the United States. In 1833, they ceded all their land on the west shore of Lake Michigan and accepted a reservation in northeastern Kansas. Several bands of the Ottawa Tribe living in Ohio had ceded their lands to the Government and moved to the Kansas reservation in 1832. After the Quapaw Treaty of 1857, they moved to Indian Territory. The main portion of Ottawa remained in scattered settlements in southern Michigan, though another portion continued to live in Canada with the Chippewa. The noted Chief Pontiac was an Ottawa, and one of the principal events in the tribe's history was known as Pontiac's War, waged near Detroit in 1763.

The Act of August 3, 1956—Public Law 84-943—terminated Federal supervision over the property and members of the Ottawa Tribe of Oklahoma. This act was repealed by the Act of May 15, 1978, which restored the Ottawa as a federally recognized tribe.

**Culture.** The Ottawa Tribe of Oklahoma belonged to the Algonquian family, which formerly occupied a larger area than any other Indian linguistic group in North America. The name "Ottawa" is from the Indian word "Adawe," meaning "to trade." It was applied to many different tribal groups which, according to tradition, carried on trade with neighboring tribes and also, later, with the French 4,500 miles away from the permanent Ottawa settlement. Though the Ottawa were great hunters, warriors, and traders, they also cultivated the soil.

**Government.** The tribe is organized under the Oklahoma Indian Welfare Act of 1936. In accordance with its constitution of 1979, ratified in 1980 and superseding that of 1938, the tribe is governed by a business committee consisting of a chief, second chief, secretary-treasurer, and two council members, all of whom are elected to staggered 3-year terms. Regular meetings of the business committee are held quarterly.

**Population Profile. 1984:** Total enrollment 2,000 (approximate); Indian resident 377; Total labor force 163; Unemployed 25; Unemployment rate 15%.


PAWNEE TRIBE OF OKLAHOMA                    Federal Trust Area
Pawnee and Payne Counties
Tribal Headquarters: Pawnee, Oklahoma

**Land Status.** Tribally owned land: 726.03 acres. Allotted land: 19,399.51 acres. Total area: 20,125.54 acres. The land was deeded in trust to the Pawnee Tribe by Public Law 90-546, approved October 2, 1868.

**History.** Pawnee prehistoric origins are still largely a mystery. Archeological studies indicate that the tribe moved northward around 1400, from an original homeland beyond the Rio Grande to the Red River near the Wichita Mountains, and then to the Arkansas River in southern Kansas or northern Oklahoma. From there, the Skidi Pawnee continued northward into southwestern Nebraska, while the Southern (or Black) Pawnee remained. The Spanish explorers Coronado (1541) and Onate (1601) probably encountered these Southern Pawnee on their explorations for a promised land rich in gold.

Until 1770, the Southern Pawnee, aided by weapons and supplies from French traders, stayed in the Arkansas River region. As French trade lessened, they migrated northward to join the Skidis in what is now Nebraska near the Platte, Loup, and Republican Rivers. The move gave the tribe renewed outlets for trade as well as good buffalo hunting south of the Platte.

The opening of the frontier brought disaster to the Pawnee. Three treaties (1833, 1848, and 1857) provided for the cession of all Pawnee lands to the United States, with the exception of a reservation 30 miles long and 15 miles wide along both banks of the Loup River, centering near present-day Fullerton, Nebraska. In 1876, this tract was also surrendered to the United States, and the entire tribe was relocated to a new reservation in Oklahoma in a difficult exodus that caused many deaths. The tribe never made war against the United States, and Pawnee scouts served admirably with United States forces against hostile Indians between 1865 and 1885, greatly aiding the construction of railroads to the Pacific. Under an agreement dated November 23, 1892, with the United States, the Pawnee gave up certain lands for a perpetual annuity payment of $30,000 per year, to be divided equally among tribal members. This annuity, which breaks down to just a few dollars apiece, is still provided. The only other tribe still to receive such payments is the Oneida.

**Culture.** The Pawnee are members of the Caddoan linguistic family. Their name probably is derived from the word "pariki," or "horn," which refers to their curved, stiffened scalp lock. Although marked by tragedy, the Pawnee have left many enduring legacies. Some hardy Pawnee varieties of seed are still used by today's farmers. The Pawnee religion is still remarkably rich in myth, symbolism, and poetic fancy, with elaborate rites and dramatic ceremonies connected with the cosmic forces and heavenly bodies. Their belief—that all of these were created by one deity, the all-powerful and omnipresent Tirawa—is highly integrated with most of their institutions and practices. Their ceremonial dances are distinguished for their dignity, rhythm, and symbolism.

**Government.** The tribe is organized under the Oklahoma Indian Welfare Act of 1936. In accordance with its constitution of 1938, the tribe is governed by a business council consisting of a president, vice president, secretary-treasurer, and five council members, all of whom are elected to 2-year terms. Regular meetings of the business council are held quarterly. A Federal Charter was adopted in 1938.

**Population Profile. 1984:** Total enrollment 2,396; Indian resident 1,997; Total labor force 1,040; Unemployed 260; Unemployment rate 25%. No Bureau of Indian Affairs schools are operated within the service boundaries. The tribe has successfully administered a Johnson O'Malley Program, an Adult Vocational Training Program, and a Higher Education Program contracted from the BIA. As of 1985, enrollment in elementary through high school totaled 749.

PEORIA TRIBE OF OKLAHOMA                    Federal Trust Area
Ottawa County
Tribal Headquarters: Miami, Oklahoma

**Land Status.** Tribally owned land: 38.79 acres. Total area: 38.79 acres.

**History.** The Peoria Tribe formerly belonged to the group of Algonquian Tribes forming the Illinois Confederacy. Upon Marquette's return from his expedition down the Mississippi in 1673, he found the Peoria living near what is now Peoria, Illinois. During the general removal of the eastern Indians to the West in 1832, the Peoria, together with a remnant of the Kaskaskia (once a leading tribe of the Illinois Confederacy), emigrated to a new reservation assigned to them on the Osage River, Kansas. In 1854, the two tribes were joined by the Wea and Piankshaw, two bands of the Miami, and in 1857-58, these united tribes moved to the Quapaw Reservation in Oklahoma.

The Act of August 2, 1956—Public Law 84-921—terminated Federal supervision over the property of the Peoria Tribe. This act was repealed by the Act of May 15, 1978, which restored the Peoria as a federally recognized tribe.

**Culture.** The name "Peoria" is from the French form of the personal name, _Piwarea_, meaning "he comes carrying a pack on his back."

**Government.** The tribe is organized under the Oklahoma Indian Welfare Act of 1936. In accordance with its constitution, approved by the Bureau of Indian Affairs in 1980 and ratified in 1981, superseding the original constitution of 1939, the tribe is governed by a business committee consisting of a chief, second chief, secretary-treasurer, and two councilmen, all of whom are elected for staggered 4-year terms. Regular meetings of the business committee are held monthly. A Federal Charter was ratified in 1940.

**Population Profile. 1984:** Total enrollment 2,000 (approximate); Indian resident 398; Total labor force 192; Unemployed 29; Unemployment rate 15%.

PONCA TRIBE OF OKLAHOMA                    Federal Trust Area
Kay County
Tribal Headquarters: White Eagle, Ponca City, Oklahoma

**Land Status.** Tribally owned land: 933.71 acres. Allotted land: 13,240.06 acres. Government owned land: 10.00 acres. Total area: 14,183.77 acres.

**History.** The Ponca were one of five tribes in the Dhegiha group of the Siouan linguistic family. This group consisted of the Ponca, Omaha, Osage, Kaw (Kansa), and Quapaw. In 1673, the Ponca were living on the Niobrara; later they moved to southwestern Minnesota and the Black Hills of South Dakota. In 1877, they were evicted from their lands by the United States, which caused such hardship among the tribe that it became the subject of a public investigation ordered by President Hayes. In a settlement, about a third of the tribe returned to their lands on the Niobrara in 1880, while the rest moved to new lands set aside for them in Oklahoma. A small group of Ponca known as the Northern Ponca live in Nebraska.

**Culture.** The Ponca have maintained their language and many of their traditions while adopting the agriculture and educational standards of the neighboring non-Indian society. Since 1881, they have sponsored the Ponca Indian Powwow, held annually in late summer at their White Eagle Reservation in Kay County.

**Government.** The tribe is organized under the Oklahoma Indian Welfare Act of 1936. In accordance with the constitution of 1950, the tribe is governed by a business committee consisting of a chairman, vice chairman, secretary-treasurer, and four committee members, who are elected to staggered 2-year terms. Regular meetings of the business committee are held three times a year. A Federal Charter was adopted in 1950.

**Population Profile. 1984:** Total enrollment 2,028 (as of 1980); Indian resident 2,272; Total labor force 1,241; Unemployed 311; Unemployment rate 25%. The Ponca tribe receives direct funding for its education programs from the Bureau of Indian Affairs. In 1985, the tribe funded 48 students in higher education institutions, in addition to those in Adult Education and the G.E.D. programs. The public school dropout rate has declined significantly in recent years; for the 1983–84 school year, the junior high dropout rate was 15 percent, and the senior high school dropout rate was 30 percent.


QUAPAW TRIBE                            Federal Trust Area
Ottawa County
Tribal Headquarters: Quapaw, Oklahoma

**Land Status.** Tribally owned land: 729.15 acres. Allotted land: 11,867.73 acres. Total area: 12,596.88 acres.

**History.** The Quapaw (from "Ugakhpa," meaning "downstream people") are a southwestern Siouan tribe. By a treaty signed in St. Louis, Missouri, on August 24, 1818, the Quapaw ceded their lands south of the Arkansas River, except for a small territory between Arkansas Post and Little Rock extending inland to the Saline River. In 1824, the Quapaw signed a treaty ceding the rest of their land to the United States, and the tribe agreed to move to the country of the Caddo, where they were assigned a tract on the south side of the Red River. The river frequently overflowed its banks, destroying Quapaw crops. Soon the tribe was drifting back to its old country, now settled by whites. Finally, a treaty signed May 13, 1833, conveyed to the Quapaw 150 sections of land in the extreme southeastern part of Kansas and the northeastern part of Indian Territory, to which they agreed to move. On February 23, 1867, they ceded their lands in Kansas and the northern part of their lands in Indian Territory to the United States. Under the Allotment Act of 1887, the Quapaw objected to Federal plans to allot each tribal member only 80 acres. They established their own program and allotted 200 acres to each of the 247 members. This action was ratified by Congress in 1895. Rich lead and zinc deposits were found on some of these allotments in 1905.

**Culture.** Early records show the Quapaw as peaceable people. They lived in dome-roofed, bark-covered houses inside palisades. They were agriculturalists and hunters, known for their beautiful pottery and decorated animal skin rugs. The Quapaw have been active in the development of Ottawa County since the turn of the century.

**Government.** The tribe is organized under the Oklahoma Indian Welfare Act of 1936. It does not have a constitution; rather, the Quapaw Tribe operates under a resolution, adopted in 1956 and approved by the Commissioner of Indian Affairs in 1957. This resolution delegates authority to a tribal business committee consisting of a chairman, vice chairman, secretary-treasurer, and four committee members, who are elected to 2-year terms. Regular meetings of the business committee are held quarterly.

**Population Profile.** 1984: Total enrollment 3,000 (approximate); Indian resident 1,340; Total labor force 750; Unemployed 112; Unemployment rate 15%.

SAC AND FOX TRIBE OF OKLAHOMA          Federal Trust Area
Lincoln, Payne, and Pottawatomi Counties
Tribal Headquarters: Stroud, Oklahoma

**Land Status.** Tribally owned land: 970.00 acres. Allotted land: 15,072.64 acres. Total area: 16,042.64 acres. The specific land area was acquired by the Acts of February 13, 1891 and May 17, 1926.

**History.** Originally separate and independent tribes of the Algonquian linguistic family, the Sac (or Sauk) and Fox Tribes have long been affiliated and allied. The original homeland of the Sac and Fox was in the Great Lakes region, where the Sac inhabited the Upper Michigan Peninsula and the Fox, the south shore of Lake Superior. By 1667, when Father Allouez made the first recorded white contact with the two tribes, Iroquois and French pressure on the Sac, and Chippewa pressure on the Fox, had pushed both groups to the vicinity of present-day Green Bay, Wisconsin. French attacks on the Sac and Fox in the 18th Century, attributed to Indians, strengthened the alliance of the two tribes, amounting to a confederation. Forced to migrate south, they attacked the Illinois and forced them from their lands along the Mississippi in the present-day States of Illinois, Iowa, and Wisconsin. Those groups that stayed near the Mississippi River became known as the "Sac and Fox of the Mississippi" to distinguish them from the "Sac and Fox of the Missouri," a large band that settled further south along the Missouri River.

In 1804, the chiefs of the Missouri band were persuaded to sign a treaty ceding to the United States all Sac and Fox lands east of the Mississippi River, as well as some hunting grounds to the west of it. Government efforts several years later to enforce the treaty embittered the Sac and Fox, most of whom knew about the treaty. Attempts to remove the Sac and Fox caused a split in the confederation. The majority of the tribe followed the conciliatory Sac Chief Keokuk, who agreed to move. The remainder supported his rival, Black Hawk, a Sac warrior who bitterly opposed the treaty and led his "British Band" into revolt (Black Hawk War). With the Treaty of Fort Armstrong (1832), the Sac and Fox power on the frontier came to an end. In 1833, the tribe were moved to Iowa, where they lived for only 13 years before being moved again, this time to the Osage River Reservation in Kansas. In 1869, the Sac and Fox were again moved, this time to Oklahoma. Keokuk, and later his son, Moses, continued to lead the conciliatory faction of the tribes, but many Fox opposed the many cessions of land to the United States and returned to Iowa in 1859 to join a small number who had steadfastly refused to be moved.

**Culture.** The Sac took their name from "Osakiwug," which means "People of the Yellow Earth" and differentiates them from the Fox, whose name is "Meshkwakihug," meaning "Red Earth People." The name Fox was applied to the entire tribe by the French, from the name of one clan, the "Wagosh" or "Red Fox" group.

Their indigenous culture, later influenced by contact with Plains tribes and the acquisition of horses in the 19th Century, was that of the Eastern Woodlands. Although they established fixed villages and practiced extensive cultivation of maize, squash, beans, and tobacco, they devoted much time to fishing, hunting small game and buffalo, and harvesting wild rice. Travel was by dugout and birchbark canoe. The two tribes lived in bark houses in warm weather and in oval reed-type lodges during winter. Their social and religious organization was a complex one in which the Grand Medicine Society played an important part.

The present-day Sac and Fox are almost completely acculturated. Their chief sources of revenue are farming, stock raising, and oil development. Jim Thorpe, one of the greatest athletes of all time, was a member of this tribe.

**Government.** The tribe is organized under the Oklahoma Indian Welfare Act of 1936. In accordance with their constitution of 1937, amended in 1980, the tribe is governed by a business committee consisting of a principal chief, second chief, secretary-treasurer, and two councilmen, who are elected to staggered 2-year terms. Regular meetings of the business committee are held quarterly.

**Population Profile. 1984:** Total enrollment 2,145; Indian resident 1,041; Total labor force 496; Unemployed 99; Unemployment rate 20%. There are no boarding schools in this immediate area, although there are two in the Anadarko area. Only a few Sac and Fox children attend boarding school; the rest go to public schools. At least 30 attend some type of higher education each year through the Bureau of Indian Affairs Scholarship Program.

SEMINOLE NATION OF OKLAHOMA                    Federal Trust Area
Seminole County
Tribal Headquarters: Wewoka, Oklahoma

**Land Status.** Tribally owned land: 380.10 acres. Allotted land: 27,968.00 acres. Total area: 28,348.10 acres. This land is held in trust by the United States by the Act of July 26, 1936.

**History.** The people who came to be known as "Seminole," meaning "runaways," were a combination of Hitchiti-speaking Oconee, Yamasee driven from the Carolinas and Muscogee (Creek) fleeing Georgia. Their ranks were swelled by fugitive slaves who found refuge and freedom among the Indians in Florida. In 1819, Spain ceded the territory of Florida to the United States. Pressure by white settlers for Seminole lands led to a Government policy that favored removal of the Seminole to Oklahoma. Attempts to force removal between 1835 and 1843 produced resistance from many able Seminole leaders, the greatest of whom was Osceola.

The United States succeeded in transporting most of the Seminole to Oklahoma in what amounted to a brutal, debilitating march. They were eventually granted a reservation of their own in the western part of the Muscogee (Creek) Nation. Many Government promises made to the Seminole were never fulfilled. Many Seminole are still in Florida, descendants of the 150 Seminole who escaped all removal efforts. They are located on three Federal reservations at Hollywood, Brighton, and Big Cypress.

**Culture.** The Seminole have some of the traditional ceremonials, dances, and ball games, as well as their language. However, most of the original crafts and skills still known by the Seminole in Florida have been lost.

**Government.** The Seminole Nation is not organized under the Oklahoma Indian Welfare Act of 1936. Prior to statehood, the Seminole Nation had its own tribal government. After statehood (1907), the principal officers of the Five Civilized Tribes of Oklahoma were appointed by the President of the United States under authority of the 1906 Act. The 1970 Act, Public Law 91-495, authorized the Five Civilized Tribes to select their principal officers by popular election. The Seminole Nation of Oklahoma now operates under a federally recognized constitution, approved by the Commissioner of Indian Affairs and ratified in 1969, which provides for election of a chief, assistant chief, and a 42-member tribal council. Elections are held every 4 years. Regular meetings of the tribal council are held quarterly.

**Population Profile.** 1984: Total enrollment 3,142; Indian resident 3,869; Total labor force 1,684; Unemployed 214; Unemployment rate 13%. The Seminole Nation operates two Head Start classes. Most tribal children attend various public high schools in Seminole County. Some students attend Seminole Junior College, which is centrally located within the county.

SENECA-CAYUGA TRIBE OF OKLAHOMA          Federal Trust Area
Delaware and Ottawa Counties
Tribal Headquarters: Miami, Oklahoma

**Land Status.** Tribally owned land: 1,093.06 acres. Allotted land: 2,934.81 acres. Total area: 4,027.87 acres.

**History.** The Seneca of the Quapaw Agency were formerly called the Seneca of Sandusky. In reality, the tribe was an affiliated group of Indian bands (of Iroquoian origin) known as Mingoes, living on the upper Ohio River and consisting of survivors of the Conestoga Tribe and a few Cayuga, Mohawk, Oneida, Tuscarora, and Onondaga that became united as a result of the Indian and colonial wars of the 18th Century. No records have been found to prove they were part of the Seneca Tribe of New York State.

Under treaty provisions with the United States in 1817, the Seneca of Sandusky were granted 40,000 acres on the east side of the Sandusky River in Ohio. By 1830, they had improved farms, had schools for their children, and were well advanced in modern civilization. Following the policy of removing the eastern Indians to the West, the Government induced them to sell their Ohio lands and accept a new reserve north of the Cherokee Nation.

A band of the Seneca of Sandusky joined the Shawnee of Ohio, who had settled near Louistown in the latter part of the 18th Century. At that time they were known as the mixed band of Seneca and Shawnee. By a treaty of 1831, the Government induced them to sell their Ohio lands and accept a new reserve adjoining the Seneca of Sandusky in Indian Territory. Both the Seneca of Sandusky and the mixed Seneca and Shawnee moved to their new country in 1832 and, like the other eastern tribes, suffered many hardships during their journey. Protesting that the lands first assigned them were unfit for cultivation, they entered into a new treaty a short time after their arrival at the Seneca Agency. By the terms of the treaty, they were assigned a permanent reservation, beginning at the northeast corner of the Cherokee cession of 1828 and situated between the Neosho River and the Missouri boundary south of the Quapaw country. In 1881, a band of over 100 Cayuga from Canada and New York came to join their kin in Oklahoma.

**Culture.** The acculturation process of the Seneca-Cayuga has been a mixture of resistance, acceptance, and adoption. Many tribal beliefs and customs have resisted change and persist in an almost pure form. Yet a great many new ideas have been adopted from neighboring tribes and non-Indians, and have been integrated into the pattern of life of the Seneca-Cayuga people.

**Government.** The tribe is organized under the Oklahoma Indian Welfare Act of 1936. In accordance with its constitution of 1937, amended in 1973, it is governed by a business committee consisting of a chief, second chief, secretary-treasurer, interpreter, and three council members. Elections are held every 2 years. Regular meetings of the business committee are held monthly. A Federal Charter was ratified in 1937.

**Population Profile. 1984:** Total enrollment 3,100 (approximate);

Indian resident 753; Total labor force 395; Unemployed 59; Unemployment rate 15%.


TONKAWA TRIBE OF OKLAHOMA            Federal Trust Area
Kay County
Tribal Headquarters: Tonkawa, Oklahoma

**Land Status.** Tribally owned land: 160.00 acres. Allotted land: 238.24 acres. Government owned land: .50 acres. Total area: 398.74 acres.

**History and Culture.** The Tonkawa belong to the Tonkawan linguistic family. They have a distinct language; and their name, as that of the leading tribe, was applied to their linguistic family. During the 18th and 19th Centuries, they lived in central Texas. In 1884, they moved from Texas to Indian Territory and were assigned 91,000 acres of land previously assigned to the Nez Perce in Kay County, Oklahoma.

**Government.** The tribe is organized under the Oklahoma Indian Welfare Act of 1936. In accordance with its constitution of 1938, the tribe is governed by a tribal committee consisting of a president, vice president, and secretary-treasurer, who are elected for 2-year terms. Regular meetings of the tribal committee are held monthly.

**Population Profile. 1984:** Total enrollment 181; Indian resident 1,292; Total labor force 688; Unemployed 172; Unemployment rate 25%.


WICHITA TRIBE OF OKLAHOMA            Federal Trust Area
Caddo County
Tribal Headquarters: Anadarko, Oklahoma

**Land Status.** Tribally owned land: 2,602.64 acres. Allotted land: 55,599.92 acres. Government owned land: 129.83 acres. Total area: 58,332.39 acres. Land is jointly owned with the Caddo and Delaware Tribes of Oklahoma. Acreage totals include all three tribes; acreage by individual tribes is not available. This land was ceded by the Caddo, Delaware, and Wichita to the United States pursuant to agreement with the United States on June 4, 1891, and ratified by the Act of May 2, 1895. The land was restored to the tribes by order of the Secretary of the Interior on September 11, 1963.

**History.** Wichita tradition indicated that the tribe migrated southward from the north and east. In 1850, the Wichita had moved from near the Red River into the Wichita Mountains region with their main village a short distance from what is now Fort Sill, Oklahoma. In 1859, the Wichita moved to a permanent site south of the Canadian River near the present Caddo-Grady County line. A reservation was established in 1872, consisting of 743,610 acres and known as the Wichita-Caddo Reservation.

**Culture.** The name "Wichita" seems to have originated from the Choctaw term "Wia chitch," or "Big Arbor." This term probably came about because the Wichita built and lived in grass lodges that were made by erecting a framework of poles placed in a circle in the ground with the tops united in an oval form and bound together with numerous withes, or wattles, the whole thatched with grass. The lodges were about 25 feet in diameter and 20 feet high, and from a distance they looked like a group of haystacks. The Wichita are closely related to the Pawnee; they entertain each other annually in an Indian powwow or celebration.

**Government.** The tribe is not organized under the Oklahoma Indian Welfare Act of 1936. The tribe has no constitution or bylaws. Its governing rules, approved by resolution and adopted by the tribe in 1961, provide for a tribal executive committee consisting of a president, vice president, secretary, treasurer, and three alternate councilmen, all of whom are elected to 4-year concurrent terms. Regular meetings of the executive council are held quarterly.

**Population Profile. 1984:** Total enrollment 1,170; Indian resident 608; Total labor force 218; Unemployed 74; Unemployment rate 34%. Almost all the Wichita children attend public school in their home communities. During the 1984–85 school year, 22 tribal members are attending colleges and universities with assistance from Bureau of Indian Affairs grant funds. The estimated average education level of tribal members is 10.5 years. In addition, many Wichita adults are participating in the various adult education programs.


WYANDOTTE TRIBE OF OKLAHOMA                Federal Trust Area
Ottawa County
Tribal Headquarters: Wyandotte, Oklahoma

**Land Status.** Tribally owned: 214.88 acres. Total area: 214.88 acres.

**History.** "Wyandot" is the English corruption of the Indian name "Wendat," a tribe of the Iroquoian family known as Huron by the French. From 1534 to 1543, on an expedition along the St. Lawrence River, the French explorer Cartier recorded an Iroquoian tribe (proven later as Wyandot) living on the present site of Montreal and Quebec. Generally, in that early period, the Wyandot or Huron made up a confederation inhabiting the land south and east of Georgian Bay, Canada. A century later, owing to many years of warfare with the Iroquois, this confederation was broken up and its refugees scattered over wide areas seeking new homes. It was not until the latter half of the 18th Century that the nucleus of the present Wyandotte Tribe was formed by the main portion of the Hurons, who, after their defeat by the French, settled along the Detroit and Sandusky Rivers. From then on, these people were called Wyandotte, and they succeeded in establishing themselves as the strongest and most powerful tribe in the Ohio country. In 1815, a large part of Ohio and Michigan was confirmed to them by treaty with the United States in recognition of their fidelity during the War of 1812. Four years later, Government representatives induced them to sell the greatest part of the land and to reserve only a small portion near Detroit. In 1842, they signed a treaty ceding their Ohio and Michigan lands to the United States.

About a year later, the tribe was moved to Kansas where they had been promised a reservation; but upon arrival there, they found this promise unfulfilled and were forced to purchase land from the Delaware. They thrived in Kansas, became prosperous, and took a great interest in education. They were declared citizens under an 1855 treaty, but this led to the loss of their lands. In 1859, the Seneca-Cayuga sold the homeless Wyandotte over 30,000 acres of land, an agreement which was confirmed by the United States in 1867. During that time, the Wyandotte's tribal organization was restored; and the last members of the once-powerful Wyandotte Tribe moved to the Quapaw country in Indian Territory. In Oklahoma, they again became prosperous through hard work.

The Act of August 1, 1956, terminated Federal supervision over the Wyandotte Tribe and its members. This act was repealed by the Act of May 15, 1978, which restored the Wyandotte as a federally recognized tribe.

**Culture.** Life in the early Huron territory centered in towns. Dwellings were of the longhouse type and were made of bark. Agriculture was the chief means of subsistence, with corn being the principal crop, followed by beans, squash, tobacco, and sunflowers. Fish was also a principal food and was probably of greater importance to their economy than hunting.

**Government.** The tribe is organized under the Oklahoma Indian Welfare Act of 1936. In accordance with its constitution, approved by the Secretary of the Interior and ratified in 1937, the tribe is governed by a business committee consisting of a chief, second chief, secretary-treasurer, and two councilmen. Elections are held every 2 years.

**Population Profile. 1984:** Total enrollment 2,400 (approximate); Indian resident 494; Total labor force 193; Unemployed 29; Unemployment rate 15%.

## OREGON

BURNS PAIUTE RESERVATION                    Federal Reservation
Harney County
Paiute Tribe
Tribal Headquarters: Burns, Oregon

**Land Status.** Government land: 771.93 acres. Allotted land: 11,014.00 acres. Total area: 11,785.93 acres.

**History.** The Northern Paiute ranged through western Nevada and southeastern Oregon. For a time, the Paiute suffered under the Shoshone who acquired horses and raided the Paiute camps taking prisoners for slaves. As a result of mistreatment of Indians by encroaching settlers, the Paiute war erupted. After two battles, the U.S. Government assigned the Paiute to reservations in 1863.

**Culture.** The Paiute Indians were of semi-nomadic Plateau Indian culture ranging over the dry uplands of Idaho, eastern Oregon, and eastern Washington. All Plateau tribes were traditionally fishermen and hunters who wandered over the country in small, loosely-organized bands searching for game, wild seeds, berries, and roots of camas. With basketry techniques that ranked among the best in North America, they wove the grasses and scrubby brush of the Plateau into almost everything they used, including portable summer shelters, clothing, and watertight cooking pots. Having no clans, Plateau Indians counted descent on both sides of the family. There was little formal organization. The few tribal ceremonies centered around the food supply. In the early 1700's, horses were introduced among the tribes, and they became highly skilled horsemen who counted their wealth in terms of the new animal.

**Government.** The governing body of the tribe is the tribal council, which has a membership of five persons, elected to 2-year terms by the general council. The tribe is organized under a constitution approved on June 13, 1968.

**Population Profile. 1969:** Tribal enrollment 225; Indian resident 150. **1980:** Indian resident 160; Non-Indian resident 7; Percent Indian of total population 95.8; Total housing units 40; Occupied housing units 36.

**Transportation.** U.S. Highway No. 70 runs east-west near the reservation. The Burns Paiute Reservation is located in the southeastern corner of Oregon where settlement population is sparse. Burns, one of the larger cities in the area, is served by all means of commercial transportation.

**Community Facilities.** A clinic located in Burns serves the residents' medical needs.


CELILLO VILLAGE                                    Federal Reservation
Wasco County
Walla Walla Tribe
Tribal Headquarters: Celillo Village, Oregon

**Land Status.** Tribally-owned land and Government land: 30.39 acres. Total area: 30.39 acres.

**History.** The tribe remaining on the reservation is not organized as a governmental entity. They are descendants of the Plateau Indians. Because of the small size of the reservation, very little information is available.

**Culture.** The Walla Walla Indians were of semi-nomadic Plateau Indian culture ranging over the dry uplands of Idaho, eastern Oregon, and eastern Washington. All Plateau tribes were traditionally fishermen and hunters who wandered over the country in small, loosely-organized bands searching for game, wild seeds, berries, and roots of camas. With basketry techniques that ranked among the best in North America, they wove the grasses and scrubby brush of the Plateau into almost everything they used, including portable summer shelters, clothing, and watertight cooking pots. Having no clans, Plateau Indians counted descent on both sides of the family. There was little formal organization. The few tribal ceremonies centered around the food supply. In the early 1700's, horses were introduced among the tribes, and the Indians became highly-skilled horsemen who counted their wealth in terms of the new animal.

**Population Profile. 1969:** Indian resident 30.

UMATILLA RESERVATION                    Federal Reservation
Umatilla County
Cayuse, Walla Walla, and Umatilla Tribes
Tribal Headquarters: Pendleton, Oregon

**Land Status.** Tribally-owned land: 15,646 acres. Allotted land: 70,616 acres. Non-Indian land: 159,537 acres. Total area: 245,699 acres. The tribe lost their fishing sites at Celila Falls, Oregon, which were reserved by treaty, through the construction of the Dalles Dam Project on the Columbia River. Judgment funds have been allocated to compensate for this.

**History.** The Umatilla, Cayuse and Walla Walla Indians are located on the Umatilla Reservation. These tribes were included as Plateau Indians and were known as fishermen and hunters, wandering over the countryside in small loosely-organized bands. When the traders and fur trappers came into the Oregon territory in the 1800's, they brought with them white men's diseases. Having no immunity to them, the Indians died in appalling numbers. In 1854, territorial governors were instructed by the Federal Government to buy out Indian rights. A period of treaty-making began under which the Indians were to be placed on reservations. Under resulting treaties, the Indians of Oregon ceded vast areas of land and began living on the reservations designated for them.

**Culture.** The Indians of the Umatilla Reservation were a semi-nomadic Plateau tribe ranging over the dry uplands of Idaho, eastern Oregon, and eastern Washington. All Plateau tribes were traditionally fishermen and hunters who wandered over the country in small, loosely-organized bands searching for game, wild seeds, berries, and roots of camas. With basketry techniques that ranked among the best in North America, they wove the grasses and scrubby brush of the Plateau into almost everything they used, including portable summer shelters, clothing, and watertight cooking pots. Having no clans, Plateau Indians counted descent on both sides of the family. There was little formal organization. The few tribal ceremonies centered around the food supply. In the early 1700's, horses were introduced among the tribes and the Indians became highly skilled horsemen who counted their wealth in terms of the new animal.

**Government.** The tribal constitution, approved in 1949, provides for a nine-member governing body, the board of trustees, which is elected by the general council. The general council, composed of all tribal members, has delegated virtually all of its powers to the board of trustees.

**Population Profile. 1969:** Tribal enrollment 1,245; Indian resident 981; Unemployment 17%; Underemployment 37%; Median family income $4,500. **1980:** Indian resident 908; Non-Indian resident 1,711; Percent Indian of total population 34.7; Total housing units 890; Occupied housing units 814. The education level for the reservation is 9th grade.

**Tribal Economy.** The tribe has an income of $35,000 from interest. The tribe has organized the Tribal Leasing Enterprise and the Tribal Farming Enterprise to manage and develop the land and agriculture of the reservation.

**Climate.** The reservation is located in the northeastern corner of Oregon where rainfall averages 15 inches per year. Temperatures range from a summer high of 100 degrees to a winter low of 25 degrees.

**Transportation.** Interstate 80N passes through the reservation southeast-northwest to Portland. State Highway No. 11 runs just west of the reservation northeast-southwest. Transportation by air, bus, train, and truck is readily available in Pendleton, which lies 5 miles from the reservation.

**Community Facilities.** The Cascade Natural Gas Corporation provides gas to reservation homes. Electricity is available from the Pacific Power and Light Company. A private hospital in Pendleton meets the medical needs of the reservation residents.

**Recreation.** In addition to the nearby Columbia River and Blue Mountain Hunting Range, there are various activities which attract the public. Pendleton Roundup is a world famous rodeo with its Indian "Happy Canyon" pageant and tepee village. The traditional Indian Festival of Arts in LaGrange promotes advancement of the Indian people. An annual Root Feast is sponsored by the Tribal Celebration Committee. Cabbage Hill is a portion of the old Oregon Trail featuring a view of the Umatilla Basin, an awe-inspiring scene framed by timbered slopes and blue mountains.


WARM SPRINGS RESERVATION                    Federal Reservation
Jefferson, Wasco, Linn, Marion, and
   Clackamas Counties
Warm Springs, Northern Paiute, and
   Wasco Confederated Tribes
Tribal Headquarters: Warm Springs, Oregon

**Land Status.** Tribally-owned land: 480,196 acres. Government land: 16 acres. Allotted land: 84,118 acres. Total area: 564,330 acres.

**History.** The Warm Springs, Wasco, and some Northern Paiute Indians are located on the Warm Springs Reservation. These tribes were Plateau Indians and were known as fishermen and hunters, wandering over the countryside in small, loosely-organized bands. When white traders and fur trappers came into the Oregon territory in the 1800's, they brought with them white men's diseases. Having no immunity to them, the Indians died in appalling numbers. In 1854, territorial governors were instructed by the Federal Government to buy out Indian rights. A period of treaty-making began under which the Indians were to be placed on reservations. Under the resulting treaties, the Indians of Oregon ceded vast areas of land and began living on the reservations designated for them.

**Culture.** The Confederated Tribes of the Warm Springs Reservation were one of semi-nomadic Plateau Indian culture ranging over the dry uplands of Idaho, eastern Oregon, and eastern Washington. All Plateau tribes were traditionally fishermen and hunters who wandered over the country in small, loosely-organized bands searching for game, wild seeds, berries, and roots of camas. With basketry techniques that ranked among the best in North America, they wove the grasses and scrubby brush of the Plateau into almost everything they used including portable summer shelters, clothing, and watertight cooking pots. Having no clans, Plateau Indians counted descent on both sides of the family. There was little formal organization. The few tribal ceremonies centered around the food supply. In the early 1700's, horses were introduced among the tribes and the Indians became highly skilled horsemen who counted their wealth in terms of the new animal.

**Government.** The tribe operates under a constitution and charter approved in 1938. The Tribal Council of the Confederated Tribes of the Warm Springs Reservation, the official governing body of the reservation, which represents all the enrolled members, is made up of eight elected members and three elected chiefs who enjoy a lifetime tenure.

**Population Profile. 1969:** Tribal enrollment 1,761; Indian resident 1,643. Unemployment 32%; Underemployment 12%; Median family income $8,900. **1980:** Indian resident 2,004; Non-Indian resident 240; Percent Indian of total population 89.3; Total housing units 627; Occupied housing units 559.

**Tribal Economy.** The tribe earns an income of $4,500,000 annually. Over half of this income is profits from the Warm Springs Forest Products Industry. Most of the remainder is income from the tribally-owned resort, Kah-Nee-Ta. Various tribally owned commercial establishments round out the tribal income. The tribe owns and operates all these establishments.

**Climate.** Warm Springs is located in the northwestern quarter of Oregon near Portland. The rainfall in this area averages 12 inches annually. Temperatures range from a high of 85 degrees to a low of 0 degrees. The climate is ideal for forestry.

**Transportation.** Federal Highway No. 26 runs northwest-southeast through the reservation. Bend, a city located 60 miles south of the reservation, is served by commercial air and trainlines. Bus and trucklines have stops on the reservation.

**Community Facilities.** Water for the communities on the reservation is drawn from wells. The Public Health Service operates a hospital at the Warm Springs Agency to serve the health needs of the tribe.

**Recreation.** The famous Kah-Nee-Ta Resort Hotel is located on the Warm Springs Indian Reservation. Facilities include mineral hot springs, motel and tepee accommodations, restaurant, camping areas, and trout fishing. The Polton and Round Butte Dams provide excellent fishing and boating.

## SOUTH CAROLINA

CATAWBA RESERVATION                 State Reservation
York County
Catawba Tribe
Tribal Headquarters: Rock Hill, South Carolina

**Land Status.** The tribe owns 100 acres. 530 acres are individually owned (quit-claim), and 2,758 acres are non-Indian owned. Total area: 3,388 acres. The tribe terminated its relationship with the Federal Government in 1962, and the tribal estate was distributed to all enrolled members, either in cash or in land. The estate totaled $187,774.40, and $296 was distributed to each member including minors.

**History.** The Catawba were a Siouan tribe, the most populous in the Carolinas after the Cherokee with whom they were continually at war. Raiding parties also traveled regularly to the Ohio Valley where they fought against the Iroquois, Shawnee, and Delaware. In 1701, they were described as a "powerful nation" in two divisions living in large villages. After the death of their chief, King Haiglar, killed in 1762 by Shawnee, the Catawba declined. They fought on the side of the Americans against the British. Further warfare and disease, particularly two sieges of smallpox, reduced the Catawba to a small remnant by 1800. Their reservation of 15 square miles was first confirmed in 1793, then leased almost entirely to whites in 1826. All but 640 acres were sold in 1841 to the State of South Carolina. Termination occurred in 1962, a step which the tribe now regrets having made and feels was done through ignorance of the full implications.

**Culture.** The Catawba were sedentary agriculturists and excellent hunters. Their women were skilled in pottery and basketry, arts which are continued into the 20th Century. The tribe earlier absorbed about 20 smaller Carolina tribes into their group. There are few "brass ankle" people of undetermined origin living in the reservation. Little traditional culture remains and much blending it with that of the surrounding communities has occurred. Indians, however, experience prejudice and discrimination from the surrounding non-Indians.

**Government.** The constitution and the bylaws of the tribe were revoked with termination in 1962. No formal organization exists now, other than the church on the reservation and its activities.

**Population Profile.** **1969:** Tribal enrollment 700 (est.); Indian resident 47; Non-Indian resident 6; Unemployment 0; Underemployment 0; Median family income $3,120. **1980:** Indian resident 728; Non-Indian resident 270; Percent Indian of total population 72.9; Total housing units 316; Occupied housing units 278. Average education level is improving. About half of the Indian residents have completed high school. Students attend school in Rock Hill. There is an area trade school in West Columbia, 65 miles from the reservation.

**Tribal Economy.** The majority of the employed Indian residents work in the textile factories in the area, averaging $60 per week income. There is no farming as the land is rocky and contains too much clay.

**Climate.** Elevation is 700 feet above sea-level where rainfall averages 43 inches annually. The lowest mean temperature in January is 34 degrees, and the highest mean in July is 89 degrees. Extremes of 8 degrees in winter and 93 degrees in summer occur.

**Transportation.** The reservation is close to major U.S. Highway No. 21 and local road service is adequate. The nearest airport is at Charlotte, 27 miles from the reservation. Trains, buses, and two commercial trucking firms serve the city of Rock Hill, 10 miles from the reservation.

**Community Facilities.** Only three houses have water facilities. These consist of pumps attached to wells. Heating is provided by bottled gas supplied by a Rock Hill company. Electricity has existed for many years, but there are no sewer lines serving the reservation. The nearest hospital, private, is in Rock Hill. The only tribal buildings now belong to the Church of the Latter Day Saints.


# SOUTH DAKOTA


CHEYENNE RIVER RESERVATION                    Federal Reservation
Perkins, Dewey, and Ziebach Counties
Sioux Tribe
Tribal Headquarters:  Eagle Butte, South Dakota

**Land Status.** Tribally-owned land: 911,467 acres. Allotted land: 503,483 acres. Government land: 4,554 acres. Total area: 1,419,499 acres. In the 1868 Treaty at Fort Laramie, the Sioux agreed to a territory encompassed by the western slopes of the Black Hills, the Niobrara River on the south, the Missouri River on the east, and the Cannonball River to the north. However, an 1889 Act of Congress established seven reservations for the Sioux, including 2,700,000 acres for the "Cheyenne River" Sioux. By Acts of Congress in 1909 and 1910, all unallocated and unsold land on the reservation was opened for homesteading to non-Indians. Currently, about 47 percent of the original reservation land area is owned by non-Indians. An additional 104,400 acres of the best agricultural and residential lands were flooded by the Oahe Reservoir.

**History.** The Dakota Sioux were driven west across the Mississippi River by the Chippewa in the early 18th Century. Rapidly adopting the horse and Plains culture based upon the horse, they roamed the Missouri Valley freely until the early 19th Century. Trappers, settlers, gold miners, and, finally, Federal troops threatened their freedom of movement and the survival of the buffalo herds. This led to constant conflict until the extinction of the all-important buffalo in 1885. The Sioux tribe's power deteriorated rapidly, and they were forcefully confined to reservations. The Cheyenne River Reservation became the center of the Ghost Dance Religion while it flourished briefly in the 1880's.

**Culture.** The Cheyenne River Sioux lived as Plains Indians with a buffalo-centered economy until the advent of reservation confinement. The buffalo provided food, clothing, shelter, and a variety of tools and equipment. The tribes were highly mobile, especially after they acquired the horse, following the buffalo herds for much of the year. The Sioux are members of the Algonquian family. This tribe speaks the Lakota dialect of the Siouan language.

**Government.** The tribe is governed by a council of 15 members elected from 13 districts for 2-year terms. The chairman, who heads the tribal government, is elected at large for a 4-year term.

**Population Profile. 1969:** Tribal enrollment 5,993; Indian resident 4,126; Non-Indian resident 3,000; Unemployment 31%; Underemployment 36%; Median family income $3,400. **1980:** Indian resident 1,529; Non-Indian resident 297; Percent Indian of total population 83.7; Total housing units 554; Occupied housing units 409. The tribe has achieved an average education level of 8.5 years. Children attend public elementary schools. The high school at Eagle Butte has boarding facilities and is subsidized by the Bureau of Indian Affairs. Forty-three tribal members attended college in 1969-70.

**Tribal Economy.** Lignite coal is currently being mined. Oil is known to exist in substantial amounts but is not being exploited. Almost half of the tribe's annual income of $300,000 is earned through farming. Twenty-five people work full time for the tribe. The tribe owns and operates a number of businesses including the Super Value Supermarket in Eagle Butte, a beef sales pavilion and a beef herd enterprise, a gas station, two laundromats, and the telephone company. Five of the 70 retail and service stores on the reservation are owned by Indians, the remainder owned by non-Indians.

**Climate.** Rainfall averages between 16 and 19 inches per year. The climate has four distinct seasons. Temperatures reach an average high of 75 degrees in July and a low of 14 degrees in January.

**Transportation.** U.S. Highway No. 212, a major east-west highway, and State Routes 65 and 63, north-south routes, pass through the reservation. Eagle Butte has train service. Pierre, 70 miles from the reservation, is the nearest location served by air, bus, and trucklines.

**Community Facilities.** Four communities have municipal water and sewage systems. PHS also operates four small systems. Gas is purchased by the tank. The Morean-Grand Electric Cooperative supplies electricity to the reservation. Health care is provided by the Public Health Service at the hospital in Eagle Butte. In addition, the PHS holds weekly clinics at Cherry Creek. Four communities have dilapidated community buildings. The Community Action Program building is located in Eagle Butte.

**Recreation.** The Oahe Reservoir, on the eastern border of the reservation, is an excellent area for hunting, fishing, and water sports. Additional areas throughout the reservation are also open for similar outdoor recreation activities including hiking and horseback riding. Each summer the Rodeo and Powwow takes place in Eagle Butte.

CROW CREEK RESERVATION Federal Reservation
Buffalo, Hyde, and Hughes Counties
Sioux Tribe
Tribal Headquarters: Fort Thompson, South Dakota

**Land Status.** Tribally-owned 31,111.92 acres. Government land: 19,079.89 acres. Allotted land: 72,339.40 acres. Non-Indian land: 114 acres. Total area: 123,531.21 acres.

**History.** The middle, or Wiciyela Sioux Division, who speak the Nakota dialect, were first met by white explorers in north central Minnesota about the end of the 17th Century. Shortly thereafter, they moved west. Although habitually at war with other tribes, the Sioux did not actively resist white immigration until the whites began to intrude in great numbers and decimate the buffalo herds. Under the Fort Laramie Treaty in 1868, all of the land held by the Sioux east of the Missouri River was released to the U.S. Government with exception of the Crow Creek, Yankton, and Sisseton Reservations. In the 1870's, buffalo herds were systematically slaughtered by white commercial hunters. With the loss of the buffalo, the food supply disappeared, and the Indians were forced to accept reservation life and rationed food.

**Culture.** The Wiciyela Sioux Division met and warred with semi-sedentary tribes during its westward migration. In the process, they adopted from those river tribes such characteristics as round earth-lodges, bullboats, horticultural techniques, ceremonies, and styles of dress.

**Government.** The Crow Creek Sioux Tribe is not organized under the Indian Reorganization Act of 1934, but has a constitution and bylaws approved in 1949. The tribal law and order department operates under the Code of Federal Regulations Section 25. The six-member tribal council, which derives its authority from the constitution and bylaws, is popularly elected and represents the entire reservation. The council chairman is the administrative head of the tribe.

**Population Profile. 1969:** Tribal enrollment 1,853; Indian resident 1,150; Unemployment 64%; Underemployment 20%. **1980:** Indian resident 1,474; Non-Indian resident 313; Percent Indian of total population 82.5; Total housing units 452; Occupied housing units 415. Education level 7.0 grades.

**Climate.** Rainfall averages 17 inches per year, most of which falls in winter months. The temperature varies from a high of 75 degrees to a low of 15 degrees. The area is dry and windy.

**Transportation.** State Highway No. 34 runs through the reservation east-west while State Highway No. 47 runs north-south. Commercial airline and train service are located in Pierre, some 60 miles from the reservation. Bus and trucklines serve Chamberlain, 20 miles distant.

**Utilities.** Water for the reservation comes from the Big Bend Reservoir. The Big Bend Dam powerhouse can produce 468,000 kilowatts of electricity. Health care is available through private hospitals in Chamberlain and Pierre.

**Recreation.** Excellent fishing and hunting are available on the reservation. Water-oriented sports are rapidly gaining favor with the public on Lake Sharpe formed by the Big Bend Dam. Plans have been made to develop the Old Fort Thompson as an historical site.


FLANDREAU RESERVATION                    Federal Reservation
Moody County
Flandreau Santee Sioux Tribe
Tribal Headquarters: Flandreau, South Dakota

**Land Status.** Tribal land: 2,180 acres. Government land: 176 acres. Total area: 2,356 acres.

**History.** In March 1869, 25 families of the most enterprising Indians at Santee Agency left and took homesteads at Flandreau, Dakota Territory, as authorized by the Sioux Treaty of 1868. They had no agent for the first four years, but after that a part-time agent looked after their affairs until they were placed under the Santee Agency in 1879. They had no reservation, and their agency was referred to as the Flandreau Special Agency until 1879. The only Government-owned property was a school, established in 1870. The reservation was established in 1935 through an Act of Congress.

**Culture.** This group was active in adopting white men's ways and today is fully integrated, economically and educationally, into the dominant culture. Unemployment, low income, and Federal dependency are no longer reported to be problems.

**Government.** The constitution, under the authority of the Indian Reorganization Act, was approved in April 1936 and revised in November 1967. The tribal charter was ratified in October 1936. The governing body is the executive committee which is elected at large in August of even-numbered years. A president, vice-president, secretary-treasurer, and two trustees form the executive committee.

**Population Profile. 1969:** Tribal enrollment 500; Indian resident 106. **1980:** Indian resident 158; Non-Indian resident 11; Percent Indian of total population 93.5; Total housing units 54; Occupied housing units 51. Employment figures for the Flandreau as a group are not available as they are thoroughly integrated with the non-Indian labor force. The unemployment rate is, however, low. The education level on the reservation is approximately 11th grade, a high average for a reservation. Between 15 and 20 tribal members are currently in college. There is a boarding school with vocational training on the reservation.

**Community Facilities.** Most of the Indians use local hospitals at their own expense. Some travel to the Winnebago PHS hospital for major medical care. The tribe has a small building for tribal activities and operations.

**Tribal Economy.** The tribe has an annual income of about $1,000. The economic status of the tribe and of the individual members is successfully interwoven with the non-Indian economy of the area.

LOWER BRULE RESERVATION                    Federal Reservation
Lyman and Stanley Counties
Sioux Tribe
Tribal Headquarters: Lower Brule, South Dakota

**Land Status.** Tribal land: 66,629 acres. Government land: 13,209 acres. Allotted land: 34,702 acres. Total area: 114,219 acres.

**History.** The Lower Brule Sioux are descended from the bands of Tetons that moved into the Dakotas from the area just west of the Great Lakes. Although habitually at war with other tribes, the Sioux did not actively resist white immigration until the whites began to intrude in great numbers and decimate the buffalo herds. With the beginning of the Plains Wars, the U.S. Government intervened and a peace council was called near Laramie, Wyoming, resulting in pledges of peace. The treaty terms were broken, and the conflict was resumed. The wars continued as additional treaties were dishonored; however, by 1890, the Sioux were relegated to their reservations.

**Culture.** The Teton division of the Sioux were originally of the eastern woodland culture with an economy based on hunting, gathering, and fishing, supplemented by limited horticulture. As the people moved westward, they acquired horses and adopted the cultural pattern of nomadic equestrians whose economic base was the horse, the bison, and trade. The Sun Dance was an annual religious ritual performed by the young men of the tribe each summer.

**Government.** The Lower Brule Sioux Tribe operates under a charter ratified in 1936 and a constitution and bylaws approved in 1960. The seven-member tribal council is popularly elected representing the entire reservation population. The council chairman is the administrative head of the tribe.

**Population Profile. 1969:** Tribal enrollment 296; Indian resident 581; Unemployment 48%; Underemployment 23%. **1980:** Indian resident 850; Non-Indian resident 173; Percent Indian of total population 83.1; Total housing units 327; Occupied housing units 243. Education level: 7.0 grades.

**Tribal Economy.** Average annual tribal income: $86,000. Approximately 55 percent of this income is revenues from grazing permits. Commercial/industrial establishments: Cal-Dak Electronics Corp.— private ownership.

**Climate.** The weather here is dry and windy. Most of the annual mean of 17 inches precipitation falls during the summer months. The mean high temperature is 75 degrees; the mean low is 15 degrees.

**Transportation.** State Highway No. 47 runs through the reservation north-south. Commercial airlines and train companies serve Pierre, 75 miles from the reservation. Bus and trucklines stop in Chamberlain, 30 miles distant.

**Utilities.** Water for the reservation comes from the Big Bend Reservoir. Electricity is generated at the Big Bend Dam in ample amounts for the reservation's present and future needs. Hospital care is available in Chamberlain and Pierre at private hospitals.

**Recreation.** Hunting and fishing on the reservation are excellent, with a wide variety of game and a well-stocked reservoir. Water-oriented sports on Lake Sharpe formed by the Big Bend Dam are rapidly gaining favor with the public.


PINE RIDGE RESERVATION                    Federal Reservation
Sheridan County, Nebraska and
Bennett, Shannon, and Washabaugh
  Counties, South Dakota
Oglala Sioux Tribe
Tribal Headquarters:  Pine Ridge, South Dakota

**Land Status.** Tribally-owned land: 372,243 acres. Government land: 48,231 acres. Allotted land: 1,089,077 acres. Non-Indian land: 1,269,159 acres. Total area: 2,778,000 acres.

**History.** The Oglala Sioux are descended from the bands of Tetons who moved into the Dakotas from the area just west of the Great Lakes. Although habitually at war with other tribes, the Sioux did not actively resist the white immigration until the whites began to intrude in great numbers and decimate the buffalo herds. With the beginning of the Plains Wars, the U.S. Government intervened and a peace council was called near Laramie, Wyoming, resulting in pledges of peace. The treaty terms were broken with conflict resulting. Further treaty agreements were similarly disregarded by the incoming whites, and, after subsequent conflict, the Sioux were relegated to their reservations by 1890. In late December 1890, troops from the U.S. Cavalry intercepted a group of Sioux under Chief Big Foot on the Pine Ridge Reservation at Wounded Knee Creek. The Wounded Knee Massacre resulted in the slaughter of Indian men, women, and children as they fled.

**Culture.** The Teton division of the Sioux were originally of woodland culture with an economy based on hunting, gathering, and fishing, supplemented by limited horticulture. As the people moved westward they acquired horses and their cultural pattern became that of equestrian nomads whose economic base was the bison, the horse, and trade. The Sun Dance was an annual religious ritual performed by the young men of the tribe during summer encampment.

**Government.** The Oglala Sioux Tribe is organized under the Indian Reorganization Act of 1934 and operates under a constitution and bylaws approved in January 1936. The 32-member tribal council is popularly elected and represents the many reservation districts. The council president is the administrative head of the tribe and heads the five-member executive committee.

**Population Profile. 1969:** Tribal enrollment 13,813; Indian resident 11,151; Unemployment 52%; Underemployment 21%. Education level: 9th grade. **1980:** Indian resident 11,946; Non-Indian resident 1,283; Percent Indian of total population 90.3; Total housing units 3,230; Occupied housing units 2,729.

**Tribal Economy.** The growing season averages 128 days. Clay suitable for pottery is present in large quantities. There are also small amounts of semiprecious stones. The annual average tribal income is $570,000.

Eighty percent of this income is derived from grazing permits. Tribal associations and cooperatives include the Land Association Enterprise, Shopping Center Enterprise, and the Construction Enterprise. Commercial and industrial establishments on the reservation include the Pine Ridge Products Company, which is privately owned and the Supermarket which is also privately owned.

**Climate.** Rainfall averages 16 inches per year. The temperature varies from a mean high of 75 degrees to a mean low of 23 degrees.

**Transportation.** State Highway No. 73, a north-south route, and U.S. Highway No. 18, an east-west route, are the major traffic arteries. The nearest commercial airline service is located in Chadron, Nebraska, 57 miles distant. Commercial trains serve Rushville, Nebraska, 25 miles from the reservation. Bus and trucklines stop in Pine Ridge.

**Utilities.** Water is obtained from individual wells. Electricity is provided by the Consumer Public Power and the LaCreek Power Cooperative. The USPHS operates a hospital for the tribe in Pine Ridge.

**Recreation.** Waterfowl hunting and trout fishing are popular at Denby Reservoir. Boating facilities are available at White Clay and Oglala Reservoirs. The Sun Dance is held at Pine Ridge each summer. Also of interest is the Wounded Knee Battlefield and the Jesuit School and Mission. Nearby attractions include the Black Hills, Mount Rushmore National Monument, and Dinosaur Park at Rapid City.


ROSEBUD RESERVATION                    Federal Reservation
Mellette, Todd, and Tripp Counties
Sioux Tribe
Tribal Headquarters: Rosebud, South Dakota

**Land Status.** Tribally-owned: 409,321 acres. Government land: 28,797.24 acres. Allotted land: 540,112.12 acres. Total area: 978,230.30 acres.

**History.** The Rosebud Sioux are descended from the bands of Tetons which moved into the Dakotas from the area just west of the Great Lakes. Although habitually at war with other tribes, the Sioux did not actively resist white immigration until the whites began to intrude in great numbers and decimate the buffalo herds. With the beginning of the Plains Wars, the U.S. Government intervened, and a peace council was called near Laramie, Wyoming, resulting in pledges of peace. The treaty terms were broken with conflict resulting. Further treaty agreements were similarly disregarded by the incoming whites, and after subsequent conflict, the Sioux were relegated to their reservations by 1890.

**Culture.** The Teton division of the Sioux was originally of woodland culture with an economy based on hunting, gathering, and fishing, supplemented by limited horticulture. As the people moved westward, they acquired horses and adopted the cultural pattern of equestrian nomads whose economic base was the bison, horse, and trade. The Sun Dance was an annual religious ritual which took place during the summer encampment.

**Government.** The Rosebud Sioux were organized under the Indian Reorganization Act of 1934 and operate under both a constitution and bylaws approved in 1935 and a charter approved in 1937. The 22-member tribal council represents the 21 reservation districts. The council president and executive committee provide the administrative leadership.

**Population Profile. 1969:** Tribal enrollment 9,400; Indian resident 7,181; Unemployment rate 50%; Underemployment 9%. **1980:** Indian resident 5,688; Non-Indian resident 1,640; Percent Indian of total population 77.6; Total housing units 2,366; Occupied housing units 1,877. Education level 1969: 9th grade. /

**Tribal Economy.** Annual average tribal income: $490,000. Tribal associations, cooperatives, etc.: Land Acquisition Enterprise; Tribal Ranch Enterprise. Commercial/industrial establishments on reservation: The Rosebud Manufacturing Co.—tribally owned; Rosebud Electronics—tribally owned; Rosebud Sign Techniques, Inc.—tribally owned.

**Climate.** Rainfall is insufficient for intensified agriculture. The temperature here varies from a high of 90 degrees to a low of -20 degrees.

**Transportation.** U.S. Highway No. 18 crosses the reservation east-west; U.S. Highway Nos. 83 and 183 pass north-south. The nearest commercial airline is located in Pierre, South Dakota, 110 miles from Rosebud. Train, bus, and trucklines serve the reservation.

**Utilities.** Water is obtained from wells. Electricity is provided by the Cherry-Todd Electric Cooperative. The USPHS maintains a hospital in Rosebud.

**Recreation.** The Rosebud Reservation offers fishing and hunting to the sportsman. Other items of interest include Crazy Horse Canyon, Ghost Hawk Canyon and camping grounds, and the annual Rosebud Fair and Powwow. There is a nine-hole golf course at Rosebud. The Geological Museum at Mission features a display of Badlands fossils.


SISSETON RESERVATION                    Federal Reservation
Day, Coddington, Grant, Marshall,
    and Roberts Counties, South Dakota
Richland and Sargent Counties, North Dakota
Sisseton and Wahpeton Sioux
Tribal Headquarters: Sisseton, South Dakota

**Land Status.** Tribally-owned land: 850 acres. Allotted land: 105,930 acres. Government land: 152 acres. Total area: 106,932 acres. The Sisseton Reservation lies in both North and South Dakota. Of the total area, 2,602 acres are in North Dakota and 104,497 in South Dakota. The reservation was created by a treaty in 1867. After allotments of 160 acres to each individual Indian, the Government purchased the remainder of the original reservation and opened it to homesteading in 1892.

**History.** The Sioux tribes originally lived in the woodlands area of Minnesota and Wisconsin. Sisseton means "Marsh Village," Wahpeton means "Village Among the Leaves." When most of the bands were driven west by the invading Chippewa, these bands moved to the lake country just within the Dakota Territory. Liking it and wanting to remain there, they withstood attacks from the Chippewa. They did not move again until driven out by U.S. troops in 1862. After the Minnesota Massacre at New Ulm during the Civil War, the Sisseton were advanced upon by U.S. troops. In an effort to prevent a massacre, the tribal council ruled that all whites on the reservation must dress like Indians. Those Indians fleeing from the Sisseton were returned to the soldiers. The tribe thus prevented the advance of the troops to their reservation. However, war ultimately broke out and the tribe was forced to flee to Canada. Tribal elders tell amusing stories about dodging the ponderous cannonball. The tribe returned from Canada in 1863 and signed a treaty at Enemy Swims Lake. Gabriel Renville was the tribe's treaty chief from 1862 until 1892. Treaties provided for the establishment of Fort Sisseton in 1864.

**Culture.** The Sioux were good hunters and fishermen, adapting to their environment in the lake country of the Dakotas. They gathered wild fruits, corn, and ground chokecherries and wild plums with meat for food. The Sioux were well organized. There has been a great deal of intermarriage with whites and adoption of new customs.

**Government.** The Sisseton-Wahpeton Sioux Council is composed of 10 members, who are elected from separate districts. Five officers, a chairman, two vice-chairmen, secretary, and treasurer, are elected at large. The tribe is unincorporated and operates under the 1966 constitution and bylaws which replaced those of 1946.

**Population Profile. 1969:** Tribal enrollment 5,000 est.; Indian resident 1,936; Unemployment 46%; Median family income $4,200. **1980:** Indian resident 2,700; Non-Indian resident 10,886; Percent Indian of total population 19.9; Total housing units 5,640; Occupied housing units 4,046. The average education level for the reservation is 10th grade. No higher education facilities are available in the immediate vicinity although several State universities are not far distant.

**Tribal Economy.** The only major mineral resources are sand and gravel which are currently being mined. The tribe has only a very small income. There are currently no commercial or industrial establishments on the reservation.

**Climate.** The rainfall averages between 20 and 24 inches annually.

**Transportation.** U.S. Highway No. 12 and Interstate 10 cross through the reservation east-west. U.S. Highway No. 81 and Interstate 29 are north-south highways. A commercial train runs through the reservation. Bus and trucklines stop in Webster and Sisseton, both on the reservation. The nearest air service is located in Watertown, 33 miles away, and Aberdeen, 72 miles from Sisseton.

**Community Facilities.** Water is provided by the Department of the Interior treatment plant, wells, and springs. Electricity is supplied by the Ottertail Power Company and the Lake Region Electric Cooperative. The Northwestern Bell Telephone Company serves the reservation area. The U.S. Public Health Service Hospital in Sisseton serves tribal members. There are also county hospitals in Britton and Day.

**Recreation.** The Old Fort Sisseton State Park is located near the reservation. In addition there are picnic and recreation areas. The many lakes provide water sports. Winter sports are good in the area. The tribe holds an annual powwow and rodeo.


STANDING ROCK RESERVATION                Federal Reservation
Sioux County, North Dakota
Corson, Dewey, and Ziebach
 Counties, South Dakota
Sioux Tribe
Tribal Headquarters:  Fort Yates, North Dakota

**Land Status.** Tribal land: 294,840.41 acres. Government land: 10,258 acres. Allotted land: 542,700.66 acres. Total area: 847,799.13 acres.

**History.** The Standing Rock Sioux are descended from the bands of Tetons which moved into the Dakotas from the area just west of the Great Lakes. Although habitually at war with other Indian tribes, the Sioux did not actively resist white immigration until the whites began to intrude in great numbers and decimate the buffalo herds. With the beginning of the Plains Wars, the U.S. Government intervened and a peace council was called near Laramie, Wyoming, at which pledges of peace were given. The treaty terms were broken, however, and conflict was renewed. Further treaty agreements were similarly disregarded by the incoming whites, and after subsequent conflict, the Sioux were relegated to their reservations by 1890.

**Culture.** The Teton division of the Sioux were originally of woodland culture with an economy based on hunting, gathering, and fishing, supplemented by limited horticulture. As the people moved westward, they acquired horses and adopted the culture pattern of equestrian nomads whose economic base was the bison, the horse, and trade. The Sun Dance was an annual religious ritual performed each summer by the young men of the tribe.

**Government.** The Standing Rock Sioux operate under a constitution approved on April 24, 1959. The 15-member tribal council is popularly elected and represents the various reservation districts. The council chairman is the administrative head of the tribe.

**Population Profile. 1969:** Tribal enrollment 7,131; Indian resident 4,712; Unemployment 43%; Underemployment 17%. **1980:** Indian resident 4,800; Non-Indian resident 4,016; Percent Indian of total population 54.4; Total housing units 2,745; Occupied housing units 2,369. Education level: 9.0 grades. Loans of up to $7,200 with $2,400 written off upon successful completion of the course are available to students continuing their education.

**Tribal Economy.** Average annual tribal income: $200,000. Sixty percent of this income is revenue from grazing permits. Commercial/industrial establishments: Five Star Cheese—privately owned; Plastic Moulders, Inc.—privately owned; Chief Manufacturing Co.—privately owned.

**Climate.** The precipitation averages 16 inches per year, most of which falls during the summer growing season. Snow during the winter is light, and the mean winter temperature is 17 degrees. The average summer temperature is 62 degrees.

**Transportation.** U.S. Highway No. 83 passes through the reservation north-south. U.S. Highway No. 12 crosses the reservation east-west. The nearest commercial airline is in Bismarck, North Dakota, some 40 miles from the reservation. Train, bus, and trucklines stop in Fort Yates on the reservation.

**Utilities.** Water is obtained from wells central to each community. Electricity and natural gas are supplied by the Montana-Dakota Utilities Company, and the Mor-Gran-Sou Cooperative. The Public Health Service operates a hospital at Fort Yates. Hospital care is also available in Bismarck.

**Recreation.** Boating, fishing, and water sports are popular on Lake Oahe. Waterfowl hunting is also excellent. Activities include the annual Sioux Indian Fair and the annual Fourth of July Rodeo. Attractions include the site of old Fort Manuel and the grave of Sitting Bull.


YANKTON RESERVATION                    Federal Reservation
Charles Mix County
Yankton Sioux Tribe
Tribal Headquarters:  Wagner, South Dakota

**Land Status.** Tribal land: 5,560 acres. Allotted land: 29,372.23 acres. Non-Indian land: 400,000 acres. Total area: 34,932.23 acres. The reservation was established by treaty in 1853. It encompassed the heart of the traditional homeland of the Yankton Sioux. Under the 1887 Allotment Act, the tribal members were allocated 40-, 80-, and 160-acre tracts, and the rest of the reservation was opened up to settlers.

**History.** Tribal tradition indicated the Yankton always lived in an area centered about the confluence of the James and Missouri Rivers. The tribe never fought against the United States and generally lived in peace with other tribes.

**Culture.** The Yankton Sioux are very similar to other Sioux in their language, customs, and culture with one exception. This small group was by nature peaceful and did not join with the mainstream of Sioux who fought other tribes and the U.S. Government.

**Government.** The tribe is nonchartered. The constitution and bylaws were adopted in 1932. In 1961, a nine-man constitutional committee was elected to revise the constitution. The constitution and bylaws were adopted as amended in July 1962. The governing body is the Yankton Sioux Tribal Business and Claims Committee. The officers, a chairman, vice-chairman, secretary, and treasurer, and committee members are elected at large for 2-year terms. Major decisions require the action of the entire tribe.

**Population Profile. 1969:** Tribal enrollment 3,600; Indian resident 1,251; Non-Indian resident 10,534; Unemployment 17%; Underemployment 53%. **1980:** Indian resident 1,688; Non-Indian resident 4,853; Percent Indian of total population 25.8; Total housing units 2,527;

Occupied housing units 2,107. The education level for the reservation is 8.0 grades. There are presently nine tribal members in college.

**Tribal Economy.** Sand and gravel deposits on the reservation are being used. Chalk shale and clays also exist in substantial quantities but are not being exploited. The tribal income of $17,800 is primarily profits from farming. Only 10 percent is interest. M-Tron Electronics has an industrial plant in Greenwood, South Dakota, which employs 17 Indians.

**Climate.** Rainfall averages 23.6 inches annually. The temperature ranges from an average high of 77.7 degrees to an average low of 19.2 degrees.

**Transportation.** U.S. Route 281 runs north from the reservation. U.S. Route 18 crosses the reservation east-west, and South Dakota Highway 50 runs south-east. Trains and airlines serve Yankton, 45 miles from the reservation. Wagner and Mitchell also have air service.

**Community Facilities.** Wagner has a municipal water and sewer system. Greenwood and the rest of the reservation use ground water and wells. Northern Natural Gas pipes gas to Wagner. Northwest Public Service Company and the Charles Mix Electric Association supply electricity to the reservation area. Health care for the Yankton Sioux is provided at the 25-bed PHS hospital in Wagner. The tribe has converted an old school building.

**Recreation.** Hunting for pheasant and other game is good. A number of historic sites provide diversion. Two powwows are held each year. On the Fourth of July is the "Struck by the Ree" Powwow. The Fort Randall Powwow is held the first week in August.


# TEXAS


ALABAMA-COUSHATTA RESERVATION          State Reservation
Polk County
Alabama and Coushatta Tribes
Tribal Headquarters: Livingston, Texas

**Land Status.** Total area: 4,400 acres. All reservation land is tribally owned. The Alabama and Coushatta were given two leagues of land by the Texas Legislature close to the present location; however, this land was taken away from the Indians by white settlers in the early 1800's. General Sam Houston, a good friend of the Indians, was instrumental in having Texas purchase 1,280 acres in 1854 for the tribes. In 1928, the State and Federal Governments appropriated funds to purchase an additional 3,071 acres to be held under State trust for the tribe. The tribe is acquiring 152 acres for forthcoming expansion of the tourist facilities.

**History.** The Alabama-Coushatta, members of the Muskogean stock, Upper Creek Confederacy, first appeared in Texas in the early 1700's. They were the first friendly tribe encountered by Coronado De Soto and his men in the southeastern United States area. When most tribes in Texas were removed to Indian Territory in Oklahoma, the Alabama-Coushatta were permitted to remain, as they had a history of peaceful relations. The two tribes were under the Federal Bureau of Indian Affairs until Public Law 280 terminated Federal affiliation. The responsibility for the tribes was then transferred to Texas. Under Texas jurisdiction, local attention has been a major factor in the progress attained. The termination of State aid was expected in 1974 at the request of the tribes.

**Culture.** The culture of the Alabama and Coushatta has now been preserved through an Indian-oriented tourist program initiated on the reservation. For many years the culture of the tribes has waned partly because of the tribes' small size and partly because they are surrounded by white communities and isolated from related tribes. The effect of the Protestant religion in undermining their own religious ceremonies and rituals was irreversible. The tribes readily took to the new religion, while much pressure was applied to disband their ceremonies which the missionaries considered evil. The Indians realized the importance of preserving their culture only after much had been lost.

**Government.** The tribes are governed by a council of seven members elected by the tribes. The governor appoints three distinguished persons to serve as the Texas Commission for Indian Affairs. The Commission's duty is to look after the best interests of the tribes. In all significant decisions handed down by the Commission, the tribal council concurrently approves or vetoes the action. In all council actions the Commission concurrently approves or gives advice. The Commission has served to promote the programs of the reservation, give legal counsel, coordinate the needs of the tribes and work with the legislature and other government bodies, and improve communications between the Indians and the complicated governmental processes.

**Population Profile. 1969:** Tribal enrollment 550; Indian resident 380; Non-Indian resident 10; Unemployment 0; Underemployment 0. **1980:** Indian resident 494; Non-Indian resident 10; Percent Indian of total population 98.0; Total housing units 186; Occupied housing units 138. Employment is readily available as there are more job openings than Indian labor available, and employers must compete for Indian labor. Eastern Texas is prospering, but the labor shortage is a problem. The average education level of the tribes is 12th grade. There are six college graduates in the tribes. The tribes provide $4,000 per year for students requiring scholarships.

**Tribal Economy.** The tribes employ 18 persons. Tribal associations include the Texas Forestry Association, the Big Thicket Association, and membership in the National Congress of American Indians.

**Climate.** The reservation area averages over 44 inches of rainfall each year. Temperatures range from a high of 83 degrees to a low of 50 degrees.

**Transportation.** The reservation lies along the east-west Highway No. 190. Livingston, 17 miles from the reservation, is served by commercial bus and trucklines. Houston, 90 miles away, offers air and train transportation.

**Community Facilities.** The reservation has installed and maintains the sewer system. Water is drawn from wells. Gas is piped in by the

United Gas Corp. The Sam Houston Electric Coop. supplies electricity. The John Sealy Hospital in Galveston as well as the Tyler County Hospital in Woodville provide medical care for the tribal members. Additional health care is available in Tyler County. Former school buildings are utilized by the community for the various functions held throughout the year which include gospel singing, basketball games, and Indian powwows.

TIGUA INDIAN RESERVATION           State Reservation
El Paso County
Tigua Tribe
Tribal Headquarters: Ysleta del Sur Pueblo, El Paso, Texas

**Land Status.** Total area: 73 acres. All the land is State trust land. This includes 50 acres at Hueco Tanks Park, 26 miles from Ysleta, 20 acres at Sabinas archeological site 20 miles from Ysleta, and 3 acres being purchased at the Ysleta Mission by the State of Texas. The Tigua Indians have no tribal lands as their 1751 Pueblo Grant of 20,040 acres was never made a reservation as was such a grant in New Mexico in 1864. This land was taken over by early American and Mexican settlers. A few families own small lots on which they have built homes; however, these were purchases from settlers and presently are personal property.

**History.** The Tigua Indians of Ysleta, El Paso, Texas are a displaced Pueblo tribe originally located at the Isleta Pueblo just south of Albuquerque, New Mexico. Their first contact with European civilization was in 1540 when Coronado spent the winter with them. During the Spanish colonization of New Mexico, they were converted to Christianity and under the Spanish padres' direction constructed a mission in 1621 at Isleta, New Mexico, dedicated to St. Anthony. During the Pueblo Revolt of 1680, the tribe was removed by the Spanish during their retreat and located at Ysleta del Sur now in Texas. The Isleta, New Mexico Pueblo and Mission were destroyed and abandoned during the revolt and were not re-inhabited for approximately 20 years. The Tigua Indians brought the tribal drums, staffs of office, and Santo or Saint Anthony with them to Ysleta, where in 1682, they built the present day Ysleta Mission. This mission today stands on the original foundation and incorporates much of the original adobe walls in the present structure. It has been in continuous use since 1682, and St. Anthony continues as the Patron Saint of the Tigua with June 13th, Saint Anthony's Day, being their main religious celebration.

**Culture.** Although these people have been pushed aside and deprived of their lands by being engulfed in the development of a modern Mexican-American civilization for almost 300 years, their tribal identity has survived, and today they still practice many aboriginal customs no longer found among other pueblo people. They have retained their form of tribal government, practice the same form of ceremonial dances and continue to live in the same adobe houses, obtaining much of their sustenance by hunting, fishing, and planting small gardens.

Herbs, roots, and plants are still used for medicine. They consider the Hueco Tanks area to be a sacred place where their ancestors lived. There is a myth that the great spirit created the Pueblo Indians in the caves which abound there. The many pueblo pictographs and relics in the area support this belief.

**Government.** The tribal government consists of a cacique mayor, captain di guerra, governor, lieutenant governor, and alguacil or bailiff. All major actions by the council are approved or ratified by a vote of the tribe. At present the tribe does not have a constitution and is not considering the adoption of a constitutional form of government.

**Population Profile. 1969:** Tribal enrollment 348; Indian resident 348; Unemployment 50; Underemployment 150. **1980:** Indian resident 365; Non-Indian resident 138; Percent Indian of total population 72.6; Total housing units 114; Occupied housing units 112. The average education level for the tribe is 4th grade. At present there is one tribal member in college. The State provides some scholarship money toward a college education. Vocational education is offered at the El Paso Technical High School.

**Tribal Economy.** The annual tribal income is $300 earned in a variety of occupations. A tribal enterprise operates Hueco Tanks Park by contract with El Paso County. Gate fees and concession rentals collected are used to employ five tribal members to maintain the park. A community arts and crafts facility is planned at Ysleta to develop and market native crafts.

**Climate.** The rainfall in the area averages 10 inches per year. Temperatures reach a high of 105 degrees and a low of 15 degrees.

**Transportation.** U.S. Highway No. 54 is a north-south route through El Paso. U.S. Highway No. 80 and Interstate 10 are major east-west routes. Twelve miles from Ysleta in El Paso, all forms of commercial transportation are available.

**Community Facilities.** Very few of the Indians' homes have running water, utilities, or sanitary facilities, although these are readily available in El Paso. The city and county provide health care at Ysleta Center. A clinic at Alameda is open to tribal members by contract. Hospitalization is available at Thomason General Hospital. The tribe is planning construction of a community building to be built in the Barrio area.

**Recreation.** Recreation and tourist facilities are numerous in El Paso. On June 13, St. Anthony's Day, the tribe holds a fiesta which includes the traditional pueblo dancing.


UTAH


SKULL VALLEY RESERVATION                    Federal Reservation
Tooele County
Goshute Tribe
Tribal Headquarters: Grantsville, Utah

**Land Status.** Tribally-owned land: 17,284 acres. Allotted land: 160 acres. Total area: 17,444 acres.

**History.** The Goshutes, related to the Shoshones, lived in the region around Great Salt Lake and northern Utah. Hunters pursued antelopes, rabbits, and birds for food. They also became harvesters of seeds, roots, herbs, sagebrush, cacti, reeds, and grasses. These resourceful people became interested in the art of healing and developed many vegetable medicinal compounds. The grim realities of survival limited the bands to extended families, and personal possessions were limited to what could be carried.

**Culture.** This tribe utilized shelters of brush, reeds, and grasses lashed to poles bent in a conical shape. Fibers from milkweed and sage brushbark reeds and grasses were woven into clothing and utensils. Each tribal member was an active contributor to the common welfare and cooperative sharing was the essence of survival.

**Government.** The tribe does not operate under a constitution or bylaws. Decisions are made on an informal basis by the entire tribal membership attending called meetings.

**Population Profile. 1969:** Tribal enrollment N.A.; Indian resident 30; Unemployment 55%; Underemployment 10%; Median family income N.A. **1980:** Indian resident 13; Non-Indian resident 0; Percent Indian of total population 100.0; Total housing units 4; Occupied housing units 4.

**Climate.** The reservation is located in an arid region south of the Great Salt Lake. The rainfall averages only 6 inches per year. The temperature reaches a high of 100 degrees in the summer and a low of 10 degrees in the winter.

**Transportation.** The reservation lies 25 miles south of U.S. Highway No. 40, with access via a county road. All means of commercial transportation are miles northeast of the reservation.

**Community Facilities.** Utilities on the reservation are scanty. Water is drawn from wells, and septic tanks are the only provision for waste disposal. The Public Health Service operates a hospital in Owyhee, Nevada, which serves these tribal members. There is also a private hospital in Tooele, Utah.


UINTAH AND OURAY RESERVATION               Federal Reservation
Uintah, Duchesne, and Grand Counties
Ute Tribe
Tribal Headquarters: Fort Duchesne, Utah

**Land Status.** Tribally-owned land: 970,273 acres. Government land: 24 acres. Allotted land: 37,855 acres. Total area: 1,008,192 acres. In addition to the land it owns, the tribe has subsurface rights on 192,000 acres.

**History.** Ute territory in frontier days comprised central and western Colorado and eastern Utah, including the eastern part of Salt Lake Valley and Utah Valley, and extended into the upper drainage area of the San Juan River in New Mexico. The white settlers in southern Utah upset an Indian plan of land "ownership" that had existed for many years. Certain lands were organized as the traditional province of particular tribes, and a ceremony was observed by strangers when passing from the land of one group to another. The white man's failure to acknowledge this ancient pattern of land rights led to misunderstanding and ill will on both sides. In October 1863, the Government of the United States extended its authority, without formal purchase, and the Indians were assigned to reservations. The tribe became a Federally-chartered corporation under the Act of June 18, 1934.

**Culture.** Ancestors of today's Utes inhabited forested mountain slopes filled with game and productive streams. A shelter of brush, reeds, and grasses lashed to poles bent in a conical shape was the typical housing. Each band member was an active contributor to the common welfare. Cooperative sharing was the essence of survival. Arrow and spearhead makers were honored individuals. The annual game drives in the fall were communal in nature. The Ute became experienced horsemen after horses were introduced by the Spaniards.

**Government.** The Uintah and Ouray Tribal Business Committee is the popularly elected governing body of the tribe. It is composed of six members who are elected for terms of 4 years. The tribal constitution and bylaws empower the business committee to act on such matters as negotiations for loans in the name of the tribe, formation of enterprises, contractual agreements with other agencies, and other responsibilities.

**Population Profile. 1969:** Tribal enrollment 1,611; Indian resident 1,274; Non-Indian resident 5,900; Unemployment 60%; Underemployment 10; Median family income $4,500. **1980:** Indian resident 2,050; Non-Indian resident 14,859; Percent Indian of total population 12.1; Total housing units 6,547; Occupied housing units 4,601.

**Tribal Economy.** The tribe's annual income of $950,000 is primarily revenue from mineral leases and forestry. The tribe also operates a cattle enterprise and recently established a furniture manufacturing company.

**Climate.** The reservation lies southeast of Salt Lake City in essentially two segments. The area is arid like much of Utah, averaging only 7 inches of precipitation annually. The temperature varies seasonally from a high of 90 degrees to a low of 0 degrees. Large quantities of gas and oil lie under the reservation and are the source of most of the tribe's income. Also present are phosphate, coal, and gravel.

**Transportation.** U.S. Highway No. 40 runs east-west through the northern portion of the reservation. There are no other highways, but towns are connected by internal roads. Bus and trucklines stop on the reservation. Commercial train and air companies serve Provo, Utah, 70 miles west of the reservation.

**Community Facilities.** The Public Health Service has installed septic tanks and dug wells for basic sanitary facilities. Gas is supplied by the Mountain Fuel Company. Three companies supply electricity to various parts of the reservation, the Moon Land Electric Association, the Utah Power and Light Company, and the Uintah Power and Light Company. The Public Health Service Hospital servicing the Indians' medical needs is located at Fort Duchesne.

**Recreation.** The annual Bear Dance of the Ute Tribe is held in April or May, and the Sun Dance takes place in July. Fort Duchesne, an old Army post, has interest to many tourists. The tribe constructed, in an unusually beautiful setting, a large tourism complex which became available for use in 1970.

# VIRGINIA

MATTAPONY RESERVATION                        State Reservation
King William County
Mattapony Indians (Powhatan)

**Land Status.** Total area: 125 acres. Deed to the reservation was granted to the Mattapony Indians in 1658 by the colonial Virginia House of Burgesses. The reservation is located on the Mattaponi River near Wakema, Virginia. Any qualifying brave may obtain permission from the tribal council for land use.

**History.** The term "Powhatan" refers to the former confederacy of Virginia's Algonquian tribes and to their most famous chief, whose proper name is Wahunsonacock, and whose daughter, Pocahontas, saved the life of Captain John Smith. At the time the Jamestown settlers arrived, the Powhatan Confederacy had about 200 villages, 160 of which were noted on Smith's map. The Indians were at first friendly to the whites, but were soon driven to hostility by the continued exactions made upon them. Under Opechancanough, an uprising was planned which, in 1622, nearly wiped out the English settlements, destroying every one except Jamestown, which was warned ahead by an Indian convert. Reprisals followed against the Indians, and, in 1625, 1,000 Indians were defeated at the great battle at Pamunkey. Other massacres of Indians, including the raid under Nathaniel Bacon in 1676, effectively decimated the tribe. By 1705, there were only 12 villages left and Pamunkey with 150 people was the only one of importance. The greatest problem the Mattapony face today is maintaining status as a tribe.

**Culture.** The Powhatan Indians practiced an animistic religion and believed in immortality. Their houses were built with saplings whose tops were bent over and tied and then covered with bark and sided with woven mats. These dwellings could hold several families. They were advanced in agriculture and cultivated maize (corn), beans, pumpkins, fruit trees, and several varieties of roots. They computed by the decimal system. Typical crafted items were clay pots and pipes and ceremonial clothing of woven turkey feathers. Some basketry and beadwork are still done today. The tribal organization has endured, although the Indian language was extinct by the end of the 18th Century, and most of the culture has been lost. Hunting and fishing are still important.

**Population Profile. 1969:** Indian resident 65. **1980:** Indian resident

68; Non-Indian resident 8; Percent Indian of total population 89.5;
Total housing units 29; Occupied housing units 26.


PAMUNKEY RESERVATION                    State Reservation
King William County
Pamunkey Indians (Powhatan)
Tribal Headquarters: Pamunkey, Virginia

**Land Status.** Total area: 800 acres. The Pamunkey Reservation
was established in 1677 by the Virginia House of Burgesses on the Pamunkey River, 20 miles east of present-day Richmond. The State provides minimal services to the reservation, principally the upkeep of
roads running to Pamunkey.

**History.** The term "Powhatan" refers to the former confederacy
of Virginia's Algonquian tribes and to their most famous chief whose
proper name was Wahunsonacock, whose daughter, Pocahontas, saved
the life of Captain John Smith. At the time the Jamestown settlers
arrived, the Powhatan Confederacy had about 200 villages, 160 of
which were noted on Smith's map. The Indians were at first friendly
to the whites, but soon driven to hostility by the continued exactions
made upon them. Under Opechancanough, an uprising was planned
which, in 1622, wiped out the English settlements, destroying every
one except Jamestown, which was warned ahead by an Indian convert.
Reprisals followed against the Indians, and in 1625, 1,000 Indians were
defeated at the great battle of Pamunkey. Other massacres of Indians,
including the raid under Nathaniel Bacon in 1676, effectively decimated
the tribe. By 1705, there were only 12 villages left, and Pamunkey,
with 150 people, was the only one of importance.

**Culture.** The Powhatan Indians practiced an animistic religion
and believed in immortality. Their houses were built with saplings
whose tops were bent over and tied and then covered with bark and
sided with woven mats. These dwellings could hold several families.
They were advanced in agriculture and cultivated maize (corn), beans,
pumpkins, fruit trees, and several varieties of roots. They computed
by the decimal system. Typical crafted items were clay pots and pipes
and ceremonial clothing of woven turkey feathers. Some basketry
and beadwork are still done today. The tribal organization has endured
although the Indian language was extinct by the end of the 18th Century
and most of the culture has been lost. Hunting and fishing are still
important.

**Government.** The Indians practice self-government and are not
taxed by the State. They elect a chief, a seven-member council, clerk,
and treasurer. These officers serve for 4 years and make the laws
for the tribe.

**Population Profile. 1969:** Tribal enrollment 350 est.; Indian resident
28; Non-Indian resident 2; Underemployment 0. **1980:** Indian resident
50; Non-Indian resident 9; Percent Indian of total population 84.7;
Total housing units 33; Occupied housing units 30. Forty percent of
the Indians living on the reservation have completed high school. The

children attend public schools nearby, and the State reimburses the local system for their educational expenses. There is one college graduate living on Pamunkey Reservation.

**Tribal Economy.** There is no tribal income. There are no industrial establishments on the reservation, although there is an arts and crafts shop which is widely known for its craftwork and artifacts. It includes a small museum. The only important mineral resource is clay which is used in pottery making.

**Transportation.** The State maintains a paved road to the reservation, but roads on the Indian land are dirt and maintained by the tribe which recently acquired a grader for the purpose. The nearest airport is at Richmond, 20 miles away. Truck, bus, and train service are also available in Richmond. The Pamunkey River runs through the reservation.

**Climate.** Pamunkey Reservation is 60 feet above sea level in elevation and averages 45 inches of rain annually. The average temperatures range from 32 degrees to 88 degrees in the summer months. A record low of 2 degrees and a high of 105 degrees have been recorded.

**Community Facilities.** Water is provided from wells and electric pumps. Both wood and bottled gas are used for cooking and heating. The Virginia Electric and Power Company supplies electricity. Septic tanks provide sewage disposal facilities. There is a hospital in Richmond supported by public funds which provides health and social services. There is one community building on the reservation.


# WASHINGTON


CHEHALIS RESERVATION                    Federal Reservation
Grays Harbor and Thurston Counties
Chehalis Tribe
Tribal Headquarters: Oakville, Washington

**Land Status.** Tribally-owned land: 21 acres. Allotted land: 1,628 acres. Non-Indian land: 2,566 acres. Total area: 4,225 acres. A claim filed with the Indian Claims Commission for loss of land and fishing rights was settled by compromises in the amount of $754,380, and funds have been distributed on a per capita basis to eligible descendants of the Upper and Lower Chehalis Tribes.

**History.** The Confederated Tribes of the Chehalis Reservation were established by Executive Order in 1864 which was amended in October 1886. The reservation was originally inhabited by bands of Chehalis, Chinook Clatsop, and Cowlitz Indians.

**Culture.** The Chehalis Indians were part of the Coastal Indian culture of the Pacific Northwest which flourished in the moist coastal strip, their lives built around a natural abundance of fish and forests. Many coastal tribes made fine basketry and wood carvings, and Indians of the Juan de Fuca Strait were famed for blankets loom-woven of dog hair. Salmon was the foremost food, and many tribal beliefs and ceremonies centered around salmon. The second most important natural resource was wood, particularly the western red cedar. In the highly materialistic culture of the Pacific Northwest, the skillfully crafted gabled lodges helped proclaim the prestige of the owners. Steamed and bent cedar was fashioned into boxes, buckets, serving dishes, and utensils. Cedar bark supplied clothing, mats, furnishings, and rope. Wealth determined leadership in this property-conscious culture, and the elaborate social structure included a hereditary nobility, a middle class, and a slave class of war captives and their descendants.

**Government.** The Chehalis Tribe is not organized according to the 1934 Indian Reorganization Act, but operates under a tribal constitution which was appproved in August of 1939. The constitution provides for a Chehalis Community Council consisting of all .qualified voters of the tribal membership who elect a six-member business committee to 2-year terms. This committee is responsible for the tribal administration.

**Population Profile.** 1969: Tribal enrollment 116; Indian resident 186. 1980: Indian resident 200; Non-Indian resident 205; Percent Indian of total population 49.4; Total housing units 140; Occupied housing units 123. The average education level for the tribe is 9th grade, and two members are college graduates.

**Climate.** The reservation lies in the eastern part of the State where the ocean currents bring an annual rainfall of 40 inches per year. The temperatures reach a high of 80 degrees and a low of 25 degrees.

**Transportation.** The reservation lies just south of U.S. Highway No. 12 which runs east-west. Olympia, 35 miles from the reservation, is the nearest location served by regularly scheduled bus, train, truck, and airlines.

**Community Facilities.** The wells and sewer system were installed by the U.S. Public Health Service. The reservation is a part of the Grays Harbor County Public Utility District which supplies electricity. A Public Health Service Hospital is located in Grays Harbor to serve members of the tribes.


COLVILLE RESERVATION                    Federal Reservation
Ferry and Okanogan Counties
Confederated Tribes
Tribal Headquarters: Nespelem, Washington

**Land Status.** Tribally-owned land: 937,240 acres. Allotted land: 74,248 acres. Non-Indian land: 7 acres. Total area: 1,011,495 acres.

**History.** The Colville Indian Reservation was established by Executive Order on July 2, 1872, which changed the boundaries of the area previously set aside by an 1872 Executive Order to the present boundaries.

**Culture.** The Confederated Tribes were of seminomadic Plateau Indian culture ranging over the dry uplands of Idaho, eastern Oregon, and eastern Washington. All Plateau tribes were traditionally fishermen and hunters who wandered over the country in small, loosely-organized bands searching for game, wild seeds, berries, and roots of camas. With basketry techniques that ranked among the best in North America, they wove the grasses and scrubby brush of the Plateau into almost everything they used, including portable summer shelters, clothing, and watertight cooking pots. Having no clans, Plateau Indians counted descent on both sides of the family. There was little formal organization. The few tribal ceremonies centered around the food supply. In the early 1700's, horses were introduced among the tribes, and the Indians became highly skilled horsemen who counted their wealth in terms of the new animal.

**Government.** The governing body of the Confederated Tribes is the Colville Business Council, consisting of 14 members representing the four voting districts on the reservation. The business council represents all segments of the Indian people. The economic development and planning committee, which also acts as the Overall Economic Development Program Committee, is assisted by an advisory committee. The Confederated Tribes are organized under a constitution which was approved on April 19, 1938.

**Population Profile. 1969:** Tribal enrollment 4,953; Indian resident 2,983; Unemployment 39%; Underemployment 24%. **1980:** Indian resident 3,500; Non-Indian resident 3,547; Percent Indian of total population 49.7; Total housing units 2,713. Occupied housing units 2,317.

**Tribal Economy.** The tribe, which has an annual income of approximately $3 million provides eight 4-year scholarships of $2,600 and 10 2-year scholarships of $1,500 to tribal members continuing their education.

**Climate.** The Colville Reservation is located in northeastern Washington where rainfall averages 15 inches each year and temperatures reach highs of 85 degrees and lows of 0 degrees.

**Transportation.** U.S. Highway No. 97 runs along the western border of the reservation north-south. State Highway No. 21 is also a north-south highway and State Highway No. 155 crosses the reservation northwest-southeast. The reservation is served by train and buslines. The closest available truck service is 15 miles away at Grand Coulee. Spokane, 97 miles from the reservation, is the nearest location of commercial air service.

**Community Facilities.** Reservation residents draw water from wells. Most areas have local sewer systems. The Washington Water Power and REA provides the electricity to the reservation. Both Bell Telephone and General Telephone serve the reservation. PHS operates one hospital at Colville Agency to serve the health needs of tribal members.


HOH RESERVATION                                    Federal Reservation
Jefferson County
Hoh Tribe
Tribal Headquarters: Forks, Washington

**Land Status.** Total area: 443 acres. All the reservation land is tribally-owned. The Hoh Tribe has shared in a recently awarded claims judgment for the Quileute and Hoh Indians amounting to $112,152.

**History.** The Hoh Reservation was established by Executive Order of September 11, 1893. The Hoh are considered to be a part of the Quileute Tribe, but are recognized as a separate tribal group. Funds from cutting timber on the reservation are in deposit for use in tribal development programs.

**Culture.** The Hoh Indians were part of the Coastal Indian culture of the Pacific Northwest which flourished in the moist coastal strip, their lives built around a natural abundance of fish and forests. Many coastal tribes made fine basketry and wood carvings, and Indians of the Juan de Fuca Strait were famed for blankets loom-woven of dog hair. Salmon was the foremost food and many tribal beliefs and ceremonies centered around salmon. The second most important natural wealth was wood, particularly the western red cedar. Although strong and durable, it was easily worked with primitive tools. In the highly materialistic culture of the Pacific Northwest, the skillfully crafted gabled lodges helped proclaim the prestige of the owners. Steamed and bent cedar was fashioned into boxes, buckets, serving dishes, and utensils. Cedar bark supplied clothing, mats, furnishings, and rope. Wealth determined leadership in this property-conscious culture, and the elaborate social structure included a hereditary nobility, a middle class, and a slave class of war captives and their descendants.

**Government.** As a result of Public Law 89-655 providing for a basic role of the tribe, a constitution was adopted on May 24, 1969, and approved on July 1, 1969. This constitution authorized the election of a tribal business committee.

**Population Profile. 1969:** Tribal enrollment 40; Indian resident 20; Unemployment 36%. **1980:** Indian resident 46; Non-Indian resident 21; Percent Indian of total population 68.7; Total housing units 26; Occupied housing units 20. The average education attainment is 9th grade.

**Climate.** The Hoh Reservation is located in the northwestern section of the State where the rainfall averages 100 inches annually. The temperatures reach highs of 80 degrees and lows of 30 degrees.

**Transportation.** The reservation is 3 miles from the north-south highway, U.S. No. 101. The nearest scheduled stop for bus, train, and trucklines is at Forks, 25 miles from Hoh. Eighty-five miles from Hoh is Port Angeles, where there is a commercial airport.

**Community Facilities.** The Public Health Service installed the wells and sewage facilities for the reservation. The Jefferson County Public Utility District supplies electricity to the reservation. There is a hospital in Port Angeles and a clinic in Forks to meet the health needs of the population.

**Recreation.** The reservation includes a beautiful ocean frontage which could be developed into a recreation facility.

KALISPEL RESERVATION                    Federal Reservation
Pend Oreille County
Kalispel Tribe
Tribal Headquarters:  Usk, Washington

**Land Status.** Indian tribal land: 409 acres. Allotted land: 4,220 acres. Total area: 4,629 acres.

**History.** The Kalispel Indians earned a livelihood based on the area's natural abundance of fish and forest. In 1855, after a treaty was negotiated in which they ceded vast areas of this rich land, the Kalispel Tribe was located on this reservation.

**Culture.** The Kalispel Tribe was of seminomadic Plateau Indian culture ranging over the dry uplands of Idaho, eastern Oregon, and eastern Washington. All Plateau tribes were traditionally fishermen and hunters who wandered over the country in small, loosely-organized bands searching for game, wild seeds, berries, and roots of camas. With basketry techniques that ranked among the best in North America, they wove the grasses and scrubby brush of the Plateau into almost everything they used, including portable summer shelters, clothing, and watertight cooking pots. Having no clans, Plateau Indians counted descent on both sides of the family. There was little formal organization. The few tribal ceremonies centered around the food supply. In the early 1700's, horses were introduced among the tribes, and the Indians became highly skilled horsemen who counted their wealth in terms of the new animal.

**Government.** The Kalispel Tribe is organized under the Indian Reorganization Act of 1934 with a constitution and charter approved in 1938. The Kalispel Business Council consists of seven members elected to 1-year terms by the community council.

**Population Profile.** **1969:** Tribal enrollment 167; Indian resident 120; Unemployment 28%. **1980:** Indian resident 98; Non-Indian resident 8; Percent Indian of total population 92.5; Total housing units 25; Occupied housing units 22. Average education level: 8th grade.

**Climate.** The rainfall in this area averages 15 inches per year. Temperatures vary from a high of 95 degrees to a low of 0 degrees in a generally mild climate.

**Transportation.** State Highway No. 31 runs through the reservation north-south. Spokane, 50 miles from the reservation, has full transportation facilities including bus, train, truck, and air service.

**Community Facilities.** The wells and septic tanks on the reservation were provided by the Public Health Service. There is no gas piped to the reservation. The reservation is a part of the Pend Oreille County Public Utility District which supplies the electricity. The nearest hospital is in Spokane.


LOWER ELWAH RESERVATION                 Federal Reservation
Clallam County
Clallam Tribe
Tribal Headquarters:  Port Angeles, Washington

**Land Status.** Total area: 372 acres. All the land on the reservation is tribally owned. For the purpose of presenting claims to the Indian Claims Commission, the three bands of Clallam Indians, living on the Port Gamble, Lower Elwah, and Jamestown Reservations, have consolidated as the Clallam Tribe. Liability has been determined, but values and offsets have not been established.

**History.** By Treaty of Point No Point of 1855, the Clallam Indians were entitled to share in a small reservation on Hood Canal with the Skokomish Tribe who were their traditional enemies. As this was Skokomish territory, very few Clallam Indians settled there. The Lower Elwah Band of Clallam located on a sandspit in Port Angeles, where their unsatisfactory living conditions aroused public protest. When funds became available under the Indian Reorganization Act of 1934, 372 acres of farmland in Elwah Valley were purchased and assigned to the 14 families which make up the band. On January 19, 1968, the land was designated as an Indian reservation.

**Culture.** The Clallam Indians were part of the Coastal Indian culture of the Pacific Northwest which flourished in the moist coastal strip, their lives built around a natural abundance of fish and forest. Many coastal tribes made fine basketry and wood carvings, and Indians of the Juan de Fuca Strait were famed for blankets loom-woven of dog hair. Salmon was the foremost food, and many tribal beliefs and ceremonies centered around salmon. The second most important natural wealth was wood, particularly the western red cedar. Although strong and durable, it was easily worked with primitive tools. In the highly materialistic culture of the Pacific Northwest, the skillfully crafted gabled lodges helped proclaim the prestige of the owners. Steamed and bent cedar was fashioned into boxes, buckets, serving dishes, and utensils. Cedar bark supplied clothing, mats, furnishings, and rope. Wealth determined leadership in this property-conscious culture, and the elaborate social structure included a hereditary nobility, a middle class, and a slave class of war captives and their descendants.

**Government.** The Lower Elwah Tribal Community Council of the Lower Elwah Band of Clallam Indians operates under the tribal constitution which was adopted on May 6, 1968, and approved on May 29, 1968. The council elects three of its members for 2-year terms to form the tribal business committee.

**Population Profile. 1969:** Tribal enrollment 135; Indian resident 135; Unemployment 34%. **1980:** Indian resident 47; Non-Indian resident 17; Percent Indian of total population 73.4; Total housing units 18; Occupied housing units 15. The education attainment level for the tribe is 9th grade. Nine tribal members are college graduates.

**Climate.** The annual rainfall in this area is 35 inches. The temperature reaches a high of 80 degrees and a low of 25 degrees.

**Transportation.** The reservation lies adjacent to the east-west State Highway No. 112. Port Angeles, which lies 10 miles from the reservation, is served by commercial bus, truck, train, and airlines.

**Community Facilities.** Water is drawn from wells which were installed by the Public Health Service. The sewer system was installed by the same agency. The tribe obtains electricity from the Clallam County Public Utility District. Tribal members obtain medical care through the private hospital in Port Angeles.

LUMMI RESERVATION                    Federal Reservation
Whatcom County
Lummi and Nooksack Tribes
Tribal Headquarters: Bellingham, Washington

**Land Status.** Tribally-owned land: 12 acres. Allotted land: 7,073 acres. Total area: 7,085 acres. The Lummi Reservation was established by treaty in 1859 and modified by Executive Order in 1873. The Lummi Tribe owns in trust all of the 5,000 acres of tidelands abutting the reservation. These tidelands include those abutting the sold-off upland areas.

**History.** A small portion of the aboriginal Lummi Indian land area was reserved as a political entity from the cession by the Muckl-te-oh or Point Elliot Treaty in the Territory of Washington, January 22, 1855. It is admitted that "presents were distributed to induce good feelings and attendance," and that the interpreter used Chinook jargon, "a mixed language not generally understood by the Indians." Also, the tribes were promised a large general reservation, but no action was ever taken by the Government. By Executive Order in 1873, certain portions of the treaty boundary were rearranged, slightly enlarging the reservation.

**Culture.** The Lummi Indians were part of the Coastal Indian culture of the Pacific Northwest which flourished in the moist coastal strip, their lives built around a natural abundance of fish and forests. Many coast tribes made fine basketry and wood carvings, and Indians of the Juan de Fuca Strait were famed for blankets loom-woven of dog hair. Salmon was the foremost food, and many tribal beliefs and ceremonies centered around salmon. The second most important natural resource was wood, particularly the western red cedar. Although strong and durable, it was easily worked with primitive tools. In the highly materialistic culture of the Pacific Northwest, the skillfully crafted gabled lodges helped proclaim the prestige of the owners. Steamed and bent cedar was fashioned into boxes, buckets, serving dishes, and utensils. Cedar bark supplied clothing, mats and furnishings, and rope. Wealth determined leadership in this property-conscious culture; and the elaborate social structure included a hereditary nobility, a middle class, and a slave class of war captives and their descendants. The Lummi Indians were always involved in fishing and the sea. The annual Stommish (meaning warrior) originated with the historical warfare between the Lummi and Haida Indians. In June, after the coastal waters settled down from the winter storms, the Haida Indians would come down from the north to engage the Lummi in battle and to capture slaves. As settlement by non-Indians developed in the mid-1800's, the Lummi were able to arm themselves with rifles. After the marauding Haida beached their canoes, the Lummi opened fire and killed most of the enemy. There were no more raids and the Lummi still celebrate with the annual Stommish event.

**Government.** The business council is the governing body of the tribe. This council, consisting of 11 members, is elected by popular vote of the adult members of the tribe. The council has the authority to regulate the conduct of trade and use and disposition of the property.

The general council, composed of all members of the tribe, meets annually and has the authority to recommend future action of the Lummi Business Council. There are seven standing committees in addition to the Lummi Planning Commission. The tribe operates under a constitution approved on April 2, 1948, and not under the Indian Reorganization Act.

**Population Profile.** **1969:** Tribal enrollment 1,200; Indian resident 669; Unemployment 12%; Median family income $3,200. **1980:** Indian resident 1,259; Non-Indian resident 1,015; Percent Indian of total population 55.4; Total housing units 1,047; Occupied housing units 750. The tribe has achieved an average education level of 8th grade. The Bellingham Technical School offers general education development classes and adult vocational training.

**Tribal Economy.** The tribe has an average annual income of $5,000. The Lummi Indian Weavers manufacture cloth with Indian designs. Lummi Arts and Crafts manufactures ceramics, baskets, and totem poles. The Lummi Indian Museum, a source of information on Indian history, is maintained by the tribe. A cottage industry, Lummi Knitters, produces sweaters, socks, gloves, and caps. In addition there are three industries on the reservation owned by non-Indians: Bellingham Marina, Fisherman's Cove Resort, and 10 residential subdivisions. All other commercial and industrial businesses are off the reservation.

**Climate.** The Lummi Reservation is in the extreme northwestern part of Washington where rainfall measures 34 inches per year. Temperature here varies from an average high of 75 degrees to an average low of 25 degrees. Sand and gravel are the only mineral resources on the reservation; however, the tidelands and timber have been important natural resources.

**Transportation.** Interstate 5, a major north-south traffic artery, is 2 miles from the reservation boundary. State Highway No. 540 crosses the reservation east-west. All internal reservation roads were turned over to the county in 1940 by the Bureau of Indian Affairs. Bellingham, 5 miles from the reservation, has a modern deep water harbor, and other transportation service is by train, bus, and truck. The nearest commercial airport is in Seattle, 100 miles to the south of the reservation.

**Community Facilities.** Water is drawn from local wells. Septic tanks provide for sewage disposal. Gas is supplied by the Cascade Natural Gas Company; electricity by the Puget Sound Power and Light. The USPHS operates a clinic on the reservation.

**Recreation.** The major recreational activity on the Lummi Reservation is the annual Stommish. The local all-Indian American Legion post is instrumental in the presentation. This involves a princess contest, war canoe trophy races, dancing, and a salmon steak barbeque. Profits have been used in the construction of a 44'x88' American Legion hall which is presently used for Head Start and kindergarten classes.

MAKAH RESERVATION                          Federal Reservation
Clallam County
Makah Tribe
Tribal Headquarters: Neah Bay, Washington

**Land Status.** Tribally-owned land: 24,526 acres. Allotted land: 2,487 acres. Total area: 27,013 acres. Claim was filed in 1950 with the Indian Claims Commission for $10,000 for loss of fishing rights and land. The Commission determined no liability for loss of fishing rights, and the land loss component is being prosecuted.

**History.** The Makah Reservation was created by the Treaty of Neah Bay in 1855. It was amended, and the reservation was enlarged by subsequent Executive Orders. It is believed that the main band of Makah Indians lived in Canada, and a few still reside there. While there is some intermingling with other groups, they have maintained a high degree of Indian blood.

**Culture.** The Makah Indians were part of the Coastal Indian culture of the Pacific Northwest which flourished in the moist coastal strip, their lives built around a natural abundance of fish and forests. Many coastal tribes made fine basketry and wood carvings, and Indians of the Juan de Fuca Strait were famed for blankets loom-woven of dog hair. Salmon was the foremost food, and many tribal beliefs and ceremonies centered around salmon. The second most important natural resource was wood, particularly the western red cedar. Although strong and durable, it was easily worked with primitive tools. In the highly materialistic culture of the Pacific Northwest, the skillfully crafted gabled lodges helped proclaim the prestige of the owners. Steamed and bent cedar was fashioned into boxes, buckets, serving dishes, and utensils. Cedar bark supplied clothing, mats, furnishings, and rope. Wealth determined leadership in this property-conscious culture, and the elaborate social structure included a hereditary nobility, a middle class, and a slave class of war captives and their descendants. Traditionally, the livelihood and major resources of the Makah Tribe were derived from the sea. The Makah ventured, hunting and fishing, far out to sea in ocean-going canoes. Expert and precise at hunting the whale, the Makah gained a reputation of respect from neighboring tribes and settlers. The Makah were quick to adopt modern techniques and equipment in pursuing a livelihood. At the turn of the century, several sailing schooners of up to 60 tons ranged as far north as the Bering Sea competing in the lucrative fur seal trade. Prohibition by international agreement of fur seal hunting due to waning seal herds rendered the highly specialized Makah fleet almost useless.

**Government.** The tribe is organized under the Indian Reorganization Act with a constitution approved May 16, 1936, and charter ratified February 27, 1937. The Makah Tribal Council is the only duly elected governing body of the Makah Indian Tribe. The council consists of five persons and has the responsibility for initiating, developing, and continuing economic and community growth. An executive director is appointed to carry out and implement the policies and programs of the council.

**Population Profile. 1969:** Tribal enrollment 558; Indian resident

515; Non-Indian resident 400; Unemployment 38%; Underemployment 19%; Median family income $4,500. **1980:** Indian resident 803; Non-Indian resident 442; Percent Indian of total population 64.5; Total housing units 435; Occupied housing units 372. Education level: 8th grade.

**Tribal Economy.** Seventy-seven percent of the tribe's annual income of $260,000 is derived from forestry, the remainder from lease income and interest. Two persons are employed full time by the tribe. The Makah Development Corporation and the Makah Housing Authority are tribal organizations formed to program tribal development. During the 1920's, the Makah Tribe negotiated a long-term contract with Crown Zellerbach Corporation beginning the development of another of the tribe's valuable resources, timber. After expiration of the contract, the tribe took advantage of the growing timber export market by selling timber on a competitive, open-bid basis. The tribe's forest yields 20 million board feet of lumber annually. Individual Indians operate a fishing fleet, and the Elbrum's Motel. Cape Flattery Company, Crown Zellerback Corporation, Evans Products Company, and two fish-buying stations are privately owned. Manganese, granite, and gravel deposits are on the reservation; however, the forest is the major natural resource in use.

**Climate.** The Makah Reservation lies at the tip of Washington on the Pacific Ocean, the westernmost Indian reservation in the nation. The climate is mild, with a bountiful rainfall averaging 105 inches per year, and temperature reaching highs of 80 degrees and lows of 30 degrees.

**Transportation.** State Highway No. 112 is an east-west route reaching the reservation. Port Angeles, 66 miles from Makah, is the nearest source for transportation by air, bus, and truck.

**Community Facilities.** Makah has a municipal water and sewer system. The Clallam Public Utilities District supplies electricity. The nearest hospital to the reservation is in Port Angeles.

**Recreation.** Makah Day is a two-day celebration held annually at Neah Bay in August. This event features canoe races, Indian dances, and games. Salmon barbeques are an added attraction.


MUCKLESHOOT RESERVATION                    Federal Reservation
King County
Muckleshoot Tribe
Tribal Headquarters: Auburn, Washington

**Land Status.** Tribal land: .29 acres. Allotted land: 1,188.28 acres. Total area: 1,188.57 acres. Approximately 22,000 acres within the original boundaries are now owned by non-Indians.

**History.** The Muckleshoot Reservation was established by Executive Order of 1857 and Presidential Order of 1874. Certain tracts of land in Washington territory were withdrawn from sale and set apart as the Muckleshoot Indian Reservation. This was the locality of Muckleshoot Prairie.

**Culture.** The Muckleshoot Indians were part of the Coastal Indian culture of the Pacific Northwest which flourished in the moist coastal strip, their lives built around a natural abundance of fish and forests. Many coastal tribes made fine basketry and wood carvings, and Indians of the Juan de Fuca Strait were famed for blankets loom-woven of dog hair. Salmon was the foremost food and many tribal beliefs and ceremonies centered around salmon. The second most important natural resource was wood, particularly the western red cedar. Although strong and durable, it was easily worked with primitive tools. In the highly materialistic culture of the Pacific Northwest, the skillfully crafted gabled lodges helped proclaim the prestige of the owners. Steamed and bent cedar was fashioned into boxes, buckets, serving dishes, and utensils. Cedar bark supplied clothing, mats, furnishings, and rope. Wealth determined leadership in this property-conscious culture, and the elaborate social structure included a hereditary nobility, a middle class, and a slave class of war captives and their descendants.

**Government.** The tribe is organized under the Indian Reorganization Act with the constitution and charter both approved and ratified in 1936. The Muckleshoot Tribal Council consists of nine tribal members who are elected to 3-year terms.

**Population Profile. 1969:** Tribal enrollment 340; Indian resident 271; Unemployment 38%. **1980:** Indian resident 375; Non-Indian resident 2,616; Percent Indian of total population 12.5; Total housing units 1,187; Occupied housing units 1,072. The average education level for tribal members is 9th grade. Two members are college graduates.

**Climate.** The rainfall averages 32 inches per year. Temperatures, generally seasonable and mild, reach a high of 85 degrees and a low of 25 degrees.

**Transportation.** State Highway No. 169 runs through the reservation north-south. Auburn lies adjacent to the reservation and has commercial train, bus, and truck service. The nearest airport is in Tacoma, 35 miles from Muckleshoot.

**Community Facilities.** Water is drawn from wells. The Public Health Service installed both the wells and septic tanks. The reservation is part of the King County Public Utility District which supplies electricity. Tribal members can go to a hospital in Tacoma and a clinic in Auburn for health care.

NISQUALLY RESERVATION                         Federal Reservation
Thurston County
Nisqually Tribe
Tribal Headquarters: Yelm, Washington

**Land Status.** Tribal land: 3 acres. Allotted land: 813 acres. Total area: 816 acres. Approximately 3,881 acres of the original reservation are now owned by non-Indians. The Nisqually Tribe has a claim pending before the Indian Claims Commission, but to date no liability has been found.

**History.** The original reservation was negotiated by the Medicine Creek Treaty of 1854 and established by Executive Order in 1857. The

Nisqually gave their name to one dialect of the coastal division of the Salishan language. They were located on the Nisqually River above its mouth and on the middle and upper courses of the Puyallup River.

**Culture.** The Nisqually Indians were part of the Coastal Indian culture of the Pacific Northwest which flourished in the moist coastal strip, their lives built around a natural abundance of fish and forests. Many coastal tribes made fine basketry and wood carvings, and Indians of the Juan de Fuca Strait were famed for blankets loom-woven of dog hair. Salmon was the foremost food, and many tribal beliefs and ceremonies centered around salmon. The second most important natural resource was wood, particularly the western red cedar. Although strong and durable, it was easily worked with primitive tools. In the highly materialistic culture of the Pacific Northwest, the skillfully crafted gabled lodges helped proclaim the prestige of the owners. Steamed and bent cedar was fashioned into boxes, buckets, serving dishes, and utensils. Cedar bark supplied clothing, mats, furnishings, and rope. Wealth determined leadership in this property-conscious culture, and the elaborate social structure included a hereditary nobility, a middle class, and a slave class of war captives and their descendants.

**Government.** The tribe adopted a constitution in 1946, according to the 1934 Indian Reorganization Act. The constitution provides for a Nisqually Community Council formed by all qualified voters in the tribe. They elect a five-member business council which carries out most of the tribe's government affairs. Members of the business council are elected for 2-year terms.

**Population Profile.** **1969:** Indian resident 189; Unemployment 29%. **1980:** Indian resident 42; Non-Indian resident 212; Percent Indian of total population 16.5; Total housing units 74; Occupied housing units 69. The average education level among tribal members is 9th grade. There are four college graduates in the tribe.

**Climate.** The rainfall averages 34 inches annually in this mild climate. The seasons are modified, and temperatures reach a high of 85 degrees and a low of 25 degrees.

**Transportation.** The reservation is near the east-west State Highway No. 510. The City of Olympia is only 10 miles from the reservation. Public transportation by bus, truck, train, and plane is available in Olympia.

**Community Facilities.** PHS installed wells and septic tanks on the reservation. Electricity is supplied by the Thurston County Public Utility District. Medical care is available to residents at a private hospital in Olympia.

OZETTE RESERVATION                    Federal Reservation
Clallam County, Washington

**Land Status.** There is no population on this reservation. As there are no members, the Makah Tribe is endeavoring to introduce legislation through Congress to allow the Ozette Reservation to become part of the Makah Reservation. The Secretary of the Interior has recommended that the land be added to the Olympic National Park. The reservation is located in northwestern Washington between Highway

No. 112 and the Olympic National Park. The nearest major city and transportation hub is Port Angeles, Washington.


PORT GAMBLE RESERVATION                    Federal Reservation
Kitsap County
Clallam Tribe
Tribal Headquarters: Kingston, Washington

**Land Status.** Total area: 1,301 acres. All the land is tribally owned. For the purpose of presenting claims before the Indian Claims Commission, the three bands of Clallam Indians, living on the Port Gamble, Lower Elwah, and Jamestown Reservations, have consolidated as the Clallam Tribe. Liability has been determined, but values and offsets have not been established.

**History.** By the Treaty of Point No Point of 1855, the Clallam Indians were entitled to share in a small reservation on Hood Canal with the Skokomish Tribe, who were their traditional enemies. As this was Skokomish territory, very few Clallam Indians settled there. Some of the Clallam located in a shack town on the Port Gamble Peninsula. When funds became available under the Indian Reorganization Act of 1934, land on the Peninsula was purchased in 1936 and the Port Gamble Reservation was established.

**Culture.** The Clallam Indians were part of the Coastal Indian culture of the Pacific Northwest which flourished in the moist coastal strip, their lives built around a natural abundance of fish and forests. Many coastal tribes made fine basketry and wood carvings, and Indians of the Juan de Fuca Strait were famed for blankets loom-woven of dog hair. Salmon was the foremost food, and many tribal beliefs and ceremonies centered around salmon. The second most important natural resource was wood, particularly the western red cedar. Although strong and durable, it was easily worked with primitive tools. In the highly materialistic culture of the Pacific Northwest, the skillfully crafted gabled lodges helped proclaim the prestige of the owners. Steamed and bent cedar was fashioned into boxes, buckets, serving dishes, and utensils. Cedar bark supplied clothing, mats, furnishings, and rope. Wealth determined leadership in this property-conscious culture, and the elaborate social structure included a hereditary nobility, a middle class, and a slave class of war captives and their descendants.

**Government.** The Port Gamble Band of Clallam Indians is organized under a constitution approved in 1939 and a charter ratified in 1941. The Port Gamble Business Committee consists of seven members elected annually and is subject to the Port Gamble Community Council.

**Population Profile.** **1969:** Tribal enrollment 181; Indian resident 122; Unemployment 26%. **1980:** Indian resident 266; Non-Indian resident 36; Percent Indian of total population 88.1; Total housing units 118; Occupied housing units 84. The average education level for the tribe is 9th grade.

**Climate.** Rainfall in this part of the State averages 40 inches annually. The temperatures vary with the seasons, reaching a high of 90 degrees and a low of 10 degrees.

**Transportation.** State Highway No. 3 runs north-south near the reservation. Port Gamble is only 30 miles from Seattle where all means of commercial transportation are readily available.

**Community Facilities.** The Public Health Service installed wells and septic tanks to meet the basic sanitary needs of the residents. Port Gamble is a part of the Kitsap County Public Utility District which provides electricity to the county as a whole. For medical care, tribal members go to the PHS Hospital in Seattle.

PORT MADISON RESERVATION　　　　　　　　Federal Reservation
Kitsap County
Suquamish Tribe
Tribal Headquarters: Bremerton, Washington

**Land Status.** Tribal land: 41 acres. Allotted land: 2,638.49 acres. Government land: .41 acres. Total area: 2,679.9 acres. Of the original reservation, 4,604 acres are now owned by non-Indians. A claim has been filed by the tribe with the Indian Claims Commission for loss of land and fishing rights. A judgment has been set at $78,500; however, the amount of Government claims as offsets has not yet been determined.

**History.** The Port Madison Reservation was set aside as part of the Point Elliott Treaty of 1855 and enlarged by Executive Order of 1864. The original inhabitants of the reservation were primarily of the Suquamish Tribe and a few from other tribes. There has been much intermarriage among the tribes and non-Indians.

**Culture.** The Suquamish Indians were part of the Coastal Indian culture of the Pacific Northwest which flourished in the moist coastal strip, their lives built around a natural abundance of fish and forests. Many coastal tribes made fine basketry and wood carvings, and Indians of the Juan de Fuca Strait were famed for blankets loom-woven of dog hair. Salmon was the foremost food, and many tribal beliefs and ceremonies centered around salmon. The second most important natural resource was wood, particularly the western red cedar. Although strong and durable, it was easily worked with primitive tools. In the highly materialistic culture of the Pacific Northwest, the skillfully crafted gabled lodges helped proclaim the prestige of the owners. Steamed and bent cedar was fashioned into boxes, buckets, serving dishes, and utensils. Cedar bark supplied clothing, mats, furnishings, and rope. Wealth determined leadership in this property-conscious culture, and the elaborate social structure included a hereditary nobility, a middle class, and a slave class of war captives and their descendants.

**Government.** The tribe's constitution, approved in July of 1965, provides for the administrative responsibilities of the tribal government to be handled by the popularly elected five-member Suquamish Tribal Council.

**Population Profile. 1969:** Tribal enrollment 300; Indian resident 190; Unemployment 26%. **1980:** Indian resident 148; Non-Indian resident 3,267; Percent Indian of total population 4.3; Total housing units 1,611;

Occupied housing units 1,320. The average education level for tribal members is 9th grade. Four members are college graduates.

**Climate.** The rainfall in the northwestern part of Washington averages 40 inches annually. The temperatures in a usually mild climate reach highs of 90 degrees and lows of 10 degrees.

**Transportation.** Although no major highway runs through the reservation, State Highway No. 3 runs north-south nearby. Seattle, 25 miles from the reservation, is served by all means of public transportation.

**Community Facilities.** To meet the basic sanitation needs of the reservation, the Public Health Service installed both wells and septic tanks. The reservation is a part of the Kitsap County Public Utility District which supplies electricity to the area. The Public Health Service Hospital in Seattle provides health service to tribal members.

**Recreation.** This reservation is known for its agate beach and excellent marine view. Traditional totem poles also attract many visitors. The Chief Seattle Park and Memorial are also located here. The tribe has an annual celebration, "Chief Seattle Days," scheduled during Seafair Week in Seattle in August.


PUYALLUP RESERVATION                    Federal Reservation
Pierce County
Puyallup Tribe
Tribal Headquarters: Puyallup, Washington

**Land Status.** Total area: 33 acres. All the land is tribally owned.

**History.** The Puyallup Tribe lived near the mouth of the Puyallup River and neighboring coast. The original Puyallup Reservation was established under the terms of the Treaty of Medicine Creek of 1855. In 1904, Congress removed the restrictions from allotted lands within the reservation with the result that most of the land was sold. The Puyallup spoke the Nisqually dialect of the coastal division of the Salishan linguistic family.

**Culture.** The Puyallup Indians were part of the Coastal Indian culture of the Pacific Northwest which flourished in the moist coastal strip, their lives built around a natural abundance of fish and forests. Many coastal tribes made fine basketry and wood carvings, and Indians of the Juan de Fuca Strait were famed for blankets loom-woven of dog hair. Salmon was the foremost food, and many tribal beliefs and ceremonies centered around salmon. The second most important natural resource was wood, particularly the western red cedar. Although strong and durable, it was easily worked with primitive tools. In the highly materialistic culture of the Pacific Northwest, the skillfully crafted gabled lodges helped proclaim the prestige of the owners. Steamed and bent cedar was fashioned into boxes, buckets, serving dishes, and utensils. Cedar bark supplied clothing, mats, furnishings, and rope. Wealth determined leadership in this property-conscious culture, and the elaborate social structure included a hereditary nobility, a middle class, and a slave class of war captives and their descendants.

**Government.** The tribe is organized under the Indian Reorganization Act with the constitution approved on May 13, 1936. The Puyallup Tribal Council consists of five members elected to 3-year terms.

**Population Profile. 1969:** Tribal enrollment 450; Indian resident 170; Unemployment 19%. **1980:** Indian resident 856; Non–Indian resident 24,332; Percent Indian of total population 3.4; Total housing units 9,639; Occupied housing units 8,974. The average education level is 9th grade. Two tribal members are college graduates.

**Climate.** The reservation lies immediately adjacent to the city of Tacoma. Rainfall here averages 32 inches per year. The temperature reaches a high of 85 degrees and a low of 25 degrees.

**Transportation.** A major north–south highway, Interstate 5, passes through the reservation. All means of transportation are readily available in Tacoma.

**Community Facilities.** The wells for water and the septic tanks were installed by the Public Health Service. The electricity is supplied by the Pierce County Public Utility District. A private hospital in Tacoma provides medical care to tribal members.


QUILEUTE RESERVATION            Federal Reservation
Clallam County
Quileute Tribe
Tribal Headquarters: La Push, Washington

**Land Status.** Tribal land: 584 acres. Allotted land: 10 acres. Total area: 594 acres. The Quileute Tribe shared in a recently awarded claims judgment for the Quileute and Hoh Indians amounting to $112,152.

**History.** The Quileute Reservation was designated in the Quinault River Treaty of 1855 and established by Executive Order of 1889. Tribal residents live in frame houses on lots assigned by the tribe.

**Culture.** The Quileute Indians were part of the Coastal Indian culture of the Pacific Northwest which flourished in the moist coastal strip, their lives built around a natural abundance of fish and forests. They also were whalers and seagoers. Many coastal tribes made fine basketry and wood carvings, and Indians of the Juan de Fuca Strait were famed for blankets loom-woven of dog hair. Salmon was the foremost food, and many tribal beliefs and ceremonies centered around salmon. The second most important natural resource was wood, particularly the western red cedar. Although strong and durable, it was easily worked with primitive tools. In the highly materialistic culture of the Pacific Northwest, the skillfully crafted gabled lodges helped proclaim the prestige of the owners. Steamed and bent cedar was fashioned into boxes, buckets, serving dishes, and utensils. Cedar bark supplied clothing, mats, furnishings, and rope. Wealth determined leadership in this property–conscious culture, and the elaborate social structure included a hereditary nobility, a middle class, and a slave class of war captives and their descendants.

**Government.** The tribe's constitution, written according to the 1934 Indian Reorganization Act, was approved in November 1936. Their charter was ratified the following year. The Quileute Tribal Council consists of five members who are elected to 3–year terms.

**Population Profile. 1969:** Indian resident 270; Unemployment 47%; Median family income $4,500. **1980:** Indian resident 273; Non–Indian resident 54; Percent Indian of total population 83.5; Total housing units 73; Occupied housing units 73. The average education level is 9th grade. Five tribal members are college graduates.

**Tribal Economy.** The tribe has an income of $14,000 annually from lease payments.

**Climate.** Rainfall in this extreme northwestern corner of Washington measures 117 inches each year. Temperatures are modified, the high being 70 degrees and the low 30 degrees.

**Transportation.** A county road connects the reservation with U.S. Highway No. 101. Port Angeles is a 70-mile drive from the reservation. Commercial bus, train, truck, and airlines serve Port Angeles.

**Community Facilities.** The Public Health Service installed wells and septic tanks on the reservation. Electricity is supplied by the Clallam County Public Utility District. A private hospital in Port Angeles treats all residents of the area. There is also a clinic in Forks.

**Recreation.** The village of La Push, on the mouth of the Quileute River, offers a protected harbor for commercial and sports fishing vessels. Salmon fishing in the area draws many people. The Indians own a beautiful coastal area with a spectacular view which is a popular summer recreation area.


QUINAULT RESERVATION                        Federal Reservation
Grays Harbor and Jefferson Counties
Quinault Tribe
Tribal Headquarters: Taholah, Washington

**Land Status.** Tribally-owned land: 4,414 acres. Allotted land: 123,524 acres. Non-Indian land: 61,105 acres. Government land: 18 acres. Total area: 127,956 acres. The Quinault Tribe's claim made with the Indian Claims Commission was settled, and an award of approximately $200,000 was authorized which tribal members voted to use for community projects.

**History.** The Quinault Reservation was authorized in the treaty made with the Quinault and Quileute Indians in 1855 and enlarged by Executive Order in 1873. The original reservation was established for use of, and occupancy by, the Quinalt and Quileute Tribes who received allotments. Later, members of the Chinook, Chehalis, and Cowlitz tribes who resided in the area were allotted land on the reservation.

**Culture.** The Quinault Indians were part of the Coastal Indian culture of the Pacific Northwest which flourished in the moist coastal strip, their lives built around a natural abundance of fish and forests. They also were whalers and seagoers. Many coastal tribes made fine basketry and wood carvings, and Indians of the Juan de Fuca Strait were famed for blankets loom-woven of dog hair. Salmon was the foremost food, and many tribal beliefs and ceremonies centered around salmon. The second most important natural resource was wood, particularly the western red cedar. Although strong and durable, it was easily worked with primitive tools. In the highly materialistic culture of the Pacific Northwest, the skillfully crafted gabled lodges helped proclaim the prestige of the owners. Steamed and bent cedar was fashioned into boxes, buckets, serving dishes, and utensils. Cedar bark supplied clothing, mats, furnishings, and rope. Wealth determined leadership in this property-conscious culture, and the elaborate social structure included a hereditary nobility, a middle class, and a slave class of war captives and their descendants.

**Government.** The Quinault Tribe has no constitution or charter, but operates under bylaws adopted by the tribe in August 1922 which have not been approved by the Secretary of the Interior. The Quinault Business Committee consists of five persons elected to 1-year terms.

**Population Profile. 1969:** Tribal enrollment 1,050; Indian resident 927; Unemployment 24%; Median family income $15,000. **1980:** Indian resident 943; Non-Indian resident 558; Percent Indian of total population 62.8; Total housing units 588; Occupied housing units 455.

**Tribal Economy.** The tribe has an annual income of approximately $23,000. A scholarship fund of $1,000 annually is set aside. The major tribal enterprise is the Fish Marketing Enterprise.

**Climate.** The reservation lies along the Pacific in the northwestern portion of Washington. Rainfall averages 110 inches annually, and temperatures reach highs of 80 degrees and lows of 30 degrees.

**Transportation.** State Highway No. 109 is the major east-west route, and U.S. Highway No. 101 runs north-south. Moclips, 15 miles from the reservation, is served by commercial train, bus, and trucklines. Hoquiam and Aberdeen, 40 miles distant, have commercial air transportation.

**Community Facilities.** The municipal water and sewer system was constructed by the Public Health Service. Grays Harbor Public Utilities District supplies electricity. The nearest hospital is in Aberdeen.

**Recreation.** Fishing along the Quinault River with guide service is available during trout season. The annual Quinault River Trout Derby is highlighted by canoe races down the Quinault River. Another celebration held by the tribe is the Taholah Days Indian Celebration. Moclips and Taholah Indian fishing villages on the Pacific Ocean feature salmon fishing and clam digging. Beautiful Quinault Lake is located on the edge of Olympic Peninsula Rain Forest.


SHOALWATER RESERVATION                    Federal Reservation
Pacific County
Quinault, Chinook, and Chehalis Tribes
Tribal Headquarters: Tokeland, Washington

**Land Status.** Total area: 335 acres. All land is tribally owned.

**History.** The Shoalwater Reservation was established by Executive Order in 1866 for miscellaneous "Indian purposes." Now, and at various other times, members of the Quinault, Chinook, and Chehalis tribes have resided on the reservation.

**Culture.** The Indians of the Shoalwater Reservation were part of the Coastal Indian culture of the Pacific Northwest which flourished in the moist coastal strip, their lives built around a natural abundance of fish and forests. Many coastal tribes made fine basketry and wood carvings, and Indians of the Juan de Fuca Strait were famed for blankets loom-woven of dog hair. Salmon was the foremost food, and many tribal beliefs and ceremonies centered around salmon. The second most important natural resource was wood, particularly the western red cedar. Although strong and durable, it was easily worked with primitive tools. In the highly materialistic culture of the Pacific Northwest, the skillfully crafted gabled lodges helped proclaim the prestige of the owners. Steamed and bent cedar was fashioned into boxes, buckets, serving dishes, and utensils. Cedar bark supplied clothing, mats, furnishings, and rope. Wealth determined leadership in this property-conscious culture, and the elaborate social structure included a hereditary nobility, a middle class, and a slave class of war captives and their descendants.

**Government.** There is no governmental organization, and all contacts are made directly with reservation residents. However, the residents are considering establishing a formal tribal government and are in the process of formulating a constitution and bylaws.

**Population Profile. 1969:** Tribal enrollment 12; Indian resident 20; Unemployment 40%. **1980:** Indian resident 28; Non-Indian resident 5; Percent Indian of total population 84.8; Total housing units 19; Occupied housing units 13. The education level attained for the tribe is 9th grade. There are no college graduates on the reservation.

**Climate.** The annual rainfall in this area is 100 inches. The temperature reaches a high of 85 degrees and a low of 30 degrees.

**Transportation.** The reservation lies adjacent to the east-west State Highway No. 105. Aberdeen, 25 miles from the reservation, is served by commercial bus, truck, train, and airlines.

**Community Facilities.** Water and sewer systems were installed by the Public Health Service. Electricity is provided by Pacific County Public Utility District. Health facilities are available in Aberdeen.

SKOKOMISH RESERVATION                    Federal Reservation
Mason County
Skokomish Tribe
Tribal Headquarters: Shelton, Washington

**Land Status.** Tribal land: 16 acres. Allotted land: 2,905 acres. Non-Indian land: 2,066 acres. Total area: 4,987 acres.

**History.** The Skokomish Reservation was established by the Treaty of Point No Point in 1855 and an Executive Order of 1874.

**Culture.** The Skokomish Indians were part of the Coastal Indian culture of the Pacific Northwest which flourished in the moist coastal strip, their lives built around a natural abundance of fish and forests. Many coastal tribes made fine basketry and wood carvings, and Indians of the Juan de Fuca Strait were famed for blankets loom-woven of dog hair. Salmon was the foremost food, and many tribal beliefs and ceremonies centered around salmon. The second most important natural resource was wood, particularly the western red cedar. Although strong and durable, it was easily worked with primitive tools. In the highly materialistic culture of the Pacific Northwest, the skillfully crafted gabled lodges helped proclaim the prestige of the owners. Steamed and bent cedar was fashioned into boxes, buckets, serving dishes, and utensils. Cedar bark supplied clothing, mats, furnishings, and rope. Wealth determined leadership in this property-conscious culture, and the elaborate social structure included a hereditary nobility, a middle class, and a slave class of war captives and their descendants.

**Government.** The Skokomish Tribe is organized under a constitution approved in 1938 and charter ratified in 1939. The Skokomish Tribal Council consists of five members elected to 3-year terms.

**Population Profile. 1969:** Tribal enrollment 200; Indian resident 150; Unemployment 34%. **1980:** Indian resident 305; Non-Indian resident 178; Percent Indian of total population 63.1; Total housing units 199; Occupied housing units 141. The education level attained by the tribe is 9th grade. The tribe has one college graduate.

**Climate.** The annual rainfall in this area is 83 inches. The temperature ranges from a high of 95 degrees to a low of 18 degrees.

**Transportation.** The reservation lies adjacent to the east-west State Highway No. 101. Olympia, 25 miles from the reservation, has the nearest commercial airline facilities. Train, bus, and trucking facilities are available in Shelton, 10 miles from the reservation.

**Community Facilities.** The water and sewer system was provided by the Public Health Service. Electricity is provided by the Mason County Public Utility District. Hospital facilities are available in Shelton.

SPOKANE RESERVATION                    Federal Reservation
Stevens County
Spokane Tribe
Tribal Headquarters: Wellpinit, Washington

**Land Status.** Tribally-owned land: 96,536 acres. Allotted land: 40,577 acres. Government land: 38 acres. Total area: 137,151 acres.

**History.** The Spokane Indians, a seminomadic Plateau group, were generally peaceful, but became dissatisfied with treaties being negotiated for their lands. In 1858, the Spokane and Coeur D'Alene united with the Palouse and Yakima to defeat U.S. forces near Rosalia, Washington. The following year, a punitive expedition overwhelmed the tribes, forcing surrender and destroying their horses. They were then placed on reservations, ceding vast areas of land.

**Culture.** The Spokane Indians were one of seminomadic Plateau Indian culture ranging over the dry uplands of Idaho, eastern Oregon, and eastern Washington. All Plateau tribes were traditionally fishermen and searchers for game, wild seeds, berries, and roots of camas. With basketry techniques that ranked among the best in North America, they wove the grasses and scrubby brush of the Plateau into almost everything they used, including portable summer shelters, clothing, and watertight cooking pots. Having no clans, Plateau Indians counted descent on both sides of the family. There was little formal organization. The few tribal ceremonies centered around the food supply. In the early 1700's, horses were introduced among the tribes, and the Indians became highly skilled horsemen who counted their wealth in terms of the new animal.

**Government.** The Spokane Tribe operates under a constitution which was approved in May of 1951. This establishes the three-member Spokane Business Council which is popularly elected to govern the reservation. Council members are popularly elected to 3-year terms.

**Population Profile. 1969:** Tribal enrollment 1,500; Indian resident 600; Unemployment 30%; Median family income $6,700. **1980:** Indian resident 1,050; Non-Indian resident 425; Percent Indian of total population 71.2; Total housing units 475; Occupied housing units 426.

**Tribal Economy.** The tribal income each year is approximately $186,000. Scholarships in the amount of $7,000 are budgeted each year.

**Climate.** The Spokane Reservation borders on the Colville Reservation in the northeast corner of the State near the city of Spokane. The rainfall here averages 15 inches each year, and temperatures reach a high of 95 degrees and a low of 0 degrees as the seasons are modified by the Pacific Ocean.

**Transportation.** State Highway No. 25 crosses the reservation north-south connecting with U.S. Route 2 at Reardan, which lies at the junction of these two highways, 22 miles to the south. Reardan has train, bus, and truck service. Spokane, 40 miles from the reservation, is the nearest city having air service.

**Community Facilities.** A private hospital in Spokane gives the closest available medical care. The PHS installed the local water and sewer system. Electricity is available through the Washington Water Power and REA.

**Recreation.** Old Fort Spokane is located near the reservation. An annual Indian Fair and Celebration is held at Wellpinit on Labor Day. Lake Roosevelt provides excellent fishing and boating.


SQUAXIN ISLAND RESERVATION                    Federal Reservation
Mason County
Squaxin Island Tribe
Tribal Headquarters: Shelton, Washington

**Land Status.** Government land: 2 acres. Allotted land: 826 acres. Non-Indian land: 668 acres. Total area: 1,496 acres. By a Federal Court decision, it was established that the tribe owns the tidelands. The tribe has filed a claim with the Indian Claims Commission, but no determination of liability has been made.

**History.** The Squaxin Island Reservation was established by the Medicine Creek Treaty of 1854. The Squaxin Indians speak the Nisqually Branch of the coast division of the Salishan language. None of the tribal members lives on the Island because regular transportation is lacking, and there are no facilities to serve the people.

**Culture.** The Indians of Squaxin Island were part of the Coastal Indian culture of the Pacific Northwest which flourished in the moist coastal strip, their lives built around a natural abundance of fish and forests. Many coastal tribes made fine basketry and wood carvings, and Indians of the Juan de Fuca Strait were famed for blankets loom-woven of dog hair. Salmon was the foremost food, and many tribal beliefs and ceremonies centered around salmon. The second most important natural resource was wood, particularly the western red cedar. Although strong and durable, it was easily worked with primitive tools. In the highly materialistic culture of the Pacific Northwest, the skillfully crafted gabled lodges helped proclaim the prestige of the owners. Steamed and bent cedar was fashioned into boxes, buckets, serving dishes, and utensils. Cedar bark supplied clothing, mats, furnishings, and rope. Wealth determined leadership in this property-conscious culture, and the elaborate social structure included a hereditary nobility, a middle class, and a slave class of war captives and their descendants.

**Government.** The tribe operates under a constitution which was approved on July 8, 1965. The government body is the Squaxin Island Tribal Council, consisting of five persons elected to 3-year terms by the general council.

**Population Profile.** **1969:** Tribal enrollment 100; Indian resident 0; Unemployment 27% (enrolled). **1980:** Indian resident 35; Non-Indian resident 21; Percent Indian of total population 62.5; Total housing units 13; Occupied housing units 13.

**Climate.** The reservation land is in western Washington near Olympia. The climate is moderate, rainfall averaging 35 inches per year, and the high temperature being 80 degrees, the low 25 degrees.

**Transportation.** Olympia, 15 miles from the reservation, is the major city of the area. It is served by bus, train, truck, and airline companies.

SWINOMISH RESERVATION                    Federal Reservation
Skagit County
Swinomish Tribe
Tribal Headquarters: La Conner, Washington

**Land Status.** Tribally-owned land: 273 acres. Allotted land: 3,098 acres. Non-Indian land: 3,692 acres. Total area: 3,371 acres. The Swinomish Reservation was established by the Point Elliot Treaty of 1855, and the north boundary was defined by an Executive Order of 1873. The reservation was set aside for the use of the Suiattle, Skagit, and Kikiallus Indians and is known as the Swinomish Indian Tribal Community.

**History.** This tribe was originally about seven separate tribes of Salishan origin occupying contiguous areas. They were generally coopera-tive and closely bound together. They united against aggression from tribes to the north and carried on a high degree of socio-economic interchange. The Swinomish were first exposed to whites in the 1850's. Interaction with whites introduced radical changes in their economic system such as the value placed on timber.

**Culture.** The groups forming the Swinomish Tribe are all Salishan groups exhibiting many similarities. They flattened infants' heads in the Pacific Coastal style. They had a tradition of wolf or dog ancestry. Rather than believe in a central deity, these people felt the presence of a personal spirit. They lived in small units having a simple political organization and an intricate society. The chief and his advisors attained their position through ability and achievement; however, the position was closely related to their social class. They operated under a system of informal democracy. Resources were abundant and wealth was attained with little effort. Social status for one's children was gained by distributing wealth at Potlatch. Prisoners of war were conscripted to slave service. There were even some intentional slave raids on other tribes. Polygamy was practiced, with marriages frequently made for political reasons. The Salishan people lived in long communal houses. Women gathered food and cooked, while men hunted and fished. Sea products were their primary food resource. The canoe, the most important means of travel on the many waterways, was also a stable unit of value. In the winter, the people were at leisure to develop an elaborate culture, as exhibited in their ceremonial life and mythology.

**Government.** The tribe is organized under the Indian Reorganization Act of 1934. The Federal charter, constitution, and bylaws were voted upon by the tribe in 1935 and approved by the Secretary of the Interior in 1936. The governing body is the 11-member Swinomish Indian Senate. Members are elected to a 5-year term, two being elected every year except in years divisible by five when three are elected. The senate is subdivided into committees and has the responsibility of planning development of human and natural resources.

**Population Profile. 1969:** Tribal enrollment 320; Indian resident 364; Unemployment 43%; Underemployment 36%; Median family income $2,700. **1980:** Indian resident 414; Non-Indian resident 976; Percent Indian of total population 29.8; Total housing units 733; Occupied housing units 527.

**Tribal Economy.** The tribe earns an income of about $15,000 each year from its businesses. These include salmon fish traps, an oyster enterprise, and a marina.

**Climate.** The reservation lies in the Puget Sound area north of Seattle. Rainfall measures 35 inches per year, and temperatures reach highs of 80 degrees and lows of 25 degrees.

**Transportation.** The reservation lies near Interstate Highway No. 5, a major north-south route. State Highway No. 536 crosses the reservation east-west. The City of Everett, 35 miles from Swinomish, has ample transportation service including bus, train, truck, and air.

**Community Facilities.** The Public Health Service installed a municipal water and sewer system on the reservation. Tribal members go to Everett to obtain health care.


TULALIP RESERVATION                          Federal Reservation
Snohomish County
Snohomish Tribe
Tribal Headquarters: Marysville, Washington

**Land Status.** Tribally-owned land: 5,171 acres. Allotted land: 3,707 acres. Total area: 8,878 acres.

**Culture.** The Snohomish Indians were part of the Coastal Indian culture of the Pacific Northwest which flourished in the moist coastal strip, their lives built around a natural abundance of fish and forests. Many coastal tribes made fine basketry and wood carvings, and Indians of the Juan de Fuca Strait were famed for blankets loom-woven of dog hair. Salmon was the foremost food, and many tribal beliefs and ceremonies centered around salmon. The second most important natural resource was wood, particularly the western red cedar. Although strong and durable, it was easily worked with primitive tools. In the highly materialistic culture of the Pacific Northwest, the skillfully crafted gabled lodges helped proclaim the prestige of the owners. Steamed and bent cedar was fashioned into boxes, buckets, serving dishes, and utensils. Cedar bark supplied clothing, mats, furnishings, and rope. Wealth determined leadership in this property-conscious culture, and the elaborate social structure included a hereditary nobility, a middle class, and a slave class of war captives and their descendants.

**Government.** The tribe is organized under the Indian Reorganization Act of 1934. The constitution and charter were approved in 1936. The governing body of the tribe is the Tulalip Board of Directors, who are elected to 3-year terms.

**Population Profile. 1969:** Tribal enrollment 994; Indian resident 490; Unemployment 36%; Median family income $2,500. **1980:** Indian resident 768; Non-Indian resident 4,278; Percent Indian of total population 15.2; Total housing units 2,091; Occupied housing units 1,771.

**Tribal Economy.** The tribe has an annual income of $27,000. Scholarships (up to $600) are provided to tribal members continuing their education. The tribe operates the Jimmicum Springs Water System.

**Climate.** The reservation lies on Puget Sound north of Seattle. The rainfall averages 35 inches per year, and temperatures for the mild climate reach highs of 80 degrees and lows of 25 degrees.

**Transportation.** The reservation lies near Interstate 5, a major north-south route along the Sound connecting Seattle with Vancouver, Canada. Everett, 10 miles from the reservation, is served by air, truck, train, and buslines.

**Community Facilities.** The reservation's water and sewer system are municipal. Tribal members obtain health care in the nearby Everett Hospital.


YAKIMA RESERVATION                                    Federal Reservation
Klickitat and Yakima Counties
Fourteen Confederated Tribes from the
   Yakima Nation
Tribal Headquarters: Toppenish, Washington

**Land Status.** Tribally-owned land: 798,754 acres. Allotted land: 296,459 acres. Non-Indian land: 133,600 acres. Federal land: 23 acres. Total area: 1,095,236 acres. Originally, all of the lands within the reservation were held in trust by the United States Government for the Yakima Tribe of Indians in a tribal status. Subsequently, trust patents were issued to individual members of the tribe under the allotment system, these individual allotments being held in trust by the United States Government for the owners until such time as the trust restrictions might be removed and fee patents issued for many of the allotments which passed from Indian ownership. This accounts for the present checker-boarded ownership which prevails on the reservation.

**History.** The name Yakima or "Runaway" is now commonly applied to a number of related and unrelated peoples. The Yakima Nation, commonly known as the Yakima Tribe of Indians, was created as a political entity by the Treaty of June 9, 1855. Before the treaty could be ratified, the Yakima War broke out. The treaty was subsequently ratified on March 8, 1859, and proclaimed on April 18, 1859. The Yakima Indian Reservation was established by this treaty.

**Culture.** The Indians of the Yakima Nation were one of seminomadic Plateau Indian culture ranging over the dry uplands of Idaho, eastern Oregon, and eastern Washington. All Plateau tribes were traditionally fishermen and hunters who wandered over the country in small, loosely-organized bands searching for game, wild seeds, berries, and roots of camas. With basketry techniques that ranked among the best in North America, they wove the grasses and scrubby brush of the Plateau into almost everything they used, including portable summer shelters, clothing, and watertight cooking pots. Having no clans, Plateau Indians counted descent on both sides of the family. There was little formal organization. The few tribal ceremonies centered around the food supply. In the early 1700's, horses were introduced among the tribes, and the Indians became highly skilled horsemen who counted their wealth in terms of the new animal.

**Government.** The General Council of the Yakima Nation was the ruling body representing and including the 14 confederated tribes. In 1944, the Yakima Tribal Council was formally established by the General Council and authorized to transact business for and on behalf of the tribe. Rules of procedure governing the Yakima General Council and Tribal Council were authorized in 1956.

**Population Profile. 1969:** Tribal enrollment 5,391; Indian resident 7,010; Unemployment 23%; Underemployment 38%. **1980:** Indian resident 4,983; Non-Indian resident 20,380; Percent Indian of total population 19.6; Total housing units 8,531. Occupied housing units 7,751.

**Tribal Economy.** The tribe has an annual income of $1,500,000, most of which is earned through forestry. A fund of $50,000 is available annually for scholarships to tribal members continuing their education. The tribe formed the Yakima Land Enterprise. There are numerous private industries on the reservation, including White Swan Industries, A.J. Industries, Utah-Idaho Sugar Company, Western Packing Company, Schaake Packing Company, Hansen Packing Company, Northrup-King Seed Company, Hitchcock Lumber Company, and various other industries including fruit processing plants, a seed cleaning plant, a fertilizer plant, a feed mill, and a concrete pipe factory. There are several commercial, retail, and service establishments, and two banks.

**Climate.** The Yakima Reservation lies in the south-central portion of Washington State. The rainfall averages 18 inches per year, and temperatures reach a high of 100 degrees to a low of 0 degrees.

**Transportation.** Interstate 82 will run along the northeastern border of the reservation. U.S. Highway No. 97 runs through the eastern part of the reservation north-south, and State Highway No. 220 runs east-west. Train, bus, and trucklines stop on the reservation. Commercial air service is available in the City of Yakima, 4 miles from the reservation border.

**Community Facilities.** There are city water and sewer systems on the reservation. Cascade Natural Gas Company provides gas, and the Pacific Power and Light and REA supply electricity to the reservation. Telephone service is through the Oregon-Washington Telephone Company. Hospital care is available in Toppenish in the eastern part of the reservation. Clinics are held in Wapato and Harrah.

**Recreation.** Recreation on the Yakima Reservation is primarily limited to the lower valley area where game includes pheasants, chukars, and duck. Grouse, deer, elk, and bear are abundant in the restricted timberland area. The Yakima Tribe sponsors an all-Indian rodeo each summer with Indian cowboys from all western states participating. The Washington State Park Service is developing an historical park at Fort Simcoe, which was built and manned by the army during the years of 1855 to 1859. The officers' courts and three parks are located at Toppenish. Wapato and Harrah both have libraries and parks.

# WISCONSIN

BAD RIVER RESERVATION                    Federal Reservation
Ashland and Iron Counties
Chippewa Tribe
Tribal Headquarters: Odanah, Wisconsin

**Land Status.** Tribally-owned land: 8,325 acres. Allotted land: 33,477 acres. Government owned: 13,110 acres. Total area: 54,932 acres. The reservation was established in the Treaty of La Pointe, 1854. The original area of 124,234 acres was allotted to 1,610 Indians, and an additional 12,164 were placed in trust for the tribe. Most of the land has been lost to Indian ownership.

**History.** The Chippewa, or Ojibway, were one of the largest Indian nations north of Mexico, and controlled lands extending along both shores of Lakes Huron and Superior and westward into North Dakota. Their migration to this area was instigated by Iroquois pressure from the northeast. Drifting through their native forests, never settling on prized farmlands, the Chippewa interests seldom conflicted with those of the white settlers. They maintained friendly relations with the French and were courageous warriors. In the early 18th Century, the Chippewa drove the Fox out of northern Wisconsin and then drove the Sioux across the Mississippi and Minnesota Rivers. By this time, they were also able to push back the Iroquois whose strength and organization had been undercut by settlers. The Chippewa of the United States have been officially at peace with the Government since 1815 and have experienced less dislocation than many other tribes.

**Culture.** The Chippewa were nomadic timber people traveling in small bands engaging primarily in hunting and fishing, sometimes settling to carry on a rude form of agriculture. These foods were supplemented by gathering fruits and wild rice. Their wigwams of saplings and birchbark were easily moved and erected. Birchbark canoes were used for journeys, but other travel was usually by foot. The tribe was patrilineally divided into clans, usually bearing animal names. Although their social organization was loose, the powerful Grand Medicine Society controlled the tribe's movements and was a formidable obstacle to Christianizing attempts of missionaries. A mysterious power, or manitou, was believed to live in all animate or inanimate objects. The Chippewa today are largely of mixed blood, mostly French and English.

**Government.** The tribe adopted a constitution and bylaws according to the provisions of the 1934 Indian Reorganization Act. The tribe elects a chairman, vice-chairman, secretary, and treasurer. These together with three elected councilmen form the tribal council. They meet monthly unless additional meetings are called.

**Population Profile.** 1969: Indian resident 423; Unemployment 50%; Median family income $3,100. 1980: Indian resident 699; Non-Indian resident 217; Percent Indian of total population 76.3; Total housing units 331; Occupied housing units 259.

**Tribal Economy.** Traces of iron and copper have been found on the reservation, and there is some ceramic quality red clay in the area. The tribe has an annual income of $6,500. Over 90 percent of this is earned through tribal businesses. The remainder is revenue from the forest industry. Four individual Indians operate commercial enterprises and employ other tribal members.

**Climate.** The climate in this area is influenced by Lake Superior, with rainfall measuring 28 inches annually. The average summer high is close to 70 degrees, the low is close to 15 degrees; however, the extremes reach 72 degrees and 2 degrees.

**Transportation.** U.S. Route 2 and State Highways No. 169 and No. 13 serve the reservation running east-west. Two buslines and a truck company serve the reservation regularly. Trucklines stop there as needed. North Central Airlines serves the reservation area. Coal and iron carriers dock in Ashland Harbor.

**Community Facilities.** The U.S. Public Health Service provides the reservation with water and waste disposal facilities. A sewer line serves 20 homes. Water is drawn from pressure wells and community pumps. Electricity is provided by the Lake Superior District Power Company and REA. Two hospitals are located in Ashland where medical needs can be met.

**Recreation.** The reservation has 17 miles of shoreline along Lake Superior. In addition to this, 100 miles of river flow through Bad River. Hunting and fishing are excellent in the area. The outdoor recreation potential offered by the lakes and rivers, game, and scenery is rapidly becoming a valuable asset, attracting many visitors from nearby urban areas.


LAC COURTE OREILLES RESERVATION          Federal Reservation
Sawyer County
Chippewa Tribe
Tribal Headquarters: Reserve, Wisconsin

**Land Status.** Tribally-owned land: 3,945 acres. Allotted land: 26,584 acres. Government-owned land: 13,190 acres. Total area: 43,719 acres. Non-Indians hold the most desirable lake-frontage property. The Lac Courte Oreilles Reservation was authorized by the Treaty of 1854. In 1860, the land was retaken by the U.S. Land Office. In 1873, the Government reallotted 69,136 acres to the Chippewa Indians.

**History.** In the early historic period, the Chippewa Tribe, a member of the Algonquian family, was among the largest north of Mexico, with lands extending along both shores of Lake Superior and westward to the Turtle Mountains in North Dakota. Friendly with the French, the Chippewa utilized French weapons to drive the Sioux westward. They joined in Pontiac's Rebellion which broke out against the British in May 1763. Later, the Chippewa joined Tecumseh along with the Potawatomi, Winnebago, and other tribes to drive out the white settlers. The defeat of Tecumseh and his death in 1813 ended the organized resistance. The Chippewa obtained territory at Lac Courte Oreilles after displacing the Sioux, who had driven out the Ottawa. An agent of the Northwest Fur Company had his warehouse here from 1800 to 1852, although during Tecumseh's War the Indians burned his warehouse. In recent years the Lac Courte Oreilles Indians have led the State in organizing Natagamie, or garden clubs, to raise vegetables and solve their economic problems.

**Culture.** The Chippewa were nomadic forest hunters. Wigwam houses were used which were portable and easily reconstructed. Travel was by foot, snowshoe, and birchbark canoe. Kinship and lineage was traced through the father's family. They believe there was a mysterious power in all objects, which they called the manitou. The Chippewa buried their dead in mounds and carried on a widespread trade in copper. Hiawatha was their warrior-hero god. Their most important society was the Grand Medicine Society, a formidable obstacle to the Christianizing attempts of the missionaries. They carried on some agriculture, supplemented by the gathering of fruits and wild rice.

**Government.** The Lac Courte Oreilles Tribe is governed by a tribal chairman, vice-chairman, two councilmen, and a tribal clerk, who meet monthly. These officials are elected by the members of the tribe.

**Population Profile. 1969:** Tribal enrollment 1,848; Indian resident 860; Unemployment 38%. **1980:** Indian resident 1,145; Non-Indian resident 554; Percent Indian of total population 67.4; Total housing units 1,362; Occupied housing units 521. Since the Indian children attend public schools and not Government schools, no records have been kept on average educational level.

**Tribal Economy.** The tribal income is $29,000 per year, 50 percent produced by farming, 20 percent from forestry, and 30 percent from leases. There are no full-time employees. The major enterprise is a tribally-owned cranberry farm. There are a small grocery store and gas station on the reservation.

**Climate.** The average annual rainfall is 29 inches. Winter temperatures average 12 degrees, and summer temperatures average 65 degrees.

**Transportation.** U.S. Highway No. 63 runs north–south. State Highway No. 527 also runs north–south. The nearest commercial airline is at Duluth, 70 miles away. Train, bus, and trucklines services are available in Hayward, adjacent to the reservation.

**Community Facilities.** Water is provided by wells and from the lakes in the area. Bottled gas and bulk gas are available at Hayward. Electricity is provided by Lake Superior District Power Company. A 30-bed hospital in Hayward provides hospital care under PHS contract, and there is a health clinic in Reserve operated by the PHS.


LAC DU FLAMBEAU RESERVATION                    Federal Reservation
Iron and Vilas Counties
Lac du Flambeau Band of Chippewa Indians
Tribal Headquarters: Lac du Flambeau, Wisconsin

**Land Status.** Tribally-owned land: 29,110 acres. Allotted land: 15,327 acres. Government land: 40 acres. Total area: 44,477 acres. Within the original reservation boundaries are 29,123 acres which are now in non-Indian ownership. Approximately 2 percent of the tribal lake-front land is leased for income purposes. The tribe has reserved nearly 10 percent of its lakefront for member-use only.

**History.** The Chippewa, or Ojibway, tribe were one of the largest Indian nations north of Mexico, controlling lands extending along both shores of Lakes Huron and Superior and westward into North Dakota. The Chippewa were pushed into this area by the Iroquois who lived farther to the northeast. The Chippewa in turn forced the Fox out of northern Wisconsin and drove the Sioux across the Mississippi and Minnesota Rivers. They lived in forest areas instead of settling on rich farmlands. Because of the differing interests in land and land use, the Chippewa had little friction with white settlers. The Chippewa Nation has been officially at peace with the United States since 1815. This reservation was first established by the treaty of 1854 to include an area of three townships and was later enlarged.

**Culture.** The Chippewa traveled in small bands through forestlands, hunting, and fishing, sometimes settling to carry on a rude form of agriculture. Foods were supplemented by gathering fruits and wild rice, which were plentiful in the area. Birchbark was widely used for crafts and building material in wigwams and canoes. The tribe was patrilineal, divided into clans bearing animal names, and loosely organized. The Grand Medicine Society had a great deal of control over the tribe. A mysterious power, or manitou, was believed to live in all animate or inanimate objects. The tribe is now experiencing a cultural revival. A committee is studying and preserving the language. Many of the young people are learning the tribal dances and songs. Older Indian women know how to weave mats and rugs from reeds and bags from a type of burlap. Several women make birchbark baskets, canoes, and moccasins, while others make beadwork for commercial sale.

**Government.** The tribe is organized under the Indian Reorganization Act of 1934. The 12-member tribal council handles the day-to-day problems of the community, together with the Bureau of Indian Affairs representative. The council which manages the tribal business meets twice monthly.

**Population Profile. 1969:** Tribal enrollment 890; Indian resident 801; Unemployment 111; Underemployment 121. **1980:** Indian resident 1,092; Non-Indian resident 1,119; Percent Indian of total population 49.4; Total housing units 2,265; Occupied housing units 723. The average education level for the tribe is 8th grade. Children attend the local grade school and the Lakeland High School in Minocqua, Wisconsin. Students receive $25 per semester for clothes when they reach the 10th grade. The tribe grants the outstanding senior a scholarship to the college of his choice. To date there are no college graduates.

**Tribal Economy.** Two-thirds of the annual tribal income of $44,200 is obtained through business leases. The remaining third is income from forestry and gravel. The tribe has organized a number of committees to plan and promote the development of tribal resources. They include the housing, enrollment, industrial development, education, and realty resource committees. The tribe is also a member of the Great Lakes Inter-Tribal Committee. The Simpson Electric Company employs both men and women. Two Indians own and operate summer resorts on tribal land. Other Indian-owned and operated businesses include a restaurant, two gift shops, an insurance agency, and a laundromat. Most of the unemployment is seasonal, with almost full employment during the summer months.

**Climate.** The rainfall averages nearly 43 inches per year. Temperatures range from a high of 80 degrees to a low of -30 degrees. The weather is highly seasonal.

**Transportation.** State Highway No. 70 passes through the southwest corner of the reservation. State Highway No. 47 passes through the reservation southeast-northwest, connecting with U.S. Highway No. 51. In addition there are several county and BIA roads within the reservation. Train service is available on the reservation. A bus stops in Woodruff, 13 miles from Lac du Flambeau. The nearest available truck and air service is located in Rhineland, 35 miles from the reservation.

**Community Facilities.** The new housing units have community public works systems. Residents purchase bottled gas, as no gas lines come into the reservation area. The Rhineland Cooperative provides electricity to the reservation area. Health care and hospitalization are available in Woodruff through the Public Health Service and Department of Indian Health. The USPHS contracts with the county nurse to visit the reservation.

**Recreation.** Lac du Flambeau is advertised as the "Vacation Capital of the North" with its 126 beautiful spring-fed lakes, sandy shores, and groves of birch and pine trees. During the summer months the Wa-swa-gon Dance Club entertains twice weekly at the "Indian Bowl" with Chippewa dances. The Indian Bowl is a stadium fronting on Lake Interlacken.

MOLE LAKE RESERVATION                    Federal Reservation
Forest County
Sakoagon Chippewa Band
Tribal Headquarters: Mole Lake, Wisconsin

**Land Status.** Tribally-owned land: 1,694 acres. Non-Indian land: 280 acres. Total area: 1,974 acres. Mole Lake is the smallest of the Wisconsin reservations. Mole Lake community on Rice Lake is made up of two general stores, a filling station, an elementary school, a tavern, and the Waba-Nun-King Chapel. The homes are scattered on either side of the highway for about a mile. There are a good number of non-Indian farms in the area.

**History.** The Chippewa, driven from the east by the Iroquois, controlled a vast area through Michigan to North Dakota. They successfully forced the Fox out of Wisconsin and the Sioux to the west, thus gaining control of the prized wild rice fields. The Chippewa lived in nomadic bands, largely in forested areas. Their interests thus did not conflict with those of the incoming settlers, and in general good relations were maintained. Pledging peace and friendship, the chief of the Mole Lake Band signed a treaty in 1826 at Fond du Lac with Federal officials. The reservation site was selected by the chief because of the abundance of wild rice growing there, which was food for his people.

**Culture.** The Chippewa were nomadic timber people traveling in small bands engaging primarily in hunting and fishing, sometimes settling to carry on a rude form of agriculture. These foods were supplemented by gathering fruits and wild rice. Their wigwams of saplings and birchbark were easily moved and erected. Birchbark canoes were used for journeys, but travel was usually by foot. The tribe was patrilineal, divided into clans usually bearing animal names. Although their social organization was loose, the powerful Grand Medicine Society controlled the tribe's movements and was a formidable obstacle to Christianizing attempts of missionaries. A mysterious power, or manitou, was believed to live in all animate or inanimate objects. The Chippewa today are largely of mixed blood, mostly French and English.

**Government.** The band adopted a constitution and bylaws in 1938, according to the 1934 Indian Reorganization Act. The Charter of Incorporation was ratified in 1939. The governing body is the tribal council, made up of a chairman, vice-chairman, treasurer, secretary, and two members-at-large. Elections are held every two years.

**Population Profile. 1969:** Tribal enrollment 121; Indian resident 113. Unemployment 32 persons; Underemployment 0. The average education level for the reservation is 10th grade. Members of the band make use of the Employment Assistance Program offered by the Bureau of Indian Affairs. The people generally do not want a changed way of life.

**Tribal Economy.** The tribe earns slightly over $500 each year in forestry. Several individuals work for the tribe through the Community Action Program. The tribe has organized a housing committee and a health committee to improve conditions on these areas. Mole Lake is also a member of the Great Lakes Inter-Tribal Council. A few of the women are engaged in beadwork and weaving. One family works full time at weaving and tanning deer hides for a subsistence income. About six families work in the woods part time. The only full-time employment available is at Conners Forest Industries in Laona, 20 miles from Mole Lake. There is a 320-acre lake which is one of the outstanding rice beds in the State. The remainder of the reservation is either low-grade timberland or unproductive swampland and upland brush.

**Climate.** The reservation lies in northeastern Wisconsin where temperatures reach a summer high of 90 degrees and a winter low of -30 degrees.

**Transportation.** The reservation lies on north-south State Highway No. 55, 36 miles from Rhinelander where commercial air and truck service are available. Pelican Lake, 11 miles from the reservation is serviced by a commercial trainline. The nearest bus stop is in Crandon, 9 miles distant.

**Community Facilities.** As the public works facilities on the reservation are inadequate, residents obtain their water from wells and lakes and utilize outdoor privies and septic tanks. Only bottled gas is available. The local REA provides electricity. Hospital and other medical care is available in Rhineland at the St. Mary's Hospital. This care is financed by the Public Health Service. There is one community building on the reservation, which was rebuilt with assistance from the Great Lakes Agency of the Bureau of Indian Affairs. VISTA workers on the reservation have helped to organize a pre-school nursery and a boy scout troop. They are advisors to the women's organization and offer study hall for high school students.


ONEIDA RESERVATION                          Federal Reservation
Brown, Oneida, and Outagamie Counties
Oneida Tribe
Tribal Headquarters: Oneida, Wisconsin

**Land Status.** Tribally-owned land: 2,109 acres. Allotted land: 466 acres. Total area: 2,574 acres. Non-Indian land is checker-boarded between Indian lands. The reservation was established by treaty in 1838 to include 65,730 acres. By 1930, only 1,000 acres were left to the tribe. A series of land purchases begun in 1934 brought the reservation to its present acreage. The Indian land is in scattered tracts. There is some of the State's best farmland, and although near the highly industrialized and urbanized Fox River Valley, most of the land is still used for agriculture.

**History.** The Wisconsin Oneida are descendants of the New York Oneida, a member tribe of the League of the Iroquois. The Oneida were second to the east, the Mohawk being Keepers of the Eastern Gate, and the Onondaga, immediately to the west, being Keepers of the Council Fire. The League reached the apogee of its power around 1700. The influx of Europeans, Iroquois involvement in the resulting struggles for power, and the Revolutionary War contributed to the decline of the League. Most member tribes sided with the British during the war with the colonies; however, the Oneida remained neutral until forced to join the Tuscarora on the side of the colonies. Following the establishment of the United States, Governor Clinton of New York took the initiative to settle New York's claims with the Indian tribes. The Oneida sold most of their land and decided to move west. By 1846, most of the New York land had been sold with the assistance of Eleazer Williams, an Episcopal priest. The Indians negotiated between 1821 and 1838 to obtain a western empire; an 1838 treaty established a reservation in Wisconsin, most of which was lost through allotments. Land was purchased for the tribe from the Menominee.

**Culture.** The Iroquois lived in longhouses, composite family dwellings owned by the women. The Indians were skilled in building log cabins, tilling the soil, and in military enterprise. Lineage and property were inherited through the mother. Their society was fundamentally democratic, placing emphasis on the dignity of the individual and the power of the clan. The League was organized for mutual defense and developed into a powerful government. Each tribe was represented by several chiefs appointed by the women of the tribe. All decisions were unanimous, discussions being continued until opposition was either reasoned away or abandoned. The effectiveness of their socio-political structure was recognized by the colonists and used as an important model for the present United States Government. Only the remnants of the three Oneida clans and the Iroquois organization were brought by the tribe to Wisconsin. The tribe displays little adoption of the woodland Indian traits of the surrounding tribes.

**Government.** The Wisconsin Oneida Tribe is organized under the 1934 Indian Reorganization Act. The Executive Committee is formed by four officers who are elected by the resident tribal members. The Executive Committee, together with the five elected councilmen, form the tribal council which directs the tribal affairs.

**Population Profile. 1969:** Indian resident 1,670; Unemployment 5%; Median family income $3,800. **1980:** Indian resident 1,821; Non-Indian resident 11,568; Percent Indian of total population 13.6; Total housing units 4,046; Occupied housing units 3,886. The average education level for the tribe is above the 9th grade. More than one-quarter of the population are high school graduates. At present, 579 have education beyond the 12th grade. The St. Norbert College is located in DePere, and the University of Wisconsin has a branch in Green Bay, where a variety of vocational schools are also located.

**Tribal Economy.** The tribe has only a minimal income, most of which is earned through farming. The remainder is earned in forestry. Because of the location near Green Bay, most of the commercial and industrial activity is located there; however, the tribe planned an industrial park that was completed in 1970 on Indian land within the city limits of Green Bay in an effort to partake of the economic activity there. There are no substantial mineral resources on the reservation.

**Climate.** The climate in the Green Bay area is modified by Lake Michigan. The average rainfall is 29 inches per year. The average summer high temperature is 79 degrees, the winter low is 2 degrees.

**Transportation.** Two State Highways, Nos. 29 and 54, cross the reservation east-west going into Green Bay. Train and buslines run through the reservation to stop in Green Bay. The same city is served by air and trucklines.

**Community Facilities.** The U.S. Public Health Service has extended water and sewer lines to a third of the reservation homes. The remainder are served by local wells or the Green Bay Water Department and utilize septic tanks. The Wisconsin Public Service Company provides both electricity and gas. Some residents purchase oil or bottled gas. Over a third of the homes have telephones which are serviced by the Wisconsin Telephone Company. There are no hospitals or other health facilities on the reservation. Tribal members obtain medical care in Green Bay. There are recreational facilities, such as parks, and ballfields, in both Green Bay and on the reservation.


POTAWATOMI RESERVATION                    Federal Reservation
Forest County
Potawatomi Tribe
Tribal Headquarters: Potawatomi, Wisconsin

**Land Status.** Total area: 11,667 acares. Most of the land (11,267 acres) is tribally owned. Allotments account for 400 acres. The reservation is made up of scattered holdings, checker-boarded with non-Indian lands. The land is rolling and rocky. Timber is the only resource. The reservation was created by Act of Congress in 1913, at which time 14,439 acres were purchased.

**History.** The first Europeans visited the Upper Great Lakes Region in the early 1600's and later came in increasing numbers to exploit the fur trade. The Potawatomi were living all along the Lake Michigan shore and were a powerful tribe. Their chief, Onanguisee, saved a band of LaSalle's men from starvation in 1680. When the Potawatomi ceded their lands in 1833 and agreed to move to the Iowa territory, about 400 remained in Wisconsin. For years they led a poverty-stricken existence, in small tar paper shacks, picking wild berries and selling maple sugar, occasionally working as lumberjacks. Their last hereditary chief, Simon Kahquados, who died in 1930, made valiant efforts to help his people and was honored by the Bureau of Indian Affairs which gave him medals but ignored his proposals.

**Culture.** The Potawatomi were expert fishermen, canoe builders, hunters, and trailmakers. They fashioned art objects of wood. Their society was organized by clans. Clothing was of deerskin and fur. They raised vegetables and corn, clearing small plots of land by girdling the trees. The tribe today is conservative in its advocacy of only Indian marriage and adoption.

**Government.** The constitution and bylaws were established in February 1937 under the Indian Reorganization Act. The governing body is the general tribal council composed of all qualified voting members, including the chairman, vice-chairman, secretary, and treasurer. The general council meets twice annually.

**Population Profile.** **1969:** Indian resident 229; Unemployment 55%; Median family income $2,600. **1980:** Indian resident 220; Non-Indian resident 4; Percent Indian of total population 98.2; Total housing units 49; Occupied housing units 47. The population has declined 1.1 percent since 1940. More than half the population is under 20 years old. Public schools are attended at Crandon, Laona, and Wabeno. State vocational school training is at Rhinelander, Wisconsin.

**Tribal Economy.** Tribal income is $10,800 annually, all of which comes from forestry. There are two full-time, six part-time tribal employees. There are no commercial or industrial establishments on the reservation.

**Climate.** Rainfall averages 31 inches per year. The average high is 82 degrees in July, and the average low is 0 degrees in January.

**Transportation.** U.S. Highway No. 8 runs east-west, 10 miles north of the reservation. State Highways No. 552 and No. 632 service the reservation. The nearest commercial airport is at Rhinelander, 45 miles from the reservation. Commercial train and buslines service Antigo and Rhinelander. Antigo is 35 miles away.

**Community Facilities.** Electricity, provided by Wisconsin Public Service Company, services 19 homes. Water is provided by individual and community wells. Sewage is serviced by septic tanks and town systems or outdoor privies. There are six telephones on the reservation. Local doctors contract with the Public Health Service to care for health needs.


RED CLIFF RESERVATION                    Federal Reservation
Bayfield County
Red Cliff Band of Chippewa Indians
Tribal Headquarters: Red Cliff, Wisconsin

**Land Status.** Tribally-owned land: 5,122 acres. Allotted land: 2,145 acres. Total area: 7,267 acres. Due to the loss of allotments sold by individual Indians, more than half of the original reservation has been alienated. Outsiders logged off the timber, the only valuable resource the Indians had.

**History.** The Chippewa Indians, members of the Algonquian family, constituted one of the largest Indian tribes north of Mexico. Their lands extended along both shores of Lake Superior and west to the Turtle Mountains of North Dakota. They were friendly with the French and used French weapons to drive the Sioux further westward. They joined Pontiac's Rebellion which broke out against the British in May 1763. The Chippewa joined Tecumseh in 1813; organized resistance ended. The Red Cliff Band of Chippewa under Chief Buffalo signed a treaty in 1854, giving them 14,442 acres of land.

**Culture.** The Chippewa were nomadic forest hunters. The wigwam houses used were portable and easily reconstructed. Travel was by foot, snowshoe, and birchbark canoe. The Chippewa carried on a widespread trade in copper. Kinship and lineage was traced through the father's family. The Chippewa believed there was a mysterious power in all objects. They called it the manitou. They buried their dead in mounds. Hiawatha was their warrior-hero god. Their most important society was the Grand Medicine Society, a formidable obstacle to the Christianizing attempts of the missionaries. The Chippewa carried on some agriculture, supplemented by the gathering of fruits and wild rice. Today the Indian people find employment at resorts, guiding, and forestry work, all of which is seasonal. Skilled workers can find employment in nearby communities.

**Government.** The Red Cliff Tribal Council is made up of a chairman, a vice-chairman, treasurer, secretary, and three council members who are elected by the tribe for a period of one year.

**Population Profile.** **1969:** Tribal enrollment 403; Indian resident 299; Unemployment 58%; Underemployment 10%; Median family income $2,900. **1980:** Indian resident 589; Non-Indian resident 97; Percent Indian of total population 85.9; Total housing units 243; Occupied housing units 179. The average education level attained by the Red Cliff Tribe is 10th grade. There are six college graduates living on the reservation. Children attend school at Bayfield.

**Tribal Economy.** Tribal income is $2,113 per year, 85 percent of which comes from forestry and 15 percent from leases. There are no full-time tribal government employees. The tribe has a park and a forestry committee and is a member of the Great Lakes Inter-Tribal Council. A garment factory is operated in partnership with Red Cliff women. There is a national recreation park on the reservation.

**Climate.** Rainfall averages 23-29 inches annually. The temperature during the summer months averages 65 degrees and during the winter 12 degrees.

**Transportation.** State Highway No. 13 serves the reservation running north-south. There is an airport in Ashland, 26 miles away, and train, bus, and truck service are also available in that city.

**Community Facilities.** Water is provided through the Public Health Service system for the public housing and adjacent homes. There are also community wells. Bottled gas is available. Electricity is provided by the Lake Superior District Power Company, and the PHS has built a sewer system for the housing units. Elsewhere, individual septic tanks are in use. There is a hospital in Ashland which contracts with PHS for the care of the Indian people. Red Cliff has a health clinic and health programs. There is a community center building in Red Cliff, and the semiannual Medicine Dances are held as major community events.

ST. CROIX RESERVATION                    Federal Reservation
Burnett, Barron, and Polk Counties
St. Croix Band of Chippewa
Tribal Headquarters: Danbury, Wisconsin

**Land Status.** Tribally-owned land: 1,715 acres. Allotted land: 515 acres. Total area: 2,230 acres. The St. Croix Tribe owns all reservation land. The land was purchased in 1938 for the Indians under the Indian Reorganization Act of 1934.

**History.** In the early historic period, the Chippewa Tribe, a member of the Algonquian family, was among the largest north of Mexico with lands extending along both shores of Lake Superior and west to the Turtle Mountains of North Dakota. Friendly with the French, the Chippewa utilized French weapons to drive the Sioux further westward. They joined in Pontiac's Rebellion which broke out against the British in May 1763. Later, the Chippewa joined Tecumseh along with the Potawatomi, Winnebago, and other tribes to drive out the white settlers. The defeat and death of Tecumseh in 1813 ended organized resistance. The Chippewa Tribe retained its cultural identity, and several bands remained in Wisconsin. The St. Croix band was landless until 1938.

**Culture.** The Chippewa were nomadic forest hunters. The wigwam houses used were portable and easily reconstructed. Travel was by foot, snowshoe, and birchbark canoe. Kinship and lineage was traced through the father's family. They believed there was a mysterious power in all objects which they called the manitou. The Chippewa buried their dead in mounds and carried on a widespread trade in copper. Hiawatha was their warrior-hero god. Their most important society was the Grand Medicine Society, a formidable obstacle to the Christianizing attempts of the missionaries. The Chippewa carried on some agriculture, supplemented by the gathering of fruits and wild rice. Today the Indian people find employment at resorts, guiding, and forestry work, all of which is seasonal. Skilled workers can find employment in nearby communities.

**Government.** Tribal government is organized under the Indian Reorganization Act of 1934. There is a tribal council with a president, vice-president, secretary, and treasurer elected for terms of 2 years. The tribe is a member of the Great Lakes Inter-Tribal Council.

**Population Profile. 1969:** Tribal enrollment 564; Indian resident 292; Non-Indian resident unknown; Unemployment 43%; Underemployment many. **1980:** Indian resident 392; Non-Indian resident 35; Percent Indian of total population 91.8; Total housing units 115; Occupied housing units 106.

**Tribal Economy.** Tribal income is $253 per year, all of which is derived from forestry. There are no full-time tribal employees. The St. Croix Tribe is a member of the Inter-Tribal Community Action Program. There are health, housing, and recreation committees within the tribal council working to develop the reservation.

**Climate.** Average annual rainfall is 27 inches. The average winter temperature is 11 degrees, and the average summer temperature is 68 degrees. A high of 95 degrees and a low of -30 degrees have been recorded.

**Transportation.** U.S. Highways Nos. 70 and 48 service the reservation east-west. State Highway No. 35 also serves the reservation. The nearest commercial airline is located in Duluth, 55 miles from the reservation. Train service is also available in Duluth, as are trucklines. Bus service is available in Danbury, adjacent to the reservation.

**Community Facilities.** Water is provided through a community system to the new housing units. Gas is available in bottle form. Electricity is provided by Barron Company or REA (St. Croix Falls). There is a community sewer system to the new units. USPHS contract hospital care is available in Superior.


STOCKBRIDGE-MUNSEE RESERVATION              Federal Reservation
Shawano County
Stockbridge (Mahican) and Munsee Tribes
Tribal Headquarters: Bowler, Wisconsin

**Land Status.** Tribally-owned land: 2,250 acres. Government land: 13,077 acres. Total area: 15,327 acres. The reservation is all tribally-owned. The Stockbridge Tribe was divided on the issue of whether land should be tribally or individually owned until 1912 when the long legal and legislative tangle was concluded. The original reservation of 23,040 acres was taken from the Menominee Reservation. By the Treaty of 1856, the Stockbridge Indians obtained the present site in exchange for the cession of their lands on Lake Winnebago.

**History.** Originally from Massachusetts, the Mahican Indians moved west into New York where they joined the Stockbridge, Brotherton, and other tribes. They fought against the colonists in the Revolutionary War, were defeated and were gradually Christianized. In accordance with a Government policy to move the eastern tribes west, the Stockbridge were moved to Wisconsin in 1822 to live with related tribes, principally the Menominee with whom they became closely affiliated. In 1856, the Stockbridge were granted land on the present reservation site adjacent to the Menominee. In the 1870's, valuable pine lands on the reservation were sold by Congress without notice to the tribe. Lumbermen removed the timber leaving the tribe with no means of subsistence beyond the sale of produce from meager gardens. In the 1930's, the Bureau of Indian Affairs acquired 14,423 acres of the original Stockbridge Reservation and returned the land to the Indians.

**Culture.** The Stockbridge were an eastern Algonquian Tribe who were moved around by the Federal Government until finally settled on Wisconsin land. They adopted the hunting and fishing economy of Wisconsin and retained their traditions and political organization. Most of the craftwork has been lost and discontinued except for the making of trinkets for tourists. The tribe has reforested its lands and finds some employment in nearby communities.

**Government.** A general council which meets twice annually elects the tribal council consisting of a president, vice-president, treasurer, and secretary, and four additional councilmen. The tribal constitution was written in 1933 and adopted in 1938 by favorable vote of the tribe in order to function as an independent, self-governing body.

**Population Profile. 1969:** Tribal enrollment 920 (est.); Indian resident 460; Non-Indian resident unknown; Unemployment 13%. **1980:** Indian resident 582; Non-Indian resident 690; Percent Indian of total population 45.8; Total housing units 591; Occupied housing units 401. Children attend public schools, and no separate records are maintained.

**Tribal Economy.** Tribal income is $1,500 yearly, 95 percent of which comes from forestry, and 5 percent from other sources including arts and crafts. The tribe has recently chartered Mohicans, Inc., a factory making fiberglass molds for various industrial uses. This enterprise is tribally-owned and operated.

**Climate.** Annual rainfall is 30 inches. Temperatures average 69 degrees during the summer months and 14 degrees during the winter. A high of 103 degrees and a low of -39 degrees have been recorded.

**Transportation.** State Highways Nos. 29 and 55 service the reservation east-west and north-south. U.S. Highway No. 45 runs north-south about 10 miles from the reservation. County roads serve the reservation directly. Trains of the Chicago and North Western Railroad cross the reservation. The nearest airline is 40 miles away at Wausau Airport. Commercial bus and trucklines serve the town of Shawano, 25 miles away.


WINNEBAGO RESERVATION                    Federal Reservation
Parts of Ten Counties in Wisconsin
Winnebago Indian Tribe
Tribal Headquarters: Wisconsin Dells, Wisconsin

**Land Status.** Total area: 4,116.62 acres. The reservation consists of 3,835.62 acres of restricted fee allotment. An additional 290 acres are held by the Government in trust for the tribe. The land is scattered among Shawano, Marathon, Clark, Wood, Adams, Juneau, Monroe, Jackson, LaCrosse, and Crawford Counties.

**History.** The Winnebago were encountered in the Lake Winnebago and Green Bay area of Wisconsin by the first Europeans to reach Wisconsin. The French Explorer, Nicolet, landed near Red Banks in 1634, finding an encampment of 5,000 Winnebago warriors. During the 17th and 18th Centuries, the Winnebago Tribe was reduced by smallpox and battles both with other tribes and with settlers. They were involved in Black Hawk's war in the mid 1700's, an effort of the Sauk and their allies to retain their lands in Wisconsin. The Winnebago chief, Spoon Decorah, a friend of whites, delivered Black Hawk to the Indian Agent at Prairie du Chien. The major portion of the tribe was removed by the Government from Iowa to Missouri, to South Dakota, and finally to Wisconsin and resisted efforts to remove them until, in 1875, they were allowed to remain. The most concentrated period of land transfer occurred between 1825 and 1837.

**Culture.** The Winnebago are timber people with houses, dress, and crafts similar to the Sauk and Fox and to the Menominee. Their language is a Siouan dialect related to the Oto, Iowa, and Missouri groups. The tribe was traditionally divided into four Upper, or Air

Clans, and eight Lower, or Earth Clans. Individuals were required to marry a member of the opposite level. The Thunderbird and Bear Clans were the most prominent, respectively, among the two groups. The two most important religious ceremonies are the Summer Medicine Dance and the Winter Feast. Winnebago artistic work, particularly the bright designs made by sewing porcupine quills, bright feathers, and beads onto buckskin, was noted for its beauty.

**Government.** In 1963, the Winnebago were officially recognized as a tribe. They adopted a constitution and bylaws. The tribe elects a chairman, vice-chairman, a secretary, and a treasurer, and five additional councilmen. There is a great deal of participation in working toward the betterment of the scattered Winnebago communities. The tribe belongs to the Great Lakes Inter-Tribal Council.

**Population Profile.** 1969: Tribal enrollment 1,330 (est.); Indian resident 1,330; Non-Indian resident unknown; Unemployment unknown; Underemployment 50%. **1980:** Indian resident 349; Non-Indian resident 67; Percent Indian of total population 83.9; Total housing units 115; Occupied housing units 104. Indian children attend public schools. Federal programs in Adult Education, Employment Assistance, Low-Rent and Self-Help Housing are helping to improve the impoverished condition of many of the Winnebago. Most present employment is seasonal: work on roads, forestry projects, tourist entertainment, and construction work.

**Tribal Economy.** There is no tribal income from the 193 acres held in trust and tribally-owned. Mineral resources are insignificant. In general, the areas where the Indian people reside are the poorer areas of the State. More than half of the Winnebago Tribe are living below the Federal poverty line. A small garment industry employs seven or eight women in the Black River Falls area. The tribe has received program help under the Economic Opportunity Act.

**Climate.** The climate varies over the 10-county area in which the Winnebago Tribe is scattered. Average rainfall runs from 25 to 30 inches per year. Winter temperatures are from 11 degreees to 14 degrees overall average, and summer temperatures average in the high 60's.

**Transportation.** All counties in which the Winnebago people live are served by both State and county roads. Several major U.S. Highways cross the State. Rail, air, and bus service are available in the larger towns and small cities.

**Community Facilities.** A small number of housing units have been constructed at Wisconsin Dells and at Black River Falls. There is a community building in the Wisconsin Dells community, and Black River Falls Mission is used for recreation, education, and social functions.

WYOMING

WIND RIVER RESERVATION                    Federal Reservation
Fremont and Hot Springs Counties
Shoshone and Arapahoe Tribes
Tribal Headquarters: Riverton, Wyoming

**Land Status.** Tribal land: 1,776,136 acres. Government land: 1,076 acres. Allotted land: 109,344 acres. Total area: 1,836,556 acres. This reservation, having a total area of 44 million acres, was originally granted to the Shoshone Tribe in 1863. Land cessions reduced the area to the present acreage. The Arapahoe Tribe was placed here temporarily in 1878. However, "temporary" gradually became permanent, and the two tribes now share the reservation. The hostility between the two tribes has diminished, but they continue to live separately and have separate governments.

**History.** The Shoshone Tribe originally lived in the Great Basin area between the Rockies and the Sierra Nevada. They entered the Plains east of the Rockies about 1500, and thereafter developed similarly to other Plains Indian tribes. From their first encounter with whites, sometime in the early 19th Century, the Shoshone found trade profitable and remained friendly. The Fort Bridger Treaty of 1863 provided that 44,675,000 acres of land in four States be reserved for the Shoshone; however, several years later this was reduced by 41 million acres. The tribe were relatively content until their enemies, the Arapahoe, were settled on the reservation with them. The Arapahoe, a Plains tribe, had competed with the Shoshone, and been at war with them frequently. They were hostile to the United States and remained so until subdued and placed on the Wind River Reservation.

**Culture.** Both the Shoshone and Arapahoe were originally sedentary farmers but were of different linguistic stocks. When they moved into the area of the Great Plains they took on the characteristics of the Plains Indians, becoming seminomadic buffalo hunters. The Shoshone, who were at war with the other Plains tribes, welcomed the white man as an ally while the Northern Arapahoe continued to battle both other tribes and the whites. The Arapahoe tribesmen were valorous and contemplative. The Sun Dance and the eight secret societies were extremely important to them. Robes and lodges were generally adorned with beadwork.

**Government.** Neither of the tribes is organized under the Indian Reorganization Act of 1934. They each maintain a separate business council of six members of the tribe. The business of the reservation as a whole is carried on by the Joint Business Council. For matters of special importance, each tribe may convene its general council which consists of all enrolled members of that tribe. At least one-fourth degree of Shoshone or Arapahoe Indian blood is required for tribal membership.

**Population Profile. 1969:** Tribal enrollment 4,594; Indian resident 4,062; Non-Indian resident 3,519; Unemployment 37%; Underemployment 26%; Median family income $4,200. **1980:** Indian resident 4,159;

Non–Indian resident 19,007; Percent Indian of total population 18.0; Total housing units 8,293; Occupied housing units 7,396.

**Tribal Economy.** The joint tribal income averages $3 million annually. Profits from the Arapahoe Ranch Enterprise form the largest portion of the income. Revenues from grazing rights and forestry supplement this. The Arapahoe Ranch Enterprise is tribally operated as a beef breeding operation. There are additional tribal associations such as the Cooperative Cattleman's and Sheep Growers Association. The land and climate are best suited to stockraising. Coal veins are curently being mined. There are also deposits of phosphate, gypsum, and bentonite on the reservation, but these are not presently being exploited.

**Climate.** The reservation is located in central Wyoming where the rainfall averages 13 inches per year. The average high temperature is 80 degrees; the average low is 10 degrees.

**Transportation.** U.S. Route No. 287 and State Route No. 26 run through the northeastern corner of the reservation. State Route No. 789 runs north–south to the eastern border of the reservation. Riverton is serviced by commercial air and trainlines. Bus and trucklines stop in all the major reservation towns.

**Community Facilities.** Water is drawn from wells. Most areas have access to electricity from either the Pacific Power and Light Company or the Riverton Valley Electric Association.

# INDEX

**N**

**O**